The theme of British economic decline is inescapable in contemporary debates about Britain's economic performance and sense of national identity. *Understanding decline* is a serious contribution to an important argument, approached in a way that is accessible not only to the specialist academic market but to students of economics, history, and politics.

Barry Supple, to whom the volume is dedicated, when Professor of Economic History at Cambridge was concerned with various aspects of this historical problem. Indeed, his 1993 Presidential address to the Economic History Society, 'Fear of failing', already a classic, is reprinted here as a highly effective keynote essay.

Other essays pick up this theme in diverse but essentially unified ways, seeking to assess British economic performance in different ways over the past two centuries. They include case-studies through which the reality of decline can be explored, while differing perceptions of decline are examined in a number of essays dealing with ideas and policy issues.

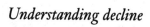

Understanding decline

Barry Supple

Understanding decline

PERCEPTIONS AND REALITIES OF
BRITISH ECONOMIC PERFORMANCE

EDITED BY

PETER CLARKE AND CLIVE TREBILCOCK
University of Cambridge

CAMBRIDGE
UNIVERSITY PRESS

CAMBRIDGE UNIVERSITY PRESS
Cambridge, New York, Melbourne, Madrid, Cape Town, Singapore, São Paulo

Cambridge University Press
The Edinburgh Building, Cambridge CB2 8RU, UK

Published in the United States of America by Cambridge University Press, New York

www.cambridge.org
Information on this title: www.cambridge.org/9780521563178

First published 1997
This digitally printed version 2007

A catalogue record for this publication is available from the British Library

Library of Congress Cataloguing in Publication data
   Understanding decline : perceptions and realities of British economic
   performance / edited by Peter Clarke and Clive Trebilcock.
      p.   cm.
   Includes bibliographical references and index.
   ISBN (invalid) 0 521 56317 8 (hb)
      1. Great Britain – Economic conditions.   2. Great Britain – Economic
   policy.   I. Clarke, Peter, 1942– .   II. Trebilcock, Clive.
   HC253.U55   1997
   338.941–dc21   97–8905   CIP

ISBN 978-0-521-56317-8 hardback
ISBN 978-0-521-03684-9 paperback

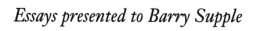

Essays presented to Barry Supple

Contents

Notes on contributors

PETER CLARKE is Professor of Modern British History at the University of Cambridge and a Fellow of St John's College.

CLIVE TREBILCOCK is University Lecturer in History at the University of Cambridge and a Fellow of Pembroke College.

DONALD WINCH is Professor of the History of Economics at the University of Sussex.

PATRICK K. O'BRIEN is Director of the Institute of Historical Research and a Professor of Economic History at the University of London.

SIMON SZRETER is University Lecturer in History at the University of Cambridge and a Fellow of St John's College.

JAY WINTER is Reader in Modern History at the University of Cambridge and a Fellow of Pembroke College.

JOSE HARRIS is a Professor of Modern History at the University of Oxford and a Fellow of St Catherine's College.

BERNARD ALFORD is Professor of Economic and Social History at the University of Bristol.

CHARLES H. FEINSTEIN is Chichele Professor of Economic History at the University of Oxford and a Fellow of All Souls College.

TONY HOPKINS is Smuts Professor of Commonwealth History at the University of Cambridge and a Fellow of Pembroke College.

DAVID CANNADINE is Moore Collegiate Professor of History at Columbia University, New York.

PETER TEMIN is Elisha Gray II Professor of Economics at the Massachusetts Institute of Technology.

Note on references

Place of publication for all works cited is London unless stated otherwise.

Preface

PETER CLARKE AND CLIVE TREBILCOCK

Like Elgar's Enigma, the theme of British economic decline possesses a haunting resonance which has inspired many variations. It remains inescapable in current debates about Britain's economic performance and sense of national identity.

Investigating the origins of this problem discloses a surprisingly long historical perspective. Arguments about the contemporary failings of the British economy soon take us back to the question, where did it all go wrong? Did the Second World War submit the nation to a ruthless audit, presaging a lost victory in the postwar years? Was the interwar period, with its variegated pattern of depression and recovery, the moment of truth for Britain's manufacturing base? Were there already signs of the onset of a harsher climate amid the Indian summer of economic prosperity in Edwardian Britain? Or, perhaps, did Victorian Britain fail? Indeed, was the first industrial nation, right from the first, somehow deficient in its industrial spirit? It is difficult to pose such questions without making allusions, which students of the literature will immediately recognise, to a long-running debate among economic historians.

Leapfrogging back through two centuries of British history, this debate in turn poses questions about the nature of British capitalism in its heroic age. Domestically, what social forces, cultural outlook, and political framework did it manifest? Internationally, what relations with the world economy and the British Empire did it imply?

Such issues have stimulated scholarly controversy during the last generation, fed by seminal statements from several contributors to this volume. But the fruitful *historiographical* debate did not arise out of thin air. It was the continuation of a long *historical* debate about decline, conducted among contemporaries who articulated and anticipated many influential contentions. Perceptions of decline have in this sense been as important as its realities. Indeed one protean issue in the debate has been how far the supposed decline has in fact been 'real'.

This is the territory which Barry Supple made his own while he was Professor of Economic History at Cambridge. The idea of marking his retirement with a volume which would move the argument forward seemed an obvious one as soon as we thought of it. Though many of the contributors have served with him at various stages in their careers and his, this is by no means an exhaustive roll-call of his colleagues and admirers. Two restrictive stipulations kept down numbers: that contributors should be younger than Barry and that they should be ready to write on the theme of decline. The plan was to produce a coherent volume rather than a conventional *festschrift*; and convention was likewise flouted by including Barry himself from an early stage. His 1993 Presidential Address to the Economic History Society, 'Fear of failing', sums up many years of reflection on his chosen theme. This address, which is already on its way to becoming a classic, is reprinted for the first time as the keynote essay in this volume; and its author has written a prologue offering his own introduction to and reflections on the essays which follow.

Barry Supple is rightly honoured as the historian of decline; but big as this subject is, it does not span the range of his interests during a long career. Born in 1930, he attended Hackney Downs Grammar School, at that time a remarkable school that produced a number of subsequently distinguished figures in academic, political, and artistic life – most of them, like Barry himself, drawn from the East London Jewish community of recent immigrants. Only after completing his first degree at the LSE in 1952 did Barry leave London for Cambridge, where he successfully submitted his PhD thesis within three years. This was the beginning of his research in seventeenth-century economic history, leading to the publication of his first book in 1959. By this time settled (so it seemed) in North America, first at Harvard for five years and then at McGill for two, his interests shifted to American railway investment, duly signalled by another big book. Returning to Britain as the foundation Professor of Economic and Social History at the University of Sussex in 1962, he again displayed his versatility with a business history of a major insurance company. He began, too, the formidable research needed to underpin his massive study of the British coal industry in the twentieth century. By the time this was published in 1987, Barry was back in Cambridge (following a three-year interlude at Nuffield College, Oxford) and had become Master of St Catharine's College as well as Professor of Economic History. Had he remained in post, his retirement age would have been sixty-seven. Instead, in 1993, he surprised us all by becoming Director of the Leverhulme Trust. Unabashed, we have nonetheless gone ahead with the plan to publish this volume in his honour on his sixty-seventh birthday.

Barry's executive efficiency has never been left in any doubt, not least to tardy colleagues, and it was harnessed thirty years ago to administrative responsibilities at Sussex that belied the youth of the rising Pro-Vice Chancellor. His responsibilities as an editor of the *Economic History Review* for nine years were fulfilled with similar dispatch, and this while he was simultaneously heavily committed to the work of the Social Science Research Council. His growing activity in the British Academy, following his election as a Fellow in 1987, was likewise concurrent with his roles as Master of a large college and as a conscientious teacher of both under-graduates and research students in Cambridge. His general equanimity survived, punctuated by splendid moments of exasperation, so that it is equally true to say that he was unusually good-humoured and that he was usually good-humoured.

Barry's conspicuous success in this demanding career has plainly rested on secure domestic foundations. His marriage to Sonia in 1958 gave him a lifelong partner throughout the vicissitudes of Boston, Montreal, Lewes, Oxford, and, finally, Cambridge, where they have made their home – a home infused with a strong sense of family. Though Barry is formidably well-read, rarely caught out on a reference, it is Sonia who has unobtru-sively cultivated a broader literary sensibility which it may not be fanciful to see as informing Barry's own recent work. For the young scholar who made his mark within the discipline of economic history, fairly rigorously defined, has surely matured into a historian of more catholic interests, regarding the economy itself as a problematic concept and reaching out for kinds of explanation which transcend purely economic analysis. This is how Barry Supple has made himself into the pre-eminent historian of British decline; and this is why our attempts at understanding decline are dedicated to him.

Introduction: national performance in a personal perspective

BARRY SUPPLE

It is with gratitude and humility that I contemplate the honour paid to me by friends and colleagues in this remarkable collection. I hope that the use of the adjective will not be attributed to any immodesty on my part. Rather, it reflects an objective view of the efforts of other scholars, which have resulted in an extremely unusual achievement – namely, a *festschrift* which appears to succeed in attaining both a thematic unity and a diverse original-ity, while tackling a problem of very great historical significance. It is, there-fore, a cause for genuine gratification that my own imperfect and 'jejune' excursions into the field of large-scale national history should have been used as a departure point for scholarly explorations which will undoubtedly endure, sustaining and focusing a debate of the greatest importance for British history and, indeed, of the greatest relevance to the evolution, aspirations, and tranquillity of the British people.

With the aid of retrospective rationalisation we can all find flattering ele-ments of consistency and therefore continuity in our interests and our scholarly efforts – even when these qualities are not always admirable (they may, after all, reflect intellectual rigidity), or are not obvious to objective observers. I should certainly not wish to claim any particularly significant consistency for my own work – on business history, on economic growth, on the state and economic performance, or on the question of Britain's putative decline. However, I hope that it is not too pretentious or far-fetched to suggest that my approach to a limited number of historical themes has been partly characterised by an interest in the perennial clash between human aspirations and social realities, in the vagaries of the links between organisations and markets, and (perhaps above all) in the need to place the world as it is or was against the images of the world as humans perceive it. Obviously, this is not to claim that social and personal images are any less historically tangible or important than some 'underlying' reality. On the contrary, since we all use images to navigate life and society, and since such images are frequently the only 'realities' available to us, to grasp their essence and operations is to grasp the essence of historical fact. But until we have fully understood the nature and workings of the images *as images*, we cannot probe historical processes fully, and above all we are likely to depart from the strict canons of scholarship and to be dragged into the unthinking ideological debates of everyday life.

For my own part, in pursuing this sort of theme in the context of the controversy about Britain's decline, I have from time to time been hard put to avoid exasperation with the pessimists – an exasperation which could (I confess) be interpreted as a fear that I might be mistaken in concluding that so much of the anxiety about decline has been 'all in the mind'. But, whatever my own motives, it seems to me beyond doubt that in this sort of discussion what we need above all is clarity and realism. In any event, it has been this type of approach which in recent years has shaped my growing interest in the nature, implications, and (above all) the perceptions of Britain's economic performance over the last hundred years or so – a concern which led me to compose the lecture, 'Fear of failing', which forms the first chapter in this book and which provided a stimulus for the themes of this *festschrift*.

'Fear of failing' made much of the potentially distorting nature of an image of performance. But the subject-matter of most of the following chapters exemplifies not merely a number of versions of that distortion, but also much broader and more fruitful themes. In particular, this book presents variations on two vital and related aspects of modern British history: the political economy of (perennial) 'modernisation', and the nation's imperial and international experience. The result is a many-sided concern with the reality, the perceptions, and the public policies associated with the huge changes in Britain's place on the world stage as a formal empire and a global power which have taken place over the last three centuries.

Compared with the traditional interpretation of Britain's economic history over that period, this concern strikingly emphasises the enduring role of the state and the persistence of debates about 'decline' (admittedly, in a variety of guises) and national power throughout far-reaching transformations of the country's actual experience. In this volume Patrick O'Brien demonstrates how far even the apparently market-based expansion of the economy on the world stage from the late seventeenth century was attributable to the exercise of state power and fiscal authority; while Donald Winch analyses not merely the sangfroid of Adam Smith's political economy and his scepticism about the value of empire, but the extent to which his calming rationality has to contest pessimism about Britain's global position. Within and yet to some extent apart from such themes, both the empire and the British economy flourished in an historically unique way between the late eighteenth and the late nineteenth centuries – although there was no period without its jeremiahs in that long and successful century. By the late nineteenth and early twentieth centuries maturity (in the first of its many manifestations) brought to the fore the curious question of whether Britain could maintain its global economic and imperial position indefinitely. Obviously, as many commentators appreciated, it could not. But contemporary developments also posed a much more sensible set of questions: Was the economy performing as well as it could? Was it adjusting effectively and rationally to the changes in economic structure and technology which (we now know) were fashioning a second industrial revolution? In this sort of context, could Britain's role as a Great Power be extended for some generations? And could the empire be harnessed to the maintenance of that role?

These issues, the economic trends of the period and later, and the multiple responses of contemporaries, provide object lessons in the contrasts and occasionally even the paradoxes of history. The empire continued to flourish, although, as Charles Feinstein confirms for a somewhat later period, its economic value to Britain was dubious. At the same time, Britain's inherited economic structure, its slow incorporation of the new industries, its funnelling of huge resources overseas, and its growing commitment to financial and other services, did not bring nemesis, nor (with the exception of the scale of its export of capital) did it contrast very much with the experience of other mature 'industrial' economies – a point stimulatingly considered by Peter Temin in relation to the USA. In the case of late-Victorian and Edwardian Britain, in spite of a multitude of commentaries suggesting that the country was on the verge of second-class rank, it entered the First World War with its superpower status little diminished. Indeed, its subsequent weakness on the world's economic stage was possibly more attributable to the impact of twentieth-century war than late nineteenth-century lethargy.

Of course, the debate about Britain's putative failure has long since transcended the simplicities of decline and ruination. And yet, as contributions to this book demonstrate, while it is difficult to argue that Britain failed, or that its entrepreneurs were culpable (rather than profit-seeking in their time and place), it remains open to question whether the state – if those who managed it had taken a longer view than we have a right to expect (over, say, two or three generations) – might have anticipated future needs. Often, those who took a long view did so in such dire terms that their despondent advocacy was seen to be unrealistic – a consideration which (as various contributors to this book suggest) establishes a bond between political-economic argument in the late eighteenth, the late nineteenth and the late twentieth centuries. On the other hand, the concern was never entirely misplaced. As Donald Winch reminds us, we live our lives looking forward, and history ought perhaps to be as interested in the things that governments failed to perceive and do, as in their achievements and interventions.

This aspect of political economy in relation to relative decline is discussed by various authors. Thus, at one level, Simon Szreter argues that individualism and the search for market conditions favourable to enterprise may have handicapped the British economy by leading successive governments to neglect investment in human and social resources. And such a challenge to the anxieties about a 'dependency culture' is a potent reminder of the potential significance of links between social policy and economic achievement and welfare. At another level, Patrick O'Brien also wonders whether Britain's long-run performance was adversely influenced by a more general sort of state failure. On this interpretation the very success of the political economy of expansion and global activity in the eighteenth and early nineteenth centuries led to a complacency and a failure to come to terms with the needs (to increase taxes, to question the ideology of Free Trade, to reverse the detachment from Europe) of a new global reality and a new stage in the economic history of Britain. And a similar *sort* of argument (albeit directed towards different sorts of lost opportunities) informs Bernard Alford's discussion of the political economy of the postwar Labour Governments, which neglected both the European dimension and the scope for structural and microeconomic change.

This 'political' interpretation of relative decline is plausible – certainly in the sense that the counterfactual of different economic and fiscal policies is conceivable. But it also raises very complex counterfactual issues: even if it is now possible to envisage scenarios which would have transformed Britain's economic position fifty or a hundred years later, is it reasonable to expect that contemporary governments could and should have anticipated the need for such transformation by state action? Indeed, in the case of both the late nineteenth century and the period after 1945, those who see government failure can also acknowledge that in the circumstances of the time there might have been little return to energetic action: the failure (if failure it was) embodied an inability to take a long, and perceptive (even prophetic), view.

At the same time, this sort of political-economy commentary on relative decline should probably not be confused with the interpretation of Britain's destiny famously associated with Joseph Chamberlain – even though he was aware of the need to measure present structures and policies against likely futures. In practice, however, as David Cannadine shows, Chamberlain's attempt to retrieve Britain's threatened position as a superpower by a reversion to mercantilist paternalism and a policy of structural conservatism is best viewed as part of a long tradition of the politics of national catastrophe. And this stimulating interpretation of a particular meaning of national decline, while it has been constantly canvassed by lesser commentators as well as by the three frail political giants discussed by Cannadine, can be thought of as the other side of a more realistic interpretation – namely, one which sees Britain's 'decline' as inevitable, and seeks to define and understand its exceptionalism in terms of the country's extraordinary supremacy and global success rather than its sadder experience as a weary Titan.

In any case, there seems little reason to amend the view that Britain was a very long time declining. And in the course of that experience the impact of the two world wars could well have been as – or even more – influential than deficiencies of culture or economic agents. On the other hand, macroeconomic and national viewpoints are not always the best ways into historical processes. In this chapter on comparative urban development, Jay Winter points out that, while the British economy was moving in many directions in the years between 1870 and 1930, metropolitan development was characterised by transformation and diversification, rather than by decline and fall, and that London's stability and growth contrasted with the experience of Paris and Berlin – at least until convergence began in the 1930s.

This is a novel viewpoint, although economic historians have for long argued that the conventional story of Britain between the wars probably underestimates the resilience and even ultimate buoyancy of the British economy and British business – a point dealt with by Clive Trebilcock in his study of the insurance industry. And more recent studies have had much to say for the achievements of the 1945–51 Labour Government. Nevertheless, there is no denying that in terms of the controversy about relative decline there is a case to answer in relation to the history of the last fifty years. In this collection, Bernard Alford's theme – the microeconomic and structural policies of the Attlee administration – has recently been subjected to much reinterpretation (in the light of the preoccupation with microeconomic policies stimulated by the excitements of Margaret Thatcher's premiership). And in expounding his theme he offers a strong criticism of the historiography which has come to claim far-sightedness, or at least efficacy, for the Attlee Government – and as already suggested, establishes an interesting parallel to Patrick O'Brien's concept of the missed opportunities of political economy and the neglect of the European dimension two generations earlier. On the other hand, as Jose Harris, suggests, it is extremely doubtful if the Attlee Government's rather constrained commitment to welfare expenditure can be blamed for the economy's 'failure' (then or later) to grow faster than it did.

Obviously, the history of Britain's economic experience in the decades after 1945, and particularly the discussion of the causes of its ultimate relative decline, can involve a multitude of perspectives. But it is perhaps significant that the contributors to this collection who are concerned with this problem focus on a question which (in different forms) has been a familiar issue for at least a century: was the British economy capable of sustaining the costs and strains of the country's inherited global role and the geopolitical aspirations of its rulers? Was the commitment to a far-flung network of economic and political relationships inimical to a more feasible, and ultimately more realistic, association with European economies and polities?

The discussion of 'overstretch' (that invariable accompaniment of imperial, and possibly social, extension) informs a large part of Peter Clarke's pungent appraisal of those who misinterpret Keynes in the context of the New Jerusalem of welfare policies (the presumed baleful influence of which is also denied, albeit in different ways, by Simon Szreter, Bernard Alford, and Jose Harris). And far from advocating a disastrous profligacy of expenditure, Keynes, as Clarke and Jose Harris respectively show, was well aware of Britain's relative weakness on a world stage where it could no longer play the economic or political role to which it aspired, and of the power of arguments in favour of financial probity and constraint. In a complementary exercise, Charles Feinstein suggests the extent to which even the abandonment of empire was a benefit rather than a cost to the mother country. And in his original assessment of Macmillan's audit of empire in 1957 Tony Hopkins provides not merely an analysis of the varying perspectives on the colonial system and the extent to which Britain's imperial position was bound up with the global strength of sterling, but an indication that in some important historical circumstances national evolution is better characterised by the concept of 'change' rather than 'decline'.

That would not have been an acceptable view to Winston Churchill, nor to Margaret Thatcher, who may have appreciated the impossibility of regaining imperial stature, but whose particular ambitions for a world-leadership role clearly ran counter to the reality which the passage of time had forced upon Britain. And David Cannadine is thereby able to contrast their ideological hopes and apocalyptic visions of Britain's trajectory through history with the innocuous inevitability of relative decline in its broadest outlines.

A more sober view of the reality of change is considered by Peter Temin in his analysis of the parallels between late twentieth-century America and late nineteenth- and early twentieth-century Britain. But the assumptions which determine the outlook and policies of the state are themselves on a par with images – and the images which interpenetrate British history are concerned with national destiny and the stage on which it might be played out, as well as with disappointment and gloom. In a variety of ways, the contributors to this book reinforce the view that political as well as popular images are often distorted visions of reality. For example, Jose Harris demonstrates the extent to which condemnations of the presumed 'burden' of 1940s' welfare expenditure were based partly on the politicised context in which Beveridge operated, but principally on the fading of social memory and the transformations of popular culture and aspirations in the 1960s. And Tony Hopkins shows the vital, if increasingly unrealistic, views of empire (and of the Sterling Area) which influenced politicians in the late 1950s.

Certainly, and with increasing intensity, the commitments generated by social responsibilities or international aspirations in the second half of the twentieth century have come to be interpreted as obstacles to economic expansion – as the burdens rather than the benefits of success and maturity. And it is a fascinating thought that Joseph Chamberlain's fears that Britain was a weary Titan were refracted into these new forms almost a hundred years after he expressed them. Yet the parallel should not be taken too far. First, Chamberlain argued that the weariness and weakness could be alleviated by augmenting economic power through the abandonment of economic policies and structures which hampered imperial co-operation and cohesion, and through the reinforcement of Britain's global power. But the modern version of the symbiosis between international posture and national efficiency has inverted this recommendation: the abandonment of the imperial and geopolitical role, which Chamberlain would have abhorred and strove to reverse, has come to be seen as a prerequisite of the reinforcement of the national economy. Second, although there is an obvious and powerful sense in which social expenditure and overseas commitments can absorb resources which might otherwise have augmented productive efficiency, it is not at all clear that this sort of 'trade-off' existed in reality, as distinct from in the minds of those who make policy and determined priorities. Obviously Britain was too small a nation and an economy to remain a great power or to make exceptional provision for its collective social needs. Nevertheless, its welfare expenditures, certainly, have rarely been distinctively high, while in any case the decision as to the proportion of the national income that can be devoted to social services is frequently as much a political and a psychological as an economic one – or, rather, the changing attitudes which surround it are themselves constituent elements in 'economic reality', and that reality can change over time. International obligations or domestic welfare are frequently (although not invariably) 'burdens' only insofar as decision-makers or the population at large decide that they prefer the things that might have to be given up in order to pursue them. To a degree, 'overstretch' is a habit of mind, while the re-ordering of priorities is a critical aspect of the changing sense of national performance.

In these respects, as in others, then, the use of the ever-changing image of 'decline' as an historical perspective gives access to much broader themes in modern British political, social, cultural, and economic history. When I first began to write about decline I envisaged pursuing these themes. But even had I possessed the qualifications for such a task, recent professional responsibilities would have prevented me from bringing it to fruition. Moreover, even within the confines of my own specialisms in economic history, I had not yet exhausted the subject of the contrast between the true and the imagined meanings of 'decline' in its more straightforward senses – or the extent to which the public at large does not find it easy to distinguish decline from change. And I therefore count myself doubly fortunate in the presentation of this *festschrift*, in which so many much better qualified historians have been willing to elaborate on this and on much broader topics, and thereby to demonstrate in so many productive ways the richness of the route from what used to be called 'good old-fashioned economic history' to the broader uplands of Britain's history in its varied aspects.

I

Fear of failing: economic history and the decline of Britain

BARRY SUPPLE

As befits such an occasion, this lecture takes a speculative view of a very broad theme: Britain's putative economic decline, and more particularly the preoccupation with failure which has intermittently characterised political, journalistic, and academic discourse over the last hundred years. I should emphasise at the outset that I am concerned primarily with *economic* decline. Other aspects of the controversy concerning national decadence – the glum sense of moral and civil decay, of social dislocation and *anomie*, of deterioration in traditional institutions – must no doubt be taken seriously. But insofar as these are genuine problems, many of their origins, or at least the obstacles to their prospective solutions, are to be found in the performance and organisation of the British economy.

There can be no doubt about the persistence with which commentators have taken a profoundly despondent view of Britain's economic record and future – certainly over the last century, and in some respects well before then. And what interests me is less the actual record than the *idea* of decline – the assumption that things are going from bad to worse, when so much evidence suggests that they are going from not so bad to something somewhat better. Admittedly, it is only really over the last generation that economic and political debate has come to be dominated by the idea that Britain is in such serious decline that it is heading for national ruin. But even then, of course, the underlying habit of lugubriousness was not new. Yet commentators have always been aware that there was a contrast between what they feared and what they knew. Here for example, is Beatrice Webb, committing her perplexity to her diary in June 1925:

Presidential address delivered at the annual conference of the Economic History Society, University of Hull, 2 April 1993. I am very much indebted to Peter Clarke, Ron Martin, and John Thompson for their detailed comments and firm advice on the first draft of this lecture – and for their patience in the face of so many idiosyncratic views. First published in *Economic History Review*, 47, 3 (1994), pp. 441–58.

What troubles me is the gross discrepancy between the alarmist views . . . about the industrial decadence of Great Britain . . . [and] the absence of all *signs* of extreme poverty among the people at large. Compared with the 80s, even the early years of the twentieth century, there is no outward manifestation of extreme destitution: no beggars, few vagrants, no great and spontaneous demonstration of the unemployed, no 'bitter outcries' or sensational description of the sweaters' dens and poverty-stricken homes . . . What is the explanation of this curious combination of the permanent unemployment of eleven per cent of the population with a general sense of comparative prosperity on the part of the bulk of the population?[1]

Familiar as this clash of perception and apprehension is, it is relevant to emphasise that it was not simply a product of twentieth-century tensions. More than a century before Mrs Webb was so puzzled, Macaulay tackled the same conundrum from a more optimistic perspective. In 1830, in the course of a counterblast to Southey's pessimism about industrialisation, Macaulay reminded his readers of the tendency of each generation to assume that the future was nevertheless bleak. He then posed the question which is crucial to the present theme: 'On what principle is it that, when we see nothing but improvement behind us, we are to expect nothing but deterioration before us?[2]

In the late twentieth-century Britain, of course, the seeming paradox of a sense of economic failure thriving in an increasingly affluent society has a simple and obvious terminological resolution: relative decline and absolute growth can and do co-exist. British national income has certainly grown; but over the last century or so that of other leading economies has grown faster. In the quarter century up to the 1970s, for example, while Britain's rate of economic growth accelerated, there was even more dramatic acceleration in other countries. As a result, anxiety and complaint about falling behind became most strident even as affluence became an accepted characteristic of British society. The figures are familiar. British Gross Domestic Product grew at about 2 per cent annually between 1873 and 1913, at a little over 2 per cent between 1924 and 1937, and at almost 3 per cent between 1951 and 1973.[3] Hence, while there may well be a British disease, there is also a British rate of growth – more or less 2 per

---

[1] N. MacKenzie and J. MacKenzie (eds.), *The diary of Beatrice Webb, vol. IV 1924–1943, The wheel of life* (Cambridge, Mass., 1985), pp. 52–3 (22 June 1925).

[2] T. B. Macaulay, 'Southey's Colloquies (January 1830)', reprinted in *Critical and historical essays* (1894), p. 122.

[3] R. C. O. Matthews, C. H. Feinstein, and J. C. Odling-Smee, *British economic growth, 1856–1973* (Oxford, 1982), p. 22. Including the wartime years, the rates of growth of GDP (per man-year in brackets) were: 1873–1913, 1.8% (0.9%); 1913–37, 1.1% (0.7%); 1937–73, 2.4% (1.9%). Ibid., p. 24.

cent. That rate of growth certainly did not fall in the long run. But it has been outstripped by the performance of other countries in the west and in Asia. Between 1950 and 1983, for example, when Britain's annual growth rate rose to about 2.4 per cent, the equivalent figure was 3.3 per cent in the United States, about 4.5 per cent in the leading west European powers, and 7.9 per cent in Japan.

It is, then, a commonplace that Britain's presumed decline is a matter of *relative* growth rates and output. But jeremiahs have not stopped there. Time and again, Britain's apparent economic difficulties and role as a world power have tempted even would-be realists into loose talk of deceleration – of a 'decline in Britain's tempo of expansion' when, quite manifestly, such an event has not taken place.[4] More that that, a few commentators have even argued that Britain was in danger of declining in the fundamental sense of experiencing an actual decrease in output – although it is hard to find any serious, let alone persuasive, attempt to explain how a positive rate of growth might be transmuted into actual decadence and even collapse, simply because it is lower than the growth rates of some other countries.

In any event, the bedrock of the debate has always been the relative 'failure' of the British economy and its associated demotion from the leading rank of industrial powers. In this respect it is, of course, possible that the historical perspective misleads us, and that we are witnessing a long-run tendency to convergence in the productivity and income levels of leading industrial societies, either as a whole or (more likely) within sub-groups of such nations. Such a process would certainly be consistent with some differences in achievement – mostly explained by the accident of natural endowments or of historical timing. To that extent, latecomers may, indeed, have advantages, although convergence theories imply that they are unlikely to be spectacular. Obviously, the evidence about convergence is still inconclusive. But we cannot yet dismiss the theory that the levels of per caput output and consumption in Britain (while constrained by the cultural, social, and economic effects of an early start) will not end up so far behind those of other European economies, or even Japan, once the diffusion of capital and technology on the one hand, and the influence of mature institutions and structural inflexibility on the other, have had their effects.

More generally, perhaps, while the Golden Age of Capitalism may be over, it is probably over for almost everyone who experienced it. And while it is clear that we have not after all enjoyed a British miracle, events in

---

[4] Quoted in W. A. P. Manser, *Britain in the balance* (1971), p. 60.

German factories or Japanese labour markets could imply that we may nevertheless have succeeded in exporting a little of the British disease. In any case, whatever the situation with regard to convergence, there is much to be said for McCloskey's view that when the long-run experience of economic growth is considered, the differences between Britain and other advanced societies are much less (and much less important) than the differences between the advanced and less developed countries.[5] A good handful of other countries have higher average living standards than the British. But on the whole those differences are trivial compared with the generally neglected differences between British living standards and those of the bulk of the rest of the world. This was a point picked up by Clapham in the epilogue of his great work on the economic history of modern Britain, written in 1937: 'Hanging behind all thought and discussion' of the issue of income inequality and redistribution in the 1920s

were – or should have been – the reflections that almost the least propertied of their countrymen was already a privileged member of the human race; that the talk of a world of plenty which needed only to be organised, a way of speech then coming into fashion among social experimentalists, was not yet relevant to a world some two-thirds of whose inhabitants had not, by Western standards, decent clothing for their backs or plain food enough to eat.[6]

Over fifty years later, the generalisation is hardly less apt.

It has to be admitted, of course, that from the present viewpoint all this has an abstruse ring to it. Historically, there can be no doubt about Britain's relative decline or about the gloomy reaction to it. In the last hundred years or so, its share of world manufacturing output has fallen from 25 per cent or more to about 4 per cent; its share of world trade in manufactures, from about 40 to less than 9 per cent.[7] In the league tables of output growth among reasonably developed countries, Britain seems (at best) to be lingering at the bottom, jostling somewhat shamefacedly between, say, Spain and Greece.

And yet in spite of all this, the British are the beneficiaries of developments which in every generation leave them richer than their predecessors. Blips there have been in plenty, and from the depths of such a slump as was experienced from about 1990, it seems difficult to envisage any decisive

---

[5] D. N. McCloskey, *If you're so smart: the narrative of economic expertise* (Chicago, 1990), pp. 46–8.

[6] J. H. Clapham, *An economic history of modern Britain, vol. III: National rivalries (1887–1914) with an epilogue (1914–1929)* (Cambridge, 1938), p. 554.

[7] P. Bairoch, 'International industrialisation levels from 1759 to 1980', *Journal of European Economic History*, 2 (1982), pp. 296, 304.

recovery. Yet the historical experience points far more firmly in the direction of a return to a modest but adequate trend rate of growth than to any descent into some abyss of apocalyptic collapse. Why, then, is there such a preoccupation with the prospect of economic failure? To rephrase Macaulay's question, why do the British worry in the way that they do about the relative decline which undoubtedly exists, when the historical experience has been one of substantial and prolonged growth in incomes and living standards?

I

The most obvious reason for this perverse anxiety is that the loss of leadership and relative power which inexorably follows lagging growth can have disturbing psychological and political repercussions – at least for some. Even when Britain has not suffered from the illusion that, because the world is getting bigger around it, it was getting smaller,[8] the fear of second-class nationhood has dogged British political and economic discussion ever since the German and American challenges first seriously manifested themselves in the 1880s. And that fear was even more keenly felt once the self-confidence produced by victory in two gruelling world wars had been dissipated.

The basic meaning of Britain's presumed failure and decline (albeit mediated by its relative inefficiency and uncompetitiveness) therefore concerns its actual position in the world. At least among the actively political and articulate nation, decline has been most often identified with the loss, not so much of income or wealth, as of relative power and international standing as a leading industrial nation. It is identified with a fear (again in Webb's words) that in spite of a 'steady improvement in hygiene and manners and in the facilities for a comfortable and interested life', 'Great Britain will slither on to a spate of relative quiescence and powerlessness in the world's affairs.'[9] This fear was clearly at the root of the concern, which surfaced in the 1890s and 1900s, about Britain's industrial future. Writing in the *Contemporary Review* in 1900, William Clarke had no doubts that 'German goods are not only rising in intrinsic value, but they oust English manufactures in every market in the world', or that 'In every great international

---

[8] This point is cogently made by Manser (*Britain in the balance*, p. 179), who also draws the analogy of passengers in a stationary train seeing an adjacent train pulling out and imagining that they were moving backwards.

[9] MacKenzie and MacKenzie, *Diary of Beatrice Webb*, pp. 86–7 (18 June 1926).

competition in machinery, America beats England.' His conclusion was clear:

> the serious decline of England as a great industrial centre has begun . . . the giant is visibly exhausted, and is slackening speed . . . Nations, like man, have their exits and their entrances. England was the first to develop the 'great industry', she will be the first to lose it.[10]

Others were much less philosophic and restrained. Joseph Chamberlain, for example, was certainly not resigned to Britain's presumed future, although at the time he found insufficient support for his disturbing view that 'The weary Titan staggers under the too vast orb of its fate',[11] or for his concomitant deduction that a revolution in political economy was needed to safeguard Britain's industrial strength and create a new imperial economic bloc. At one level, therefore, tariff reform was sustained by a sweeping geopolitical view of impending decadence. And it was from that perspective that its adherents deduced the vital need to use tariffs and preferences to redress the threatened imbalance of Britain's international power. This, they argued, could be attained by using trade policy to form a more coherent imperial unit, which would take its place beside the USA, Germany, and Russia as a twentieth-century power.

Clearly, the Edwardian anxiety about Britain's total wealth proved premature. Not only did a continued buoyancy override the vagaries of the trade cycle, but Britain entered and successfully fought the First World War as a major power. Nor was it immediately obvious at that war's end (with an empire larger than ever before and its principal competitor on its knees) that Britain had lost its pre-eminence. In retrospect, the Second World War stands out as a more potent cause of geopolitical decline, although even that conflict did not involve an immediate and obvious indication of national decay when set against the exhaustion and devastation of actual and potential rivals.

International decline, reflected in the reduction in the share of world output and relative material power, therefore took time to manifest itself in dramatic ways. But when all is said and done, it was inevitable – as more and more countries entered the ranks of the industrial economies, as other and bigger countries grew more rapidly, as the empire first loosened its ties and then disintegrated (along with other traditional empires), and as the

---

[10] W. Clarke, 'The social future of England', *Contemporary Review*, 77 (July–Dec. 1900), pp. 858–62.

[11] Quoted in front matter of A. L. Friedberg, *The weary Titan: Britain and the experience of relative decline, 1895–1905* (Princeton, 1988).

resources and commitments necessary for world power status became ever more extensive and expensive, until they receded well beyond the reach of Britain's modest economy. Given the size and natural endowments of other countries, it was inconceivable that Britain could permanently play a very significant or autonomous part in international affairs. It simply lacked the resources necessary to maintain anything like its 'historical' role, first as a major policeman in imperial and quasi-imperial affairs, and then as a premier 'player' on the world scene.

Disturbed as some observers have been at what they see (in Barnett's apprehensive words) as 'the bleak and even terrifying reality of Britain's fallen place in the world',[12] such a diminution of power could hardly have been avoided. A country with such a small proportion of the world's resources and population cannot indefinitely deal on equal terms with developed nations bigger by anything between 50 and 400 per cent. Indeed, Britain's transformation from imperial power to global innocuousness turned out to be a relatively (and surprisingly) sluggish process. And it is perhaps the slow pace, rather than the rapidity, of Britain's decline on the world scene that is the more interesting historical problem.

Beyond this, we should surely bear in mind that status as an imperial or world power does not of itself enhance the material welfare of the mass of the people. And it is, therefore, not at all clear that this aspect of decline has been of central concern to the majority of the population. Rather, it is reasonable to suppose that the greatest sensitivity to Britain's diminishing international role would have been felt by a small and exclusive minority. This consisted of the people who principally determined economic and political policy and were therefore more directly involved in formulating explanations of Britain's economic performance. Their patriotic sensibilities, as well as their personal self-confidence and their rewards as wielders of authority in an erstwhile imperium, were affronted by the loss of national status. The rest of the population, however, have very little direct and personal experience of Britain's power in the world. No doubt it is in some sense reassuring, even flattering, to be a citizen in a superpower. But for the men and women on the Clapham omnibus, work and income, social networks and quality of life – the prosaic essences of daily existence – take precedence over geopolitics and cartographical prominence in the ultimate calculation of welfare. Of course, politicians (especially dictatorial ones) would have us think otherwise. But they mislead us. And appreciating that

---

[12] C. Barnett, 'Obsolescence and Dr Arnold' in P. Hutber (ed.), *What's wrong with Britain?* (1978), p. 34.

fact can be a bitter lesson – one which has been learned with tears over seven and a half decades, by millions of people in the USSR. 'In the Second World War', wrote Taylor at the end of his *English history, 1914–45*:

the British people came of age . . . Imperial greatness was on the way out; the welfare state was on the way in. The British empire declined; the condition of the people improved. Few now sang 'Land of Hope and Glory'. Few even sang 'England Arise'. England has risen all the same.[13]

There is another reason for scepticism about the 'objective' existence of decline in terms of relative standing (or, rather, for believing that such failure, while nonetheless keenly felt, is largely 'in the mind'). In the last resort only one country can be top nation. If not being top is failure then Britain has been in good and abundant company – and always will be. Of course, it may be that the anguish is caused by not being in the top four, or top six, or top twelve, or top twenty economies. But there seems little intellectual satisfaction or exactitude to be found in that direction.

On the other hand, the idea of 'failure' through demotion does have potential force in the realm of collective memory. For example, if a people are worse off than those who have never recently been inferior to them, there seems to be no cause for alarm. Thus, the British accept without too much anguish the fact that the USA has a higher average level of material welfare than Britain. And if they were to discover that there is life on Mars, and that its living standards and economic power are three times theirs, they would not, presumably, feel the more a failed nation. But we are all much more sensitive to comparisons closer to home, and which reverse customary rankings. Nations as well as individuals can experience relative deprivation. Hence, the British do feel keenly the humiliation of decline from a remembered position of economic pre-eminence, power, and influence in relation to others who were once their inferiors. Few Britons old enough to recollect the postwar decades can really, in their heart of hearts, comfortably accept that the per caput income of the French, let alone the Italians, exceeds theirs. The real hurt is to have been top dog (or at least a leading dog) in a fairly recent period which can be painfully contrasted with an inferior contemporary status.

This is not to deny the complex historical significance of the transition from leading to second-rank nation. As Chamberlain had divined, since continued national independence would ineluctably lead to Britain's steady demotion through the league tables of national standing and power, the

[13] A. J. P. Taylor, *English history*, 1914–1945 (Oxford, 1965), p. 600.

maintenance of international influence could only be achieved by a closer association with other, similarly placed, countries. Yet his preferred solution to this problem – an imperial federation – proved entirely unrealistic (even at the time). In fact, it took another generation and two world wars before the search for collaborative great power status was seriously renewed. And the resulting quest for a framework of co-operation, for allegiances and networks which might generate mutual support and strength, dominated much of British foreign policy after the war. The quest turned out to be long and frustrating: neither the Sterling Area nor the Commonwealth nor the 'special relationship' with the USA nor the European Free Trade Association provided the strength and continuity that was needed. And when Britain joined the European Economic Community in 1973 (having spurned it in the 1950s, and been rejected in the 1960s), that step acknowledged, as few others could have done, the relative weakness rather than the international strength of the policy and the economy.

II

So far I have concentrated on economic might – the global leverage of Gross Domestic Product – and the sense that this was being eroded, which lay at the root of the discussion of decline. But once decline was considered in terms of power and standing, critics of Britain's economic performance and policy also become exercised at the changing pattern of economic activity and its implications for the country's leverage in world affairs. 'Decline' has come to be interpreted in terms of the structure of the economy – and in particular of the balance between manufacturing and services (especially financial services), and of the presumed human costs of economic change.

Again, of course, there was intensive debate about this ninety years ago. Then, Chamberlain and his fellow tariff reformers were no doubt guilty of some special pleading on behalf of vulnerable industries. But they also took a bleak view of the future precisely because of their apprehension that competition with protected manufacturers abroad would destroy Britain's great staple industries (and therefore its military potential), reduce the demand for labour, and erode industrial skills. In other words, it would undermine core industrial activities and distort an economy which might be only flimsily rich. What was needed, they urged, was a policy to maintain a healthy (that is, a large and traditional) manufacturing base. This meant reducing the incentives and institutions which encouraged the export of capital, and redressing the balance between manufacturing industry and financial and other services.

From this viewpoint, there seemed to be two reasons why, even if national income were substantial, its composition might be enfeebling. First, if international competition were allowed full play, while resources stayed within the manufacturing sector, the resulting restructuring would stimulate inferior industries and skills and demoralize social classes. 'Look how easy it is', Chamberlain said scornfully during his campaign of 1903:

Your once great trade in sugar refining is gone; all right, try jam. Your iron trade is going; never mind, you can make mouse traps. The cotton trade is threatened; well, what does it matter to you? Suppose you try dolls' eyes . . . believe me . . . although the industries of this country are very various, you cannot go on for ever. You cannot go on watching with indifference the disappearance of your principle industries, and always hoping that you will be able to replace them by secondary and inferior industries.[14]

On this view, structural change would both dilute the quality of industry and work and social life, and reduce Britain's power to make war by undermining its heavy and sophisticated industry. In some respects, however, this was to beg the question. For it assumed that the only direction in which structural change could proceed was 'down' (towards 'secondary and inferior industries') – whereas the change we see in expanding economies is upwards on the scale of sophistication, towards new technologies and higher value-added sectors. Chamberlain had a point in assuming that a frail manufacturing sector would enfeeble military potential. But structural change could as well have increased war-making power. In this respect, it is significant that he neglected to discuss chemicals or scientific instruments or electrical engineering or the embryonic motor vehicle industry.

The fact was that Chamberlain's approach also subsumed a more entrenched fear – a fear of structural change in itself. He even entered a caveat about the intergenerational costs of even efficient structural change:

Even if it could be proved in the long run that the country did not suffer in wealth, that there had been a transfer from one trade to another, still I should say, when you count up all the families that have been reduced to misery, all the heart-burnings, all the suffering that has been caused by these changes to the individual, when you think of all the honest men who have gone to the workhouse and can never be brought back again to the ranks of continuous labour – when you think of all these things, then I say, even if the country were enriched, its wealth would have been dearly purchased.[15]

[14] C. W. Boyd, (ed.), *Mr Chamberlain's speeches* (1914), vol. I, p. 248.
[15] Ibid., pp. 218, 224.

In making these points, Chamberlain was in good company – at least in the sense that contemporary economic historians were, like him, dissidents on the subject of structural change. 'Mainstream' economists asserted the continued importance of free trade and the effectiveness of the very factor mobility and competitive adaptation that Chamberlain feared. Economists, he said, 'forget altogether the difference between wealth and welfare'. And economic historians (or, rather, the historical economists as many thought of themselves) also took issue with established economic theory. Ashley, for example, lent his pen to a favourable assessment of protectionism. The low wages and unemployment resulting from a slump in staple industries, he wrote, have 'a negative and degrading effect, far greater than the positive and elevating effect of a period of high wages and overtime'.[16] Other pioneers of economic history (notably, Hewins and Cunningham) joined in on the side of tariff reform and, more generally, on the side of state intervention and neo-mercantilism. For such men, their suspicion of the effects of the operation of untrammelled markets naturally spilled over into a suspicion of free trade. And they were joined by other powerful academic voices – like that of Mackinder, for example, who argued that every great irregularity of employment 'involves terrible wreckage of the capital fixed in humanity . . . Are not our slums to a very great extent the scrap-heaps of abandoned and disused portions of our national man-power?'[17] Such sentiments, now joined to impassioned pleas for interventionist 'industrial policies', are, of course, still familiar – on both sides of the Atlantic.

On the other hand, the fear of structural change and its identification with 'decline' have not always dominated the economic history profession. Ashton and Clapham, for example, representing an intermediate generation, had a greater respect for factor mobility and the benefits as well as the costs of change. In a 1942 lecture on the likely postwar future, Clapham accepted the need for unemployment if society were to avoid the dangers of complete immobility. 'I want industries and ways of service to change', he said, 'and that means to decay; and if I did not I should expect them to do so in my despite.' Nor did he agree that public control was the answer to unemployment resulting from change:

---

[16] W. J. Ashley, *The tariff problem* (1903; 3rd edn 1911), p. 116. Also p. 79: 'Adam Smith . . . relying on the transferability of capital, expected that the lessening prosperity of one particular home industry owing to foreign competition would result in the transference of capital to another home industry. But, as we have seen, it may lead to the transference of capital to the same industry in another country.'

[17] H. J. Mackinder, 'Man-power as a measure of national and imperial strength', *National Review*, 45 (1905), p. 142.

from the standpoint of economic efficiency, a nation placed as we are, and even more placed as we shall be, cannot afford very much of that kindly well-paid under-employment which is to me, as a student of English character and history, a real, if seldom discussed, danger of 'socialization' schemes when they are carried through as anything of the sort in this country is likely to be, in a spasm of national kindliness towards a distressed industry . . .

And if we cannot afford much pain under-employment, either in the service of a hypothetical cotton corporation or under Morris Ltd., we must have either the perfectly mobile man or a measure of recurrent unemployment, as industries contract and expand, are born and die.[18]

On the other side, of course, for a generation after 1945, with peace, full employment and the advent of an apparent golden age, such a viewpoint rarely found any strong political support. More recently, with a change in the economic climate, the deleterious consequences of 'spasms of unthinking kindliness' towards distressed industries have become more intrusive. Obviously, as has been shown in the case of the first, if not the second, reaction to the threatened closures of coal mines of 1992–3, the arguments from social need and sentiment remain strong. But the fact remains that perplexity rather than self-confidence still characterises and distorts the discussion of structural imbalance as a practical problem of industrial policy. Above all, holding on to what Chamberlain had called 'principal industries' after their competitive advantages had been eroded has proved a recipe for relative decline.

There was, and is, a second, over-arching reason why pessimists were, and remain, concerned about structural change. This has been the long lasting fear of 'deindustrialisation' – of the relative, perhaps even absolute, shrinking of the manufacturing sector as a whole. And it was this consideration that enabled the tariff reformers, like their modern counterparts, to brush aside as irrelevant the statistics which suggested that national prosperity was assured because the service sectors were booming, and the GDP was holding up. Critics of the City of London were by no means enthusiastic about Britain's continued dominance of the world's financial and commercial systems. The spectacular expansion of services and investment income, they argued in terms familiar to historians, reduced employment and starved British industry of capital. In Chamberlain's words, it 'may mean more money, but it means less men. It may mean more wealth, but it means less welfare.'[19] It was, therefore, one more reason for fearing that Britain's prestige and power would decline, that the country might sink

---

[18] J. H. Clapham, *The historian looks forward* (Barnett House Papers: Sidney Ball Lecture, 4 June 1942), pp. 9–10.   [19] Boyd, *Mr Chamberlain's speeches*, vol. I, pp. 267–8.

into the position of a mere rentier, like Holland (that universal stereotype of decline and structural enfeeblement – which, we are now told, is currently one of the strongest economies in Europe). Holland, Chamberlain asserted, 'is richer – richer than ever it was before – but is still an inconsiderable factor in the history of the world'.[20]

It is, of course, true that in the years before the First World War income from foreign investments was so great that it financed the continued accumulation of yet more capital overseas. But it is surely misleading to isolate investment income from all other sources of overseas earnings – the export of goods and services, for example – as if Britain was, or ever had been, a genuine rentier, in the words of the Chancellor of the Exchequer in 1947, 'living on our nineteenth-century investments'.[21]

More generally, however, it is the structural relationship between the City and industry which has provided that vein of analysis and concern which has been abundantly mined by economic historians. The apparent imperfections of the capital market which favour overseas as against domestic investment, the gentility of capitalism which (it is held) distances enterprise from industry, the distortions seemingly produced by the pride of finance and the Treasury's defence of sterling – all these have been offered as elements in the saga of Britain's presumed competitive deficiencies. And economic historians have on the whole reflected, and perhaps sustained, views about structural change and Britain's consequent humiliating future as an inflated leisure centre which have for long been commonplace among manufacturing interest groups and journalists. 'If something is not done', said a wool manufacturer before the protectionist Tariff Commission of 1903:

if we are to go on looking after the consumer in this country, and leaving the producer to take care of himself, I can conceive the time when this country will be the home of a great many millionaires, making their wealth abroad, and employing large numbers of servants and gamekeepers here, whilst many of the great productive industries we now carry on will be transferred to other countries.[22]

This sort of worry is, if anything, more intense today. It should, perhaps, be called the 'Weinstock effect' – for it was G.E.C.'s Lord Weinstock, in his evidence to a House of Lords Committee on overseas trade in 1985, who asked:

what will the service industries be servicing when there is no hardware, when no wealth is actually being produced? We will be servicing, presumably, the produc-

---

[20] Ibid.   [21] Quoted in Manser, *Britain in the balance*, p. 63.
[22] *The report of the Tariff Commission*, vol. II, pt. II: 'The woollen industry' (1905), para. 1484.

tion of wealth by others. We will supply the Changing of the Guard, we will supply the Beefeaters around the Tower of London. We will become a curiosity. I do not think that is what Britain is about. I think that is rubbish.[23]

For most of this century, the presumed dominance of finance over industry has been persistently interpreted as both a symptom and a cause of decline. 'Sound money', it has been assumed, has been the enemy of growing industry. And on this there is a very broad consensus (albeit not unanimity) among historians. In fact, few of us look with equanimity at structural change which affects our livelihood. Most of us have a sense that the manufacture of hardware – of *things* – is a more solid basis for national affluence than the sale of intangibles. Consequently, the literature on the bias towards the City and sterling, and the supposed neglect of industrial finance and enterprise, is huge.

And yet it is not clear that all these points are well taken. Why is the manufacture of ping-pong balls more worthy than the sale of educational services? Is the production of cigarettes or tanks inherently more useful than the supply of nurses or violinists? More generally, every economy passes through a trajectory of structural change, and time was when it was assumed that the process which led from primary to secondary to tertiary concentrations was benign and progressive. As Clapham argued during the Second World War, in any changing economy, people have to leave industries where there is insufficient work, moving

to some expanding occupation, say chocolate-making or chorus singing . . . as machines do more and more work for us, an increasing number of people must make popular luxuries or brighten other people's leisure. The tendency that way is marked already and is all to the good.[24]

Further, the decline in the relative significance of manufacturing is in any case an ambiguous indicator of comparative national well-being. Quite apart from the fact that industrial activity has never accounted for as much as 50 per cent of employment or output, and that manufactured exports have never paid for all Britain's import needs, the absolute importance of industry must not be ignored. In spite of competitive inadequacies, British manufacturing remained a powerful element in the indigenous economy and the world at large for decades after its imminent demise was announced – and the maintenance of national integrity in two world wars can in part be attributed to the fact that British manufacturing industry was decidedly

[23] House of Lords, *Report from the select committee on overseas trade* (HMSO HL 2381–I, 1985), pp. 42–3.   [24] Clapham, *The historian looks forward*, p. 9.

not defunct. More pertinently, however, while it is obviously disconcerting to witness the rapid shrinkage of formerly important industries, it is as well to bear in mind that much of what is conventionally labelled 'deindustrialisation' is both very recent and fairly general among developed nations.

On the first score – the chronology of structural change – the percentage of the British labour force employed in manufacturing, mining, construction, and public utilities varied very little between the middle of the nineteenth century and the early 1970s (it was about 43 per cent at both dates, having peaked at about 46 per cent in the early 1950s). However, by 1981, with the decline in Britain's international position and the growth in oil production, the proportion had fallen to 38 per cent.[25] By the end of the 1980s it had fallen below 30 per cent – a proportion matched by the value added in industry. Even more spectacularly, if we take manufacturing alone, its share of employment, which had been 35 or 36 per cent in the 1960s, and 31 per cent in 1975, had fallen to barely 26 per cent ten years ago and is now only about 20 per cent.

Indeed, just as the application for membership of the Common Market had borne out Joseph Chamberlain's perception of the need to belong to a larger and more coherent power bloc, so the profound slump of the early 1980s seemed the culmination of a process which appeared to justify his prophecies concerning deindustrialisation. Depression struck new as well as old industries. Mouse traps and dolls' eyes as well as iron and cotton were now in trouble. And, while the state withdrew from large parts of British industry, 'rationalisation' – the reduction in capacity and the ruthless streamlining of operations – broached with such meagre results in the 1930s, had at last come into its own. Between 1977 and 1983 British Steel lost 61 per cent of its labour force, British Leyland 53 per cent, British Shipbuilders 28 per cent – and major private firms such as Courtaulds, Tube Investments, Dunlop, and Talbot each lost over 50 per cent. And at a different level, the experience of the coal industry after the mid 1980s is a dramatic example of apparently catastrophic decline.

But will such changes *necessarily* prove catastrophic? No one would wish to claim that the fact that we are now a net importer of manufactured goods is a sure demonstration of economic health. But the reduction in industry's share of employment as an economy matures is hardly surprising, and in itself and alone it is of dubious significance in the context of the debate about decline. For one thing, and contrary to the new mythology, Britain

[25] R. E. Rowthorn and J. R. Wells, *De-industrialisation and foreign trade* (Cambridge, 1987), p. 10.

is not exceptional in its present level of industrialisation. The exceptional cases are, in fact, Germany and Japan. In 1989, for example, the proportion of the labour force engaged in industry in Britain was more or less the same as that in France, Belgium, and Sweden, and exceeded that in the USA, Norway, Holland, Denmark, and Canada. Of the leading developed economies only Germany and Japan had significantly larger percentages of their workers in industry, while the proportion of value added derived from industry was more or less the same in Britain, the USA, Belgium, Canada, France, Holland, and Sweden. (Again, only Germany and Japan were significantly more 'industrial'.)[26]

In any case, if British industry had been more dynamic, with higher levels of labour productivity, it is possible that the share of manufacturing in total employment would still have fallen, and perhaps significantly. Fewer people would still have been capable of producing more goods.[27] Mature economies simply need to devote less resources to the fabrication of material products – although they possibly do not need to shed resources with quite the precipitate and painful speed of Britain in the last 10 years. At the same time, and at a more sophisticated level of argument, the implications for real incomes of a continued deficit on trade in industrial goods are not particularly hopeful. And (more generally) it is important to sustain the potentially vital relationships between the production of high value services and the presence of a sophisticated industrial base.

In relation to structural change, therefore, the argument from inevitability and sophistication may be taken too far. Part at least of the process can be attributed not to the inexorable progress towards maturity, but to stagnation and/or low productivity in hitherto important industries, although even here the pain of structural dislocation in the face of trends in more rapidly developing non-European economies is no longer a singularly British phenomenon. But it does help explain why, until recently, industrial decline has most often been taken to mean the decline of specific industries and depression in particular regions – that is, structural change *within* manufacturing – especially when unaccompanied by commensurate shifts of labour to new and advanced industries. Indeed, it is in these senses

[26] N. F. R. Crafts, *Can de-industrialisation seriously damage your wealth?* (1993), p. 21.
[27] Rowthorn and Wells, *De-industrialization*, pp. 3–6. The authors point out that if British industrial productivity had been greater, then manufacturing output and national income would both have been higher (and the manufacturing balance of trade stronger – but not by much). Nevertheless, precisely because productivity would have been higher 'almost as many manufacturing jobs as were lost due to closures and lay-offs would have disappeared as a consequence of the automation and modernisation which would have characterised industrial success'.

that the image of decline has had perhaps the most significant actual effects on Britain in the twentieth century – if only because of the resulting tension between policies designed to defend and assuage the industries under pressure, and those designed to encourage more positive responses to adversity and more rapid adaptations of the industrial structure.

Nevertheless, it would be simplistic in the extreme to deduce decline from structural changes which are widely shared. And more than this, it is now clear that structural changes are not confined to intra-national developments.[28] The evolution of the global economic system is redefining the whole concept of the British economy, to the point at which it can hardly be compared with the economy of the 1890s. Some 25 per cent of the British GDP is now produced by foreign firms; and another large slice is owned and controlled by foreign multinationals. On the other side, any discussion of the performance of the 'British' economy must surely take account of the activities and income streams of British-owned firms worldwide. That alone indicates the need for caution when assessing such a protean concept as 'Britain's share of world manufacturing trade'.

III

So far I have considered two very large meanings of decline which have excited comment and debate for a century or more: a reduction in relative economic power on the world stage and in the relative significance of manufacturing. But there is a third sense in which Britain is said to have declined, in spite of the rise in living standards. Increasingly, national failure is interpreted in terms of the inadequacy of the Gross Domestic Product in relation to the changing objectives of expenditure, its inability to hit the constantly receding target of private and public aspirations.

Since about 1950 it has been found that the costs of retaining Britain's erstwhile military, imperial, and political position in the world grew very much faster than the British economy. Indeed, they grew until they first strained and then exceeded the potential of that economy to meet them. And it was probably the attempt to maintain an international role for the pound sterling and for British power overseas that, more than any deficiency of the British character, created the problems which led first to disproportionate attention being paid to the balance of payments, and subsequently to a compulsive anxiety about productivity and output in the

[28] I am indebted to Ron Martin for the line of reasoning in this paragraph.

export industries.[29] 'Export or die' was perhaps a surprising slogan for a nation getting richer by the year. But it adequately reflected the sense of malaise and inadequacy which characterised attitudes towards national economic performance in the third quarter of the twentieth century. In any event, the inevitable reaction – a change in aspirations and a withdrawal from that costly international role – reflects the most common meaning of the phrase 'national decline', just as the reluctant search for alternative arrangements (culminating in a still grudging membership of the European Community) was the principal example of a national reaction to the fact of that decline.

Yet ambitious (and ultimately frustrating) aspirations are subjective in character. They are therefore liable to disconcerting change. As a result, keeping up with the Joneses – or, rather, a sense that one is failing to keep up with the Joneses – has become one of the prime determinants of the psychology of welfare and dissatisfaction with economic performance. This is no doubt in large part a straightforward question of simple invidious comparison with Americans or Germans or Frenchmen. And on that basis the overhauling of British living standards by others over the last few decades is significant. More critically, however, and the reason why this image of decline has become a more pressing issue, is the spread of global communication, enhanced social aspirations, and the visible decay of facilities which are increasingly costly to update.

In important respects, of course, the statistical reality presents a different picture from the subjective perception: if the older citizens of Britain who were so enthused by the Beveridge Report in 1942 had been magically transported into even the recessionary Britain of 1992, they would undoubtedly be astounded at the advances in welfare services and private living standards. On the other hand, to those who have known little worse, or who want improvement measured by the most modern criteria, contemporary living standards (and, perhaps even more, contemporary public services) seem inadequate to the point of deprivation. We are most likely to think that things are going downhill when we forget how much higher we are than our predecessors. Yet elsewhere in the world – in Eastern Europe, for example, or in those parts of Asia where even more millions aspire to join British labour markets – it seems as if Britain is already at the summit of an Everest of material welfare and expectation. It is the index number problem – insoluble and frustrating – in another guise. And yet, while it is

[29] Manser, *Britain in the balance*, esp. ch. 4.

easy to assert that the sense of poverty is a subjective matter, it is difficult to persuade those who feel relatively poor or who are inconvenienced by an aging infrastructure, that their disappointments and sense of failure (or of being failed) are psychological in origin.

We are, then, back with problems not merely of interpersonal comparison, but the transmutation of individual appetite. The fact is that expectations and aspirations change. This is obvious in terms of private consumption. But it is doubly a problem in the public sphere. There, the expected and feasible standards of service (in health, education, and transport, for example) constantly rise. But at the same time the cost of providing either increasingly sophisticated technologies or inflexibly labour intensive services grows steadily in relative and real terms. Whether public services have actually deteriorated is a matter of controversy. But one thing is beyond doubt: spurred by the potential of modern technology and the example of other developed economies, the appetite of British society for consumption and investment (for public services and collective welfare, for household and leisure goods, for health and welfare) has grown appreciably faster than the actual output of British goods and services. The creation of wealth is insufficient to satisfy collective, let alone private, wants. Indeed, there does appear to be a potentially chronic problem (albeit a social and political as much as an economic one) in that the characteristic British rate of growth of 2 per cent in the medium run is simply insufficient to match the appetites and costs of post-industrial consumption patterns in the public and private domains – although it is a moot point whether other, even more 'developed' societies have a more contented population.

The dissatisfaction generated by any particular rate of industrial or economic development is therefore a function of ambition and aspiration, and the ambitions and aspirations of the British people are certainly not abating. Indeed, the speed and ubiquity of communication by the mass media, and the resulting observation of standards of consumption in wealthier nations, serve to excite expectations as never before. In the late twentieth century such knowledge – of what is now possible, of what other societies enjoy, of what seems desirable – exceeds the growth of wealth. Appetites expand because of what is known about developments elsewhere, or about new possibilities. But the ability to satisfy those appetites is constrained by developments within the available pool of British resources. And the British think that they are declining because, as their wants change, they are less able to satisfy them than their forefathers were able to satisfy, not modern wants, but their own much simpler requirements. All this

points to the need for a history of welfare and aspirations and consumption
– of the 'bounded rationality' of consumer expectations and satisfactions.
Even the purely material (or economic) measures of performance cannot be
approached solely in terms of comparative rates of change in output and
productivity. They must also be assessed in terms of an economy's success
in fulfilling expectations in an arena where those expectations change
because the achievements of other performers can be perceived. In the
tension between wants and satisfactions, perceptions play at least as important a role as statistics. We need an economic and social history of expectations.

Many Britons have lived through a period of extraordinarily drastic
transformations in the criteria of private affluence and of what is an acceptable provision of social and public services. And those changes have shown
beyond doubt that the problems of welfare and satisfaction are neither
trivial nor ephemeral. But by the same token they have shown that 'decline'
is neither an absolute concept nor even, perhaps, a statistical one.

IV

Each of the concepts of failure – the humiliation of the loss of international
power, the insecurity of deindustrialisation, and the frustration of felt needs
and aspirations – raises distinctive issues as far as the 'objective' validity of
the resulting anxieties is concerned. Decline is itself an ideology, and like
all ideologies it has its own history. Other countries have outpaced and, at
the margin, overtaken Britain. Structural change and decay have undoubtedly shaped and depressed modern British attitudes. In the course of the
depression of the early 1990s the national sense of decline became almost
pathological. Nor should we forget the more profound effects on attitudes
and institutions of the fall from international pre-eminence experienced by
Britain since the 1880s. These considerations are all critically relevant to
the political, social, and psychological evolution of Britain. But it also has
to be said that they give special meanings to 'decline' which are different
from those most often in the minds of pessimists.

As always, it is as well to take a long view. Of course, in this respect it may
be that there are depths still waiting to be plumbed – that the present recession may prove a turning point. But past experience does not support such
a conclusion. Rather, it warns against an apocalyptic interpretation of the
economic future. The fact, that needs frequent recall, is that over the last
100 years of complaint, and in spite of constant pessimism and its

unambiguous move to the wings of the world stage, the British economy has brought ever increasing material and social welfare to its participants. Little in recent history suggests cataclysmic change in the long-run course of British development. As Adam Smith reminded an anxious correspondent almost 200 years ago, 'be assured, my young friend, there is a great deal of ruin in a nation'.[30]

[30] *The correspondence of Sir John Sinclair, Bt* (1831), pp. 390–1. I am much indebted to Donald Winch for help in locating this quotation.

2

'A great deal of ruin in a nation'

DONALD WINCH

... five years have seldom passed away in which some book or pamphlet
has not been published, written too with such abilities as to gain some
authority with the publick, and pretending to demonstrate that the wealth
of the nation was fast declining, that the country was depopulated, agriculture neglected, manufactures decaying, and trade undone.
Adam Smith, *Wealth of nations*, II. iii. 33

I

Adam Smith's response to an alarmist comment on the likely consequences
of Britain's defeat at Saratoga in 1778 gives me my title, the epigraph supplies the theme. Anyone familiar with Smith's writings, whether as moral
philosopher or as political economist, will recognise the sceptical, perhaps
also stoical, tone of voice. Smith's 'phlegm, composure, and indifference',
real or assumed, was remarked upon even when he applied for the post of
Commissioner of Customs.[1] When dealing with the far less personal
matters raised by the 'economy of greatness', Smith rarely conceded much
to conscious wisdom and was decidedly hostile to that 'insidious and crafty
animal', the politician who was guided by the 'momentary fluctuations of
affairs'. While it is characteristic of Smith to maintain that economies
thrive in spite of the 'absurd nostrums' of politician-doctors, he was not
prepared to excuse them from responsibility for making things worse than
they might have been. Just as he attributed the defeats suffered at the hands
of the American militia to poor British generalship, so he was notoriously

I am grateful to Stefan Collini, Richard Whatmore, and Brian Young for their comments
on an earlier version of this chapter.
[1] See letter to Smith from Sir Grey Cooper, 7 November, 1777 in *Correspondence*, p. 228. This
and other references to Smith employ the conventions of *The Glasgow edition of the works
and correspondence of Adam Smith*, published by Oxford University Press, in 6 volumes,
1976–87. *WN* = *Wealth of nations*, *TMS* = *The Theory of moral sentiments*.

harsh in his judgement of the deleterious effects on the public interest of mercantile-influenced legislation in economic affairs.[2]

When faced by what appeared to be disastrous omens, or by the conceited claims of 'men of system' to reorder human affairs, then, Smith self-consciously adopted the contemplative stance of the impartial spectator – the person who was capable of keeping a cool head and taking the long view.[3] The stance was sometimes galling to contemporaries who felt that more commitment was required. Thus, when faced with the larger pattern of revolutionary events within which Saratoga was to prove an important turning point, Adam Ferguson, who rightly described himself as 'a war-like philosopher', criticised Smith for writing solely with posterity in view. As Ferguson saw it, Smith had chosen to write books 'that look big upon the shelve' rather than to support 'present action' – in this case to summon up the nation's resolve to administer a 'sound drubbing' to the colonies.[4] Ferguson was wrong in suggesting that the differences between himself and Smith were purely a matter of temperament, a clash between his own activist and patriotic sympathies and those dictated by a mandarin-like phlegmatism. Smith's coolness was the result of a great deal of thought and practical experience in advising on imperial matters. In the *Wealth of nations* this was expressed in the form of a detailed analysis and history of the colonial relationship which concluded that empire was merely a mercantile project that had mainly benefited a small part of the community, some of its merchants and manufacturers, leaving the chief burdens to be borne by taxpayers and consumers. Neither Britain's naval power nor her long-term economic prospects were endangered by the loss of empire. As the peroration of the *Wealth of nations* makes plain, forsaking the 'splendid and showy equipage of the empire' was the best means of reducing the domestic burden of taxation and public debt, and hence of allowing Britain 'to accommodate her future views and designs to the real mediocrity of her circumstances'.[5] Accommodation and mediocrity implied realistic assessment of strengths and weaknesses rather than avoidance of imminent decline, but Smith's conclusion is a reminder that he was far from indifferent to the

---

[2] 'England, tho' in the present times it breeds men of great professional abilities in all different ways . . . seems to breed neither Statesmen nor Generals'; see letter to W. Strahan, 3 June 1776 in *Corr.*, pp. 196–7.

[3] Smith regarded his Scottish provincial location, away 'from the seat of great scramble of faction and ambition' as one that made it easier to become 'more indifferent and impartial spectators of the conduct of all'; see *WN*, V.iii.90.

[4] See letter to Sir John Macpherson, 27 October 1777, Edinburgh University Library.

[5] *WN*, V.iii.92.

ruinous possibilities of public prodigality financed by Britain's system of public debt.

Writing books that do, indeed, look big upon the shelf was entirely compatible with down-to-earth appraisal of the opportunities and limits within which legislators, as well as politicians, were called upon to operate. Expressed in our inelegant language, Smith taught his contemporaries and successors not only how to gauge 'trade-offs', where these included 'non-economic' factors that were not susceptible to precise measurement, but the far more difficult lesson of how to make decisions to suit a world that is always 'second-best'. A principled knowledge of the best solution under ideal conditions was helpful when making such decisions, but it needed to be tempered by concern for what was possible and an estimate of the costs of moving from one imperfect state of affairs to another. In any collection of essays devoted to perceptions as well as to the realities of economic decline, therefore, no apology is needed for focusing on Smith. Whether seen as economic historian or as economist, it would be hard to match his credentials as the person who did most to create the mentality, as well as provide the criteria, by which the long-term economic performance of modern societies continues to be assessed by members of these two academic tribes. It could be argued – though it will not be here – that Smith's relationship with economic history, especially in this country, has been more intimate than the relationship many modern economists could now legitimately claim to have with their founding father.[6] Nor should it be necessary to state that the Smithian stance – even when correctly understood, still more when not – continues to excite controversy.

One ancient caricature of this stance is that normally labelled as *laissez-faire*. When translated into a programme for writing the economic history of Britain, it has antagonised a wide range of the political spectrum, from Tory paternalists to social democrats and Marxists, by its unwillingness to accord any positive role to the state in economic affairs. The caricature can be traced back to the early decades of the nineteenth century when the ideological stereotypes were being forged during the period of Britain's transition towards becoming a manufacturing nation. In an era that has

---

[6] In partial support let me cite two stylised facts, one quantitative the other qualitative. T. S. Ashton's *An economic history of England: the eighteenth century* (1955) contains twenty-five references to the *Wealth of nations*: no other author, contemporary or modern, receives anywhere near that number. In Donald Coleman's book on *History and the economic past: an account of the rise and decline of economic history in Britain* (Oxford, 1987), Smith furnishes a standard according to which a large number of his successors as economic historians are found wanting.

seen at least one Prime Minister pledge wholehearted allegiance to Smith's wisdom, and the birth of an Adam Smith Institute, the image has received powerful reinforcement during the last decades of the twentieth century. Showing that *laissez-faire* – what Thomas Carlyle castigated as 'do-nothingism' – is a caricature of Smith's position has been the object of scholarly attention for many years, beginning, perhaps, with Jacob Viner's seminal article on the subject written for the sesquicentenary of the *Wealth of nations* in 1926.[7] Having devoted some efforts of my own to showing that Smith's views on government generally, and politics in particular, were neither exiguous nor uninteresting in their own right, I would have to report little success in overcoming a popular idea that seems important to the identities of those on both the left and right of the political spectrum.

The divergence of view exemplified in the differences between Smith and Ferguson over the American revolution has also manifested itself in disputes between economic historians charting secular changes and those who take a more urgent view of the role of the historian as crusader, responding, or claiming to be more responsive, to human suffering, more anxious to achieve outcomes in accordance with ideal standards or political preferences. It features in the old debate between 'optimists' and 'pessimists' on the consequences of the industrial revolution, those whom Donald Coleman, borrowing from Peter Clarke, rechristened more informatively 'neutrals' and 'reformists'.[8] It can also be seen in the revisionist histories of the interwar period, where the comment of contemporaries was understandably more dramatic than those who came along later to point out that what filled the headlines did not accord with what was happening more slowly in the background, namely that unemployment in the regions where the staple industries were concentrated was compatible with rising living standards for those employed, and with evidence of growth and technological innovation elsewhere in the economy.

Over the last ten years or more Barry Supple has been engaged on detailed studies of the political economy of industrial decline in Britain during the twentieth century.[9] Reflecting on this work, he has recently reminded us of some recurring themes in the debate on the actual or presumed decline of the British economy over the past century. As my epigraph

---

[7] 'Adam Smith and laissez-faire' reprinted in his *Long view and the short* (Glencoe, Ill., 1958), pp. 213–45.

[8] See *History and the economic past*, chapter 5; and P. Clarke, *Liberals and Social Democrats* (Cambridge, 1978).

[9] See especially vol. IV of *The history of the British coalmining industry, 1913–46: the political economy of decline* (1987).

shows, Smith was engaged in similar controversy with those who contributed to the equivalent eighteenth-century literature of jeremiad. Indeed, an extension backwards in time to include what was, in some respects at least, a more justifiable set of anxieties, could place those expressed during the industrial and post-industrial periods of British history in better perspective. Potential sources of ruin, absolute and relative, were every bit as numerous in the eighteenth century as they were to become a century or more later, even if the range of comparative evidence and the statistical precision with which it could be marshalled was far more limited and shaky. One could, indeed, play an immediate high trump card by simply pointing to the fact that there could be no more solidly grounded fear of ruin than that posed by famine and dearth. While there was no recent experience of famine in eighteenth-century England, and some grounds for congratulation on the subject of agricultural improvements, the history of the Corn Laws and food riots throughout the 'long' version of the century is ample proof of the preoccupation of producers, consumers, and governments with the vagaries of harvest yields and grain prices. Periods of extreme grain scarcity punctuated the period over which Smith was writing the *Wealth of nations*, and they were to return with greater ferocity in 1795–6 and 1800–1 – significantly perhaps, as we shall see, after Smith had passed from the scene. Less dramatically, though equally telling, the historical experience of sustained improvement in standards of living was far more restricted and still inherently contestable on a variety of grounds that went well beyond what we now think of as the economic variables.

Precisely because Smith was so successful in creating a new agenda and the associated criteria for assessing economic performance, however, there is a risk of underestimating what was entailed in sustaining a position of 'phlegm, composure and indifference' during the third quarter of the eighteenth century. An appreciation of some of the peculiarities of Smith's position can best be acquired against the broader context of the literature of jeremiad, with Smith's silences on some of its themes sometimes being as eloquent as his positive pronouncements. Consideration of this context could also help to explain something else that deserves to be treated as problematic, namely what Smith does or does not have in common with those later 'classical' authors whose own speculations on economic growth began where the *Wealth of nations* ended. Although I have written on these topics at greater length elsewhere, I would now like to bring them into closer contact with some of the themes that have been prominent in the writings of the person who is the object of this *fest*. Nothing in my long friendship with Barry Supple suggests immodesty on his part – or, for that matter, undue modesty – but he would be a hard man to please if he was not flattered by an offering that links his preoccupations with those of Smith.

II

One should begin where much eighteenth-century discussion began, namely with increasing population treated, as Smith conventionally described it, as 'the most decisive mark of the prosperity of any country'.[10] In the literature of jeremiad, depopulation was often attributed to the spread of commerce and luxury, largely because of an association with the growth of unhealthy towns at the expense of those rural activities which produced the necessities of life. Much the same dire result could be attributed, as Oliver Goldsmith famously maintained in his *Deserted village*, to the conversion of rural estates into stately pleasure parks. The 'consumer revolution' that is now believed to have taken place during the eighteenth century, therefore, did not always lead contemporary observers to be confident in the permanency or desirability of its results.[11] Nor was it clear how far the benefits of luxury consumption by the rich had spread beyond the urban middling ranks to the populace at large, or whether it was wise in the interests of social stability that they should be so diffused. From the point of view that Smith sought to establish, defending the possibility of a modest revolution in rising expectations on the part of the mass of society had higher priority than celebrating its actual achievement. Those who adopted the 'modern' position – first scandalously epitomised by Bernard de Mandeville's slogan relating public benefits to private vices – could argue that luxury was an antidote to inequality. Others, adopting an 'ancient' viewpoint, including Goldsmith, in his poem at least, clung to the simpler view that the relationship between urban riches and rural poverty was of the zero-sum rather than positive feedback variety.

Spokesmen for the ancients and moderns on the connections between commerce, luxury, and populousness sometimes conducted their disputes in such simple binary terms. More often, however, the debate was devoted to establishing the golden mean – another translation for what Smith meant

---

[10] *WN*, I.viii.23.

[11] In speaking of a 'consumer revolution' I am, of course, referring to the work of N. McKendrick, J. Brewer, and J. H. Plumb, *The birth of consumer society: the commercialization of eighteenth-century England* (1982). For an indication of the range of work that has followed from this book see J. Brewer and R. Porter (eds.), *Consumption and the world of goods* (1993).

in speaking of 'mediocrity'. How should a balance be struck between a complex mixture of variables, positive and negative? At what point did losses outweigh benefits, rise become decline? If, as E. A. Wrigley has persuasively maintained, Smith and his immediate successors, Malthus and Ricardo, were more impressed by the asymptotic features of economic growth than its exponential properties, one could say that their immediate predecessors were more often attracted to images based on 'seeds of decay' and the inevitability of flux in human affairs – revolution in its original meaning, sometimes taking the form of inexorable cycles of rise and fall. Such images were, of course, more potent to a generation educated in the classics and mindful of the double-edged qualities of any comparison between their own age and that of Augustan Rome.[12] Against such a background of belief, the impact of confirmed omens of decay was all the more powerful. After all, speculative financial bubbles did in fact burst; and public debts were actually escalating and might threaten the form of government created in 1688.[13] Even if England looked like establishing primacy as a commercial and manufacturing power, it was still possible for some well-informed 'moderns' to dispute the durability of wealth founded on commerce and manufacturing: was it not a law of change that rich countries, simply because they were rich, would eventually be overtaken by those enjoying some of the main advantages of poorer aspirants to wealth, low wages and a capacity to copy the innovations of leaders?[14] Moreover, even if general depopulation could not be decisively proved, there were always likely to be some villages becoming deserted as London and other cities grew. Goldsmith certainly did not think he was imagining the state of Auburn that he depicted so elegiacally.

Judged by Benjamin Franklin's widely used estimates of the rate of population increase in the North American colonies (doubling every twenty to twenty-five years), something extraordinary was clearly happening across the Atlantic. But it was taking place under circumstances that were so peculiarly favourable as to make it seem utopian as a guide to anything that might happen in even the most advanced nations of Europe.

---

[12] On the double-edged meaning of 'Augustan' see J. W. Johnson, *The formation of English neo-classical thought* (Princeton, 1967), chapters 1 and 2.

[13] For what is still the authoritative work on this subject see P. M. G. Dickson, *The financial revolution: a study in the development of public credit, 1688–1756* (1967), especially chapter 2.

[14] This question was extensively debated by David Hume, Josiah Tucker, and others. For its significance see I. Hont, 'The "rich country–poor country" debate in Scottish classical political economy' in I. Hont and M. Ignatieff, *Wealth and virtue: the shaping of political economy in the Scottish Enlightenment* (Cambridge, 1983), pp. 271–315.

Although usually treated as an 'optimist' on questions of economic growth – a judgement that should not be accepted without significant qualification – Smith's estimate of current population increase in Europe was far more modest (doubling every 500 years).[15] Other experts, notably Richard Price, took a more dismal view, and there were those who, right up to the eve of the first census in 1801, were convinced that Britain's population was either at a standstill or in decline. Smith's conventionality in accepting population increase as the mark of improvement was not matched by an interest in contributing to the debate on the detailed causes of populousness conducted by others in his circle of acquaintances, notably David Hume, Robert Wallace, and Sir James Steuart. Smith was certainly not in favour of Steuart's agenda for the legislator on this question, giving him responsibility for achieving that balance between domestic manufacturing and agricultural activities which would ensure the most rapid increase of population. On Smith's interpretation, this result was best regarded as a by-product of the growth of opulence achieved by less direct means, chiefly through high rates of capital accumulation and the removal of restrictions which prevented the optimal allocation of capital and labour between employments according to a hierarchy which assumed that there were still unexploited opportunities in agriculture.

Equally, Smith did not bother to mount a frontal assault on the more colourful anti-luxury diagnoses advanced by Goldsmith and others. Nevertheless, it is not difficult to reconstruct the answers he would probably have given. While Smith would not have condemned all forms of durable magnificence (Versailles, Stowe, and Wilton were given favourable mention), he was more impressed by the benefits of making land the subject of trade. Freed from those feudal relics, the laws of primogeniture and entail, land would fall, as it had on the other side of the Atlantic, into the hands of those who were most likely to make the best use of its commercial and productive potential. On the general issues raised by luxury, of course, Smith became the leading spokesman for the 'modern' position, bypassing much of the moralising which characterised earlier discussions, and going well beyond what had become commonplace arguments on its benefits as a source of employment to the poor that was superior to alms. For example, Hume, in distancing himself from the Mandevillian paradoxes connecting private vices with public benefits, had felt it necessary to distinguish between 'innocent' and 'blameable' luxury. Smith, on the other hand,

---

[15] *WN*, I.viii.23.

though agreeing in the *Theory of moral sentiments* that Mandeville had merely been perverse in attempting to obscure such distinctions, makes little, if any, concession to the moralising strain in most contemporary comment on the subject. Although the luxuries of the rapacious rich are typified as mere 'baubles and trinkets' in both of his major works, the unintended public benefits that arise from their pursuit are given prominence. Moreover, the latter work is rightly judged to be innovative, not merely in its unwillingness to entertain moral distinctions when defining necessaries, conveniences, and luxuries, but in undermining the 'utility-of-poverty' doctrine by refusing to endorse 'the common complaint that luxury extends itself even to the lowest ranks of the people'.[16] When coupled with the distributional or welfare criterion that Smith added to his definition of what constituted a 'flourishing' or 'happy' state of affairs; when complemented by an account of the improvements in labour productivity which result from the extension of markets at home and abroad; and when completed by a demonstration that it was private 'frugality' rather than 'prodigality' that united the universal urge to private self-improvement with public good, the end result is a comprehensive overthrow of prevailing opinion, moralistic and Mandevillian, on the connections between luxury and economic growth.

The coolness of this position was supplemented by an increase in length of perspective. In place of the balance of trade as a barometer, Smith proposed the annual balance of consumption and production, considered not merely year by year, but over long periods of time. It was this balance – whether nations were maintaining, adding to, or running down their capital stock, and at what rate they were doing so – that now determined their growth prospects, and hence whether they should be classified as progressive, stationary, or declining. The same diagnosis could also be used to explain regional disparities within nations as well as between them. The 'annual labour' of a nation provided a measure of aggregate output that corresponded with the harvest year. Labour-time, treated as a measure of 'toil and trouble', furnished a welfare index of the declining effort that needed to be expended in order to exercise command over necessities, comforts, and luxuries over longer periods of time. Employing this criterion, Smith was able to conclude that the living standards of those whose labour fed,

---

[16] 'Under necessaries therefore, I comprehend, not only those things which nature, but those things which the established rules of decency have rendered necessary to the lowest rank of people. All other things, I call luxuries; without meaning by this appelation, to throw the smallest degree of reproach upon the temperate use of them.' *WN*, V.ii.i.3. The only concession to moral judgement is the word 'temperate'.

clothed, and housed the English nation had advanced during the two hundred years that had elapsed since the beginning of the reign of Elizabeth. With perhaps the hint of a concession to the cyclical mentality, he also estimated that it was 'a period as long as the course of human prosperity usually endures'.[17] Again, however, it is the modesty that needs to be stressed: although he believed that living standards had advanced during this period, the most Smith was willing to claim (perhaps a good deal in the circumstances and knowledge available at that time) was that the wages of the common labourer were 'no-where in this country regulated by [the] lowest rate which is consistent with common humanity'.[18]

The relevant span over which national success or failure should be judged had been lengthened to the decades and generations over which nations were capable of accumulating capital. Indeed, bearing in mind what Smith has to say about the decline of feudalism in Book III of the *Wealth of nations*, centuries were the relevant timescale for some of his observations. What we would now call a long-term macroeconomic indicator enabled Smith to place in much longer perspective the kinds of adverse structural or micro-economic changes on which so much of the literature of jeremiad focused. Although this does not mean that Smith was indifferent to structural change, the contrast with the response to economic crises, the 'short-termism' of much of the mercantile literature on economic policy, the subject of one of the chapters in Barry Supple's first book, is manifest.[19] It also gave Smith another opportunity to press home the best-known part of his attack on the economic valetudinarianism encouraged by spokesmen for the mercantile system:

There is no commercial country in Europe of which the approaching ruin has not frequently been foretold by the pretended doctors of this system, from an unfavourable balance of trade. After all the anxiety, however, which they have excited about this, after all the vain attempts of almost all trading nations to turn that balance in their own favour and against their neighbours, it does not appear that any one nation in Europe has been in any respect impoverished by this cause. Every town and country, on the contrary, in proportion as they have opened their ports to all nations; instead of being ruined by this free trade, as the principles of the commercial system would lead us to expect, have been enriched by it.[20]

This seems to confirm the familiar optimistic image of Smith, even possibly to reveal him as someone who was so convinced of the benefits to be

---

[17] *WN*, III.iv.20.   [18] *WN*, I.vii.28.

[19] See *Commercial crisis and change in England, 1600–1642* (Cambridge, 1959), chapter 9.

[20] *WN*, IV.iii.c.14.

derived from free trade that he minimised the costs of structural change and was oblivious to possible interruptions to the career of growth. In attacking balance-of-trade fallacies and preoccupations, Smith may have been guilty, as later historians of mercantile thinking have argued, of gaining polemical purchase by means of an assault on a straw man. The same cannot be said of his most daring application of the principles of free trade – namely to the internal and external trade in subsistence goods – where he claimed that free trade was the only viable long-term remedy for famine and dearth. This was a far bolder substantive stroke on Smith's part, one which has earned him the dubious reputation among the 'pessimists' or 'reformists' for almost single-handedly undermining the entire 'moral economy' of the domestic trade in the necessities of life.[21]

Against this, however, must be placed Smith's assumption that establishing a regime of complete free trade was a utopian dream as far as Britain was concerned: 'Not only the prejudices of the publick, but what is much more unconquerable, the private interests of many individuals, irresistibly oppose it.'[22] In addition to this political assessment, however, it would have run counter to Smith's entire approach to such matters to portray free trade as the *sine qua non* of economic advance. To have done so would have made him guilty of the fault he condemned in the French économistes. They were so attached to the completeness and perfection of their remedies that they overlooked the natural curative properties of economic life, forgetting the wise maxim that: 'If a nation could not prosper without the enjoyment of perfect liberty and perfect justice, there is not in the world a nation which could ever have prospered.'[23] Prudent management of the problems of transition is a prime feature of the advice Smith offered to legislators. Sensitivity to the constraints of living in a second-best world also led him to counsel an 'equitable regard' for established interests which required 'that change . . . should never be introduced suddenly, but slowly, gradually, and after a very long warning'. In attempting to calm fears about the economic consequences of the loss of mercantile empire, Smith first pointed out that there was a difference between recovery from the debilitating effects of an over-rich diet and true sickness, but he also recognised that where a 'great multitude of hands' had been employed in protected trades, 'humanity' required that 'freedom of trade should be restored only by slow gradations,

---

[21] As was extensively argued by E. P. Thompson. For what was destined to be his last and longest treatment of this question see 'The moral economy of the English crowd in the eighteenth century', originally published in 1971, but reprinted with an answer to his critics in *Customs in common* (1991), pp. 185–351.   [22] *WN*, IV.ii.43.   [23] *WN*, IV.ix.28.

and with a good deal of reserve and circumspection'. Provided that the underlying sources of capital were not impaired, however, manufacturing usually allowed for compensatory expansion in collateral trades. In nations that were already embarked on a career in commerce and manufacturing, it was always easier 'to change the direction of industry from one sort of labour to another, than to turn idleness and dissipation to any'.[24] Adopting the long view of causes carried with it an obligation to extend the same perspective to problems of adaptation to new circumstances and policies.

III

Although very little of this seems to suit the conviction politics and macho-style of micro- and macroeconomic management encouraged by some of Smith's late twentieth-century admirers, there are clear parallels between Smith's attempts to steady the nerve of his contemporaries and Barry Supple's own exercises in the same art. But first one needs to consider briefly the evidence that E. A Wrigley has marshalled to show that Smith, Malthus, and Ricardo were still wedded to an asymptotic view of future possibilities that can be attributed to living in a pre-industrial world confined to animate sources of energy.[25] This alone would differentiate them from the assumptions of Barry Supple's complainants, all of whom make exponential growth their fundamental axiom – so much so, indeed, that failure to achieve the expected or hoped-for rate of increase in comparison with other nations is often taken as evidence of decline. For reasons that it would take another essay to rehearse, I think that Smith's approach to growth is more open-ended than that of his two main successors, largely because what is rightly known as the Malthusian dilemma – rapid population growth against a presumed background of diminishing returns in domestic agriculture – features less prominently in the *Wealth of nations* than it does in the writings of his disciples. The possibilities of stationariness, stagnation, and even immiseration that exist in the models (if not empirical assessments of British prospects) of Malthus and Ricardo, take second place in Smith to the opportunities on offer through expanding markets and increasing returns. Moreover, faced with the problem that was to become central to Ricardo's speculations, falling rates of profit, Smith gave an answer that was diametrically opposed to that of his successor. Low

---

[24] *WN*, IV.ii.40–4.
[25] See 'The classical economists and the Industrial Revolution' in *People, cities and wealth* (Oxford, 1987).

profits should be welcomed as a sign of progress rather than as a warning of impending capital flight and the exhaustion of sources of accumulation. High profits were usually a sign of successful abridgment of competition that was inimical to parsimony, the effective management of resources, and the rate of accumulation.[26]

Rather than enter into the complex mixture of doctrinal and other issues that underlie these differences, however, it may be better on this occasion to stick with the objective external factors that help to explain why Smith's successors, even if they fully shared his opinion on the unlikelihood of imminent ruin, were more preoccupied with conceivable limits to growth. In headline fashion, these arose from recognition, especially under conditions of war and attempted economic blockade, that Britain had become a regular net importer of foodstuffs; that her population was expanding at a rate far higher than anything Smith or Malthus had originally anticipated (doubling every fifty-five years); and that in spite of rapid growth under conditions of war, there was an alarming upward trend in expenditure on poor law relief. It might also be possible to argue that the reports of select committees on agriculture during the Napoleonic wars suggested, wrongly as it turned out, that improvements in agricultural technology were not regular or strong enough to offset tendencies towards diminishing returns.

As befitted their role as Smith's self-conscious disciples, neither Malthus nor Ricardo gave way to the kinds of jeremiad common among business-men under postwar circumstances of deflation and depression. Ricardo was, if anything, far more sanguine than Smith or Malthus about the efficacy of monetary disciplines and market incentives in bringing about rapid read-justment to policy change and economic upheaval. In this respect at least, and overlooking some unfortunate associations of Ricardianism with Marxism, less caricature would have been involved if Thatcherites had chosen to form a David Ricardo Institute rather than one based on Smith.

Ricardo and Malthus also resisted extreme 'patriotic' and paternalistic diagnoses of impending doom from those who thought, as Samuel Taylor Coleridge put it, that 'the nation that cannot exist without the goods of another nation is the slave of that nation'.[27] The long-term interest of con-sumers was still the criterion by which economic success should be judged, even if the empirical and political assessments of Malthus and Ricardo on

---

[26] 'A great stock, though with small profits, generally increases faster than a small stock with great profits.' *WN*, I.ix.11. For a fuller treatment of this argument see my *Riches and poverty: an intellectual history of political economy in Britain, 1750–1834* (Cambridge, 1996).

[27] See *Table talk* in *The collected works of Samuel Taylor Coleridge* (Princeton, 1969–93), volume XIV (1), pp. 476–7.

this subject differed. Malthus, having made population pressure an ever-present problem, rather than one that might lie in some distant future, was always more responsive to the problem of secure food supplies. He was also less convinced than Smith or Ricardo had been about the inevitability of aggregate demand expanding in line with aggregate production. Hence Malthus's apostasy on the Corn Laws in 1815, and his revival of some aspects of the pre-Smithian concern with 'seeds of decay' to express his anxieties. Those 'natural' conditions which Smith had assumed as part of the underlying reality of a 'landed nation', such as Britain still appeared to be in the third quarter of the eighteenth century, now needed to be recreated, possibly by artificial expedients that would slow down an unbalanced form of structural change in which commerce and manufacturing were growing more rapidly than the domestic capacity to support a steeply rising population.

In hindsight, of course, the asymptotic vision that can be found in the theories of Malthus and Ricardo, and the cautious way in which Malthus greeted the emergence of Britain as a manufacturing nation reliant on exports to feed its population, now seem either wrong-headed or faint-hearted. Yet given what we now know of the unprecedented nature of population growth in Britain during the first decades of the nineteenth century, a case can be made for saying that anxiety about 'deagrarianisation' and Britain's emerging dependence on foreign trade was every bit as justifiable as late twentieth-century anxiety about 'deindustrialisation' and a falling share of world trade in manufactured goods. Unequivocal signs of relief from earlier pressures on the standards of living of most wage-earners did not appear until the 1830s, after both Ricardo and Malthus had died. Smith's successors had their own reasons for not going much beyond the cautious hope that economic growth, if accompanied by control over the rate of population increase, was *capable* of delivering its benefits to the populace at large.

In another respect, however, Smith's early nineteenth-century successors could be more confident that Britain was on the way towards establishing itself as the leading commercial and manufacturing power in every sense of the term. Having survived the loss of the jewel in the crown of its western empire, as Smith had confidently said Britain would, the defeat of France in 1815 put an end to a military threat that had existed, intermittently, throughout the eighteenth century and had made a dramatic reappearance during the Napoleonic war period. From Samuel Taylor Coleridge's protectionist position, therefore, while he was right to think of political economy as having cosmopolitan overtones, he was merely giving way to journalistic exaggeration when he went on to condemn its 'tendency to make love of country a foolish superstition'.[28] Offering new indices of plenty did not mean that opulence was being separated from power, merely that an alternative way of achieving both power and plenty was being advanced. When Smith said that defence was more important than opulence, he was purveying a common-sense truth rather than making a significant concession or uttering a thought-provoking paradox. Considerations of power and plenty were as much part of his vision as they were to the mercantilists he attacked, or – to revert once more to Barry Supple's cast – to post-Boer-War tariff reformers at the beginning of the twentieth century. Following the example of his friend, David Hume, Smith had ridiculed 'jealousy' of other nations by showing the inappropriateness of perceiving international trade as a zero-sum game. But this did not make him a starry-eyed internationalist in a world of warring nations. Nor, by the same token, did it mean that he was creating a neo-mercantilist tradition that would later seek British industrial hegemony at any cost. To portray Smith and his followers as free-trade imperialist wolves in cosmopolitan sheep's clothing, as those who have followed the example of Alexander Hamilton and Friederich List have done, is merely to replace Coleridge's exaggeration with another on the opposite side of the account.[29]

There was a genuinely cosmopolite dimension to Smith's ideal solution to the American dispute. With free trade established, commerce could become 'a bond of union and friendship' between nations rather than 'the most fertile source of discord and animosity'.[30] Although not particularly sympathetic towards the constitutional claims of the American revolutionaries, or even towards the republican system of government they put in place of Britain's mixed constitution, Smith could calmly contemplate the time when America, the 'progressive' state *par excellence*, would overtake Britain in wealth and taxable capacity. Risking a rare long-run prediction, he said that this would probably happen within the next century (was it true as early as 1876?). Despite Ferguson's suspicions to the contrary, however, Smith was also capable of lending discreet support to such essentially patriotic enterprises as the ex-Loyalist George Chalmers's *Estimate of the compar-*

---

[28] See ibid, p. 487.
[29] For a couple of studies that err in this respect see B. Semmel, *The rise of free trade imperialism; classical political economy, the Empire of Free Trade, and imperialism, 1750–1850* (Cambridge, 1970); and M. Panic, *National management of the international economy* (1988), chapter 7 on 'The doctrine of Free Trade: internationalism or disguised mercantilism?'
[30] *WN*, IV.iii.c.9.

ative strength of Britain in 1785. One of Chalmers's targets was Richard Price, whom Smith described as a 'factious citizen'. Price's pessimistic assessments of Britain's population and finances were certainly not a neutral exercise in political arithmetic. Not only did Smith have a low opinion of the statistical reliability of such exercises, but he understood that jeremiad was rarely an exercise in impartial spectatorship. Price's predictions, like those of Thomas Paine later, were part of an effort to convince the British public that pursuit of war against the new American nation, and later the infant French republic, was not only unjust, but could only end in national disaster. The late eighteenth-century equivalent to Joseph Chamberlain's despondency on the subject of Britain's isolation and loss of competitiveness, the background to his ambitious plans for imperial preference combined with domestic welfare reforms, can be found in the writings of those who hoped that the example of America and France would undermine monarchy as a form of government in Britain. In 1796 Paine actually predicted the collapse of Britain's financial and banking system within the lifetime of Pitt, the present Prime Minister.[31] Although, like some of Chamberlain's more dire predictions, this could be cited as yet another example of a jeremiad that misfired, that does not mean that the underlying concern was entirely without foundation to those living through the episode.

By then, of course, Smith was no longer available to supply a calming response. While he would certainly not have approved of Paine's estimates or motives, he could, as has already been noted, entertain the possibility of 'impoverishment' arising out of public prodigality, aided by the institution of public debt. When dealing with this institution in Book V of the *Wealth of nations*, Smith endorsed the conventional position that the burden of debt would 'in the long-run probably ruin all the great nations of Europe'.[32] In this case, however, not only did he take a less calamitous view than Hume, but he wisely did not venture a prediction of how long the long run would prove to be. Indeed, having pointed out that Britain's economic growth had made the burden easier to bear, he had drawn attention to the most important factor postponing ruin.

It is one of the many ironies surrounding Smith's reputation that a few decades after his death in 1790 he should have been thought to be overly cautious, even overly cynical, in his assessment of the chances of the adoption of free trade in Britain, if not the world at large. By the middle point

---

[31] See Thomas Paine, *The decline and fall of the English system of finance*, 1796.
[32] *WN*, V.iii.10.

of the century, the movement for which he was regarded as the patron saint was the source of a good deal of national self-satisfaction. It was also giving rise to apprehensions about world domination from foreign observers of the British monster. In an essay dealing with perceptions of greatness and ruin, therefore, it seems worth balancing Barry Supple's later British cast with the fears of an earlier commentator on British hegemony. Writing in 1837, Friederich List viewed the outcome of Smith's 'cosmopolitical economy' with that mixture of admiration and fear that words like *Schadenfreude* were surely coined to describe:

How vain do the efforts of those appear to us who have striven to found their universal dominion on military power, compared with the attempt of England to raise her entire territory into one immense manufacturing, commercial, and maritime city, and to become among the countries and kingdoms of the earth, that which a great city is in relation to its surrounding territory: to comprise within herself all industries, arts, and sciences: all great commerce and wealth; all navigation and naval power – a world's metropolis which supplies all nations with manufactured goods, and supplies herself in exchange from every nation with those raw materials and agricultural products of a useful or acceptable kind, which each other nation is fitted by nature to yield to her – a treasure house of all great capital – a banking establishment for all nations, which controls the circulating medium of the whole world, and by loans and the receipt of interest on them makes all the peoples of the earth her tributaries.[33]

List also predicted what would happen if Britain succeeded in convincing other nations to accept a free-trade world:

All England would . . . be developed into one immense manufacturing city. Asia, Africa, and Australia would be civilised by England, and covered with new states modelled after the English fashion. In time a world of English states would be formed, under the presidency of the mother state, in which the European Continental nations would be lost as unimportant, unproductive races. By this arrangement it would fall to the lot of France, together with Spain and Portugal, to supply this English world with the choicest wines, and to drink the bad ones herself; at most France might retain the manufacture of a little millinery. Germany would scarcely have more to supply this English world with than children's toys, wooden clocks, and philological writings . . . It would not require many centuries before people in this English world would think and speak of the Germans and the French in the same tone as we speak at present of the Asiatic nations.[34]

As always, hindsight lends irony to such exercises in futurology, particularly when one thinks of what is happening to manufacturing on the world's Asiatic rim, or when considering recent speculations about the effects on

---

[33] *The national system of political economy* (1885 edn), p. 365.   [34] *Ibid.*, p. 131.

Britain of living with a European common currency dominated by the Bundesbank. Nevertheless, it may still be worth remembering that there was a time when List could gain a ready hearing outside Britain by expressing such fears. I would rather leave to economic historians the task of estimating for how long after 1837 List's forebodings had any credibility, but my personal guess would be for about three or four decades.

IV

Smith's sangfroid is still capable of perplexing those with more warm-blooded sympathies and hopes. For example, his diagnosis of the debilitating effects of the division of labour on all those confined to specialised manual tasks is so comprehensive that it offers no scope for a solution that could be applied at the work-place. It was undoubtedly easier for an eighteenth-century moral philosopher than for a modern economist to accept that the civic and moral deficiencies of an emerging mode of economic existence were not entirely susceptible to *economic* remedies. Some of his followers, notably Frederick Morton Eden, found Smith's diagnosis 'somewhat too highly coloured'.[35] Others, notably Karl Marx, found Smith's educational and other remedies for the condition contemptibly moderate, 'mere homeopathic doses'.[36] The divergence between utopian and non-utopian or meliorist styles of thinking could not be clearer: Smith believed that it was his duty as an impartial spectator to draw up a balance sheet of the gains and losses that accompanied economic progress, and having done so to propose means of minimising those losses that could not be eliminated. Inability to do everything did not excuse one from doing something.

Nor would Smith have claimed that commercial opulence was immune from what he described, again with what might seem like infuriating distance, as 'the *ordinary* revolutions of war and government'.[37] Instead of this being regarded as taking refuge in a world-weary or purely contemplative stance, it should be taken as a reminder of the extent to which outcomes depended on human folly and wickedness that could only be imperfectly controlled by legal and other institutional constraints. A 'science of the legislator' would not have made much sense if it left no scope for the exercise of prudence and will. Smith's voluntarism in such matters is perhaps too audacious for generations brought up on the social sciences he helped to create. Smith's form of realistic conservatism – by which I simply mean that

[35] *The state of the poor* (1797), 3 volumes, vol. I, p. 420.
[36] *Capital* (Moscow edition), vol. I, p. 362.   [37] *WN*, III.iv.24. My italics.

combination of belief in permanent imperfection with a preference for explaining events as unintended consequences – has obvious historiographic virtues when interpreting the human record over long periods. But like patriotism, conservatism is not enough. We live our lives looking forward, thinking of our children and grandchildren, forming new expectations and standards by which we judge our successes and failures. Smith did not believe that it was possible to offer advice to the legislators of the future. Yet it is impossible to avoid seeking answers to that ultimate counterfactual: would we be better, wiser, and richer if we were not as we are? It is certainly preferable to complacency, regret, and nostalgia – the defects of long memory and old age, with the last of these having the most natural of cures. Looking sideways at others who seem to be more successful can merely be an exercise in fruitless envy, but it is also one essential way of formulating answers to the counterfactual question. The communications revolution, along with foreign travel, let alone the barrage of comparative statistics now available, disturbs national complacency and fuels our discontents. As might be anticipated, Smith also supplied us with an aphorism on this subject: 'The most sublime speculation of the contemplative philosopher can scarce compensate the neglect of the smallest active duty.'[38] It does not need to be said, perhaps, that by philosopher Smith also meant political economist and economic historian. I like to think he might even have included historians of economics, if he had not been preoccupied with making that trade a more interesting possibility.

[38] *TMS*, VI,ii,3.6.

3

The security of the realm and the growth of the economy, 1688–1914

PATRICK K. O'BRIEN

I

Braudel insisted that the rise and decline of nations can only be comprehended by taking very long time spans, which will allow persistent or structural parameters conditioning economic performance to be exposed and evaluated. By focusing on *la longue durée*, a historian might locate significant conjunctures or discontinuities, which, looked at retrospectively from some vantage or end point, can shape a narrative and endow it with some rhetorically persuasive power.

My approach to 'understanding Britain's decline' surveys two and a quarter centuries of political economy from the Glorious Revolution in 1688 to the outbreak of the First World War in 1914 in an attempt to reintegrate the significance of state power into economic analyses concerned with inseparable connections between the rise and the decline of the British economy. Furthermore, the chapter will try to reinstate metropolitan and central government into the still dominant Ashtonian and Mancunian traditions in the writing of British economic history; traditions which connect the growth of national output to private consumption, private capital formation, and technological change supposedly emerging in large part as the outcome of investments of time, money, and skill by private firms and gifted artisans from the north of England. Ashton says almost nothing about government in his classic on the industrial revolution except that 'the instinct of the industrialist was to eschew politics. It was not by the arts of lobbying or propaganda but by unremitting attention to their own concerns . . . they became a power – perhaps the greatest power – in the state.'[1] I wish to argue that economic histories that implicitly denigrate govern-

---

[1] T. S. Ashton, *The Industrial Revolution, 1760–1830* (Oxford, 1948), p. 132. The proportions allocated to discussions of government and economy by two recent texts are: 7 per cent by P. Hudson, *The Industrial Revolution* (London, 1992) and about 10 per cent by M. Daunton, *Progress and poverty. An economic and social history of Britain, 1700–1850* (Oxford, 1995).

ment by ignoring its contribution to long-term growth of the kingdom are underspecified. Furthermore, too many of the accounts that attempt to deal with the state are 'Smithian' and basically celebrate a trajectory from the corrupt, costly aristocratic and militaristic regime that ruled from 1688 to 1832 to the economically benign liberal *laissez-faire* governments of Victorian times – a history that now looks seriously misleading.

II

A long perspective also exposes the conjuncture or discontinuity in the role of the state that certainly did not occur in the wake of the publication of the *Wealth of nations* in 1776, or after the passage of the first reform bill in 1832, but rather with the final defeat in 1815 of Iberian, Dutch, and above all French pretensions to countervail the Hanoverian kingdom's conjoined strategy for the safety of the realm, for the dominance of global trade, and for the preservation of a maritime Empire in Asia, Africa, and the Americas.

At sea, Europe's mercantilist age came virtually to an end at Trafalgar and on land at Waterloo. When Castlereagh signed the Treaty of Vienna, which successfully preserved the balance of power for several decades before the unification of Germany, Britain had emerged as *the* hegemonic naval and commercial power in Europe and was, moreover, in the middle of its industrial revolution.

Massive and sustained public investment in military and naval power had been required to reach a position from which national security could be taken for granted and London's dominance in servicing global commerce and British industry's leading position in the sale of manufactures on world markets seemed assured for decades to come. In an era of mercantilism and frequent resort to warfare among European powers, the costs of that 'public investment' had, however, developed into a real burden on British taxpayers and their economy. Between the Glorious Revolution and victory at Waterloo, Parliament agreed to mobilise the forces of the crown on nine occasions and in real terms taxation rose by a multiplier of eighteen. When honourable members and peers deposed James II and called upon William of Orange to preserve the protestant succession, the share of taxes came to only 3 to 4 per cent and the nominal capital of the public debt amounted to a mere 5 per cent of the national income. In 1819 when Lord Liverpool's administration returned the currency to gold and more or less completed the return of the financial system to a peacetime footing, the scale of public debt amounted to more than double Britain's gross national product and the share appropriated by central government as taxes came to 16 per cent, a decline from a high of 19 per cent in the closing years of the war to defeat of Napoleon.[2]

An overwhelming proportion (perhaps up to 90 per cent) of all the money raised in the form of loans or appropriated as taxes over these 127 years was allocated to sustain and equip the forces of the crown (including the troops of Britain's allies) and the Royal Navy. Their mission was to defend the realm, to prevent the domination of Europe by a 'universal monarch', to protect the kingdom's foreign trade, and to secure territory, populations, natural resources, fishing rights, and access to markets across the Atlantic, in Africa, the Middle East, and in India and China.

Whatever the ebbs and flows of intellectual discourse and political debates over strategy, or the hesitations and expediency that year by year accompanied Britain's rise to the status of Europe's hegemonic naval and imperial power, recently plotted fiscal trends represent hard statistical evidence of sustained commitments on the part of the crown and Parliament to a permanent enlargement of the military capacity of the Hanoverian state, which was harnessed to preserve national security, conjoined, indeed conflated, with the protection of trade and empire.[3]

Economists find it difficult to theorise with their accustomed rigour about defence. They decline to regard military expenditures as investment and are reluctant to recognise the enormous and wide-ranging benefits that flow from national security as an inseparable component of any properly formulated social welfare function. But looking back at the sequence of wars fought during the eighteenth century, economic historians have acquired the perspective to appreciate that public investment in the navy, in the acquisition of bases and colonies, and in the deployment of military power to secure access to markets beyond the borders of the kingdom mattered for the long-term growth of foreign trade during the industrial revolution.[4] Alas, and by ignoring inseparable connections between trade and the security and the stability of the regime, they have preferred latterly

---

[2] The data related to the taxation, borrowing, and expenditures by the British governments from 1688 to 1815 are available from the Economic and Social Research Council Data Archive (ref. ESFDB obrien/engm.ool.ss.d). In a calibrated form the data are referenced in P. K. O'Brien, 'The political economy of British taxation, 1660–1815', *Economic History Review*, 2nd ser., 41 (1988), pp. 1–32.

[3] For a nuanced and fully documented narrative which eschews structural explanations, see J. G. Black, *British foreign policy in the age of revolutions* (Cambridge, 1994).

[4] K. Harley, 'Foreign trade, comparative advantage and performance', in R. P. Floud and D. McCloskey (eds.), *The economic history of Britain since 1700* (Cambridge, 2nd edn 1994), vol. I, pp. 300–31.

to concentrate on static equilibrium exercises designed to assess the overall importance of exports and imports for the development of the economy. That debate has also become ideologically and anachronistically suffused with modern concerns about a proper role for governments in an economy. Those who deplore 'state interference' know that if the historical significance of foreign trade could be minimised, then the gains to British society imputable to expenditures by the government will seem disproportionately small compared to the 'costs' of the taxes and the 'crowding out' effects of the loans it raised to secure markets and sources of supply beyond the frontiers of the realm.

The overall significance of external demand and inputs from overseas must certainly be compared to the nation's natural endowments, internal trade, rising agricultural productivity, technological change, urbanisation and several other 'forces for growth' only indirectly connected to international commerce. Any satisfactory depiction or quantified assessment of the relevant interconnections seems to require the construction of an imaginative counterfactual scenario for the long-term development of the British economy proceeding without help or hindrance from its ever closer integration into the evolving international economy of the period.

Taking a cue from David Hume and quotations from Adam Smith and other critics of mercantilism, a predominantly North American group of economic historians have risen to the challenge and used cliometric techniques to demonstrate that the material gains from state-supported participation in global commerce could well have been small and dispensable components of British industrialisation.[5] Their heuristically provocative hypotheses rest, however, upon a drastically foreshortened timescale for the analysis of the essentially long-term nature of the industrial revolution. Their parsimonious models of the multifaceted connections between trade and growth are underspecified, ignore externalities, and for purposes of econometric measurement are compelled to assert the persistence of full employment and, what is less probable, to assume that the deployment of the resources (used by both private and public sectors to engage in global trade) could well have been only marginally more productive and profitable than their allocation to domestic production for purposes of internal trade.[6]

[5] The classic statement appeared in R. P. Thomas and D. McCloskey, 'Overseas trade and empire, 1700–1860', in R. P. Floud and D. McCloskey (eds.), *The economic history of Britain since 1700* (Cambridge, 1st edn 1981), vol. I, pp. 87–102.

[6] P. K. O'Brien and S. L. Engerman, 'Exports and the growth of the British economy from the glorious Revolution to the Peace of Amiens', in B. L. Solow (ed.), *Slavery and the rise of the Atlantic system* (Cambridge, 1991), pp. 177–209.

In order to evaluate the costs of investment in colonisation conjoined with protection for British commerce, some cliometricians have even resorted to the counterfactual of a liberal international economic order operating between 1688 and 1815 under competitive conditions virtually free from interference by governments and untroubled by warfare among the great powers.

Needless to say, the chronology, assumptions, and latterly the data upon which the derogation of trade, mercantilism, and empire rest, have all been revised.[7] Since Smith, the critique of Hanoverian commercial and imperial policy has dominated too much of the high ground for academic discourse. It is surely time to rescue the widespread political consensus that marked the period from the condescension of posterity. Very few of its 'enlightened' and far-sighted critics writing between 1688 and 1815 (selected for inclusion in the canon of economic thought) developed an alternative strategy for national development that offered to carry Britain to the expensively acquired position within the international economic and political order that the country occupied when Castlereagh signed the Treaty of Vienna. Over the period nearly everyone (statesmen, Members of Parliament, Anglican scholars, mercantilist intellectuals, and above all merchants) perceived that economic progress, national security, and the integration of the kingdom might well come from sustained levels of investment in global commerce, naval power, and, whenever necessary, the acquisition of bases and territory overseas. Cliometricians who, with hindsight, now suggest that realistic counterfactual strategies were in fact available, might lay them out for inspection, and explain why a polite but 'commercially aggressive' people failed to adopt their prescriptions between 1688 and 1815. They might also care to suggest how rival European powers might have responded to a unilateral declaration of free trade and withdrawal from colonisation by the Hanoverian state.[8]

Meanwhile, burdens of taxation certainly increased dramatically over time. No doubt taxes distorted and constricted the growth of the economy. Nevertheless, the degree of compliance, secured from Parliaments (disposed, rhetorically at least, to resist all taxes) and from a traditionally recalcitrant body of taxpayers, suggests that a strong degree of consensus existed about the broad objectives of state expenditure. That consensus, embedded

---

[7] For recent revisions to the data, see J. Cuenca Esteban, 'Britain's terms of trade and the Americas, 1772–1821' (unpublished paper, University of Waterloo, Ontario, April 1994).

[8] The debate is judiciously reviewed by J. Mokyr in J. Mokyr (ed.), *The British Industrial Revolution. An economic perspective* (Boulder, Col., 1993).

in the commercial and imperialistic cultures of British society, had to be sustained, however, by fiscal policies that avoided direct forms of taxation, exempted the 'necessities' of a potentially disorderly underclass from indirect taxes and structured their incidence in ways that kept the economy on course. Furthermore, borrowing by the state (represented in figures published regularly and showing an alarmingly rapid accumulation of the national debt) funded the immediate and sharp rises in expenditures on the naval and military force required to combat Britain's foes and rivals at times of conflict. 'Crowding out' certainly occurred but there is no hard evidence that borrowing by central government occurred on a scale sufficient to depress significantly private investment in the infrastructural facilities and capital goods required in the long term for the development of the economy.[9] On the contrary, there are valid arguments (well rehearsed in the mercantilist literature of the period) to conceive of high levels of public 'investment' in naval power and military force as complementary and necessary to sustain what were, in international terms, rather impressive rates of capital accumulation by the private sector. For a mercantilist age, marked by persistent recourse to warfare among European powers, it seems anachronistic for historians to classify expenditures under antithetical labels (derived from a modern national-accounts framework) into 'public consumption' and 'private investment'. At the time such allocations were more realistically regarded as connected and inseparable elements of a package of policies that aggregated into a successful strategy for the economic development and the defence of the realm.[10]

III

Apart from its core commitments to defence conjoined with the pursuit of power with profit in global commerce, the Hanoverian regime continued to be as deeply concerned (as its Stuart and Tudor predecessors had been) with internal security and the establishment of rules for the efficient operation and development of a capitalist market economy within the British Isles.

Good order provided conditions within which business could be carried on without hindrance from groups who refused to recognise the sovereign's

---

[9] The debate concerned with 'crowding out' is surveyed and referenced in C. Heim and P. Mirowski, 'Interest rates and crowding out during Britain's Industrial Revolution', *Journal of Economic History*, 47 (1987), pp. 117–40.

[10] L. Stone (ed.), *An imperial state at war. Britain from 1689 to 1815* (1994).

authority over particular provinces of a nominally united realm. Production everywhere had also to be protected from challenges to property rights, established and enforced under the law. Finally, stable levels of economic activity could only be assured if risks from crime were kept to some minimal and predictable level.

England had been united with Wales as early as 1536. In 1707 Scotland was formally incorporated into a common British market with no legal barriers to trade, migration and capital flows; a market which operated, moreover, with a single currency. Alas, these formal conditions, established for the economic integration of Scotland into a Protestant and linguistically unified kingdom, did not ensure good order, particularly in the Highlands. Jacobite threats to trade and property (even within England) persisted even beyond 1745. Scotland's integration into a 'British' economy took place gradually and in large part as the outcome of an enthusiastic response from Scots' capital, labour, and merchants to opportunities to engage in global and in imperial commerce, under the tutelage of London's businessmen and financiers and the protection of the Hanoverian navy.[11]

Irish troops fought at Culloden. Serious revolts against the crown occasioned savage repression in the 1690s and a century later in 1798. Although Pitt's union of 1801 created the legal framework for a single market, the 'province' never developed into just another region of the economy, free from challenges both to the sovereignty of the Westminster Parliament and to 'English'-owned rights to land and other property located in Ireland. As with Scotland, concessions and opportunities accorded by Westminster to allow for full participation in domestic and imperial trade, helped to alleviate a justified sense of discrimination that existed before the Union. Thereafter religious toleration, flexibly implemented demands for taxes, and the extension of tenants' rights, helped up to a point to reconcile the Irish to English 'domination'. Nevertheless, as Gladstone, and some segments of the Liberal party recognised decades before the troubles of 1916 to 1922, if free trade and a common currency had been coupled with some sort of 'home rule', that might well have lowered the costs of government and integrated Ireland efficiently into a more economically united kingdom.[12]

Owners of private property in England and Wales enjoyed a more or less clear, secure, and enforceable system of rights to land, minerals, houses,

---

[11] A. Grant and K. Stringer (eds.), *Uniting the kingdom. The making of British history* (1995).
[12] S. Connolly, R. A. Houston, and R. J. Morris (eds.), *Conflict, identity and economic change in Ireland and Scotland* (Edinburgh, 1992).

industrial and commercial capital, inventories, and other productive assets long before the Glorious Revolution.[13] Challenges to the system came, however, whenever those with legally enforceable powers over their own assets clashed with other social groups, who believed that they possessed customary or moral rights of access to rivers, to public rights of way, to the game and produce of forests, to common grazing land, to minerals, to shelter, and to cheap food and fuel, as well as privileges ostensibly guaranteed by Elizabethan statutes to control entry to gilds and to monopolise the skills acquired to manufacture a wide range of industrial commodities.[14]

Social histories covering the period 1688 to 1815 are full of episodes of social protest and appeals to Parliament by the many sections of the working class against the 'encroachments of capitalism'.[15] In general the Hanoverian state and its équipe of local magistrates dealt without sympathy with most popular claims based upon memories of a traditional, more moral economy. Although local police forces were not then available either to check crime or to restrain collective protests that spilled over into intimidation, justices of the peace rarely hesitated to call upon troops, militias, and yeomanries to quell local disturbances. Attacks upon and crimes against property could, moreover, be severely punished under the bloody code which eighteenth-century Parliaments extended to include even trivial cases of theft and dishonesty.[16]

Before 1815 social protest and crime did not constitute and were not allowed to develop into serious constraints on technological change or to hinder the spread of commodity and factor markets. Gentlemen of substance and birth ran the offices of government (central and local), the forces of the crown, the law, and the Anglican church. Businessmen recognised that, under aristocratic command, the protection of their property and their own prerogatives to manage labour remained in safe hands. Within Britain the 'authorities' confronted a population that increased and became more urban over time. But most true 'Britons' were protestants, ethnically similar and obsequious towards men of rank and breeding. As citizens of a nation involved, generation after generation, in armed struggles against Catholic powers, Jacobites, American rebels, and French Revolutionaries, Britons

---

[13] C. J. Moynihan, *Introduction to the Law of Real Property. An historical background of the Common Law of Real Property and its modern applications* (St Pauls, Minn., 1977).

[14] G. Claeys, *Machinery, money and the millennium. From moral economy to socialism* (Cambridge, 1987).   [15] E. P. Thompson, *Customs in common* (1991).

[16] D. Phillips, 'Crime, law and punishment in the Industrial Revolution' in P. K. O'Brien and R. Quinault (eds.), *The Industrial Revolution and British society* (Cambridge, 1993), pp. 156–82.

merged their identities into the pervading culture of patriotism, loyalty, deference, and good behaviour towards property.

That economically functional culture did not change much over the decades that followed Britain's final victory in 1815. Popular conceptions of customary rights and a moral economy faded into folk memory, and social movements (even Chartism) became more focused on reforms to the constitution and upon legislation perceived adversely to affect the welfare of large segments of the population: for example, upon the Anti-Combination Acts rescinded in 1819; the New Poor Law passed in 1834 but implemented slowly; and the Corn Laws, repealed in 1846. Aristocracy and gentry survived up and down Victoria's realm in positions of political power and authority by gradually making modest concessions to demands for the extension of the franchise. 'Gentlemanly capitalists' and possibly more virtuous and respectable statesmen, continued to rule over a population whose culture had been ordered not only by the Anglican church but also by traditions of loyalty, patriotism, and imperialism maintained by a successful state that had acquired and retained the largest occidental empire since Rome.[17] Victoria's ministers realised, however, that towns and cities required police forces for the day-to-day protection of property, if only because the troops, militias, and yeomanry were no longer mobilised or preparing for war as they had been in Hanoverian times. Nevertheless, and perhaps because the incidence of crime declined, the police took several decades to appear on the streets. First came acts which enabled and encouraged municipalities and then rural councils to recruit police forces. In 1856 their formation became compulsory. As late as 1914 some 50,000 policemen protected the rights of property against all forms of challenges from social protest, including by then a powerful trade-union movement, as well as risks from crime. Among a population of more than 40 million, such a thin blue line must represent a tribute to the good behaviour of all but a minority of Queen Victoria's law-abiding subjects.[18]

IV

Since the demise of command economies, faith in private enterprise has become ubiquitous. What different societies expect from the operation of 'free' markets varies, however, from country to country. Almost everywhere the direct engagement by governments in production is viewed with scep-

---

[17] P. Mandler, *Aristocratic government in the age of reform* (Cambridge, 1990).
[18] E. Royle, *Modern Britain. A social history, 1750–1985* (1987), pp. 208–19.

ticism. Most economists now argue that the economic functions of states should be confined to ameliorating the excesses of markets and complementing their benign role by providing necessary public goods that would not become available without governmental intervention funded by taxes. Above all the economic functions of governments are defined as legislating for the rules required for the efficient operation of markets for commodities, labour, and capital.

Except for military purposes (and even then on a minor scale), neither the Hanoverian nor the Victorian states engaged to any marked or direct degree in production. Before 1914, and in contrast to other European, North American, and the Asian economies, this observation applies virtually *tout court*, even to the formation and management of social overhead capital and to investment in research and development required for technological innovation.

Both regimes concentrated on deregulating commodity markets. Except for duties upon coal, minerals, and stone carried coastwise, the movement of goods within the kingdom had been virtually toll free for centuries. Once transportation by canals and railways became available, it no longer made sense to tax coastal trades. Entirely limited and unenforceable price and quality controls on grain, bread, and upon certain manufactures conducted under the supervision of gilds in corporate towns impinged upon the otherwise free operation of commodity markets in Hanoverian England. With a national system of poor relief in place, the protection of consumers on subsistence incomes from adverse price fluctuations in the price of bread was not seen as a government priority. Traditional statutes against the 'sharp practices' of engrossing, forestalling, and regrating grain at times of poor harvests lapsed or were enforced in a desultory way. After 1815 the 'poor' lost all recourse to protection from price controls on bread and grain and (until 1875) from the adulteration and pollution of their food.[19]

Businessmen also traded with each other. Throughout the period, intra-firm relations continued to be conducted in large measure on the basis of mutual trust that had evolved over the centuries into a culture of prudential and efficient behaviour. At moments of breakdown British businessmen could, however, turn to the established legal system for assistance with the definition and enforcement of contracts.

Alas, the evolution of the law related to contract is too complex to summarise and too under-researched at the level of enforcement by the courts in Hanoverian and Victorian times. In their transactions with each

---

[19] C. Petersen, *Bread and the British economy, 1770–1870* (Aldershot, 1995).

other businessmen seem, however, to have 'coped' without a cheap and easily enforceable system of commercial law. Apparently they found both common and statute law badly designed to safeguard contracts and the courts of the realm too slow and expensive for their purposes.

Under both regimes and for most transactions, businessmen relied upon traditions of honour, reinforced by networks of kin and by religious communities concerned to safeguard the reputations of their members of integrity. These cultural contexts operated in economically efficient ways that minimised the risks and costs of going to law.

Those in charge of production and trade also required long-term loans to support their decisions to invest in fixed capital, as well as access to the credit they needed to carry on their day-to-day dealings with each other and their customers. As a consequence of the Bubble Act of 1720, the formal market for raising long-term capital remained in an unsatisfactory condition. Corporate forms of enterprise with limited liability did not appear until long after the industrial revolution. Businessmen, advised by lawyers, utilised several legal but hardly secure or efficient forms of organisation to circumvent the difficulties of raising and associating capital with entrepreneurship and flexible arrangements for the management of firms. Nevertheless, Britain's institutional framework for the formation and expansion of business enterprises does not look as well designed as alternative European models. It may have constrained the growth of the British economy and almost certainly contributed to the instability of banks and insurance companies that became a feature of business crises for long stretches of the nineteenth century.

Reforms came with a 'big bang' between 1856 and 1862 when British company law moved from a strictly regulated system to the most permissive legal framework in Europe. Alas, this sudden lurch to *laissez faire* can be represented in retrospect as 'too much too late'.[20] For example, the almost total removal of protection for shareholders did little to encourage widespread investment in newly floated limited liability companies. Most existing firms, organised as family enterprises, partnerships, and closed trusts, quickly registered as limited liability companies, which simply preserved and protected many of the more complacent and unprogressive families and managers in charge of British industry and commerce in the late nineteenth century from competitive pressures to change.[21]

---

[20] D. Sugarman, *Company law and the rise of capitalism* (forthcoming).
[21] W. P. Kennedy, *Industrial structure, capital markets and the origins of British economic decline* (Cambridge, 1987).

Already in 1688 the kingdom's commodity, capital, and credit markets could be represented as relatively 'free' from governmental regulation. Yet a similar claim could hardly be made for the Hanoverian labour market, enveloped by state-enforced laws, institutions, and codes of behaviour which left a majority of the workforce uneasily suspended between repressive servitude and the voluntaristic and contractual relationships between employers and employed depicted in liberal theory.[22]

Within Britain's Atlantic Empire, the industrial revolution coincided with the rise of slavery and indentured labour. In the metropolis apprenticeships, residential service, and long-term contracts for sailors, miners, agricultural labourers, and other groups maintained hierarchical and authoritarian systems of control over substantial sections of the English and Celtic workforces. The employment rights of women, children, and families claiming poor relief to withdraw or negotiate terms for their unskilled labour or to move about in search of work remained rather rigidly circumscribed by statutes dealing with vagrancy and poor relief for the able bodied. Combinations of skilled male workmen emerged for some trades but they could be prosecuted under both common and statute law and were outlawed as subversive of good order during the war against Revolutionary France. Although the system of public welfare provided for under the old poor law ameliorated the risks to subsistence which attended the mobility of workers from agriculture to industry or from job to job, the investment costs of acquiring any sort of education or skill fell almost entirely upon workmen and their families. The publicly funded and otherwise under-employed time and education of the clergy and their wives did make some contribution, however, to raising standards of literacy and presumably ambition towards independence among the poor.

After 1815, when real wages rose, the condition and status of labour under the law improved. That transformation is clearly apparent in the sequence of statutes promulgated by Parliament between 1824 and 1906–13 to provide workers with the legal rights necessary to form and sustain trade unions and to engage effectively in collective bargaining with their employers.[23] Until just before the twentieth century, the proportion of the workforce which enjoyed union membership remained below 15 per cent but it doubled between 1905 and 1914. For most of the period unions meant craft unions. Their activities hardly operated to constrain the growth

[22] R. J. Steinfeld, *The invention of free labour. The employment relation in England and American law and culture, 1350–1870* (Chapel Hill, 1991).
[23] R. Price, *Labour in British society* (1986).

of the Victorian economy. On the contrary, they can be seen as part of the patriarchal system for the management of work, for apprenticeship and training, and for maintaining (albeit more benignly) traditions of control over the behaviour of the unskilled, the young, and over female workers.

Most of the Victorian working class quickly recognised that the poor law amendment act of 1834 had not been designed to improve welfare for their families. Indeed the proportion of gross national product transferred to them for the relief of poverty, sickness, desertion, old age, unemployment, and other disabilities, declined sharply between 1834 and 1914, compared to the equally authoritarian but more benign system that operated for eight decades between 1754 and 1834. Some historians and economists claim that the act reduced the culture of dependency that had grown up under the old poor law, promoted self-help and independence and put pressure on families to invest in skills rather than more children and all in all removed many imperfections to geographical and social mobility that had placed obstacles in the way of the efficient operation of the Hanoverian labour market.

That could be argued, but before the 1860s the state did virtually nothing to help British families to improve the quality and motivation of adolescent entrants to the workforce by allocating taxes for public investment in education. Even then the cabinet started at the top by reforming the blatantly inequitable and inefficient ways that the public and grammar schools and the ancient universities utilised their endowments. Free and compulsory primary education came on stream as late as the 1880s and not until 1902 did the government impose clearly defined duties on local authorities to provide both elementary and secondary education for the population at large.[24] On the eve of the First World War, when the competitive challenges of the second industrial revolution could no longer be evaded, 12 per cent of tax revenues were being allocated for education, arts, and sciences. By then the state had clearly made its first and direct commitment to provide resources for the long-term development of the British economy.

V

A persistent discourse and some degree of discord attended the rise in the share of national resources appropriated by the Hanoverian regime as loans (serviced from taxation) and of course the taxes themselves in order to pursue

[24] G. Roderick and M. Stephens (eds.), *Where did we go wrong? Education and economy of Victorian Britain* (Lewes, 1981).

and fund a strategy for the security of the realm and the development of the economy. At the time 'liberal' critics of the *ancien régime* concentrated upon the social and economic costs of paying for Britain's rise to a hegemonic position in the international order. Mercantilists, who refused to separate the pursuit of power from the pursuit of profit, emphasised its achievements in terms of national security, the acquisition of an empire, and gains from trade.

Despite the crowding out of 'some' private investment by the accumulation of public debt and the malign economic effects of taxation, at the Vienna settlement the realm's benefits from consistently high levels of public investment in naval power became highly visible to envious statesmen from elsewhere in Europe.[25] Over time threats to national security had been contained within limits that preserved confidence for investors; and possible invasions between 1689 and 1713, and 1803 and 1815 had been fought off. After 1688 the state allocated serious amounts of money to help clients and allies on the mainland to preserve some sort of balance of power, which countervailed Bourbon and Napoleonic ambitions towards universal monarchy. Apart from odd years between 1805 and 1812 the navy kept European markets open for trade. At every peace treaty from Ryswick to Vienna (except Paris in 1783) Britain made net gains in the form of bases, colonies, territory, and above all in securing ever-increasing access to the markets of the Portuguese, Spanish, Dutch, French, Mughal, and Chinese Empires. British merchants and the City of London obtained extraordinary shares of global commerce.[26] Their enterprise facilitated and promoted the export of domestic manufactures and at the same time covered the growing import surplus on the country's balance of trade.[27]

At the conjuncture of 1815, the Hanoverian regime bequeathed three 'structurally constricting legacies' to its Victorian successor: firstly, a polity and an economy irrevocably committed to international trade and to playing a hegemonic role in servicing and policing the global economy; secondly, levels of public debt and taxation that had been unthinkable before the Glorious Revolution; and thirdly, a boundless territorial empire in Asia, the Americas, and the Pacific of such linguistic, ethnic, and cultural diversity that the problem of retaining and defending it might well have terrified the Romans.[28]

[25] H. T. Dickinson (ed.), *Britain and the French Revolution* (1989).

[26] F. Crouzet, 'The Second Hundred Years War: some reflexions', *French History*, 10 (1997), pp. 432–50.

[27] E. S. Brezis, 'Foreign capital flows in the century of Britain's Industrial Revolution: new estimates, controlled conjectures', *Economic History Review*, 48 (1995), pp. 46–67.

[28] H. V. Bowen, *Elites, enterprise and the making of the British overseas empire, 1688–1775* (1996).

Previous sections have compared and elaborated upon the successes, failures, and above all the essential continuities between the two regimes in implementing policies designed to create institutions and legal conditions for the free and efficient operation of markets for commodities and factors of production within a united kingdom and its integrated domestic economy. Continuity also marked the policies pursued by successive Victorian governments in the realm of international economic relations. Apart from the politically symbolic but economically unimportant gesture of protecting arable agriculture with the new Corn Law of 1815, politicians did nothing to de-link the economy from its dependence on exports and imports and its engagement with the servicing of world trade. On the contrary, the whole thrust of Victorian commercial diplomacy, as well as the tariff, monetary, and exchange rate policies pursued after 1815 (and particularly after 1846), integrated Britain ever more closely into an evolving global economy. As List observed, the moves towards free trade and the ideological trumpeting of the universal virtues embodied in that persuasively powerful slogan represented a change of tactics not of strategy, a change that made sense, moreover, in the more peaceful order that prevailed in Europe for several decades after Waterloo.[29]

Throughout the long nineteenth century (1815–1914), Victorian statesmen and economists complained continuously (none more loudly than Gladstone) about their fiscal legacy. When Nicholas Vansittart restored the monetary system to gold in 1819 (at too high a parity of course), the situation looked desperate enough. Deflation and depression continued to afflict the economy in the 1820s when the Liverpool administration collected around £60 million a year in taxes.[30] By that decade taxation had risen some three times in real terms compared with the interlude of peace between the wars, from 1783 to 1793, and the proportion of gross national product appropriated by the state had jumped from around 8 per cent to 10 per cent before the outbreak of the French Revolution up to 16 per cent, down from 20 per cent immediately before the end of the long war with France. Unfortunately, in 1816 a Whig-inspired campaign had produced Parliamentary majorities for the repeal of Pitt's wartime income tax, which meant that more than 80 per cent of government revenues came from indirect and socially unprogressive forms of taxation. During the 1820s more

[29] F. List, *The natural system of political economy* (1837), translated by W. O. Henderson (London, 1983), ch. 27.
[30] B. Gordon, *Political economy in Parliament, 1819–23* (1976) and *Economic doctrine and Tory liberalism* (1979).

than half of these tax revenues were immediately transferred to the government's creditors and serviced the debt; around 30 per cent funded the empire's naval and military establishments, which left very little public money to support whatever other commitments the government had already acquired or wished to undertake. After the most expensive war in British history, it seemed not only logical but inevitable for fiscally constrained, but otherwise paternally inclined cabinets of aristocrats to embrace *laissez-faire*, initially as more of a rhetoric for doing nothing to alleviate the social distress and dislocation arising from rapid population growth, industrialisation, and urbanisation. Later in the century, when the benefits then flowing from the Hanoverian investment in power came to be taken for granted and the constraints imposed by the annual costs of servicing such a massive debt became visible, liberal attacks on the profligacy of the whole enterprise (labelled as old corruption) hardened into dogma and *laissez-faire* matured into a dominant ideology in favour of low taxes and a small state.[31]

Over time the steady rise in the national product and the grave fiscal crisis that confronted governments immediately after the war passed away. Between 1820 and 1850 while the real levels of tax revenues remained roughly constant, in per capita terms they declined by 28 per cent and taxes as a share of national income fell continuously on trend from around 16 per cent in 1820 to approximately 6 per cent by 1870. The ratio then fluctuated around that mark until after the turn of the century when rearmament combined with spending on welfare pushed it back up to the 7 to 8 per cent range over the decade before the outbreak of the First World War. Meanwhile, and as the government's debt declined from a multiple of over two to a fraction (25 per cent) of national income, the share of taxes reserved or mortgaged to service obligations to its creditors had fallen to a mere 10 per cent of total revenues around 1913.[32] Fiscal data show that victory over Napoleon's ambitions to dominate the continent and the virtual cessation of nearly three centuries of warfare among European powers for empire and hegemony at sea, provided Victorian statesmen with an enormous 'peace dividend'. Between 1815 and 1914 they took charge of their inheritance, espoused a liberal rhetoric of free trade and *laissez-faire* and rolled back the state to the macroeconomic position that central

---

[31] P. Harling, *The waning of old corruption* (Oxford, 1996).

[32] The data on government revenue borrowing, the debt, and expenditures, 1815–1914, are in process of being assembled for a data base that will be deposited in 1997 in the ESRC Data Archive (see n. 2).

governments had held in terms of national expenditure under Walpole. French power waned; Germany's *Sonderweg* and *Weltpolitik* took decades to emerge as a clear threat to European stability; Russian imperialism moved east and south. A fortuitously peaceable international order allowed 'Britons' to continue to dominate global commerce without serious challenge; and to defend the realm and run their formal and informal empire on the cheap.

Apparently no imperial historian has collected the relevant data but it would be illuminating to aggregate and to tabulate decade by decade the populations, the square kilometres of territory, the discounted values of natural resources and productive assets, and above all the kilometres of frontier, included within the post-1815 realm and its formal empire overseas, that Britain's army, the Royal Navy, and its taxpayers were committed to protect from external aggression and to preserve from internal insurrection.

Imperial borders turned out to be the cabinet's central and persistent obsession. Not only did they lengthen willy-nilly but Victorian governments found they were no longer defending a kingdom surrounded by a moat of water but involved with the security of frontiers adjacent or near enough to the colonies, territories, and armed forces of the major powers, including France, Russia, Germany, the USA, Spain, Portugal, China, Turkey, and Japan. What is more, the diffusion of railways from continent to continent invariably brought the prospects, however remote, of attacks overland by troops from those rival powers closer to British possessions and populations. Statesmen, diplomats, admirals, and generals became increasingly preoccupied with the manifold and extraordinarily complex problems of imperial security, which became conflated in their minds with the defence of the realm. Decade after decade their responsibilities grew unsteadily and unpredictably but all the time more rapidly than the resources appropriated by the state to fund anything more than minimal levels of defence and protection for the realm and its empire.

Meanwhile, in terms of shares of tax revenues allocated in peacetime to the army and navy, Victorian governments emerge again from fiscal records as being as preoccupied as their Hanoverian predecessors with security. Although Indian taxpayers made a substantial contribution, expenditures on the Imperial Army increased year after year and it came to cost much more than the Royal Navy, the senior – and the people's favourite – service. Despite the enlargement of a not so United Kingdom to include the troublesome province of Ireland and the seemingly irresistible extension of responsibilities for imperial defence, the share of the kingdom's income appropriated for both services fell some way behind the kind of ratios that became modal and acceptable to taxpayers when Britain fought to achieve hegemonic status in the international order between 1688 and 1815.

Once British aspirations to become the dominant global power had been satisfied, the Victorian political elite, under pressure to make concessions to an expanding and less bellicose electorate, settled into an altogether more conciliatory, quiescent, and non-interventionist style of diplomacy in their relations with erstwhile political rivals and economic competitors from the mainland.

The broad and consistent thrust of the foreign, strategic, and commercial policies pursued by the Victorian regime down to (and perhaps even beyond) the entente concluded with France in 1904, all added up to the kind of sensible response to immediate circumstance that led inexorably to myopia and complacency. No further and really serious political or military challenges re-emerged from Portugal, Spain, Holland, and above all from France to the nation's empire and hegemony over world trade and commerce. Russia turned east and south to consolidate a territorial empire and Romanov ambitions could be checked by diplomacy and a small Crimean War to prop up the Ottoman Empire. With Hanover gone, Britain seemed to have no immediate and direct interest in interfering with the redrawing of frontiers, or reacting to unexpected changes in ruling dynasties and other machinations in European power politics that accompanied the reunification of Italy, the decline of Habsburg dominion, and, above all, the really serious threat to the balance of power posed by the unification of Germany.

Furthermore, support among the electorate for liberal antipathies to dynastic power politics grew stronger with the extension of the franchise. In any case Victorian statesmen had their hands and minds full with more popular policies for the preservation of empire and the defence of trade.[33] For political (as well as the more familiar economic) reasons they concentrated commercial diplomacy on the removal of barriers to trade among nations. Although Cobdenite visions of peace, flowing from universal free trade, probably never took hold of the 'official mind', the Foreign Office and the Treasury saw the point of placating the political hostility of foreigners with an economic interest in securing entry to the home market and access to markets in the Americas, Africa, and Asia under formal as well as informal control of the British state. Between 1823 and 1827, Huskisson concluded the earliest of a long sequence of treaties and bilateral bargains

---

[33] G. L. Bernstein, *Liberalism and Liberal politics in England* (1986).

which embodied most-favoured-nation clauses with several European powers, including France. That strategy of negotiation which usually opened the markets of the realm, its empire and client states to foreign imports, capital, and migrants in exchange for concessions towards British manufactured exports more or less continued down to the signing of the famous Cobden-Chevalier Treaty with France in 1861.[34] Shortly thereafter, and despite the rise of neo-mercantilism among the great powers, patient bilateral negotiation and the occasional use of gunboat diplomacy to open up markets in the Third World to European traders, changed to one of rather rigid, unilateral adherence to free trade. Patrician statesmen (Liberal and Conservative), backed by gentlemen of the Foreign Office, declined to use reciprocal bargaining, retaliation, or threats of 'force' of any kind to check the general upswing in tariffs and other discriminatory obstacles to flows of exports and imports across frontiers imposed by rival European powers and by the United States between 1873 and 1914.

At home serious political campaigns to persuade the Victorian state to deploy power to 'relevel the playing field' in international economic relations (including the Fair Trade League, 1881–91, the Pressure Group for Bimetallism (in effect for the devaluation of sterling), and the famous movements led by Joseph Chamberlain for Tariff Reform and Imperial Preference, 1900–6) all failed to do much more than promote a re-examination of the ruling consensus in favour of the unilateralist version of free trade.[35]

In contrast to the situation that prevailed in Hanoverian times, Victorian commercial and strategic policies never recombined, largely because 'free trade' matured into a powerful and enduring national ideology that rested upon a set of arguments that hardly changed between 1846 and 1932. Such arguments maintained, for example, that moves to retaliate against foreign imports would lead to trade wars that could only hurt the British economy more than the economies of its rivals. Open trade preserved peace, attenuated jealousies of Britain's huge empire, and kept down taxes appropriated for its defence. The negotiation of tariff preferences among the dominions and colonies could only endanger the fragile unity of the empire. Above all, liberals held fast to the rigour (and never questioned the historical or contemporary relevance) of Ricardian theories of comparative advantage. In that mathematical context, Britain's industrialisation, the provision of

---

[34] P. K. O'Brien and G. Pigman, 'Free trade, British hegemony and the international economic order in the nineteenth century', *Review of International Studies*, 18 (1992), pp. 89–113.

[35] E. H. Green, *The politics, economics and ideology of the Conservative Party, 1880–1914* (1994).

cheap food for the working class, and industry's still pre-eminent place in the world economy were all imputed to benign effects flowing from the adoption of free trade. Whatever foreign governments and businessmen predicted, protection would only serve, given time, to weaken the competitive powers of rival American, German, and other European economies. There could be no point in taking risks with the security of the realm or in raising more taxes to fund a proactive stance for the defence of a liberal international economic order.[36]

Meanwhile, penetration of the home market by imported manufactures and the loss of export markets to subsidised European and American competitors, could be ascribed to a short run impact of 'unfair competition'. Temporary compensation could, moreover, be found by exporting more of the same to imperial and Third World markets. Commitments by the Victorian regime to long-established commercial and monetary policies could be maintained and the promotion of adjustments required by the economy postponed, pending a return to the sound economic sense and that mystical equilibrium provided by a competitive international order, alas, after 1873, visibly passing away by the year.

Laissez-faire and optimistic liberal assumptions lay behind the external as well as the internal strategy for economic development pursued by Victorian statesmen over the last quarter of the nineteenth century. They also saw themselves as a fiscally constrained ruling elite, threatened by an expanding and potentially demanding electorate. They were certainly aware that expenditures on the forces of the Crown were already rising rapidly to visibly augment the burdens of taxation (especially the detested burden of direct taxes) carried by the voters. After half a century of slow growth, by 1906 to 1914 the annual amount of tax revenue collected by central government had multiplied by a factor of 2.4 compared to the low point attained by the nightwatchman state some four decades before. In per capita terms burdens on taxpayers had risen by some 60 per cent over this same period and the tendency (deplored by Gladstonian rhetoric) to appropriate higher shares of the revenue in the still widely unpopular form of direct taxes on income and wealth became unmistakable and politically contentious in the 1890s. Without much success the Treasury tried to shift some of the costs of imperial defence onto the dominions and to levy taxes more rigorously on the Celtic provinces of the realm.[37]

---

[36] F. Trentman, 'The strange death of free trade: the erosion of the liberal consensus in Great Britain, 1903–32' in E. F. Biagini (ed.), *Citizenship and community. Radicals and collective identity in the British Isles, 1865–1931* (Cambridge, 1996).

[37] F. Trentman, 'The transformation of fiscal reform and the fiscal debate within the business community in Britain', *Historical Journal* (forthcoming).

Free riding on Britain's defence budget certainly occurred and could not be negotiated away. Memories of the American War of Independence reminded the Victorians not to push the dominions and colonies too far. Nevertheless, the national income continued to rise. Thus while the share taken as taxes remained in the 6 per cent range for nearly three decades before 1900, it moved but slowly upwards even after the turn of the century when Tirpitz began to mastermind the construction of a fleet to rival the Royal Navy.

Recent debates on the costs and benefits of the empire have revived the radical, Cobdenite–Hobsonian, views that the Victorian realm's imperial commitments represented little more than an incubus on the development of the British economy.[38] They have been concerned to remind historians that as the liberal international economic order evolved after 1815, the gains to British society as a whole from imperial trade and investment in or from migration to colonies and dominions overseas (when placed in the context of commerce with the global economy as a whole) do not emerge either as indispensable or particularly profitable.[39] Meanwhile, the opportunity costs borne by the British economy and British taxpayers for imperial defence have been represented as increasingly expensive and potentially avoidable. After patient and careful analysis of the data for several great powers, Hobson's grandson (*sic*) has shown that expenditures by the state on the Royal Navy and the British army can no longer be depicted as excessive at least in comparative terms. Between 1870 and 1913, on average the share of the national income appropriated for military purposes was discernably higher for France, Russia, and Japan, comparable for Italy, the Habsburg Empire, and Germany but three times the enviably low ratio of around 1 per cent maintained by the USA after the Civil War.[40]

Obviously these and other ratios constructed only recently by historians did not inform perceptions of the day. Victorian statesmen may have surmised that the 'military extraction ratios', achieved under far less propitious economic and administrative conditions in Hanoverian times, may have been much larger but such ratios were also, from their perspective, onerous and deplorable. As liberals ideologically committed to *laissez-faire* and a small state but coming under democratic pressure to spend more on educa-

---

[38] L. Davis and R. Huttenbach, *Mammon and the pursuit of empire: the political economy of British imperialism, 1860–1912* (Cambridge, 1986).

[39] P. K. O'Brien, 'The costs and benefits of British imperialism', *Past and Present*, 120 (1988), pp. 163–200; M. Edelstein, 'Foreign investment and accumulation, 1860–1914'; in Floud and McCloskey (eds.), *The economic history of Britain*, 2nd edn, vol. II, pp. 173–96.

[40] J. M. Hobson, 'The military extraction gap and the weary Titan: the fiscal sociology of British defence policy, 1870–1913', *Journal of European Economic History*, 22 (1993), pp. 461–506.

tion and social welfare, Victorian statesmen remained deeply concerned with burdens of taxation and military expenditures rising visibly year after year.[41]

Both political parties, and an increasingly jingoistic electorate, disdained the Cobdenite programme to de-link the realm from its expanding empire, even though they paid more and more for its defence. Meanwhile, strategic thinking at the Foreign Office, the Admiralty, and the War Office, remained dominated for more than three decades after the reunification of Germany with possible attacks across imperial frontiers in Asia and Africa by Russia and France and even in North America by the USA.[42] Hanoverian aristocrats had never displayed the myopia involved in ignoring potential threats to the realm and its stake in global commerce emerging from changes to the balance of power just a short distance away on the mainland.

Alas, the Victorian regime's detachment from Europe had originated quite early in the nineteenth century when Palmerston and his successors neglected to countervail the lead assumed by the Hohenzollern dynasty in formation of the Zollverein. Victorian diplomacy then adopted a *laissez-passer* stance towards the deployment of Prussian military power against Denmark in 1864, Austria two years later, and France in 1870, when Bismarck created and consolidated a Prusso-German empire in central Europe. For more than two decades down to the formation of the entente with France, statesmen (too many of them pro-German!), diplomats, admirals, and generals responsible for the security of the realm, displayed the kind of complacency towards the threat to British interests posed by the Kaiserreich that would have been unthinkable to their Hanoverian counterparts.[43]

The stance of the late Victorian regime is, however, entirely explicable. Had not the continental commitments of the Hanoverians been expensive and wasteful for British taxpayers and unprofitable for the economy, central in fact to the old corruption which they had cleaned up? Around the globe, France, the traditional enemy, and the autocratic Romanovs, not Germany, menaced the frontiers of the empire.[44] Would the electorate countenance and pay for the build-up of a professional standing army on the scale required to convince the Kaiser's high command that Britain would or

---

[41] H. V. Emy, 'The impact of financial policy on English party politics before 1914', *Historical Journal*, 15 (1972), pp. 103–31.   [42] B. Semmel, *Liberalism and naval strategy* (1986).

[43] P. Kennedy, *The rise of Anglo-German antagonism, 1860–1914* (1982).

[44] I. Beckett and J. Gooch (eds.), *Politicians and defence: studies in the formulation of British defence policy, 1870–1945* (Manchester, 1981).

could intervene to preserve a balance of power in Europe?[45] Statesmen and strategic planners knew, moreover, that the nation's massive reserve of force in the shape of the Royal Navy could always be pulled back to 'home waters' to deter and repel any feasible threats of invasion from the mainland. They also banked upon mobilising imperial, including Indian, troops for help with any continental commitments that might unfortunately emerge.

For these and other reasons (which historians discover unfurling day-to-day in diplomatic records that expose and supposedly explain a logic of events) for at least two decades after the Franco-Prussian War, Britain's strategic policy can now be observed to be seriously unconcerned with the balance of power in Europe. Even after the entente of 1904, the Liberal Cabinet's foreign and strategic stance towards the continent continued as late as the summer of 1914 to be too understated and ambivalent to convince the Prussian generals that Britain could be counted on to mobilise to aid her French and Russian allies. Before the outbreak of war there was no Triple Alliance just a Triple Entente![46]

VI

Historical explanations for the relative decline of the British economy are inseparable from accounts of its rise. My survey, covering a very long period of British history, has attempted to 'grasp' major structural parameters within which first Hanoverian, and, after Waterloo, Victorian governments operated as they collected taxes, borrowed savings, allocated resources, and formulated policies that conditioned the evolution of the economy. On the whole, Hanoverian aristocrats did not legislate into place a framework for the progress of capitalist enterprise in Britain that differed much from the rules and institutions promulgated by the more liberal and increasingly democratic regime that took over the state in 1815. The labour market became less 'feudal'. Both regimes underspent on human capital formation. Incentives and obstacles to private investment appeared and disappeared decade by decade. The weight of praise for and complaints against government from businessmen in charge of the economy would probably not have varied very much over the period from 1688 to 1914.

Fundamental and economically significant contrasts can be traced, however, in the strategic, diplomatic, and commercial policies pursued by the liberal state. As the ruling elite of a great and fiscally well-endowed impe-

[45] R. J. C. Adams and P. Poirier, *The conscription controversy in Britain, 1900–18* (Basingstoke, 1987).   [46] K. M. Wilson, *The policy of entente* (1985).

rial power, Victorian politicians are too often exonerated of responsibility for the pursuit of policies towards the outside world that 'troublemakers' of the day recognised as potentially dangerous.[47] Perhaps as a recent synthesis persuasively suggests they had become altogether 'too gentlemanly'.[48] Anyway their Hanoverian and mercantilist ancestors had never neglected Europe as they actively protected and aggressively encouraged British merchants and manufacturers, endeavouring to seize an extraordinary share of trade and commerce with Africa, Asia, and the Americas. Unless the outbreak of the First World War is regarded as inevitable, unavoidable, or simply contingent upon the assassination of an Austrian archduke, the failure of Victorian statesmen to tax more and to spend more to maintain free trade, to foster a co-operative international economic order, and above all to preserve the balance of power in Europe must be regarded, albeit in retrospect, as a serious indictment of the liberal imagination.[49]

Both the immediate and long-term costs that flowed from four years of global warfare are incalculable.[50] Any audit of the First World War will surely reveal that the Victorian state's failure to invest more resources and to allocate them more perceptively, in order to preclude the outbreak of the most expensive and far-reaching conflict among European powers since Napoleon, seriously constrained Britain's prospects for growth (absolute and relative) after 1918.[51] Its explicably myopic but avoidable approach to Europe perhaps mattered far more than any waning of the nation's industrial spirit, entrepreneurial lethargy, institutional sclerosis, under-investment in science, neglect of the nation's human capital, or any of those familiar economic forces behind the nation's decline?[52]

Designed along Braudelian lines to look back beyond the conjuncture of 1815 to 1688, my narrative has been 'emplotted' (to use Paul Ricoeur's felicitous term) in order to persuade that Britain's economic inheritance which emanated in large part from Hanoverian investment in power, had turned out by 1918 to be a two-edged sword.[53]

---

[47] A. J. A. Morris, *The scaremongers: the advocacy of war and rearmament, 1896–1914* (1984); A. J. P. Taylor, *The troublemakers. Dissent over foreign policy, 1792–1939* (1957).

[48] P. Cain and A. G. Hopkins, *British imperialism. Crisis and deconstruction, 1914–1990* (1993).

[49] H. J. Mackinder, *Democratic ideals and reality: a study in the politics of reconstruction* (1919), pp. 179–90; A. L. Friedberg, *The weary Titan: Britain and the experience of relative decline, 1895–1905* (Princeton, 1988).

[50] A. D. Harvey, *Collision of empires: Britain in three world wars, 1793–1945* (1992), chs. 2, 8, and 13; B. W. E. Alford, *Britain in the world economy since 1880* (1996), ch. 4.

[51] G. Hardach, *The First World War, 1914–18* (1977); K. Robbins, *The eclipse of a great power. Modern Britain, 1870–1975* (1983).

[52] B. Porter, *Britannia's burden: the political evolution of modern Britain* (1994).

[53] D. Wood (ed.), *On Paul Ricoeur. Narrative and interpretation* (1991).

4

British economic decline and human resources

SIMON SZRETER

I

There has always been something more than a little disconcerting about the discrepancy in modern British historiography between the apologetic story of the seemingly unstoppable decline of the nation's economy from the 1870s onwards and the apparently equally inexorable rise of liberal democracy, healthy citizens, living standards, the welfare state, and an affluent society during approximately the same time period.

Barry Supple's classic address, republished here, explores precisely this paradox of parallax. He offers a deft explanation of the linkage between the two perspectives. The rise of an affluent society has resulted in rising aspirations, both for provision of public services and for consumption of private goods. In a British citizenry increasingly aware of higher living standards abroad this has produced a perception of chronic inadequacy in the mere 2 per cent per annum long-term growth rate which appears to be a permanent, constitutional feature of British life, if the last two centuries of economic history are a reliable guide. These troublesome and rather unrealistic popular expectations are mainly of postwar provenance but they are superimposed upon a longer preoccupation with decline among the professional gloom-mongers of the national elite. This group has experienced unrelenting relative deprivation as the twentieth century has worn on, with the loss of the role of global political and cultural leadership which the economy's precocious industrial expansion had briefly and gloriously conferred upon during the course of the previous century.

Barry Supple has offered us a persuasive and eloquent essay on the power of perceptions. The British economy has been 'in decline' throughout the

I wish to record my thanks to the editors of this volume and to Christel Lane and Alastair Reid for their several helpful suggestions; and in particular to Hilary Cooper, for numerous improving comments on an earlier draft.

last century or more because there have been increasingly compelling cultural and psychological reasons for the British people to believe that this is so. The relationship between this perception and the actual performance of the British economy – whether good, bad, or indifferent when compared against a meaningful yardstick – has been decidedly of secondary importance in accounting for the pervasiveness of the 'decline' attitude.

There remains the implication in all this that our economic historiography of modern Britain has perhaps embraced and reflected too willingly, or too exclusively, a widespread and rather popular general view, instead, perhaps, of seeking to question its premises. In another classic article a decade earlier, David Cannadine made a similar suggestion: that trends and counter-trends over the last hundred years in the historiography of the industrial revolution might be more closely related to discernible intellectual fashions in the contemporary policy arena than economic historians might care to have acknowledged.[1] Undoubtedly, probing questions have been asked about Britain's economic decline, ever since that resounding rhetorical: 'Did Victorian Britain fail?'[2] Important articles and reputations have been built through the cut and thrust of productive dispute on this central preoccupation surrounding 'decline'. But have the premises of the popular perception been subject to serious question? Has not the very vigour and undoubted scholarly excellence of many of the contributions to this long-running debate rather, instead, engrained those premises into our thinking; so that it is now hard for social and economic historians of modern Britain to see what serious alternatives might look like?

For, underpinning this lively debate about the British economy's performance lies a puzzle and a further question, which economic historians seem to have been more reluctant to broach explicitly: what *are* the identifiable sources of sustained high rates of economic growth over the long run for a developed economy in a competitive world environment? Can these be defined, either in a general way or in a way that is specific to the British economy and people? Historians may smell here a hypothetical, an invitation to theorise, and therefore something to be avoided at all costs, or at least something to be respectfully delegated to the economists. Nevertheless all historians who have participated in this scholarly forum on Britain's economic decline, whether they like it or not, have been implicitly addressing this theoretical question all the time.

---

[1] D. Cannadine, 'The past and present in the English industrial revolution 1880–1980', *Past and Present*, 103 (1984), pp. 131–72.

[2] D. McCloskey, 'Did Victorian Britain fail?', *Economic History Review*, 23 (1970), pp. 446–59.

In an historiographically significant recent intervention, Nick Crafts has pointed out that the long-established postwar orthodoxy in growth economics, 'Solow style neoclassical growth economics, which underlies the growth accounting framework familiar to economic historians', has been under increasingly critical review and revision during the last ten years or so.[3] Much of the new work has been developed through attempts to analyse the reasons for variations in the performance of the most developed economies during the relatively high growth era, from 1950 to 1973, compared with each of the more sluggish periods before and after. The neoclassical models ascribed economic growth primarily to 'technological improvements'. How the latter came about was not investigated in detail for each economy as an historical process, but rather emerged as a definitional residual, sometimes called Total Factor Productivity, from the national accounting statistical exercise of measuring the surplus value of all outputs over all inputs for the national economy in question. The newer approaches have been prepared to probe further and to look more closely at this black box of 'technological improvement', in the attempt to distinguish the reasons for the different growth performances of different economies; or of the same economy at different points in time. As a result, a number of more specific findings and hypotheses have emerged concerning the conditions influencing high rates of economic growth in highly developed economies. Crafts has concluded from his review that:

In sum, recent research in growth economics tends to admit . . . more scope for policy and institutions to affect growth, and stresses much more the role of human capital in growth than did the mainstream growth economists of the 1960s.[4]

and

It seems quite probable that relative weakness in human capital formation may have played a greater part in British relative decline than used to be thought.[5]

The predominant character of the historical debate over the last three decades or so has been to focus on examination of the dynamism of entrepreneurs and management, those most obviously responsible for generating the economy's 'technological improvements'. Commencing with the straightforward accusation that late-Victorian entrepreneurs failed the nation, early historiographical skirmishing in the 1960s and early 1970s

[3] N. F. R. Crafts, 'The golden age of economic growth in Western Europe, 1950–73', *Economic History Review*, 48 (1995), pp. 429–47, p. 430.
[4] Crafts, 'The golden age', p. 434.   [5] Ibid., p. 443.

showed that this was a simplistic form of scapegoating.[6] Many such entrepreneurs, when their decisions and strategies were properly examined in the appropriate historical contexts in which they operated, proved to be as rational, resourceful, clever, and capable as their forefathers or their foreign competitors. The process of exculpating the entrepreneurs through the admission of exonerating circumstances has identified an ever-widening list of suspects for investigation as the truly guilty parties, the real causes of Britain's loss of economic competitiveness. Hence, the City's predilection and expertise in outward, rather than inward investment, associated problems with the functioning of domestic capital markets, the flagging of the 'enterprise culture' itself, the haemorrhaging of talent out of business and into safer and more respectable activities, and the underprovision of technical and scientific training have all been thoroughly investigated as specific hypotheses which explained why entrepreneurs and managers might have underperformed, even though many individual businessmen were doing as well as they could in the circumstances.[7]

Most recently, the field has benefited from the development of two distinct, though far from incompatible, grand theses, which generalise and synthesise much of the earlier findings. The 'gentlemanly capitalism' thesis of Cain and Hopkins argues that the economic and political dominance of southern and metropolitan finance and gentility was never seriously disturbed by the northern entrepreneurs' manufacturing revolution.[8] To adapt the terminology of the history of science, Cain and Hopkins have provided an 'externalist' account of the decline of British economic performance: how it was that, despite early success, the national political and institutional *environment* in which British business operated remained inhospitable and that this increasingly mattered.[9] The metropolitan south was only too happy to enjoy the fruits of the accessions to national wealth and power

---

[6] The case for the defence was principally mounted by: H. J. Habakkuk, *American and British technology in the nineteenth century* (Cambridge, 1962); D. McCloskey, *Economic maturity and entrepreneurial decline: British iron and steel 1870–1913* (Cambridge, Mass., 1973); L. Sandberg, *Lancashire in decline. A study in entrepreneurship, technology and international trade* (Columbus, Ohio, 1974).

[7] Even a selective and illustrative list of the contributions involved would have to be lengthy. For helpful reviews, see P. L. Payne, *British entrepreneurship in the nineteenth century* (2nd edn 1988); S. Pollard, *Britain's prime and Britain's decline* (1989); M. Collins, *Banks and industrial finance in Britain 1800–1939* (1991), chs. 4–5; M. W. Kirby, 'Institutional rigidities and economic decline: reflections on the British experience', *Economic History Review*, 45 (1992), pp. 637–60.

[8] P. J. Cain and A. Hopkins, *British imperialism: innovation and expansion 1688–1914* (1993); P. J. Cain and A. Hopkins, *British imperialism: crisis and deconstruction 1914–1990* (1993).

[9] On 'internalist' and 'externalist' accounts of the history of science, see, for instance, the articles in the *Macmillan dictionary of the history of science*.

which directly resulted from the economic dynamism of the coalfields, but the self-generated success of the world's first industrialists meant that the southern power elite never had to embrace 'industrialism' as a primary national goal in order to benefit from it. The nation's economic, like its political fate has been principally determined by the continuity and interests of this rather small, metropolitan, and imperial social group: landed and mercantile in its origins; rentier, administrative, and professional in its twentieth-century preferences. The principal institutions through which this section exerted control over the nation's economic destiny were a formidable combination: the House of Commons, the central civil service, particularly the Treasury, the Bank of England, and the City.[10] They have never voluntarily considered that the competitiveness and productivity of British industry and the urban masses in the north and midlands was of absolutely paramount importance (the repeal of the Corn Laws was foisted upon them). Critically, there has never been an attitude of possession and responsibility towards the industrial side of the economy. To the south, the north and its industry has remained an upstart distant cousin: fine while it is doing well, faintly embarrassing when not; but definitely not 'our' responsibility.

By contrast, Elbaum and Lazonick give a complementary 'internalist' analysis, with their exploration of 'institutional rigidities' or 'constraints'.[11] Their concern has been to show why there was a relative failure within British industry during the first half of the twentieth century to develop the larger, vertically integrated and amalgamated business structures and associated managerial systems which predominated elsewhere in the world's most developed economies. If it is correct that a greater preponderance of these kinds of firms in the German and US economies at and after the turn of the century enabled the businesses of those countries to develop and market more effectively a range of new, 'higher technology', and more mass consumption oriented goods, such as in the chemicals, pharmaceuticals, electricals, energy, and transport industries, then this, it is argued, is a key to Britain's flagging performance. Although there are certainly important exceptions to the generalisation (notably in retailing and financial services, though arguably these do not refute the case for manufacturing industry), Elbaum and Lazonick and their colleagues have documented the

[10] G. Ingham, *Capitalism divided?: The city and industry in British social development* (1984) has provided important research in relation to this aspect of the analysis.
[11] B. Elbaum and W. Lazonick (eds.), *The decline of the British economy* (Oxford, 1986). Their work develops themes addressed in: L. Hannah, *The rise of the corporate economy* (1976) and A. P. Chandler and H. Daems (eds.), *Managerial hierarchies* (1980).

persistence in Britain of old-fashioned, proudly independent, relatively small, family-owned and even family-run firms, without proper 'R&D' or marketing divisions – those areas most likely to drive corporate expansion and diversification. Theirs is a persuasive amplification and empirical exploration of the consequences of the old 'early start' thesis: that British family firms and their too-cossetted workforces enjoyed too easy and prolonged success by virtue of being the first in the field, exporting for too long the same old goods using the same old methods, to relatively soft, formal, and 'informal' empire markets.[12]

There can be no doubt that there is much of truth, insight, and value in each of these two grand theses, along with so many of the other contributions which have been published over the last three decades, exploring the complexity of the factors hampering the performance of British industry and industrialists. By pursuing this line of attack a range of important findings have emerged and the two theses briefly summarised above can be combined to produce a sophisticated and wide-ranging historical interpretation of Britain's economic decline. As the principal agency directly responsible for technological improvement within the economy, the enterprise record of business leaders is the obvious and proper place to look for evidence of success or failure in 'technological improvement', the factor which conventional neoclassical growth models deemed to be the key to high performance. But this direct approach may not provide *all* the answers. There may be other important causes of this long-term fall-off in economic competitiveness, when measured against the most productive economies in the world.

II

This, then, is where a human resources perspective may offer a helpfully different viewpoint for assessing the performance and diagnosing the weaknesses of the British economy during the last two centuries or so. Such a perspective invites us to look at the economy principally in terms of the long-term social and demographic evolution of its stock of human and social resources, rather than in terms of the efficiency and decisions of its entrepreneurs and managers.

The most obvious, relevant feature of the historical landscape of the last two centuries, when viewed through the demographic telescope, has been

---

[12] D. Landes, *The unbound Prometheus: technologies change and industrial development from 1750 to the present* (Cambridge, 1972).

the dramatic fall in the nation's mortality and morbidity.[13] This occurred with ever-increasing momentum from the 1870s through to the interwar decades, thereafter continuing to the present day at a more sedate pace as asymptotic limits to human longevity improvement have increasingly come into play. However, an equally significant mortality and morbidity feature, which has been somewhat obscured from view until recently, was the serious *deterioration* in urban mortality and morbidity which occurred during the second quarter of the nineteenth century and which persisted throughout most of the third quarter.[14] This urban problem was sufficiently severe that the national aggregate measure of mortality conditions, the nation's average expectation of life at birth, failed to register any improvement from the 1820s until the 1870s, having previously experienced a trend rise for almost a century, from the 1730s onwards.[15] Thus, when the historical profile of the primary index of mortality change, expectation of life at birth, is placed alongside the trajectory of national economic growth, the kind of paradoxical relationship mentioned at the outset of this chapter appears to have a long history in Britain's case. During the century of relatively gradual economic growth from the early eighteenth until the early nineteenth century the nation's health improved substantially, whereas

[13] Note that James Riley has claimed, on the basis of his analysis of Friendly Society records of claims for illness from insured workers, that morbidity and mortality showed an inverse, not a positive correlation in nineteenth-century British history, with morbidity rising in the late nineteenth century, as mortality fell. However, as Sheila Ryan Johannson has cogently argued, Riley's is a fundamentally misconceived interpretation because it simply ignores the changing social and cultural, medical and popular construction of illness across the period in question. As the anthropometric evidence presented by R. Floud, K. Wachter, and A. Gregory, in *Height, health and history. Nutritional status in the United Kingdom 1750–1980* (Cambridge, 1990), makes clear, when the incidence of mortality – predominantly from infectious diseases – was high, so too was growth-restricting illness among the children who survived to be measured; conversely, children's height attainments only began to rise during the last third of the nineteenth century, signifying a less serious morbidity experience with the gradual abatement of the range of fatal diseases. J. C. Riley, *Sickness, recovery and death: a history and forecast of ill-health* (Iowa, 1989); S. Ryan Johansson, 'The health transition: the cultural inflation of morbidity during the decline of mortality', *Health Transition Review*, 1 (1991), pp. 39–68; J. C. Riley, 'From a high mortality regime to a high morbidity regime: is culture everything in sickness?', *Health Transition Review*, 2 (1992), pp. 71–8; Ryan Johansson, 'Measuring the cultural inflation of morbidity during the decline in mortality', *Health Transition Review*, 2 (1992), pp. 78–89.

[14] R. Woods, 'On the historical relationship between infant and child mortality', *Population Studies*, 47 (1993), pp. 195–219; E. A. Wrigley, *English population history from family reconstitution* (Cambridge, 1997), p. 260 and fig. 6.8; S. Szreter and G. Mooney, 'Urbanisation, mortality and the standard of living debate in Britain in the nineteenth century: new estimates of the expectation of life at birth in large British cities', *Economic History Review*, 51 (1998) forthcoming. On morbidity and heights, see Floud, Wachter, and Gregory, *Height, health and history*, esp. pp. 205–7, 288–95.

[15] E. A. Wrigley and R. S. Schofield, *The population history of England 1541–1871. A reconstruction* (1981), table 7.15.

during the half-century of most spectacular growth across the central decades of the nineteenth century, the health of the population faltered, especially in the cities which were the engines of growth. It was only during the era of 'decline' in Britain's economic performance, from 1870 onwards, that national average life expectancy again began to edge upwards. In fact expectation of life at birth rose most rapidly and most substantially in the entire nation's history (from under fifty years to almost seventy years) during the first five decades of the twentieth century, the most prolonged period of relatively low economic growth rates experienced by the modern British economy.

The argument that will be developed in the remainder of this essay will focus on the primary importance, for a country in Britain's position, of the full development of its human resources in order to be able to *sustain*, over the long term, the highest rates of economic growth in a competitive, international trading context. It will be argued that the fact that Britain has consistently failed to sustain such high rates of growth since the 1870s has been due, in addition to all the problems identified by previous contributors to the debate, to the demonstrable lack of political commitment to this goal over the long term. This has been due to a pervasive failure, both within British public opinion and among her economic and historical analysts, to take seriously the proposition that truly comprehensive – and therefore inevitably 'expensive' – investment in the full panoply of social institutions which develop human resources is not some form of utopian or 'socialist' luxury, but actually a crucial ingredient for the perpetuation of the highest rates of free-market-based economic growth.

This argument is premised on the self-evident proposition that the history of modern economic growth throughout the world since the seventeenth century shows that the necessity of the accumulation of a nation's social and cultural capital (the quality of its human resources) is every bit as fundamental an accompaniment of the process of economic growth as is the accumulation of its material capital. It is unquestionable that every society which has experienced full 'economic development' during the last two centuries has also seen a substantial, widely dispersed increase over the same period in the health, literacy, numeracy, personal living standards, public services, and amenities of its general populace. But until recently, there has been a strong consensus, especially among growth economists and Britain's economic historians, that these particular developments principally represent the social *consequences* and fruits of successful economic growth. According to this, the strong, universal correlation has no particular significance in helping us to understand the processes of economic growth because the primary direction of causation has been from the material and the economic to the social and cultural. Marx's challenging dialectical materialism has, perhaps, fastened the attention of generations of apologists and critics of the growth of the capitalist system too exclusively on this primarily economic approach to the process. Certainly, Davenant's insistence that 'People are the real strength and riches of a country' was a commonplace of economic thought, before 'the materialist turn' of the late eighteenth and early nineteenth centuries.[16] However, as Crafts' survey of the latest research and thinking among liberal economists of growth shows, there is now emerging a serious interest in exploring the significance of the role of human capital in accounting for different rates of economic growth. Although approaching the subject from a quite distinct social and demographic perspective, this essay also seeks to argue for the importance of these aspects in influencing the characteristics of the long-term performance of the British economy.

Of course, a country can experience strong economic growth simply through the unique exploitation of abundant, essential natural resources in scarce supply elsewhere. There was an aspect of this to Britain's spectacular nineteenth-century growth, when she enjoyed for several decades a quasi-monopoly on the exploitation of the world's supply of steam power; and some of the oil-producing economies have been benefiting from this finite effect in recent decades. But virtually all national-scale economies, including Britain's, are not, over the long term, in such a simple position. For these real economies, lacking such 'natural' monopolies, the continual development of their human resources is as essential to their continued high growth as is the accumulation of productive material capital.

This proposition, concerning the long-term competitive development of human resources, relates not merely to the technical skills and training of the labour force – the narrow definition of human capital to be found in economics textbooks – but to the question of the broader, national commitment to as thorough and effective an investment in all dimensions of the nation's social and cultural capital as any international competitor. For this, it is necessary to endow the population with the best possible communications and information infrastructure, health and social

---

[16] Cited in J. Hoppit, 'Political arithmetic in eighteenth-century England', *Economic History Review*, 49 (1996), pp. 516–40, p. 525. Charles Davenant (1656–1714) was a disciple of William Petty and Gregory King; his *Discourses on the public revenues, and on the trade of England* (1698) was well known to Adam Smith. On materialism and the Scottish Enlightenment, see J. W. Burrow, *Evolution and society* (Cambridge, 1966).

services, social security/insurance system, and housing environment. Generous and comprehensive social provision of these basics provides the population with a competitive edge in the international race for the most well-trained, flexible, and effectively educable set of citizens. For, the growing economy is, in the last analysis, utterly dependent on the commercial (income-earning) value of these human working-parts. This, after all, precisely describes the environment which the educated, wealthy, and privileged elite of every society strive to provide for their own children, in order to endow their own small contribution to the nation's future human resources with the greatest range of personal opportunities and income-generating potential.

According to this argument, the long-term, high-achieving national economies are distinguished from the rest by the capacity of their socio-political and cultural systems to generalise this dynastic winning strategy – maximising investment in the encompassing human resource environment of the rising generation – to the greatest proportion of its citizens. Japan and Germany, the two large national economies which qualify as the most obvious, consistent high performers since the late nineteenth century, both score very highly in this respect. In both of these societies there has been continual strong commitment to the improvement of human resources, seen as a source of economic advance, reflected both in state policy and in companies' employment practices. During the last five years or so both of these 'high performers' have encountered serious economic problems for the first time since the 1950s. In Japan's case this has been principally because of her runaway economic success and consequent appreciation of the yen and in Germany's case because of the predictable problems of re-unification. There has been speculation of a welfare crisis promoting cuts in social provision in Germany and of Japanese companies abandoning past employment practices in response to these problems. Neither of these possible new developments, however, alters the argument here, which is an historical one. It is, however, an implication of the argument presented here that both countries could be making a mistake , in terms of their long-term growth potential, if they react too strongly in this way to their current problems.

The Prusso-German state's pioneering, nineteenth-century, universal education system and the equally innovative Bismarckian social security legislation of the 1870s and 1880s are probably the two most well-known historical markers of the German state's approach towards economic growth: *Eisen **und** Blut*. As for general patterns of company policy towards its human resources, in her recent comparative study Christel Lane has shown that this cannot be divorced from the way in which financial investment, ownership, and accountability is organised. Contrasting Britain and Germany, where she notes that little has changed in this respect in each country since the end of the last century, she finds that:

> Whereas British companies are run primarily in the interest of shareholders, German companies do not see the maximisation of profit to shareholders as their prime purpose. Managers are more concerned to safeguard the long-term stability of the company which is seen 'as a "social institution" within a local community, providing wealth and employment'.[17]

It is notable that the latter description would have applied to the attitude of many British businessmen in the early, paternalist phase of industrialisation and has been a characteristic that a small number of the most successful (measured by historical survival and growth) companies, such as Cadburys, Unilever, Marks and Spencer, have striven to maintain. But since the rise of the limited liability company and shareholding as the predominant form of ownership during the later nineteenth century, this has certainly ceased to be a general feature of British industry and of company employment practice.

Meiji Japan's Ministry of Education, established within three years of the 1868 Restoration, was as energetic as its German equivalent, claiming to have delivered 100 per cent literacy by 1900, a decade in advance of Britain.[18] Japan's leading economic historians have argued that it was this which endowed Japan with the vital 'social capability' to be able to assimilate and 'japanise' so quickly such a wide range of alien technological and organisational ideas, which in turn helps to account for the rapidity of her twentieth-century growth.[19] The postwar employment practices of Japan's famous *zaibatsu*, the great trading houses like Mitsui and Mitsubishi which survived their attempted suppression after the Second World War to become some of today's largest industrial conglomerates, are almost legendary. Although they have undoubtedly demanded high output from their workers, this has been accompanied by high levels of job security and social

---

[17] C. Lane, *Industry and society in Europe. Stability and change in Britain, Germany and France* (Aldershot, 1995), p. 47, citing G. Binney (ed.), *Debunking the myths about the German company* (Anglo-German Foundation, with RSA, 1993), p. 18.

[18] W. J. McPherson, *The economic development of Japan c. 1868–1941* (1987), p. 37.

[19] K. Ohkawa and H. Rosovsky, *Japanese economic growth. Trend acceleration in the twentieth century* (Stanford, 1973), esp. p. 118. Note, of course, that Japan was considered in this respect to constitute a special case within the framework of orthodox neoclassical growth economics of the 1960s and 1970s, because of the peculiar importance accorded to its human resources. See also S. Tsuru, *Japan's capitalism* (Cambridge, 1993)

support in the workplace and relative equality of social relations between different grades of workers, including management.[20]

Historically, the policies pursued by both German and Japanese states were, of course, strongly associated with defensive and, subsequently, expansionist nationalist goals, which produced catastrophic results for the militaristic regimes responsible. Nevertheless, as the continuing examples of both these countries' social, economic, and business practices since the Second World War demonstrate, a strong belief in the importance of the nation's investment in all its human resources can exist in a liberal democracy which has formally renounced both militarism and expansionism. It is also the case, of course, that several European states – notably the Danish, which lays claim to having created the first true welfare state during the early twentieth century – have also exhibited strong historical commitment to the development of human resources, in the widest sense, without this entailing expansionist aspirations.

Indeed, it is highly relevant that Denmark has the strongest claim to be considered alongside Japan and Germany, as one of the four most consistent economic high performers of this century, particularly throughout the postwar era.[21] The fourth such consistent high performer is Switzerland. Of course pacific Switzerland has derived many economic benefits from her unique geopolitical and financial position in modern history. But research has also shown that labour relations between management and employees are extraordinarily harmonious in Swiss firms, reflecting a pervasiveness in Swiss society of extremely positive attitudes and practices with respect to the nation's human resources.[22]

The employment practices, health, welfare, and educational policies of these economically successful societies reflect their citizens' and businessmen's common belief (sufficiently deeply held that it may be termed an 'assumption') that collective resources devoted to the health, security, and education of any member of the society is a serious benefit to all and an addi-

---

[20] R. Dore, *British factory – Japanese factory. The origins of national diversity in industrial relations* (Berkeley, 1973). M. Aoki and R. Dore (eds.), *The Japanese firm* (Oxford, 1994).

[21] In 1950 Switzerland, the UK, Sweden, and Denmark were the four countries which exhibited the highest GDP per person of all sixteen west European countries (excluding Iceland and Luxemburg from the comparison). By 1992, only Switzerland and Denmark remained in this position, having been joined by Germany and France, while Sweden had slipped to eighth position and the UK to twelfth. Crafts, 'The golden age', table 2, using data derived from A. Maddison, *Monitoring the world economy* (Paris, 1995).

[22] R. M. Solow, *The labor market as a social institution* (Oxford, 1990), pp. 18–20, citing the research of J-P. Danthine and J-C. Lambelet, in particular their article 'The Swiss recipe: Conservative policies ain't enough', *Economic Policy* (October 1987), pp. 147–79.

tion to the nation's wealth and that therefore a high level of collective, social provision is appropriate and legitimate. By contrast, the British people, and to a great extent the Americans, too (with their common libertarian roots), have displayed a strong historical and continuing predilection for 'individualist' (in fact 'familistic', or 'dynastic') political ideologies, which preach that each should look after his own: the Hobbesian *bellum omnium contra omnes*.[23] Families, not 'society', are the principal compelling moral collectivity; and each independently pursues its own best interests, willing to offer discretionary assistance to others in the local community on an *ad hoc* basis; but essentially viewing the wider society as a pool of competitors for the scarce resources of status and income. Hence the profoundly important role of charity, as a self-aggrandising activity, in modern British history and the continuing antipathy to 'bureaucratic' state-provided services, which fail to provide a status-enhancing activity for the donors.[24] Of course, the British (as the American) political tradition also clearly exhibits the alternative voices of radicalism and socialism, stressing the claims of common rights and humanity. This was even sufficiently powerful to exist as an orthodoxy in popular political rhetoric for a generation during the period from 1945 to 1979. But in the longer perspective of modern British history since the seventeenth century this set of ideals and associated agenda appears to have acted for most of the time as the counterplot, rather than the dominant story.

This, then, is the working hypothesis which provides this essay's proposed answer to the general question which the study of Britain's economic decline raises. It is sustained national commitment to investment in all of the nation's human resources that is the key to maintaining high rates of economic performance over the very long term for a national economy in the competitive international market. Individual entrepreneurs of ability are also essential, but, however heroic the latter may be, they will be inadequate, alone, to the task of maintaining the highest rates of national economic growth over the long run, without the necessary support of the full development of the whole society's human resources.

---

[23] C. B. Macpherson, *The political theory of possessive individualism* (Oxford, 1962); B. Bailyn, *The ideological origins of the American revolution* (Cambridge, Mass., 1967); S. Lukes, *Individualism* (Oxford, 1973), K. H. F. Dyson, *The state tradition in Western Europe. A study of an idea and institution* (Oxford, 1980). As the work of Peter Laslett and colleagues has shown, English 'individualism' has been institutionally nurtured in the patriarchal, 'dynastic' nuclear family household: P. Laslett, *The world we have lost* (1965), esp. chs. 1, 4; A. Macfarlane, *The origins of English individualism* (1978).

[24] On charity, see, for instance, G. Stedman Jones, *Outcast London* (Oxford, 1971; with new preface, Harmondsworth, 1984); R. J. Morris, 'Voluntary societies and British urban elites, 1780–1850: an analysis', *Historical Journal*, 26 (1983), pp. 95–118.

According to this viewpoint, a weakness in the historiography of Britain's economic decline has been too much emphasis only on the importance of the range of factors which influence the motivation and decision-making of individual entrepreneurs and managers. Although the issue of human capital has been raised and examined in the historical debate on decline, this has been from within the relatively confined view of its relation to the provision of scientific education and technical training, especially in the period from 1870 to 1914 when it has been claimed that British industry first showed signs of failing to innovate in new, more scientific areas of production as effectively as its major competitors.[25] While that may be a valid analysis of this specific problem, it is not the same scale of argument over the importance of human resources as that which is opened up here by the demographic and social long-term perspective.

III

What, then, beyond an outline review of certain demographic indices, is the substantial historical evidence, such as can be mobilised within the vehicle of a single chapter, which can support the thesis that it has been deficiencies in Britain's historical record of investment in human resources which lies at the heart of an explanation of long-term persistent decline in economic performance? Perhaps the first place to start with building such an interpretation is to examine the possible role of these factors in contributing to Britain's initial spectacular success, as the first national economy in the world to sustain high rates of economic growth.

On the eve of the industrial revolution, during the first three-quarters of the eighteenth century, Britain's social infrastructure and quality of human capital was extremely advanced by the standards of the day. The British people were free from lethal dearth and subsistence crises and had been for some time, quite unlike the subjects of the French monarchy, the other principal European case where sufficient historical evidence exists to study the incidence of 'crisis mortality' in the early modern period.[26] The British nation's physical and information communications systems – in other words, the components of the national market – were already well devel-

---

[25] M. Sanderson, *The universities and British industry, 1850–1970* (1972).

[26] A. Appleby, *Famine in Tudor and Stuart England* (Liverpool, 1978); R. Schofield, 'Crisis mortality', *Local Population Studies*, 9 (1972), pp. 9–22; P. Slack, *Poverty and policy in Tudor and Stuart England* (1988).

oped by the mid-seventeenth century because of the natural advantages of an abundance of navigable inland and coastal waterways, bettered only by the natural endowments of its principal trading competitor of the seventeenth century, Holland. Without even mentioning the subsequent combined canal, enclosure, and turnpike road revolution in the physical communication networks of the provinces, we can be quite certain of Britain's global advantage over even Holland in respect of the density and efficiency of her populace's commercial information and communications system by the last quarter of the eighteenth century, simply because of the enormous size of her principal entrepot, London.[27] Before the advent of telecommunications, large city agglomerations represented the most efficient form of information concentration and exchange possible. This quintessentially social property of a city is, of course, the primary economic function and virtue of a 'market', which is itself the foundation for trade and economic growth. Cities grow through the expansion of their trade; but the relationship is entirely reciprocal.

Although no other single city in Britain was anywhere near even one-tenth of London's size until the industrial phase of urbanisation began in earnest in the nineteenth century, historians consider there to have been a widespread 'urban renaissance' throughout Britain during the period from 1660 to 1760.[28] The commercial and communications revolution should certainly not therefore be seen as an exclusively metropolitan phenomenon, for all that the capital city was providing its main motive power.[29] The highly communicative 'polite and commercial people' of mid-eighteenth century Britain provided a buoyant market for the cheap printed word.[30] The first provincial weekly, the *Norwich Post-Boy*, was founded in the first year of the eighteenth century and there were over a hundred such weeklies in existence by the beginning of the next century.[31] Not surprisingly, the British were apparently a highly literate populace on the eve of the industrial revolution, recording just over 60 per cent male literacy and

---

[27] Already larger than any other city including Amsterdam at the beginning of the eighteenth century, at 1 million inhabitants by the last quarter, London had come to dwarf even Paris, which was approximately half that size.

[28] P. Borsay, *The English urban renaissance. Culture and society in the provincial town, 1660–1770* (Oxford, 1989).

[29] J. Brewer, *Party, ideology, and popular politics at the accession of George III* (Cambridge, 1976), ch. 8, esp. pp. 157–9.

[30] C. Langford, *A polite and commercial people. England 1727–83* (Oxford, 1992).

[31] D. Read, *Press and people 1790–1850* (1961), p. 59.

about 40 per cent female literacy in England by the 1740s and 1750s.[32] The social security system of the old Poor Law was considered generous to a fault by its late eighteenth century detractors (infamously so by parson Malthus) and almost certainly it was the most generous in the world at that time;[33] while voluntary and charitable hospitals, pursuing an ever more exacting science of medicine, had been founded in great numbers and in most cities during the course of the century. With mortality having fallen over the second half of the eighteenth century and with rising average height attainments of successive cohorts of children indicating falling morbidity, too, this completes an all-round picture in Britain of rude health and enviable advantages in the development of social infrastructure and human embodied capital by the last quarter of the eighteenth century.

This, then, was the era which gave birth to the world's first sustained episode of rapid per capita economic growth. Risk-taking entrepreneurship, the accumulation of capital, key inventions, and dramatic organisational innovations within the supply side of the economy, along with an explosive surge in demand, were also vital in driving the nation's economic growth rates upwards from that time onwards.[34] But compared to the fulsome historiographical attention lavished upon consideration of these aspects of the story, the significance of the nation's rich endowment in social infrastructure and its depth of high-quality human resources has tended to be treated merely as a given, with 'social improvements' seen principally as a fruit borne of successful economic growth, rather than as an integral part of the germinating process.[35]

---

[32] R. Schofield, 'Dimensions of illiteracy in England 1750–1850', in H. J. Graff (ed.), *Literacy and social development in the West: a reader* (Cambridge, 1981), pp. 201–13; p. 207 (percentages of grooms and brides signing at marriage in a random sample of 274 English parish registers). It seems likely that, with the exception of Scotland, these literacy rates were at least as high as, and probably higher, than those achieved elsewhere in Europe at the time, including even Prussia and Sweden, though, as is well known, the latter peculiarly recorded much higher proportions able to read than able to write: E. Johansson, 'The history of literacy in Sweden', in Graff, *Literacy and social development*, pp. 151–82.

[33] P. H. Lindert, 'Unequal living standards', in R. Floud and D. McCloskey (eds.), *The economic history of Britain 1700–1860* (Cambridge, 1994), pp. 357–86, 382–3.

[34] On demand, see N. McKendrick, J. Brewer, and J. H. Plumb, *The birth of a consumer society: the commercialisation of eighteenth-century England* (1983); J. Brewer and R. Porter (eds.), *Consumption and the world of goods* (1993).

[35] But note that recently some economists have become interested in the possible importance of gross deficiencies in human-resource quality, in the form of undernutrition and malnutrition for the productive capacities of the very poor in a country such as India: P. Dasgupta, *An inquiry into well-being and destitution* (Oxford, 1993), ch. 16. However, R. W. Fogel's recent suggestion that these kinds of consideration may have been important for increasing British work-rates during the period of the industrial revolution does not seem well grounded, especially since infectious diseases *increased* in their incidence among

Furthermore, if the high quality and quantity of the nation's infrastructure, its social security and health-promoting institutions, and its human capital are all viewed as essential components of the strength and sustainability of the initial phase of long-term economic success enjoyed by Britain in the nineteenth century, rather than as an optional extra or a by-product, then this may also offer assistance in explaining Britain's subsequent trajectory of gradual, but apparently inexorable economic decline after the mid-Victorian boom. A review of the available evidence, however, indicates that if there was failure in these terms, it was far from a general one across the range of all aspects of relevance to the vitality of the nation's human resources. Given the precocious development of her domestic rail network from the 1830s, the continued expansion down to the First World War of London as the world trading system's primary entrepot, the City as its principal money-broker, and the British merchant and military navies' respective positions as the premier fleets of their kind, the physical and information communications systems would not seem to be a promising aspect of social infrastructure to pursue, in order to identify underperformance in British society's investment in its human resources.

However, when the supporting social services and health and educational institutions for promoting human resources are examined, a set of more ominous signs emerges, in the middle of the nineteenth century. Firstly, there is the catastrophe of the Irish famine, the first major subsistence crisis on British soil for centuries and yet the worst in modern west European history. This shows that the British state had not merely allowed itself to become semi-detached from the supervision of the market economy, but it had, by the 1840s, taken the almost complete abdication of responsibility for social security advocated by the ideologues of political economy and the New Poor Law to an absurdly inhumane and irresponsible extreme. In another area of social support, it has been shown that by the 1840s the previous century's voluntary hospitals had become submerged under the weight of local demand in the fast-growing cities, without any compensatory building programme having been undertaken to expand such facilities.[36] Consistent with this, there is the rising tide of emigration from Britain during this period (additional to that leaving

the urban workforce across the relevant period: R. W. Fogel, 'Economic growth, population theory, and physiology: the bearing of long-term processes on the making of economic policy', *American Economic Review*, 84 (1994), pp. 369–95, esp. p. 386.

[36] S. Cherry, 'The hospitals and population growth: the voluntary general hospitals, mortality and local populations in the English provinces in the eighteenth and nineteenth centuries', parts 1 and 2, *Population Studies*, 34 (1980), pp. 59–75; 251–66.

Ireland after the Famine): a persistent and large flow overseas of those seeking something better and greater personal security than could be found in urban Britain.[37]

Apart from the mortality disaster in Ireland, there was also a poor showing on the mainland. As noted above, urban death rates in the second and third quarters of the nineteenth century were probably higher than they had been earlier in the century and there was also a measurable decline in children's height attainments at this time. Finally, contrary to the subsequent experiences of Germany and Japan during their initial periods of industrial expansion, literacy rates in England and Wales registered only a slight improvement from the 1770s to the 1850s, despite the enormous urbanisation of the population that occurred across those eight decades; indeed, by the second quarter of the nineteenth century the literacy rates of the new industrial cities were actually well below the national average (while those of non-industrialised market towns were above it).[38]

Thus, there is substantial evidence of decline and deterioration in supporting social infrastructure and in measurable dimensions of the human resource base in the urban heart of the mid-Victorian industrial economy of mainland Britain. The proximate reason for this was failure of adequate social, public health, and infrastructure investment in the fabric and environment of Britain's industrial cities throughout the first three-quarters of the nineteenth century. This was not simply an inevitable consequence of their fast expansion. The reasons were complex and related to the nation's evolving politics, and to the social institutions and property relations in these cities.[39] However, the rise to prominence of the 'dismal science' of classical, *laissez-faire* political economy, as the dominant ideology of the age in social and economic affairs during the first half of the nineteenth century, can perhaps be singled out as a cause of primary importance. For it was this mode of thought among the governing and business classes which legitimated the curious process whereby the dramatic accumulation of national and individual wealth occurred while social infrastructure,

---

[37] D. Baines, *Migration in a mature economy. Emigration and international migration in England and Wales, 1861–1900* (Cambridge, 1986).

[38] M. Sanderson, 'Literacy and social mobility in the industrial revolution in England', *Past and Present*, 56 (1972), pp. 75–104; Schofield, 'Dimensions of illiteracy' pp. 209, 213; D. Cressy, 'Literacy in context: meaning and measurement in early modern England' in Brewer and Porter, *Consumption and the world of goods*, pp. 305–19, p. 318.

[39] This is a vast and complex area. See, for instance, E. P. Hennock, *Fit and proper persons* (1973); D. Fraser, *Urban politics in Victorian England* (Leicester, 1976); C. Bellamy, *Administering local–central relations 1871–1919. The Local Government Board in its fiscal and cultural context* (Manchester, 1988).

health, and educational investment was permitted to lapse and fall into increasing abeyance for two or more generations.

But if the importance of human resources is so critical to long-term, sustained economic growth, why didn't the dire situation which had developed in the industrial cities by the 1830s and 1840s halt Britain's economic progress? The reason for this is that at this point in time the British economy's early start advantages, primarily in terms of dominant share of the world's mechanised production processes and its access to mass markets, were at their absolute maximum in relation to all other economies (the two principal future rivals, the USA and Germany, were still politically bitterly divided peoples with fragmented economies until the late 1860s). The predominant form of labour power required to exploit these enormous advantages was not such as would be seriously affected by the deterioration in its quality that had occurred: after all, young and illiterate children could and did do much of the work around the new, unguarded machinery in the mills, with the blessing of the state until the more restrictive Factories and Workshops Acts of the 1870s. Thus, the British economy's enormous and protracted, highly general (because relating to a revolution in the power source for multiple productive processes) comparative advantages in industrial production permitted the deficiencies in human resources to accumulate over decades without apparent harm to the economy's competitive productivity.

Serious international competition finally emerged with the political and economic unification of both Germany and the USA in the course of the 1860s and 1870s and their rapid, simultaneous economic expansion (American society, like German and Japanese, also valued education sufficiently highly for US literacy levels of over 80 per cent in 1865 already to be substantially higher than Britain's at that time).[40] Although immediately aware of, and anxious over, this international competition, the British political response was extremely sluggish because the governing class remained committed to an economic belief system, the classical political economy of *laissez-faire*, which envisaged a highly circumscribed role for the state in relation to social and economic affairs. Although the unacceptable condition of the nation's industrial cities, the unsatisfactory health of their inhabitants, and deficiencies in the nation's educational resources were clearly acknowledged to be pressing problems by a range of official and unofficial

[40] R. B. Nye and J. E. Morpurgo, *A history of the United States*, vol. II (1955; Pelican edition), p. 576.

bodies during the 1860s, it took almost half a century for a long, evolving series of piecemeal measures to emerge, which eventually effectively addressed these issues.

Only with the gradual weakening and popular questioning of classical, liberal political economy over two to three decades from the 1870s onwards was the neglect and damage to human resources slowly repaired. In default of any strong central government policy, it was municipal councils which innovated, increasingly spending on their environments and social services by devising various financial mechanisms for mobilising the funds of the wealthy towards these purposes.[41] The last decade before the First World War witnessed something of a revolution in Britain's national social policy, with the establishment in 1903 of a coherent, secular national education system (from elementary through to university levels) and with the ensuing creation of insurance-based national social security schemes for health, unemployment, and old age, albeit incomplete in their coverage of the populace's needs (women not in employment were a major category of omission, for instance).[42] However, this revolution remained a partial and stymied one through the interwar decades of unemployment and government retrenchment. It has been shown that the principal departments of state responsible for human resource development, those of Reconstruction, Health, Education, and Labour were severely circumscribed in the scope of their activities in the 1920s and 1930s. There was in effect severe rationing and gross regional disparity in the extent to which the British populace actually gained access to the range of health services, to the better quality of housing, and to the opportunities for secondary and higher education or technical and vocational training, which its social and political leaders had almost unanimously agreed to be desirable national aims for the post First World War society.[43]

[41] R. Millward and S. Sheard, 'The urban fiscal problem, 1870–1914: government expenditure and finance in England and Wales', *Economic History Review*, 48 (1995), pp. 501–35.

[42] B. B. Gilbert, *The evolution of national insurance in Great Britain: the origins of the welfare state* (1966); E. P. Hennock, *British social reform and German precedents. The case of social insurance 1880–1914* (Oxford, 1987); G. R. Searle, *The quest for national efficiency: a study in British politics and thought 1899–1914* (Oxford, 1971); M. Freeden, *The New Liberalism* (Oxford, 1978); P. Thane, *The foundations of the welfare state* (1982).

[43] On health, see J. Boyd-Orr, *Food, health and income* (1936); C. Webster, 'Healthy or hungry thirties?', *History Workshop Journal*, 13 (1982), pp. 110–30; E. Peretz, 'The costs of modern motherhood to low income families in interwar Britain' in V. Fildes, L. Marks, and H. Marland (eds.), *Women and children first. International maternal and infant welfare 1870–1945* (1992), pp. 257–80. On education see G. Sutherland, *Ability, merit and measurement. Mental testing and English education 1880–1940* (Oxford, 1984); on labour issues, see R. Lowe, *Adjusting to democracy: the role of the Ministry of Labour in British politics, 1916–1939* (Oxford, 1986).

It was not until the needs of the home front in the Second World War once again brought a unanimity of purpose in public opinion, while concentrating the minds of politicians, administrators, and local government on the health, morale and efficiency of the civilian side of the war economy, that many of these problems of access and local disparity of provision were addressed. The implementation of a truly comprehensive welfare state and national health service were both logical and administrative, as much as symbolic, political, sequelae of the wartime experience, confirmed by the fact that the originator and architect of the ambitious Beveridge Plan was a figure at the centre of the wartime administrative and planning apparatus, not a leading political figure.[44] As a result, it was only in the 1940s that the long, slow process of raising the level of investment in human resources from the slough of despond into which it had fallen by the third quarter of the nineteenth century had finally produced a set of facilities, in terms of health, social security, and education (if not training) which could compare, in their comprehensive scope and coverage of the population, with those of the other most advanced economies and societies, principally those of continental northern Europe.[45]

Hence, the period from the beginning of the twentieth century until the 1970s witnessed a long, slow process of socio-economic 'equalling upwards' in modern Britain. This was encouraged by the increasing acceptance of a progressive, strongly redistributive fiscal regime funding a widening range of social and health services, which was extended to a formal welfare state and a full-employment policy from the 1940s. The net outcome of this process and its far-reaching nature can be gauged in summary fashion from the results of research on the distribution of wealth. This shows that whereas 1 per cent of the populace still owned almost 60 per cent of the nation's wealth in the 1920s, this had been cut in half, to under 30 per cent, by the beginning of the 1970s. Conversely, the poorest 80 per cent of the population had seen their share in the nation's wealth almost triple over the same period, from just 6.4 per cent in the 1920s to almost 20 per cent by 1970.[46]

---

[44] J. Harris, 'William Beveridge in Whitehall: maverick or mandarin?', in R. MacLeod (ed.), *Government and expertise* (Cambridge, 1988), pp. 224–41; and see also C. Webster, 'Conflict and consensus: explaining the British health service', *20th Century British History*, 1 (1990), pp. 115–51.

[45] The leading nations in this respect were the Danish, Swedish, and German: D. Levine, *Poverty and society. The growth of the American welfare state in international comparison* (1988), part 4.

[46] W. D. Rubinstein, *Wealth and inequality in Britain* (1986), p. 95. Figures derived from original research reported in A. B. Atkinson and A. J. Harrison, *The distribution of personal wealth in Britain* (Cambridge, 1978).

One consequence of the gradual but protracted rise in investment in the full range of the nation's human resources across the first half of the twentieth century was a return, for a quarter of a century from the 1950s onwards, of the highest economic growth rates yet seen in British history, consistently in excess even of the halcyon mid-Victorian decades. Although this development was certainly not the *only* cause of this strong economic performance, the argument here is that it was a necessary, enabling condition. It is often pointed out that Britain nevertheless experienced lower growth rates in these postwar decades than the other economies of western Europe and Japan. However, many of these were economies shattered and distorted by war and occupation, now literally rebuilding everything and therefore growing very rapidly from relatively low base values of per capita national product. Many enjoyed substantial US capital assistance, and had no outgoings on defence expenditure. It is not really appropriate to compare countries in this position with Britain's growth performance, when she was growing from a much higher initial level of per capita GDP, while attempting to honour an enormous war debt to the USA and continuing to shoulder the military costs of world power status. It should be noted that the other non-occupied belligerents, Canada, Australia, New Zealand, and even the USA, all also failed to experience the spectacular growth rates of the recovery economies.[47]

IV

But why then, if the uneven history of Britain's investment in its own people and their social infrastructure is so important in contributing to the explanation of long-term phases of strong and weak economic performance, did the success story of the post Second World War decades come to such an abrupt end in the 1970s? And why has the problem of economic decline still remained such a haunting theme and a persistent feature of the British economy since the 1960s? The first of these two questions is amenable to a relatively obvious answer, in that the British economy succumbed – albeit somewhat more so than most others – to the general trade dislocation and unemployment problems suffered by all developed western economies in the wake of the 1973 oil crisis, following upon the host of

[47] Crafts, 'The golden age', pp. 435–6, 441–2, also makes several of these points and additionally argues that most of the usually fast-growing economies of the period were either experiencing war recovery or rapid conversion towards manufacturing from agriculture (such as Ireland and Spain).

complex problems lying behind the sudden US abandonment of the gold–dollar standard in 1971.[48]

But what of the continuing relatively poor performance ever since? The answer to this question returns us to the main thesis of this chapter: the central role of human resources and of national commitment to their supporting institutions, in sustaining high rates of economic growth over the long-term. Despite the ambitious schemes of the 1940s and their implementation over the ensuing decades, there has been a continuing failure of British public opinion, government policy, and economic historiography to perceive investment in health, housing, social services, and education (except for technical training) as fundamental and essential for the promotion of economic growth. The Beveridge plan and the postwar Labour Government in fact presented their revolution in social provision of the 1940s as a matter of the defensive rights of citizens – securing negative freedoms (from wants), in Sir Isaiah Berlin's terminology, rather then the promotion of positive freedoms – including economic ones. This was really conceived as humane and advanced charity, not as the essential basis for raising national economic productivity.

The 1940s, therefore, was a false dawn, as far as the popular British ideology of economic growth is concerned. An earlier 'great individuals' model of economic growth was never really ousted or abandoned. Such a view could hardly, of course, be considered an accurate description of the postwar practice of managed economic growth in a mixed economy under 'Keynesian' command of the budgetary and fiscal heights. Nevertheless, when this postwar form of economic management appeared to be coming unstuck in the 1970s an important part of the thinking and the populist political rhetoric of the New Right, which enabled the Thatcher government to win power, was its promise to revive the spirit of individual free enterprise from the shackles of 'socialist' state control and so return Britain to its rightful historical position as a leading world economy. This successfully appealed to the nostalgic folk memory of Britain's unique period of early industrial leadership, when economic dynamism supposedly flowed in an uncomplicated fashion from the personal achievements of commercially successful individuals – the *Upwardly-mobile* (the title chosen for the political autobiography of Norman Tebbit, the minister who was popularly considered to personify most completely the values of the Thatcherite 'revolution').

---

[48] H. Van der Wee, *Prosperity and upheaval. The world economy 1945–1980* (1986), chs. XI–XII.

Furthermore, this analysis of the cause of and remedies for Britain's economic decline was not confined to electioneering rhetoric but actually acted as the principle upon which social and economic policy was formulated. Since 1979 the leading theme of the British Government's economic policy under the Conservative administrations of both Margaret Thatcher and John Major has been consistent with the fundamental premise that the vigour and efficacity of business leadership is the key to long-term economic success. The Conservative Government developed and carried through a series of rigorous policies aimed at remedying the principal, identifiable causes of Britain's supposedly lacklustre economic performance, which it believed lay in a range of deadly inhibitions upon the dynamism of her managerial 'captains of industry' and entrepreneurial 'wealth-creators'. The British suffered a national sickness, christened by the evangelical New Right the 'dependency culture', created by a too-generous welfare state which deprived employers of cheap, mobile labour; an associated redistributive tax system drove entrepreneurial talent overseas and deprived potential businessmen of incentives to act because their personal profits would be too paltry; and trade unions were a further crippling problem in the labour market, acting as overmighty bulwarks against productive innovations in working practices – another handicap on the would-be entrepreneur's capacity to transform the country's economic performance.

However, despite all the rationalising of the early 1980s, the subsequent war against the unions, and the downsizing of the 1990s, the incentivising of the low-paid labour market through the fear of indigent unemployment and of the entrepreneurs through reduction of their personal taxation burdens, the net effect has only been a growth rate for the British economy since 1979 no higher than during the supposedly disappointing, previous decades of too much state intervention, strong unions, and dependency culture; and this has even been despite the substantial windfall of North Sea oil boosting the nation's trading position during these most recent decades.[49] The failure of these determined policies to reverse the long-term

[49] During the period 1960 to 1973 (peak to peak) UK growth of real GDP per capita was 2.6 per cent per annum; if the period of international difficulties, from 1973 to 1979, is included, then the growth rate measured in this way was 2.2 per cent for the period 1960 to 1979. The growth rate, peak to peak, for the period 1979 to 1989 was also 2.2 per cent (the next peak turning point has not yet definitely arrived and so no comparable figure is available for the period since 1989; however, the post-1989 figure is highly unlikely to be higher than that for 1979 to 1989 because of the prolonged and deep nature of the recession of 1990 to 1993). *Statistics Directorate* (OECD 1995), table 3.2, p. 50. During the period of greatest North Sea oil production, from 1982 to 1987, oil exports were contributing approximately 5 per cent of Britain's GDP: S. Pollard, *The development of the British economy 1914–90* (4th edn, 1992), pp. 402–3.

trend of economic decline also strongly suggests, therefore, that a model of sustained high rates of economic growth which focuses too exclusively on creating the appropriate market conditions for entrepreneurs and managers to act vigorously may be fatally flawed. The Thatcherite revolution has not, therefore, delivered the anticipated improvements to Britain's economic performance in either the short or medium run. But in addition it has almost certainly inflicted serious damage on the economy's capacity to generate very high rates of economic growth over the longer run, if the thesis presented here, concerning the vital importance of the accumulating development of human resources, is correct.

In the nineteenth century, the key tell-tale statistics illustrating the problems generated by a form of economic growth and an associated political ideology which eschewed the significance of building up human resources can be found in the most direct and blunt measures of the quality of human capital: debilitating mortality and morbidity experience of the urban industrial proletariat in the second and third quarters of the century. In the late twentieth century in a highly developed economy, it is not, of course, to such basic measures of the physical health of the populace as these that we should expect to look for key indicators of the state of the nation's human resources (although highly significant health variations do, of course, continue to exist).[50] Instead, it is to measures of the extent and commitment of the nation's investment in its populace's education and training that we should look for the most relevant and discriminating contemporary measures of the kind of human resources development which is of primary relevance to the long-term growth potential of the economy. This follows because a high-income economy which is to continue to compete with the highest growth rates among its peers requires from its workforce the co-ordination of a vast range of highly specific literacy and numeracy-derived skills in order to create the high value-added goods and services which alone can enable growth to be sustained as fast as its most developed competitors.

Comparative international statistics for educational provision, enrolment, and attainments are notoriously difficult to interpret. Qualifications and course contents are quite different in different cultures. Measures of per capita national expenditure are fraught with pitfalls, as educational institutions are classified in diverse ways and are funded through a complex

---

[50] For an extremely important exposition of the socio-economic provenance and political significance of continuing health problems in high-income societies, see R. Wilkinson, *Unhealthy societies: the afflictions of inequality* (1996).

mix of public, voluntary, and private means. The extent and importance of private educational outlays often goes unrecorded. However, it is at least possible to make statistically valid comparisons of an index over time within the same country: that is, to examine a key aspect of the recent British record in this area of human resource development, regardless of questions of international comparison. In this respect a useful, basic key indicator is the pupil–teacher ratio. Official statistical series exist for this index for the UK from 1970 onwards, distinguishing primary from secondary schools, and also all private from all public schools. Furthermore, the utility of a measure as basic as this is that it does allow a relevant international comparative judgement to be made on the British record. This is because two very general observations can be made with confidence from the international data that is available, without having to go into detailed consideration of how each country's statistics were collated. Firstly, it is clear that developed, higher income per capita countries have the lowest pupil–teacher ratios. Secondly, it is clear that most countries, in particular higher-income ones, have been reducing their pupil–teacher ratios during the course of the last two to three decades.[51]

In line with these general patterns, during the 1970s pupil–teacher ratios in Britain were substantially reduced by about 25 per cent in all categories of school: primary and secondary, public and private. This was quite simply achieved by an approximate 25 per cent increase in the number of teachers employed throughout the country (from 419,000 to 512,000 in the public sector), while the overall pupil population remained fairly constant (at about 10 million in the state schools). At the end of this decade Britain was still probably lagging somewhat behind its most developed competitors in terms of pupil–teacher ratios.[52] But there is at least clear evidence of strong government commitment across the 1970s to building up this dimension of the nation's human resources. From the beginning of the Thatcher administration onwards, however, there has been a withdrawal of government support for this policy.

The sharpness of the policy difference between the 1970s and the 1980s has been masked to a great extent by contingent demographic effects. Hence, pupil–teacher ratios in all schools continued to improve (reduce) slightly right through to 1990, but this was not through continued expan-

---

[51] International comparative data on pupil–teacher ratios in 124 countries, relating to the years from 1965 and 1992, were published in the education tables of each of the *World Development Reports* from 1990 to 1995.

[52] *World Development Reports*, 1990 to 1995, education tables.

sion in the nation's teaching corps. It was entirely because of falling school rolls, as the 1960s baby-boom cohorts passed out of the system. As a result the ratios in maintained schools (both primary and secondary state-funded) were in fact at their historical lowest as late as 1990. Yet, rather than using this demographic contraction as a windfall opportunity finally to equal the superior, even smaller pupil–teacher ratios of other west European countries, the government instead took this as an opportunity to reduce its own costs by cutting the number of teachers employed in the public sector (from 512,000 in 1980/1 to 464,000 in 1994/5). Consistent with the 1980s policy a subsequent, moderate rise in the trend of the pupil population of both primary and secondary schools during the 1990s has not elicited a compensatory increase in the employment of teachers. In 1993/4 and 1994/5 the pupil–teacher ratio was just over 3 per cent *higher* than during the period of its demographically induced historic low from 1987 to 1990, a deficiency concentrated in the state secondary schools where the pupil–teacher ratio was actually 6 per cent higher in 1994/5 than in 1990/1.[53]

However, the official statistics also show there has been a significant exception to this pattern: non-maintained (private) schools. They have always had substantially lower average pupil–teacher ratios than maintained schools; but the gap between the two sectors has grown substantially since the 1970s. Private schools' advertising stresses small class sizes and all the associated advantages of greater staff time per student as a leading advantage of the service they can offer, and there is insistent market pressure on them to remain competitive in this respect. Contrary to the government policy for the rest of the nation's human resources, the period since 1979 has seen a continual, gradual increase in the number of teachers employed in the private sector, regardless of trends in pupil enrolment. The number of pupils in private schools rose slightly during the 1970s and has since declined slightly, standing at 591,000 in 1994/5 (as against 606,000 in 1970/1). Meanwhile the number of teachers employed has risen by 37 per cent, from 43,000 to 59,000. Whereas the pupil–teacher ratio in state schools (primary and secondary combined) stands in 1994/5 in almost exactly the same place as in 1980/1, at 1 teacher per 19 pupils, over the same period the private school ratio has improved by 25 per cent from 13 to just 10 pupils per teacher: little more than half the public sector figure and equal to some of the best national ratios found in the western world, according to

---

[53] All statistics from the relevant annual editions of the official publications: *Social Trends*, section 3, education; and *Education Statistics* (1995), table 14.

the *World Development Reports*.[54] The problem for the British economy's long-term growth prospects is that only 6 per cent of the school population benefit from this superior pedagogic environment.

The Conservative Government benches are drawn predominantly from this small section of the nation who prefer their children to attend private schools, despite the very high personal outlay involved. As individuals they apparently value very highly precisely the kind of intensive investment in human resources for their own children which, as a government, has been deemed a negative priority for the children of the country as a whole. The apparent paradox here is explicable in terms of these ministers' and MPs' adherence to the Hobbesian attitude towards education and this can here be seen as the logical corollary of the 'individualist' myth that it is principally entrepreneurs who create economic growth, not society's human resources in general. According to this viewpoint, investment in education is not seen as an issue of vital importance for the nation's international competitiveness, but is, instead, approached as a matter of *intra*-national competition between individuals and families, jostling for scarce, income-earning credentials; and it is a competition with their fellow citizens which Conservative party politicians are personally prepared to compete for very keenly.

Apart from the school environment, the home is the other most significant institution involved in the social formation of a nation's human resources. Here, the widening gap between the institutional resources available per student in the public and private sectors of education has a mirror image in the national trend of income distribution since 1979. The wealth-distribution research, cited above, showed that the differences in resources available to wealthy and poorer households had been reducing since the first quarter of this century. To study the most recent trends, it is necessary to look instead at income distribution. The latest date for which comparative official figures are available shows that, whereas in 1979 the poorest 20 per cent (quintile) of households had 10 per cent of the nation's disposable income (after allowing for housing costs) and the wealthiest had 35 per cent, by 1990/1, the poorest quintile had only 6 per cent and the wealthiest now had 43 per cent.[55] In fact the Rowntree Trust's research showed that fully one in six of the population had experienced an actual absolute fall in real disposable income measured in this way across this

[54] *World Development Reports*, 1990 to 1995, education tables.
[55] *Social Trends*, 24 (1994), table 5.20, p. 77.

period.[56] In terms of the differential investment in and relative opportunities available to the rising generation of the nation's human resources, this trend means that whereas 5 million people were in 1979 living in households with less than half the national average income, by 1989 this had risen to 12 million, the latter embracing one in four of the nation's children.[57]

This necessarily brief review of the relevant evidence therefore indicates that despite the poor rates of national economic growth registered during the 1970s (the lowest for any full decade since the Second World War), the governments of that decade, of both right and left, were in fact pursuing the optimal strategy, according to the thesis developed here regarding the most important ingredients for *long-term* high growth in a developed economy: raising the nation's level of investment in all of its human resources. Obviously, it is not enough to pursue the optimal strategy for the long-term alone, since the short and medium term must be lived through first; and something was clearly awry here in the 1970s. However, in attempting to right the economy's capacity to deliver strong growth over the shorter-term, the succeeding governments of the 1980s and 1990s have abandoned the previous policy of a national commitment to the promotion of all the society's human resources because this was at variance with their faith in the redeeming powers of restoring the 'Victorian' virtues of private enterprise and individualist competition to British society.

By contrast with the British experience, the world's long-term economic high performers, notably the Germans and Japanese, have more consistently and more generally invested in the promotion of their nation's total pool of human resources through a wide range of institutions. The libertarian political traditions and 'individualist' cultural predilections of the British have militated against this. Keen competition within society was undoubtedly a powerful engine of national economic growth during Britain's industrial revolution era and there is no reason why it cannot continue to function as an important source of individuals' motivation. But the British historical record shows that this ideology and practice cannot, alone, sustain the highest rates of national economic growth over the long term. This is because it leads to the degradation of too great a proportion of the nation's human resources, as occurred in most graphic form in the mid-nineteenth-century cities. Without the strong commitment of the state, employers, and public opinion to the goal of providing as many of its

---

[56] S. P. Jenkins, *Winners and losers: a portrait of the UK income distribution during the 1980s* (1994).
[57] *Households below average income 1979–1988/9* (HMSO 1992).

citizens as possible with the kind of environmental advantages which the rich seek to provide for their own, there are too many 'losers' in this kind of economy for it to remain internationally competitive. As the consumption of more sophisticated goods and services steadily becomes an ever more valuable component of international trade, it is the nation with the most sophisticated stock of human producers – its citizen-workers – which can best respond to these demands on the appropriate large scale and reap the most substantial benefits, in terms of rents from high value added products.

Thus, it has been argued here that a review of the course of modern British economic, demographic, and social history shows that it conforms, both in its ups and in its downs, with one of the very few general laws of history. This is the proposition that in order to sustain the highest rates of economic growth over the long term it is necessary (though not, alone, sufficient) for a society to commit itself to that scale of comprehensive and continuous investment in its full stock of human resources which can effectively match that of its rivals. British public opinion and government policy appears, however, to have remained too firmly attached to a diametrically opposed libertarian and 'individualist' conception of the processes involved in economic growth, which gives pride of place to creating the economic conditions which most favour the interests of individual entrepreneurs and managers. This is a viewpoint whose premises have not previously been sufficiently challenged in the historiography of 'decline'.

According, therefore, to the thesis developed here, the politically successful revival and encouragement of the ideology of libertarian individualism during the last twenty years, far from delivering the British nation from further economic decline, has only compounded its historic problems of long-term low growth potential. This has been due to a pronounced tendency towards chronic under-investment in the institutions which form and develop a large part of the nation's human resources: the homes and neighbourhoods and schools and colleges of the poorer half of the populace. Of course, it may be that, in the end, the British people value their libertarian individualism above the goal of world-beating economic performance. In that case, as Barry Supple counsels, there needs to be a more realistic accommodation of popular consumer expectations to the relatively modest 2 per cent per annum growth rate which is the best that such a political ideology appears to be capable of producing over the long term.

5

The myth of decline: an urban perspective

JAY WINTER

Going downhill is the natural way: so says a hoary proverb borrowed in much writing about the economic history of Britain in this century. Proverbs, treated as 'time-honoured truths', frequently turn out to be nothing of the kind; they are simply dead wrong. The vast literature on British 'decline' is a case in point. Sooner or later most Cassandras return to the question of economic decline. The problem remains, though, that like all economies, the British economy in the period 1870–1930 moved in many different directions at once. Aggregate indicators conflate these vectors into one resultant, measured through national accounts. Politicians and scholars recite them as if they have the sanctity of the Talmud, despite the huge elements of error and estimation embedded in even the most professional calculations.[1]

It is the purpose of this essay to suggest that such a national framework of analysis is at best only the most rudimentary guide to an understanding of economic processes. What Adam Smith called the *Wealth of nations* may have been a judicious guide to an earlier period, but in a century when the definition of national identity and boundaries is a highly contested issue, and when international enterprises, services, and communications penetrate national frontiers virtually at will, perhaps today it is wisest to nod in the direction of the sage of Canongate and move on.

Some like-minded scholars have turned from rigidly national frameworks into the field of regional or global economic analysis.[2] I would like to take another tack and explore the concept of economic decline on a smaller, but no less robust level, that of the metropolis.

---

[1] O. Morgenstern, *On the accuracy of economic observations* (Princeton, 1963).
[2] E. A. Wrigley, *Industrial growth and population change* (Cambridge, 1962); on regions, the literature is vast: see R. Leonardi and R. Y. Nanetti (eds.), *The regions and European integration* (1990); G. Day and G. Rees, *Regions, nations and European integration* (Cardiff, 1991); on multinational corporations, see I. M. Clarke, *The spatial organisation of multinational corporations* (1985); A. Idris-Soven, E. Idris-Soven, and M. K. Vaughan (eds.), *The world as a company town* (The Hague, 1978), and many corporate histories.

The approach of this chapter is strictly comparative. In essence, this is not new, though the kind of comparison I try to develop has been rare in the historical literature. The economic history of London is a well-known field, full of diverse and erudite tomes. When comparisons emerge, almost all set London in this period alongside other areas of Britain, beset by problems arising from reliance on one staple trade.

This is the conventional path. But what if we move horizontally across Europe rather than vertically within the British Isles? What do transnational comparisons of similar geographic areas tell us about the viability of the notion of decline? Was London in this period a 'declining' metropolis – declining not in comparison with Scunthorpe or Wigan, but with Paris and Berlin? My central claim is that when we survey the metropolitan scene in comparative perspective, London's history – in demographic, economic, or social terms – is hard to describe in terms of decline.

A word or two is necessary about the structure of comparison. Why choose these three cities? First, their salience in the history of their countries is obvious. Secondly, they have social similarities arising from their serving as the home for large administrative and political institutions. All were entrepots; all three served as the hub of important rail and communications networks. All had strong artisanal traditions, and faced similar problems of suburbanisation. All have abundant documentary records on which to base comparisons.

In a host of ways, this evidence points to underlying continuities in the social and economic history of all three cities. To compare London to both Paris and Berlin suggests that the vibrancy of the British capital in the 1870s was still there sixty years later; so were vast differences in wealth and housing, though some of the worst features of Victorian London had vanished by the 1930s.

When we enter that decade, other elements complicate the story. First, the onset and incidence of the world economic crisis varied; secondly, the Nazi seizure of power created new conditions which transformed and ultimately levelled Berlin (and large parts of London as well). Before the 1930s, comparisons are less fraught with difficulties.

It is important to register a caveat here. London was a conurbation of 7 million, whose economic and social patterns defy any uniform interpretation. Paris and Berlin were hardly homogeneous either; what matters, though, is that we can see much more clearly on the metropolitan than on the national level what 60 years of economic and social change meant to those who lived through it. From this perspective, transformation and diversification, rather than decline and fall, dominate metropolitan history in the period 1870–1930.

I

For purposes of comparison,[3] whenever we refer to each city, we refer to two urban entities. First, there was the city core, defined in 1864 for Paris as the twenty arrondissements; for Berlin, as the 'old Berlin' of urban inner districts, constituting the city proper prior to 1920; and in London from 1889, as the twenty-eight Metropolitan Boroughs. Secondly, there was a larger administrative entity, incorporating the urban core, but extending beyond it. This larger area had its own administrative identity: the Département de la Seine, for Paris; the urban and rural districts which were amalgamated with 'old Berlin' to become 'Great Berlin' in 1920; and both the Administrative County of London and 'Greater London' beyond it. The rudimentary urban profile which follows here refers both to the smaller and the larger entities.[4] It involves comparisons of relevant evidence on demographic change, population growth and structure, industrial characteristic, and urban geography. This evidence will suggest that the history of London in the years 1870–1930 was anything but a downhill slide.

The first way of demonstrating this point is demographic. London's growth was part of a broader process of urbanisation in Europe. In the period prior to 1914, the twenty arrondissements of Paris added approximately 1 million inhabitants to its numbers, reaching about 2.9 million in 1910. Over the same period, Berlin's expansion was even more remarkable. From a modest city of 800,000 on the eve of the founding of the empire, the Wilhelmine capital was home to over 2 million people in 1910. Greater still was the increase in the population of London. Including its outer ring,

---

[3] This comparison rests on the work of a collective, which Jean-Louis Robert of the University of Orléans and I organised over the years 1989 to 1996. Ten scholars wrote a study of Paris, London, and Berlin in the First World War, entitled *Capital cities at war: Paris, London, Berlin: 1914–1919* (Cambridge, 1996). The writing of individual chapters was done collectively, with one person assigned the task of presenting the findings of the group. Jean-Louis Robert reported in chapter 2 on the prewar demographic and industrial position of the cities, but his work – and indeed the chapter I have written for this *festschrift* – reflects the contribution of all ten of us.

[4] For aggregate figures, the sources are: Census of England & Wales, 1911; Recensement de la population de la France, 1911; Statistik der Stadt Berlin, vol. 32. For birth rates and death rates, the sources are: for London, *London statistics; Annual reports of the Registrar-general of England & Wales*; for Paris, *Annuaire statistique de la ville de Paris et du Département de la Seine*; for Berlin, *Monatsberichte Gross Berlin*, 1914–18.

Greater London's population rose from approximately 3.9 million in 1871 to over 7 million in 1911. The core London County Council population rose from 3.3 million in 1871 to 4.5 million in 1911. Suburbanisation was therefore more rapid than urban growth.[5] Even allowing for inevitable inaccuracies due to changes of boundaries, the overall trend is clear. This unprecedented wave of demographic growth changed the density, the geometry, and the character of these cities, and put an enormous strain on their pre-existing infrastructure.

These cities were not only huge housing districts for permanent residents. They were also stations for temporary residents and for people moving to other destinations. All three cities had large alien populations. Their numbers grew in the two generations before the 1914–18 war, when a strong migratory wave swept westward across Europe and for many, further still across the Atlantic Ocean. Paris, London, and Berlin were frequently points on the way to another destination. As a result, the numbers passing through these cities *en route* added substantially and intermittently to the resident population.[6]

Natural increase was responsible primarily for London's growth in this period. In the case of Paris and to a lesser degree Berlin, migration was of greater importance in this process of metropolitan population growth. Indeed these developments took place against the backdrop of declining fertility rates. From a level of approximately 36 per 1,000 in the 1870s, Berlin's birth rate fell to about 20 per 1,000 in 1910. The same secular trend may be observed in the other two capitals, though in Paris, as in the rest of France, fertility rates were lower than in other European countries. French fertility decline after 1870 was the second state of an earlier process of *dénatalité* beginning a century before.[7]

Mortality rates also declined from the late nineteenth century. But this trend played a smaller role than migration in the pattern of metropolitan growth, largely because the strain of demographic expansion on housing and other urban amenities was so great as to counteract some of the posi-

---

[5] B. R. Mitchell, *International historical statistics. Europe 1750–1988* (3rd edn. 1992), table A4.

[6] For recent research and references, see D. Baines, *Migration in a mature economy: emigration and internal migration in England and Wales, 1861–1900* (Cambridge, 1985); D. Hoerder (ed.), *Labor migration in the Atlantic economies: the European and North American working classes during the period of industrialisation* (Westwood, Conn., 1985); A. Glazier and L. de Rosa (eds.), *Migration across time and nations: population mobility in historical contexts* (New York, 1986); P. E. Ogden and P. E. White (eds.), *Migrants in modern France: population mobility in the later nineteenth and twentieth centuries* (1989); and the classic study by Brinley Thomas, *Migration and economic growth* (2nd edn, Cambridge, 1972).

[7] A. J. Coale and S. C. Watkins (eds.), *The decline of fertility in Europe* (Princeton, 1986).

tive effects of municipal improvements in sanitation and water supply. Some facets of urban growth pushed death rates up while other forces helped contain them.[8]

Over the years 1870 to 1900, infant mortality rates in London remained stable, but those in Paris declined slightly. The onset of rapid infant mortality decline in both Paris and London came after 1900, starting at a higher level in Paris. In Berlin in contrast, infant mortality began to decline from its dizzying heights in the 1870s, and continued to drop after the turn of the century.[9] Nevertheless, even after thirty years of progress, Berlin's infant mortality rates in 1900 – 202 per 1,000 – were at the level registered by Paris in 1871 to 1875, and still well above early Victorian levels in London.

On the eve of the war of 1914, London was clearly the healthiest of the three cities. Life expectancy was longest and adult mortality rates were lowest of the three conurbations. Paris, in contrast, had the highest death rates, with Berlin located between the two.[10] Berlin's adult mortality levels were lower than those of Paris, but its infant mortality levels remained higher. Levels of infant mortality registered in London and Paris had converged, though Parisian infants who were sent out to wet-nurses had much higher infant mortality rates. Consequently, the mortality rates of infants born in Paris were significantly higher than those born in London.[11] Londoners still held a huge demographic edge in survival chances compared to Parisians or Berliners. No decline here, either in absolute or relative terms.

Some parts of London were as unhealthy as Paris and Berlin as a whole.[12]

---

[8] S. Szreter, 'The importance of social intervention in Britain's mortality decline *c.* 1850–1914: a reinterpretation of the role of public health', *Social History of Medicine*, I (1988), p. 1–34. V. Berridge, 'Health and medicine' in F. M. L. Thompson (ed.), *The Cambridge Social History of Britain* (Cambridge, 1990), vol. III, pp. 198–220. On the strains on London, see D. Owen, *The government of Victorian London 1855–1899: the Metropolitan Board of Works, the Vestries and the City Corporation* (Cambridge, Mass., 1982); and J. Davis, *Reforming London: the London government problem, 1855–1900* (Oxford, 1988).

[9] Sigrid Stockel, 'Sauglingssterblichkeit in Berlin von 1870 bis zum Vorabend des Ersten Weltkriegs – Eine Kurve mit hohem Maximum und starkem Gefalle', in W. Ribbe (ed.), *Berlin-Forschungen*, vol. I (Berlin, 1986), pp. 219–64.

[10] A. de Foville, 'Enquête sur le dépeuplement de la France', *La revue hebdomadaire*, 5 (1909), pp. 101–29.

[11] C. Rollet, 'Nourrices et nourrissons dans le département de la Seine et en France de 1880 à 1940', *Population*, 3 (1982), pp. 573–604; G. D. Sussman, *Selling mother's milk: the wet-nursing business in France, 1815–1914* (Urbana, Ill., 1982).

[12] R. Spree, *Health and social class in Imperial Germany*, trans. S. McKinnon-Evans (Leamington Spa, 1988); J. M. Winter, 'The decline of mortality', in T. Barker and M. Drake (eds.), *Population and Society* (1982), pp. 100–20; L. Hersch, *Pauvreté et mortalité selon les principales causes de décès d'après les statistiques de la Ville de Paris* (Rome, 1932).

But the variation between rich and poor districts on the continent was much greater than in Britain. The infant mortality rate of Shoreditch was twice that of Hampstead; the ratio of poor Belleville to rich Elysée in Paris was four to one.[13] The district of Spandau was just outside metropolitan Berlin before the 1914–18 war, and was to become an area of rapid wartime expansion. In 1900 its infant mortality rate stood at 290, while that for Berlin as a whole was about 200.[14] Before its rapid prewar growth, Spandau's overall death rate was lower than that for Berlin as a whole. By 1900, the reverse was the case.[15] The poor and overcrowded inner-city quarter of Wedding registered infant mortality rates well above those for Berlin as a whole; again, compared to the more prosperous Tempelhof quarter, Wedding was much further from Tempelhof than Shoreditch was from Hampstead.[16] The gap between rich and poor was simply greater in Paris and Berlin than in London.

A second kind of evidence is that of growth trajectories. One reason why Berlin was unhealthier than London was the sheer pace of the growth of the German capital. Over five decades, the population of Berlin quadrupled. Growth in Paris and London was about half as rapid in this period. Whereas in 1871 Berlin's population was half that of Paris, by 1914 the two cities were virtually the same size. This growth spurt, unprecedented in European urban history, was not unique to Berlin; a similar trajectory marked the expansion of other German cities in this period.[17]

Berlin's growth was exponential from relatively low levels; London's was modest from very high levels. Taken as a whole, London's nineteenth-century growth was greater than that of Paris, though after 1871 their growth paths tended to converge. Decadal rates of growth diminished for London from 23 per cent in the period 1871 to 1881, to 18 per cent in 1881 to 1891, to 17 per cent in 1891 to 1901, and to 10 per cent in 1901 to 1911. This demographic retardation is something of an optical illusion: the sheer size of London made its growth rates more modest than continental capitals.[18]

---

[13] L. Hersch, 'L'inégalité devant la mort d'après les statistiques de la ville de Paris', *Revue d'Economie Politique* (1920), p. 297.

[14] R. Gehrmann, 'Zielsetzungen und Methoden bei der historisch-demographischen Auswertung von Berlin-Brandenburgischem Kirchenbuchmaterial das Beispiel St. Nikolai (Spandau)', in Ribbe (ed.), *Berlin-Forschungen*, vol. I, p. 285.

[15] Gehrmann, 'Zielsetzungen', p. 282.   [16] Stockel, 'Sauglingssterblichkeit', p. 246.

[17] Jürgen Reulecke and Gerhard Huck, 'Urban history research in Germany: its development and present condition', *Urban History Yearbook* (1981), pp. 1–23; Horst Matzerath, *Urbanisierung in Preussen, 1815–1914* (Berlin, 1985).

[18] B. T. Robson, *Urban growth: an approach* (1973).

At first sight, Paris seems to be an intermediate case between London and Berlin. Fully 10 per cent of the national population of France lived in Paris, evenly situated between London (16 per cent) and Berlin (6 per cent). If on the eve of the war Paris resembled Berlin in terms of total population, the French capital also paralleled London in terms of relatively slow rates of natural increase. The specificity of Paris lay elsewhere. We must place its demographic history in the context, first, of feeble rates of national population growth, much lower in France than in Britain or Germany; and secondly, in the context of slower national rates of urban growth in France. Between 1850 and 1914, the French urban growth rate was 1.3 per cent per year; that of Britain, 1.9 per cent, and of Germany, fully 3 per cent.[19] Paris was the dominant element in the urban sector, constituting 30 per cent of the French population living in cities of more than 5,000 people. In contrast, London's population was 23 per cent, and Berlin's 12 per cent, of this national urban population.

The vitality of London in this period was in part a function of the social composition of its population. One of the most striking characteristics of London is the weight of its population of young people, fully 38 per cent under the age of twenty in 1911. This is surprising, in the light of earlier observations on a slowdown in London's rates of demographic growth in the later nineteenth century. The paradox is resolved in part by noting that by the eve of war in 1914, London had become a relatively minor centre of in-migration. Only 32 per cent of London's population were born outside the Greater London area, compared to over 60 per cent in both Paris and Berlin. This relative absence of newcomers and preponderance of families drawn from within London itself contributed to the relative stability of London's social structure. To be a Londoner in the late nineteenth century meant for most to be born there and to have one's sense of identity emerge from a particular urban environment, the rhythms of which were perhaps more settled than those of an immigrant city. To be sure, the diminution of migratory movements into London, while marking the city's social structure, did not eliminate or obscure the diversity of its indigenous population, or the ethnic character of some districts – in particular the East End, in which Irish and eastern European Jews continued to settle throughout this period.

Low rates of in-migration were balanced in part by a relatively high birth rate. Despite sharing the overall decline in fertility which marked all urban

[19] J. L. Pinol, *Le monde des villes au xix siècle* (Paris, 1991), p. 19.

centres in Europe in the last decades of the nineteenth century, London's birth rate stood at about 25 per 1,000, and higher still in some working-class districts. It is for this reason that much photographic evidence about prewar London presents the image of a city of children. This old metropolis is therefore the youngest of the three, a feature of social history both contributing to and reflecting social conditions and family forms. Once more, here is a clue to the city's economic vitality, and to its impact on the growing light consumer goods industries.

Paris was almost the opposite of London in demographic terms. The under-twenty population was less numerous (25 per cent in Paris as opposed to 38 per cent in London), and young adults more numerous. This was the inevitable outcome of the wave of in-migration which marked Paris's demographic development; since most migrants were young adults, it is they who predominated in a city with 62 per cent of its inhabitants born elsewhere. Most were from provincial France, but a growing number came from abroad. About 6 per cent of the total population of Paris were non-French; no other major city had as high a population of 'aliens' in this period.[20] Balancing this inflow was an outflow, especially in times of economic and political crisis, which helped reduce the net growth of Paris to London levels before the 1914–18 war. In effect, Paris was a city, the development of which was marked by the high degree of geographic mobility of its inhabitants. This demographic turbulence may have weakened earlier forms of urban sociability, identity, and custom set earlier in the nineteenth century. At the very least, the turnover of the Parisian population presented extremely diverse spatial conditions in which this identity was formed.[21]

With 33 per cent under the age of twenty, the age-structure of Berlin rested roughly between that of London and Paris. Berlin's striking demographic growth was the resultant of both high in-migration and high fertility. Balancing these factors in the 1870s was a higher death rate than in either of the other two capitals, though the disparity between Berlin's mortality rates and those of Paris and London was shrinking in the decade prior to the outbreak of war in 1914.

Immigration was formidable; about three of every five Berliners came from elsewhere, in particular from Brandenburg and East Prussia, rather than from Saxony, as had been the case earlier in the nineteenth century.

---

[20] See introduction to *Résultats statistiques de Recensement Générale de la population effectuée le 6 mai 1911* (Paris, 1913–16).

[21] Guy Pourcher, *Le peuplement de Paris, origine régionale, composition sociale, attitudes et motivations*, Cahiers de l'INED no. 43 (Paris, 1963).

Out-migration was also significant, though it led less to the countryside than to the outside world. Between 1901 and 1910 perhaps 2.6 million people arrived to live in Berlin; about 2.1 million left for other destinations. Those who remained in Berlin helped form the identity of the city in this, its most robust phase of growth.

In sum, London's population was the most stable of the three; its immigrant population from eastern and central Europe rose around the turn of the century, but these newcomers entered an urban framework under less pressure than either Paris or Berlin.

II

London's vitality in this period was also a function of diversification of trades and occupations. Most of this story is too well known to detain us. 'One had to live or at least to work abroad to appreciate to what degree London was part of the daily commercial life of all foreign countries', noted Felix Schuster, one of the great bankers of the City of London.[22] This is hardly surprising, given the massive flow of British capital abroad in the later nineteenth century. Perhaps 40 per cent of all capital outflow from Europe were British in origin, a figure well in advance of French or German venture capital in this period.

The service sector is hard to define precisely, but if we include finance, commerce, and transport, it is clear that all three played a role in creating a distinctive labour force in these capital cities. Banking and insurance employed 2.7 per cent of the active population in London, 2.1 per cent in Paris; of much greater significance was commerce, accounting for 16.6 per cent in London, 14.7 per cent in Paris. The total engaged in the service sector was about the same in the two cities: approaching one-half of the labour force. London's advantage was in the Port of London: transport workers constituted 12 per cent of London's labour force compared to 7 per cent in Paris.

London was still a major manufacturing centre in the decades after 1870.[23] Paris was not far behind.[24] In London roughly 38 per cent were employed in manufacture, with particular concentrations in the food and printing industries. A real difference in the two cities emerges in a comparison of women's work. Roughly one-third of all workers in London were

[22] Youssef Cassis, *La City de Londres, 1870–1914* (Paris, 1987), p. 18.
[23] P. G. Hall, *The industries of London since 1861* (1962).
[24] L. R. Berlanstein, *The working people of Paris 1871–1914* (Baltimore, 1984).

women, a lower proportion than in Paris. The midinette, so familiar a figure in Paris, was less well known in London, where female domestic service predominated to a greater degree than in any other European city.[25]

In the vicinity of the City, and all along the Thames, dockland drew in a multitude of 'casual' workers, or men and women in 'sweated' trades, locally born, eastern European or Irish, who for a pittance handled the flow of merchandise passing through the city.[26] This unskilled labour force existed in all three cities, but given the size of the Port of London – unmatched by anything in Paris or Berlin – this pool of underpaid labour was most significant in the British capital.

Comparisons between London and Paris are based on census returns of roughly comparable years and parallel categories of analysis. Unfortunately, the data on Berlin present greater problems for our comparative study. Census returns and social taxonomies for the German capital have their own characteristics, difficult to correlate directly with Parisian and London data. Nonetheless, it is clear that prewar Berlin was more of an industrial city than either Paris or London. A majority of the labour force (between 55 and 60 per cent) was employed in this sector. The corresponding figures for Paris and London are 43 per cent and 38 per cent, respectively. If we take account of industrial employment in the suburbs surrounding these cities, the industrial character of Berlin becomes clearer still. The metal and electrical industries employed 15 per cent of the Berlin labour force, compared to 7 and 6 per cent in London and Paris respectively. The giant operations of the Siemens firm, creating its own industrial city of 100,000 people in Siemensstadt, or of the Rathenau firm of AEG in the industrial quartier of Wedding are landmarks of European industrial history. The Ringbahn, the network of Berlin's canals, linked industrial enterprises stretching from the south-east to the north-west of the urban region.[27]

A visitor to the three cities would have little difficulty in seeing that Berlin was much more of an industrial city, indeed a proletarian city, than either of the other two capitals. Not surprisingly, Berlin had the lowest rates of female participation in extra-domestic employment; perhaps 38 per cent of women aged 15 and above in Berlin worked outside the home. Much of this industrial activity was geared towards export, a phenomenon in line with the overall robust performance of the German economy as a whole

---

[25] Theresa McBride, *The domestic revolution, 1820–1920* (1976).

[26] G. Phillips and N. Whiteside, *Casual labour: the unemployment question in the port transport industry, 1880–1970* (Oxford, 1985).

[27] Cyril Buffet, *Berlin* (Paris, 1993); F. G. Dreyfus, 'Berlin, capitale du Reich, 1871–1933', in E. François and E. Westerhalt (eds.), *Berlin: capitale, mythe, enjeu* (Nancy, 1987), pp. 55–62.

which, after the turn of the century, was approaching the status of the world's leading exporting power.

Only recently the imperial capital, Berlin employed a relatively small proportion of its labour force in the service sector. Roughly 36 to 40 per cent worked here, both for private employers and in the state sector, growing out of the older traditions of Prussian bureaucracy, still buoyant even though Berlin was not the garrison town it had been in the early nineteenth century.[28] Still, the presence of soldiers striding down Unter den Linden was a commonplace feature of the German capital. Less dominant was the service sector, despite the growth of banking and finance after the turn of the century. By 1914 the Berlin stock exchange had surpassed even those of Frankfurt and Cologne, and had become the premier financial market in Germany.[29]

Berlin had its army of civil servants too, but they were less numerous than in the other two capitals. Paris (like London) had a predominant service sector. Fully 50 per cent of the active population was thus employed, a trace perhaps, of the older Jacobin tradition of public service. This may account for the greater role of public employment in the labour force in Paris (12 to 13 per cent) compared to London (under 10 per cent), a sector traditionally masculine, as in the world of Balzac. As in London, these men worked in a well-defined part of the city, captured well by Jules Romains:

What really marked the centre was its human rhythms . . . the way the streets channelled more than a million men in convergent directions. These streets described the contours of an absorptive area the capacity of which appeared unlimited. They stretched from west to east, a kilometre from the river . . . On one side it touched the Opéra. On the other the old *marché du Temple*. The largest part, which absorbed the greatest number, were stuffed into lodgings between rue Réaumur near the Stock Exchange and the *rue du Paradis*. But at night this spongy mass of streets sent out the millions of men saturating it.[30]

With 58 per cent of women aged fifteen or more engaged in extra-domestic employment, Paris was one of the great centres of female work at the turn of the twentieth century. *Les glaneuses,* or the gatherers working wherever and however they could, were indefatigable in Paris.[31] The principal roles they played were in the textile, flower, and millinery trades,

[28] Etienne François, 'Berlin au xviiiè siècle: naissance d'une capitale', in François and Westerhalt, *Berlin: capitale, mythe, enjeu,* pp. 33–42. [29] Dreyfus, 'Berlin', p. 57.

[30] Jules Romains, *Les Hommes de bonnes volontés. Le 6 octobre 1908* (Paris, 1st edn 1932, 1958 edn), p. 190.

[31] M. Perrot, 'Les classes populaires urbaines', in F. Braudel and E. Labrousse (eds.), *Histoire économique et sociale de la France* (Paris, 1979), pp. 454–535.

covering fully 40 per cent of the female labour force in the French capital. Older trades were more masculine, in particular the furniture and jewellery trades located in the centre and east of Paris. While in general Paris was less of an industrial centre than either London or Berlin, the weight of skilled labour, the artisanat, still remained considerable.

III

So far I have emphasised three advantages London held over Paris and Berlin in the period: London's population was healthier, more stable and supported a stronger service sector than either Paris or Berlin. These advantages helped facilitate a transition London went through in this period. Suburbanisation and spatial relocation were the order of the day.[32] The other capital cities also passed through this phase of urban development, though at a different tempo and with different consequences.

In the three capitals, the city centre, once densely populated, shrank substantially by the early twentieth century. The City of London had 130,000 inhabitants in 1851; 20,000 on the eve of the First World War. Similarly old Berlin had lost half its population in this period; the four central arrondissements of Paris also dwindled both absolutely and relatively with respect to neighbouring districts.

In contrast, suburban growth was formidable, though different administrative definitions of city, county, and region in the three cases make direct comparisons difficult.[33] In the case of Berlin, the outer suburbs – integrated in the city only in 1920 – constituted fully 50 per cent of the prewar population of Greater Berlin. Fully 37 per cent of Greater London's population lived outside the twenty-eight Metropolitan Boroughs; 30 per cent of the Département de la Seine lived outside the twenty arrondissements.

This massive relocation had profound implications for housing patterns. Legal and tax issues were embedded in urban housing policy. In Berlin, private ownership of land was dominant, favouring dense and profitable housing construction. In contrast, some Rhineland municipalities had a broader range of publicly owned property.[34] In Berlin, the parameters of

[32] A. Sutcliffe, *Paris and London: capitals of the nineteenth century* (Leicester, 1994).

[33] P. Meuriot, 'De la valeur du terme de banlieue dans certaines métropoles: Paris, Berlin, et Londres', *Bulletin de l'Institut International de Statistiques* (1915), pp. 320–30; Meuriot, 'Dans quel sens se développe les métropoles européennes?', *Journal de la société de statistiques de Paris* (1913), pp. 238–50.

[34] H. Teuteberg and J. K. Wischermann, *Wohnalltag in Deutschland 1850–1914. Studien des Geschichte der Alltags* (Munich, 1985); P. Deschamps, *La formation sociale du Prussien moderne* (Paris, 1916).

housing were fixed municipally: the width of streets was to be a generous 15 metres and the maximum height of buildings, approximately 18 metres. Such standardisation gave the city's domestic housing a uniform character. What were commonly called *Mietkasernen* (rented rooms in tenements) became the rule in popular housing in Berlin. These constituted buildings of five or six stories, with inner courtyards extending well beyond the facade, catering (theoretically) for about 60 inhabitants per house.

Another Berlin characteristic was the preponderance of one-room apartments. In Luisenstadt, 70 per cent of all apartments were single rooms; the figure was 50 per cent in Wedding, and 49 per cent in old Berlin in 1900. In all these areas, sub-tenancies were normal practice, catering for perhaps one in four residents of the city before the war. Some conditions resembled the older slums of London, and the unhygienic pockets of poverty in Paris, but in other areas of Berlin, the housing stock was at least as good as that in the other two capitals. What distinguished the Berlin case, though, was massive overcrowding. What other explanation is there for the fact that 60,000 Berliners lived in cellars in 1911? Here we see the mark of an extremely mobile and unstable population, recently arrived and frequently in transit.[35]

British experience in urban development was familiar in Berlin, and knowledge of parallel developments helps account for some more generously endowed developments like Staaken and Siemensstadt, with their small apartments in a more spacious green environment.[36] But such constructions constituted only 5 per cent of all urban building in 1914. To the south-west of the city, around the city's lakes, the bourgeoisie erected comfortable villas far removed from the landscape of the city centre. In sum, therefore, the image of Berlin as a tenement city, widespread throughout Europe before the war, was based on reality.

Once more in sharp contrast to Berlin, London's urban habitat was much less densely populated. On average eight Londoners (as opposed to sixty Berliners) occupied each dwelling. From the middle of the nineteenth century, urban planning aimed to cleanse the city of its pockets of illness and crime. By 1914, almost all of the slums of Dickens's London had been eradicated. In several waves, private housing came to dominate the city. These dwellings by and large were privately owned or rented or held on

[35] M. G. Daunton (ed.), *Housing the workers: a comparative history, 1850–1944* (Leicester, 1990); Teuteberg and Wischermann, *Wohnalltag in Deutschland.*

[36] Ilse Costas, 'Management and labor in the Siemens plants in Berlin, 1896–1920' in L. Haimson and G. Sapelli (eds.), *Strikes, social conflict and the First World War. An international perspective* (Milan, 1991).

long-term (99-year) leases. Houses were rarely sub-divided into Berlin-like cells. Much land was in the hands of a small group of proprietors and institutions, many with aristocratic connections. In the majority of cases, it was not in their interests to create very dense housing, as in the case of Berlin, catering for a massive immigrant community.[37]

Fully 76 per cent of households lived in individual houses, mostly rented. In contrast 20 per cent lived in apartments and 7 per cent in rooms adjacent to shops or offices. The dimensions of such accommodation varied greatly, but popular housing was generally of two types. One was extremely simple, composed of a kitchen downstairs and a bedroom above, or a small house shared by two families, one on the ground floor, one a floor above. For the fortunate, housing was available in the new 'garden cities', much admired in Paris or Berlin. In sum, on the eve of the 1914–18 war, London registered a relatively low rate of overcrowding (however defined); its housing stock, while far from flawless, compared favourably both with that of continental cities and of the provincial cities of England and Wales.

Two problems remained troubling on the eve of the war. The first was the level of rents, roughly double or triple that of Paris. Consequently, Londoners had to devote a much larger part of their earnings to housing. Secondly, urban renewal caused major problems of displacement. Between 1902 and 1913, 70,000 lodgings in working-class districts were demolished, but only 15,000 new units were constructed in the same period.[38] It was inevitable that there would be a housing shortage, reflected in the fact that in 1914 only 1 per cent of the housing stock was unoccupied. We have noted that the period of London's massive growth was over, but housing problems remained a chronic headache.

Once more Paris appears to be a city midway between London and Berlin. More crowded than London, Paris accommodated on average thirty-four people per dwelling. Like Berlin, Paris was a city the majority of whose inhabitants lived in rented apartments. In the suburbs, separate owner-occupied houses did exist and flourish, before the postwar vogue of housing estates.

The specificity of the case of Paris rests on the convergence, first of the older character of its housing stock (compared to Berlin); and, secondly, of the absence of a policy, similar to that undertaken in London, of destroying unsanitary districts. The real estate market in Paris is as yet not well

---

[37] Harold Carter and C. Roy Lewis, *An urban geography of England and Wales in the nineteenth century* (1990); Richard Rodger, *Housing in urban Britain 1780–1914* (1989).
[38] S. Merrett, *State housing in Britain* (1979).

researched, but what we know points to high mobility and complex manipulations of real property.[39]

Paris more than London was an overcrowded city. Fully 43 per cent of lodgings were deemed overcrowded, and most of these were unsanitary as well. Some progress was registered through municipal action, though, especially in terms of the modernisation of heating, lighting, waste and garbage removal, and water supply.

Another special feature of Paris was the sharp contrast between the east and west of the city with respect to the quality of construction. In the east, the poor quality and dimensions of housing walls built in the second half of the nineteenth century precluded the construction of multi-storied dwellings. In the west of the city, beautiful dwellings constructed in stone could support easily five, six or even seven stories. Here is one of the sources of the imbalance between the west, with an abundance of housing units, and the east, with a serious shortage.

For purposes of comparison, it may be useful to envision three types of housing in the prewar period: the London house, detached or semi-detached; the one-room flat in Berlin; and the diverse apartments of Paris. Certainly, the individual household in London describes a fundamental element in what Londoners understood as well-being. Different standards applied on the continent; in smaller quarters, Parisians were not necessarily less well satisfied with their accommodation. Overcrowding on the Berlin scale was clearly undesirable. But the density of Paris offered some compensations: access to leisure, a shared urban culture and social life. In effect, the Parisian worker paid less attention than his London counterpart to housing and the comforts it provided.

Once again, the comparison does little to remove the sight of London's slums. They were both an eyesore and an assault on the dignity of many of those forced to live in them. But compared to Paris and Berlin, London's popular housing was on average less crowded and better maintained. Shaw's aesthetic principle that the least ugly is the most beautiful is perhaps the best way to state the comparison. Here, too, the urban fabric of the British capital compared well to that of its two continental rivals.

Housing patterns had a demonstrable effect on survival chances in these three cities. Here is the link between the social inequalities described above and housing in cities with very different growth trajectories. With respect to both infant mortality and tuberculosis, Paris was the worst off of the

---

[39] For urban housing in Paris, see Christian Topalov, *Le logement en France, histoire d'une marchandise impossible* (Paris, 1987).

three capital cities.[40] The character of the housing stock and patterns of overcrowding are partly to blame. But so is the rudimentary level of public health activity on the municipal level, much better developed in Berlin and London than in Paris. One observer caught this contrast well on the eve of the 1914–18 war:

if, with mediocre water supply, three times the population, poor air, a sky filled with clouds polluted by oil fumes, London has a rate of infant mortality lower than that of Paris, where the air is often pure and radiant, where the climate is more temperate, where the water and food are superior, this must arise from the hygienic and moral merits of the English household.[41]

Whatever the effect of morality, better housing, public hygiene, and probably better nutrition lay behind the fact that at all ages, female mortality was lower in London than in Paris. For all ages, the death rate in Paris was 15 to 17 per 1,000. In Berlin, the rate was 13 to 15, and in London, 11 to 13 per 1,000.

Berlin's level of overcrowding was also notorious, but still survived at higher rates than did that of Paris. Here is another indicator of the importance of health policy in London and Berlin, and the advantages accruing to these cities rather than to Paris, where such policies were less well developed.

IV

I have tried to evaluate the strengths of London as a prewar metropolitan centre by setting some aspects of its demographic and social history alongside those of Paris and Berlin. This can only offer some preliminary findings, encouraging future comparisons of sectors, industries, and districts. But the outline of the story already seems clear: London maintained a superior position in survival rates, compared to Paris and Berlin, in part because it was a more settled population, whose housing was on balance less overcrowded and insalubrious, compared to both Paris and Berlin, and in part because urban improvement was the subject of direct administrative action. Here Berlin and London shared certain structures and aims not present in the French capital.

Elsewhere we have examined the impact of the war on urban population,

[40] T. H. C. Stevenson, 'The social distribution of mortality from different causes in England and Wales, 1910–12', *Biometrika*, 15 (1923), pp. 382–400.
[41] Gaston Cadoux, *La vie des grands capitales. Études comparatives sur Londres, Paris, Berlin* (Paris, 2nd edn, 1913), p. 23.

and the significance of London's robust urban economy to the Allied war effort in the First World War. We also noted the devastating effects of the proximity of theatres of military operations to the Parisian economy, and the process of reorganisation and remobilisation that took place in all three cities throughout the war.[42] But what of the post-1918 period? Did the British capital lose its comparative advantage over her two sister cities. The answer before the 1930s is negative. Why? Mainly because the growth of the service sector after the war drew upon London's assets and reinforced the momentum of earlier developments.

My contention is that the source of London's stability and growth was primarily structural. Central government policies intersected with the city at numerous points, but they did not shift the fundamental parameters of urban development. Suburbanisation and the expansion of the service sector went on apace under different political regimes. The outward movement of urban populations to the periphery of Greater London and away from the centre of the old city reduced the proportions living in run-down tenements. Their new districts were frequently drab and under-serviced, but they were remote from the *ilôts insalubres* of the late nineteenth century.

By the 1930s, the other two metropolitan capitals had had their own spurt of suburbanisation. Berlin had become 'Greater Berlin', splicing onto the old urban core 183 urban and rural districts. Paris's Red Belt tightened around the city in the 1920s too.[43] Suburbanisation, relocation, and the inevitable extensions of traffic, transport, and communication were international events.

In another sense, these two European cities caught up with London by the 1930s. One of the striking features of the interwar years is the convergence in vital rates as among the three metropolitan centres. Table 5.1 demonstrates that the birth rate in London remained higher than that in Paris and Berlin throughout the 1920s, while on the eve of the Second World War there was essentially no difference between them. This reflected the steep decline in interwar fertility in London, contrasting sharply with signs of rising fertility in Berlin under the Nazis. The same narrowing of prewar differentials occurred with respect to mortality rates. London's death rate was lower than that of the other two cities between 1920 and 1927; thereafter, they were roughly at the same levels. The most striking convergence was in infant mortality rates. The level of infant mortality in Berlin in the early 1920s was roughly twice that of London.

[42] See Winter and Rober, *Capital cities at war*, chs. 5–8.
[43] A. Fourcaut, *Banlieu rouge 1920–1960* (Paris, 1992).

Table 5.1. *Birth, death, and infant mortality rates in Paris, London, and Berlin, 1920–39 (first quarter of each year, per 1,000)*

Year	Birth rate			Death rate			Infant mortality rate		
	Paris	London	Berlin	Paris	London	Berlin	Paris	London	Berlin
1920	20.9	28.3	17.8	19.4	12.5	13.2	103	62	129
1921	19.2	23.3	14.6	14.3	10.9	11.9	79	59	123
1922	16.7	22.2	12.6	13.9	13.1	14.4	95	76	141
1923	17.0	21.4	10.9	15.8	12.5	16.3	99	63	183
1924	16.7	19.8	9.9	17.8	17.8	15.6	104	96	144
1925	17.2	19.1	13.0	17.3	14.1	13.3	104	73	110
1926	16.7	18.5	11.5	15.1	11.1	11.7	93	50	95
1927	16.6	17.2	10.8	17.0	16.8	14.4	105	76	101
1928	15.9	16.7	10.2	16.8	14.4	13.5	105	80	96
1929	15.7	16.3	9.9	22.1	24.1	17.5	113	106	116
1930	15.5	16.3	10.1	15.3	13.7	12.3	95	78	87
1931	15.5	15.2	9.5	17.8	16.7	13.3	100	84	75
1932	13.4	14.0	7.9	12.8	12.2	10.8	76	79	68
1933	12.6	12.9	7.6	12.4	11.6	11.0	85	73	69
1934	12.6	12.9	7.6	12.4	11.6	11.0	85	73	69
1935	11.7	12.3	13.4	11.7	11.0	12.2	63	65	57
1936	11.0	13.5	13.8	9.1	9.0	10.8	45	42	56
1937	11.1	13.6	13.9	12.0	12.3	15.3	68	66	63
1938	10.8	12.6	13.8	12.4	12.5	12.7	58	63	53
1939	10.2	10.2	14.4	11.3	10.9	13.2	64	55	58

Source: Registrar-General of England and Wales, *Quarterly Returns of Births, Deaths, and Marriages,* 1920–39.

Paris was between the two. By 1931, Berlin had reached London's level, and actually fell below it in the subsequent seven years. From 1932, Paris too had narrowed the gap with London so fully that there was little to choose between them. In effect, the end of the 1920s marks the fading away of one of the salient features of European urban history. The comparative lethality of living in Paris or Berlin, rather than London even in peacetime, was by the Second World War just a memory.

Some of these gains were results of postwar social policy; some a reflection of medical improvements and the onset of the chemotherapeutic revolution from the mid-1930s, which transformed the balance between infectious and non-infectious diseases in European public health. But the coming together of vital rates reflected no failure on London's part but rather the successful eradication of many unsanitary conditions in parts of Paris and Berlin, conditions which had been eliminated decades earlier in London.

Another convergence of urban history was the blight of unemployment, higher in Paris and Berlin in 1919, then higher in London in the mid 1920s. Precise figures are difficult to find in this area, but here too there were structural reasons why the worst of the interwar depression did not hit London. No one would deny the deleterious impact of unemployment on substantial parts of the London population. West Ham, for example, was devastated.[44] But in other parts of the metropolitan area, the weight of the service sector actually protected London from the worst of the interwar depression.[45] Inevitably, commerce and trade suffered from the downturn in markets for British exports; the London re-export markets were hit too by difficulties in other parts of Europe and beyond. Consider a straightforward comparison of unemployment levels in 1931 in the industrial district of West Ham, in Greater London as a whole, and in England and Wales. The structural buffer of London's employment profile is eminently visible. In England and Wales as a whole, 11.5 per cent of the labour force were out of work. In Greater London, 8.5 per cent were jobless. Among those working in commerce, 1.3 per cent were out of work in London, compared to 6.8 per cent in the country as a whole. Even in depressed West Ham, those lucky enough to work in commerce registered 'only' 7.7 per cent jobless; they had a much better chance of weathering the interwar storm than those in the metal trades, shipbuilding, and in the water works, where

[44] J. Marriott, '"West Ham: London's industrial centre and gateway to the world". II. Stabilization and decline', *London Journal*, 14, 1 (1989), pp. 59–67.
[45] R. Porter, *London. A social history* (1996), ch. 13.

unemployment was double or triple these figures. Throughout the 1930s, West Ham had between one-sixth and one-quarter of its workforce unemployed, roughly double the rate for London as a whole.[46]

Unemployment in Paris and Berlin is much harder to measure, due to differences in reporting procedures and in their political manipulation. As bad as the figures for industrial London were, they were probably worse for Berlin. Just as in 1919, the city was devastated by the slump.[47] Paris faced the storm later, but here too the service sector was not hit as hard as was the industrial sector.[48]

With the onset of the 1930s, we can mark the end of a phase of European urbanisation. By the decade London, the pioneer, the city without parallel in 1700 as in 1900, was joined by other cities, as robust and vital as the original metropolitan capital. They retained their particular topography and flavour of life, but had more in common than many city dwellers realised. This convergence of experience was no evidence of London's decline. It signalled the completion of one phase of the transformation of urban space which created the European form of the modern city, the iconic environment of the twentieth century.[49]

---

[46] Marriott, 'West Ham', p. 51.
[47] Winter and Robert, *Capital cities at war*, ch. 7; R. Bessel. 'Unemployment and demobilization in Germany after the First World War', in R. J. Evans and D. Geary (eds.), *The German unemployed* (New York, 1987), p. 31; and in the same volume, E. Rosenhaft, 'The unemployed in the neighbourhood: social dislocation and political mobilization in Germany, 1929–33', pp. 194–227.
[48] R. Salais, 'Why was unemployment so low in France during the 1930s?' in B. Eichengreen and T. J. Hatton (eds.), *Interwar unemployment in international perspective* (Dordrecht, 1988), pp. 247–88.
[49] A. Sutcliffe (ed.), *Metropolis 1890–1940* (1984); T. Barker and A. Sutcliffe (eds.), *Megalopolis: the giant city in history* (New York, 1993).

6

Phoenix: financial services, insurance, and economic revival between the wars

CLIVE TREBILCOCK

Precisely when, and how, the non-manufacturing parts of the UK economy may have shared, or failed to share, in the 'decline of Britain' since 1870 is a strand in recent history which still requires systematic unravelling. It is a commonplace of contemporary observation that the revived City of London of the 1970s, 1980s and 1990s has generated economic life beyond the manufacturing base, but the relationship between industrial retardation and non-industrial resilience in the century after 1870 is more obscure.

Financial services, primarily banking and insurance, have traditionally escaped the strictures which many economic historians have showered on the faltering British economy of Victorian and Edwardian England. Whatever degree of failure the manufacturing sector may, or may not, have exhibited in the critical time-period of 1870 to 1914, the men of the City – usually, of course, public-school men – get full marks for sustained dynamism in promoting the great boom in UK invisible exports which characterised the last years of the high imperial age. This is almost certainly too kind an appraisal of the more venerable institutions which had their home within the Square Mile.[1]

Two solid points may be made against it. Some of the great financial houses, and certainly the older insurance offices, maintained practices and practised cautions that were quite as outmoded as any to be found among the 'practical men' of manufacturing. Some of the largest insurers – the Sun, the Royal Exchange, and the Phoenix – were as old as any trade of the classical industrial revolution period and could scarcely be expected to escape the marks of age or the corporate memory that went with it. The company histories suggest that conservatism and risk avoidance formed the

---

[1] See Clive Trebilcock, 'The City, entrepreneurship and insurance: two pioneers in invisible exports – the Phoenix Fire Office and the Royal of Liverpool, 1800–90' in N. McKendrick and R. B. Outhwaite (eds.), *Business life and public policy, essays in honour of D. C. Coleman* (Cambridge, 1986), pp. 137–72. From 1984 Phoenix was a member of the Sun Alliance Insurance Group, and, since 1996, has been part of the Royal and Sun Alliance Insurance Group.

hall-mark of more than one of the great nineteenth-century offices.[2] The lesson surely is that no economic sector is homogeneous: the City was no single entity and certainly not a consistently dynamic one; it contained its older as well as its newer technologies.

The second point is that many financial entrepreneurs in Britain may simply have encountered their competitive crisis later than their manufacturing brethren, in the interwar years, and proved just as deficient – and just as committed to their own antiquated process of the 'automatic' Gold Standard, the prewar parity, and the balanced budget – in responding to a new world financial order in which London no longer stood unchallenged.[3]

Intriguingly, the insurance sector did not share in this financial gloom: structural change within the industry and social change within the UK gave the underwriters a surprisingly secure path through the dangerous terrain of the interwar recession. The records of Phoenix Assurance identify this plan with some precision.

If not all insurers deserved the plaudits heaped on the service sector before 1914, quite a lot of insurers deserve exculpation from the widespread financial failures of the interwar years. Perhaps it was in this era, rather than in the prewar one, that this financial service most notably defied the general tendency of the economy.

Insurance men certainly did not anticipate such an outcome. Financial markets in the 1920s and 1930s were notoriously unstable and the money men were understandably chastened by them. Insurers fully expected to share this experience. In some markets, this expectation was fulfilled, but, over a surprising range of activity, it was not (see table 6.1). Pessimism was justified in the sector of fire insurance, could not be rejected in the accident sector, and was impossible to overstate in the marine market; but this was still not the whole picture.

Fire insurance in the interwar decades fully reflected the troubled state of the world economy. There is a natural, if unwelcome, relationship between high unemployment, idle plant, and high fire wastage, and the insurers of property paid the price. Between 1921 and 1930, the Phoenix fire-loss ratio exceeded the 'safe' level of 50 per cent in six years of the decade. In 1922, in the US market, fire loss was higher than in any year since that of the great San Francisco earthquake of 1906, and both 1922 and

---

[2] This is an easily identified refrain in Barry Supple's, *The Royal Exchange Assurance* (Cambridge, 1970); see also P. G. M. Dickson, *The Sun Insurance Office, 1710–1960* (1960); for institutional memory see C. Trebilcock, *Phoenix Assurance and the development of British insurance*, vol. I (Cambridge, 1985), pp. 414, 427, 701, 757.

[3] C. Trebilcock in McKendrick and Outhwaite, *Business life*, p. 139.

Table 6.1. *Total premium income of UK offices: fire, accident, life, 1920–37 (£ million)*

	Fire	Accident	Ordinary life
1920	58.5	45.1	41.9
1929	58.4	66.1	69.8
1935	48.8	67.3	74.3
1937	49.8	75.6	80.5

Source: Supple, *The Royal Exchange Assurance*, p. 427.

1923 were particularly awful in Canada. All major offices experienced rising loss ratios in the crisis years 1927 to 1930. Total UK fire premiums remained fairly stable during the 1920s but suffered heavily at the end of the decade. They fell by 14.7 per cent between 1929 and 1937. At the same time, costs of operation, especially for large foreign insurers, ran at worrying levels, the two pressures together narrowing profit levels. The Phoenix Fire Department sustained a peak-to-trough fall in premium income between 1928 and 1935 of nearly 21 per cent, with its North American markets again inflicting considerable damage.

By contrast, both accident and ordinary life business strongly resisted the world economic recession of the interwar years. Both grew most rapidly during the 1920s – accident by 46.6 per cent, life by 66.1 per cent – but continued to register progress, in each case by around 14 to 15 per cent, between 1929 and 1937. Fire began the era as the leading branch of insurance but was soon overtaken by both accident and ordinary life. The remarkable expansion of life business was accompanied by high profitability but the growth of accident business was altogether more problematic.

For most large insurers, accident premiums increased rapidly in the interwar years but failed to drag accident profits up with them. This was because the dominant sectors of accident insurance at this time were workmen's compensation and motor. The first was unlikely to prosper in an era of jobless workers and failing businesses and the second was equally undependable at the time when the ownership of cars, and collisions between them, were both increasing at breakneck speed. These dangers were redoubled if the workers or the automobiles were located in North America. The Phoenix Group accident account – which was heavily exposed to the USA – fell into the red in 1923, 1924 and 1926, recorded slender profits for most of the 1930s and recovered only in 1938.

If fire and accident were buffeted by heavy winds during the depression years, marine business was laid abeam by a howling gale. Worldwide contraction in international trade after the First World War led to a precipitous decline in the demand for shipping services, ship construction, and ship insurance. At the Phoenix, the marine share of the company's total income dwindled from 18.3 per cent in 1919 to a low of 5.3 per cent in 1925 – a foul year for the industry – and wallowed along at 6 to 7 per cent for the rest of the period. Not even the ships that were built afforded the insurers much joy. While humble freighters and tramps rusted in docks or estuaries, taking cargo and carriage from no-one, a succession of luxury liners swept down the slipways; and all too frequently towards disaster. They were a Blue Riband menace. Three major liners were lost in 1928 alone; and the *Europa* burned on the stocks in 1929. If they got as far as the sea, their cargoes could be as big a risk as they were. For, during the economic crisis of the 1920s, the liners were the parcel carriers of doom: they shipped the bullion that was leaking from the vaults of the central banks. In 1931, the Phoenix bewailed 'the unprecedented . . . shipments of gold'. But at least the Phoenix managed to conjure up a marine profit; it was the first for eight years. Few marine insurers managed to extract any kind of positive outcome from markets like these. The corporate sector of the sea trade earned only £22 million in premiums in 1922, and averaged a paltry £11 million between 1931 and 1937.

I

By the 1920s, most big UK insurance companies were composite offices, writing all the main lines of insurance – at that time fire, accident, marine, and life – across a single 'counter'. Theoretically, therefore, activity in one sector could compensate for high levels of embarrassment in others. It will already be obvious that insurers who were dealing at one and the same time with torched factories, expanding housing estates, luxury liners, compensated workers, a soaring market in endowment assurances, and irate motorists were exposed to the full variety of the interwar economy. Such diversity between insurance sectors could explain the surprise frequently expressed by underwriters of this era that they were not faring *worse* than was actually the case.

The main source of diversity in these years was the life sector. Throughout the 1920s, both for the Phoenix and the UK assurance sector as a whole, record takings for total new insurances were continuously set and broken. Similarly, the growth of life funds and interest income upon them was notably strong, especially in the second half of the 1920s. At the Phoenix the disjunction was sharpest over the Crash years: while fire, accident, and total premiums shrank by 15 to 20 per cent over the period 1929 to 1933, new life sums assured notched up eight successive records between 1928 and 1938, and four of these were within the 'bracket of distress', 1929 to 1933. Life business showed remarkable resilience and sailed gaily through the troubles of the world economy.

The puzzle then is why assurance did not obey the logic of the depression. Insurers, though gratified by its waywardness, could offer no easy explanation. Phoenix's Chairman, the formidable Sir Gerald Ryan, perhaps the leading actuary of his generation and a notable specialist in corporate acquisitions, was as puzzled as anyone. But, characteristically, he was more fertile than most with possible explanations. In his last annual report on the post-Crash year of 1930 he recorded that 'no unfavourable element exists' in the office's life business, and that the new sums assured, at just below £3 million 'now seems to be our normal stride'.[4] The 1930s then proceeded to prove him wrong. But in an unexpected way: the pace increased. Records continued to tumble, and by 1938, 'our normal stride' was closer to £5 million.

Most big life assurers did well during these years. The total UK life market expanded its new sums assured from £146.5 million in 1920 to £260 million in 1937, an increase of 78.2 per cent. Yet the Phoenix did better still, pressing new sums assured up from £2.5 million in 1920 to £4.9 million in 1937, an increase of 96 per cent.

Generally, the UK assurance industry felt even the Crash itself only lightly, in marked contrast to its US counterpart. The British specialist press was struck in 1931 by the fact that, 'life assurance usually suffers in times of commercial depression, but the contrary was the experience last year'.[5] Their American equivalents could not say the same. While UK new life business was still rising, US new life business was down 12.3 per cent in the first half of 1931 against the same period of 1930. Life offices were at the centre of the US Crash. Policy-holders unable to get cash from failing banks pursued the offices for cash values from surrendered policies. And the offices, unable to get cash from the same banks, could not pay them. Nearly 200 American insurance ventures failed or were absorbed between 1929 and 1933. Meanwhile the worst that UK life assurers faced was the dilemma

---

[4] Phoenix Chairman's Annual Report, 10 June 1931.
[5] *Bankers' Magazine*, 131 (1931), p. 321.

presented by the cheap-money policies of the early 1930s: this brought them a great accession of new business but created a shortage of rewarding prospects in which the new money might be invested.[6]

Among the dozen companies in Table 6.2, there is little sign of weakness. The strong growth of Prudential and Legal and General hardly betrays a trace of the Crash and at a lower level of expansion it exerted little pressure on the growth patterns of the UK Provident, the Phoenix, the Scottish Widows, the Alliance, or the Royal Exchange. Together with the Standard and the Atlas, this group represented the Phoenix's closest peers in the life market. Within this cohort, ranking just below the elite of giant life operators, the Phoenix's performance was notably steady. The Atlas demonstrated a tendency to slip somewhat and the Scottish Widows to climb. More often than not the Phoenix was very close to, or just ahead of the Alliance, and was always comfortably clear of the Royal Exchange. Such a performance, in such generally troubled years, more than validates Ryan's claim that the Phoenix had firmly established itself among the UK's top life offices.

But he still spent much time casting around for reasons which might explain this. In 1920 he had offered as possibilities the higher level of real incomes or the effect of depreciating stock markets in making life policies more attractive as investments.[7] By 1927 he was having to work harder: perhaps the recent war, by severely altering the value of money, had alerted the public to the need for saving; or maybe the passing of the 'lost' wartime generation had created a new sensitivity to the need for life assurance. The further assurance gains of the late 1920s, which again surprised the underwriters, forced Ryan to seek more compelling arguments. By 1928, he had found unmistakable evidence of 'growing habits of *thrift* . . . among our people', and even thought that this should be 'set against the common denunciation of the age as one of extravagance and luxury'.[8] But, in reality, the most distinguished life man of his day never achieved before his retirement any clear idea of why the UK life market was behaving as it so gratifyingly was.

It is likely, of course, that there was more than one answer, and that different life offices tapped into different versions of these answers. The strong rebound in life business immediately after the First World War clearly represented both the postponed demand which had not been able to

[6] Ibid., 132 (1931), p. 636; 137 (1934), p. 361.
[7] Phoenix Chairman's Annual Report, 28 April 1920.
[8] Ibid., 24 April 1928.

Table 6.2. *Rankings by new sums assured on ordinary life business: twelve selected companies, 1927–1933*

Company	1927		1930		1931		1932		1933	
	£m	Rank	£m	Rank	£m	Rank	£m	Rank	£m	Rank
Prudential	16.9	1	18.2	1	19.5	1	19.0	1	23.0	1
Pearl	10.2	2	10.4	2	8.0	4	7.6	5	8.8	5
Norwich Union	9.3	3	8.0	5	8.2	3	8.0	4	8.9	4
Legal and General	6.7	4	11.4	4	9.7	2	10.3	3	12.0	3
Commercial Union	4.0	7	4.4	7	4.0	7	4.0	7	3.9	9
UK Provident	3.3	9	3.1	14	3.5	9	3.6	11	3.9	10
Standard	3.0	10	3.2	12	n.a.	n.a.	2.7	17	3.5	12
Atlas	2.9	11	4.1	9	3.0	12	2.5	19	2.8	18
Phoenix	2.9	12	2.9	15	3.1	11	3.4	12	3.5	13
Scottish Widows	2.7	13	3.5	10	3.5	8	3.6	10	4.1	8
Alliance	2.5	14	3.2	11	3.2	10	3.4	13	3.2	14
Royal Exchange	2.2	17	2.5	17	2.4	16	2.9	16	3.0	16

Note:
Ranks were allocated before rounding the sums assured to one decimal place.
Source: Extracted and calculated from the *Bankers' Magazine.*

find acceptance during the war, and also the needs of demobilised service-men returning to family, and often newly married, life. Wartime inflation had also halved the worth of life policies; so there was plenty of ground to be made up. But these are short-term explanations which work best in rela-tion to the upswing in life sales of 1918 to 1920. The formidable life boom of 1924 to 1939, in which total UK new sums assured by all offices more than doubled, must have originated from more persistent or more numer-ous influences.

One rather raffish possibility was the tax efficiency (to use an indulgent phrase) of a certain kind of single premium endowment policy. This type of policy came from nowhere to account for just under 20 per cent of all Phoenix life premiums at its peak in 1925, and other offices experienced similarly striking growth patterns. It was an ingenious device. The client took out the single premium policy. The company loaned the client the money to pay the single premium. The premium attracted tax relief. When the endowment matured, it repaid the loan and the client walked away with the balance. As tax scams went, this was fairly blatant and the Exchequer noticed; in the Finance Act of 1930, the Chancellor called an end to the fun. Immediately, the Phoenix was faced with £2 million worth of surrender demands and premium income from this source collapsed. But, in any event, no single insurance vehicle could go far in explaining the resilience of the entire life market.

II

Something more substantial and enduring was needed. Phoenix officials argued two possible explanations from the supply side. Firstly, they pointed out that the office no longer used just the Life Department for selling life policies; one of the advantages of composite status was that the whole organisation could be used for pushing what was selling well. Secondly, they pointed out, with some pride, that they could dress these policies in some very alluring bonuses; life assurance could be shown to be a good investment.

The successful life specialist, Standard Life, was maintaining a bonus of 2.2 per cent at this time and it has been argued that this was a particular magnet for Standard's impressive new business.[9] Yet the non-specialist

---

[9] J. Butt, 'Life assurance in war and depression: the Standard Life Assurance Company and its environment, 1914–39' in O. M. Westall (ed.), *The historian and the business of insurance* (Manchester, 1984), pp. 163–4.

Phoenix was paying one point higher, 2.3 per cent, in 1925 and 2.5 per cent by 1930. If the Standard had a magnet for new business, it would seem that the Phoenix had a more powerful one.

This is confirmed by an unusual piece of oral evidence from an official who first joined the Phoenix in 1926, and retired from it in 1970. His first job was to fill out valuation cards for new endowment policies. He remembered in retirement in *1990*, and correctly, the level of bonus paid to December 1925, and that it was considered a particular selling point of Phoenix policies at the time. But then, of course, less dynamic and less attractive life assurers than the Phoenix were also selling a lot of policies in 1925.

More compelling explanations lie on the demand side, with the policy-holders rather than with the insurers. Where the pre-1914 life market had revolved around the 'old' professional and capitalist middle classes, that of 1919–39 centred on the 'new' lower-middle class of white-collar suburbanites.

The advent of this salariat is probably an undervalued feature.[10] The extension of the government administrative apparatus in wartime had greatly swelled the army of middle-ranking officials. The advance of new mass production assembly industries had vastly expanded the demand for supervisors in quality-, stock-, and cost-control. While the matching growth in the services sector – high-street retailing, entertainment, banking, and indeed insurance itself – had multiplied the ranks of shop, cinema, and branch managers. These groups formed a natural market for clever adaptions of endowment assurances to provide a whole range of insurance 'consumer' goods which could do anything from paying school fees, through creating teenage nest eggs or protecting family income to financing house purchases. At the same time, rising real wages for that 80 per cent of the workforce which was almost always employed, pumped up demand for 'industrial' insurances and the cheaper ordinary policies.

As socio-economic changes operated to create new demand, so did demographic ones. Average life expectation for a male at birth improved between 1906 and 1922, from 48.5 to 55.6 years.[11] As people lived longer, so they gave up work earlier. In 1881, nearly 75 per cent of men over sixty-five years of age still worked; by 1931 barely 50 per cent did so.[12] Increasing

---

[10] Although both John Butt and Barry Supple took note of its potential importance. See Butt, 'Life assurance', p. 161 and Supple, *Royal Exchange Assurance*, pp. 434–5.
[11] *Bankers' Magazine*, 124 (1927), p. 743.
[12] L. Hannah, *Inventing retirement; the development of occupational pensions in Britain* (Cambridge, 1986), p. 123.

life expectation was clearly a major influence in switching the emphasis of assurance away from insuring against death and towards insuring for life after work. This helps explain, of course, the very marked swing towards endowment policies – geared to provide a lump sum at a particular retirement date – which affected the whole industry after 1900: by 1925, between 50 per cent and 75 per cent of all new life business came in the form of endowments.[13]

However, Leslie Hannah has argued persuasively that the demand for endowments, and the associated demand for occupational pensions, was not only a product of longer lives but followed rather from a *combination* of advancing life expectation, technological change, and rising prosperity levels. He gives priority to the third of these variables: the phenomenon of post-employment income fitted into the patterns of the inter-war economy as a luxury consumer good developed on the back of rising real incomes and more evenly distributed wealth. The most rapid *increase* in the market for after-work income came in the period 1930 to 1950, not in the more recent postwar decades.[14]

The 'invention' of retirement for large sections of the community, and the need to finance it, made the yield upon insurance investment a crucial matter. In the shaky stock markets of the 1920s and 1930s, life policies offered good prospects of outperforming the conventional investment alternatives. Not least, income-tax relief on life assurance – running at 2 shillings in the £ – gave policies an edge. By the late 1920s, some financial opinion argued that 'the tax advantages put life policies ahead of all other investments'.[15] Furthermore, the proliferation of brokers and life salesmen made insurance products more accessible than other forms of investment. Not least, the life policy had resisted inflation, 'one of the few things that had not increased in price', since the war, opined the *Bankers' Magazine* in 1923.[16] Indeed, by the late 1920s, it was falling in price, as the offices reduced life premiums, particularly on non-profit policies.[17]

The attractions of insurances as investments were clear by the early 1920s and were further promoted by the Great Crash. By the mid-1920s,

---

[13] G. H. Recknell, 'Life assurance versus investments', *Post Magazine and Insurance Monitor*, 7 November 1925.   [14] Hannah, *Inventing Retirement*, pp. 122–7.

[15] *Bankers' Magazine*, 123 (1927), p. 186. This journal calculated that the maximum available rebate amounted to 10 per cent of premiums paid, up to a ceiling of one-sixth of one's income. Endowment capital sums payable on maturity were free of tax. Even after Chancellor Snowden raised income tax by 6d to 4s 6d in the £ in 1929, and adjusted the allowances, thus facing policy-holders with a 12.5 per cent increase in tax payable, the advantages remained considerable, especially given the performance of other investments after the Crash.   [16] Ibid., 116 (1923), p. 130.   [17] Ibid., 126 (1928), p. 820.

a twenty-year, with-profits endowment, taken out in 1904, would have yielded 3.6 per cent, against the 3.5 per cent achieved by a leading municipal stock, or the 1.3 per cent earned by Consols. The disparity widened in the 1930s due to the fall in stock market yields after the Crash. 'Never', said the *Bankers' Magazine*, 'has the value of life assurance been more strikingly demonstrated than by the Wall Street collapse. A life policy is one of the few investment media that has preserved steadiness and convertibility into cash throughout the present prolonged economic crisis.'[18] The government's cheap money strategy after 1932 also reduced yields on competing investment products and further favoured insurances. Under these conditions, life offices could present themselves increasingly as 'great investment trusts not only providing the people with protection against the financial loss resulting from death or old age but with the means of systematically investing their savings under expert guidance'.[19]

One other prospect for assurance growth, linked to these economic and social currents, was the advance of group life and pension schemes offered by employers to their workers but managed through insurance companies. Simple group life schemes were first launched in the USA in 1912 and introduced from there to the UK market in 1918; but they advanced only slowly in Britain, partly because many employers already incurred National Health Insurance liabilities, and partly because most firms in the 1920s were seeking ways of *reducing* costs.[20] Full group pensions were not properly marketed in Britain before the later 1920s.[21] Progress was no more rapid than in group life and it took the insurers some time to develop the necessary skills. The initiator of this type of life business in the UK was

---

[18] Ibid., 129 (1930), p. 325; 135 (1933), p. 350.   [19] Ibid., 125 (1928), p. 341.

[20] Ibid., 123 (1927), p. 27. By 1927 by contrast, group life schemes in the USA covered 5 million people. Ibid., p. 1075. However, when contrasts between US and UK levels of cover are drawn, and under-insurance inferred in the latter, the variable of National Health Insurance should be remembered (but rarely is). The best early performer in the UK group life market was probably the Provident Mutual which made 'remarkable' progress in a slack market, and offered a product superior to the American one, giving the employee an independent contract which could be continued if employment was transferred. Ibid., 131, (1931), p. 153.

[21] Supple, *Royal Exchange Assurance*, pp. 435–6; although insurance companies had managed pension schemes for individual firms before this. See Butt, 'Life assurance', p. 164. A leading full-scale group scheme, which was expected to encourage others, was that arranged with Legal and General by the National Joint Industrial Council for the Flour Milling Industry on behalf of some seventy member firms in 1932. *Bankers' Magazine*, 133 (1932), p. 670. The great innovator at Legal and General, and the leading group pensions expert in the UK, was T. A. E. Layborn. See H. Cockerell in the *Dictionary of business biography*, vol. III (1985), pp. 687–9.

probably the American operator, Metropolitan Life.[22] This venture transferred its business to Legal and General, which had developed its own
scheme by 1930 and became the UK market leader. Metropolitan withdrew
from the UK market in 1934, by which time a further threesome of insurers – Eagle Star, Prudential, and Standard Life – had joined the group
pension business. Most other companies did not enter the sector until the
late 1930s, or until after the Second World War.[23]

But perhaps the biggest single opening for new assurance business in the
interwar years was created by the exceptional activity in house purchasing.
The upswing in residential construction between 1920 and 1938, which
created many of the suburbs of modern Britain, was one of the most active
features of the interwar economy. It created demand for the 'new industries'
of motor vehicles, electricity generation, durable consumer goods, and artificial fibres. New suburban houses needed transport services, power, electrical devices for cooking and entertainment, and soft furnishings. Over 4
million houses were constructed in this period, 2.7 million of them between
1930 and 1938, and the rate of growth of the building industry between
1920 and 1938, at an annual average of 5.4 per cent per annum, was exactly
twice that of industrial output as a whole. Measured over the slightly different time-period, 1924 to 1937, the building industry grew faster than at any
time in its history over the long span 1856 to 1973 (see table 6.3). Construction activity was actually concentrated into two separate booms: gov-
ernment-subsidised housebuilding accounted for 60 per cent of dwellings
built in the 1920s and helped fuel a particular surge between 1925 and 1927,
while a second larger wave, based more centrally on private owner-occu-
pier purchasing occurred between 1933 and 1938.[24]

The buyers of these houses, particularly the buyers of the 1930s, were
characteristically the white-collar employees of the 'salariat'. An insurance
product which could draw upon the house-buying urge of this group would
link itself to one of the strongest socio-economic movements of the day.
The endowment-related mortgage was clearly a vehicle for the times.

The life offices responded to these prospects with alacrity. The *Bankers'*

---

[22] Metropolitan set up a UK branch in 1928. Its arrival was treated by the press as an
'American invasion' and an 'insurance war'. By contrast the UK life industry coolly pointed
out that group life was a small part of the market, formed a tariff for it and invited the
'invader' to join. This was the first ever common scale in life business. Competition for
ordinary non-profit business remained particularly keen. *Bankers' Magazine*, 125 (1928), p.
1017; 127 (1929), p. 333.

[23] Butt, 'Life assurance', p. 166; Hannah, *Inventing retirement*, pp. 35–8.

[24] See D. H. Aldcroft and H. W. Richardson, *Building in the British economy between the wars*
(1968), ch. 10; and also their *British economy 1870–1939* (London, 1969), pp. 46–7, 244.

Table 6.3. *Annual average growth rates of UK construction output, 1856–1973 (per cent)*

1856–73	3.1	1937–51	−1.2
1873–1913	1.1	1951–64	3.8
1924–37	4.6	1964–73	1.8

Source: R. C. O. Matthews, C. Feinstein, and J. Odling-Smee, *British economic growth 1856–1973* (Oxford, 1982), p. 228.

Magazine had noticed 'numerous house purchase policy schemes' as early as 1922, and by 1925 was convinced that this was 'a very desirable field for the life offices to cultivate'.[25] For the companies there was a particular incentive on the investment side; for entry into mortgage-related business permitted a very welcome diversification of their portfolios away from tricky stock exchange holdings, and especially, from the mountains of government bonds which war finance had heaped on them. This need for postwar financial innovation was not unfamiliar to long-lived insurance offices. For the inclination towards house-purchase loans after the investment strains of the First World War was precisely analogous to the inclination of sharp-eyed insurers towards the annuity loan after the financial strain of the Napoleonic Wars, a century before.[26] And again each device was precisely matched to the social currents of its respective era: the mortgage-linked endowment served the virtuous needs of the increasingly substantial white-collar bourgeoisie of the early twentieth century, while the annuity-loan had served the less-than-virtuous needs of the decreasingly substantial lesser aristocracy of the early nineteenth century.

In wooing the housing market, the offices sought advantage over the building societies, by offering lower interest rates on the loan for house purchase, as well as income-tax relief on the endowment needed to secure it, not to speak of the life cover in the policy. If this did not work, they could propose, as a second best, that a loan supplied by a building society should be secured by one of their endowments. They were active in both strategies in the 1920s but particularly followed the upswing in private residential construction after 1933.[27]

[25] *Bankers' Magazine*, 113 (1922), p. 909; 120 (1925), p. 569.
[26] See *Phoenix Assurance*, vol. I, pp. 630–43. Also *Bankers' Magazine*, 123 (1927), p. 223.
[27] Ibid., 134 (1932), p. 907; 137 (1934), p. 181.

III

How did the Phoenix exploit the various developments in the market for new types of insurance products? Clearly, it faced the same general demand currents as the other offices. But output was not determined solely by demand; the offices could respond to new demands with different designs of product, and many did so, across a wide range of the new fields which had been opened up. Most were aimed primarily at a white-collar market and took stock of the special economic features of the time. Thus Standard Life produced the Acme policy in 1921–2, featuring guaranteed surrender, paid-up and bonus features, a Family Provision policy in 1923, aimed at future inheritance or marriage settlement requirements; and in 1928, a minimum-cost/maximum-cover policy. The Royal Exchange went early into group life – for the Musicians Union in 1921 – and into 'Bachelor' endowment policies to cover the tricky period between employed liberty and married employment. Allied Insurance in 1924 added disability provisions to certain types of life policy. And the Phoenix, true to its tradition of dealing with the more up-market life clients, developed specialities in policies to cover death-duty entanglements and super-tax minimisation.[28] Family income policies were introduced in 1930 by Legal and General and became all the rage in the early 1930s with endless variations, almost every office producing a twist of its own. Under the constrained economic conditions of the 1930s, much actuarial ingenuity also went into producing policies with maximum cover for minimum premium and an entire arsenal of easy-payment schemes.

The Phoenix's promotional literature provides a good guide to the office's reaction to the new features in the life market. The purpose of these brochures was precisely to attract attention to new products. Indeed, the Guard Book containing the prospectuses is effectively the only way of detecting new policies – unless they are mentioned elsewhere in minutes or memoranda – since all policies entered the accounts under the conventional basic classes. The prospectuses contain a number of clusters, each of them lightly promoted before 1921, much more heavily between 1921 and 1940. Three of these were: family insurance devices; cheap-cover policies; and income-tax-related instruments.

In the first cluster, children's assurances and endowments were advertised by eight prospectuses in the period 1908 to 1921 but by twenty-nine in the

---

[28] Butt, 'Life assurance', pp. 163–4; Supple, *Royal Exchange Assurance*, p. 451.

period 1922 to 1940; educational endowment and school fee policies scored only once 1908 to 1921 but thirteen times, 1922 to 1940; family mainte-nance policies arrived only in 1930 and were then pushed by six pamphlets before 1940. This was again fast going, since the family income policy had been introduced by the leading assurance innovator, Legal and General, in the same year, 1930, and then rapidly copied, 'by every office in the land' by 1932.[29] Somewhat strangely, the Phoenix caught on to the 'wild oats' cover, the 'Young Man's Policy' only in 1936.[30] In 1937 the office developed a famous 'First Essential' policy, a low-cost, high-benefit cover for young marrieds. This was suspended at the outbreak of war but proved sufficiently far-sighted to be worthy of re-introduction in 1950.[31]

In its cheap policy promotions, the Phoenix was clearly trying to broaden its appeal to the new white-collar buyers and step back from its earlier reliance on high-value policies. There can be no doubt about the Phoenix's energy in chasing a new class of clientele: various kinds of economical or easy-payment policies were promoted in only three prospectuses between 1908 and 1921 but by no less than forty-five between 1922 and 1940. The emphasis on easy-payment schemes commenced, fittingly enough, in 1930, and received massive emphasis – fourteen separate publications – in the ensuing decade.

Generally, here the Phoenix showed a rapid response to new opportuni-ties, competitor's initiatives, and changed economic circumstances, but nowhere more so than in the Guaranteed Savings Policy introduced in 1929. This was designed to pay on death the sum assured plus a further sum equal to all the premiums paid by a man aged thirty in 1929, and thus to guarantee that the death benefit should be larger than all the premiums paid. This was a very swift way of cashing in on the blow to investor confi-dence delivered by the Crash and exploiting the superior security of the life product. The *Bankers' Magazine* was impressed: 'Our life offices quickly seized the opportunity presented by the great depreciation in Stock Exchange values.'[32]

The Phoenix's attempts to give the Revenue a run for its money had a longer pedigree. Policies aimed at income-tax exemption or benefit, or at death duty and supertax minimisation, were advertised by fourteen separ-ate publications as early as 1908 to 1921 but by twenty more between 1922

---

[29] *Bankers' Magazine*, 131 (1931), p. 973; 133 (1932), p. 329.
[30] Life Policy Proposal and Prospectus Guardbook.
[31] Phoenix Bristol Life File 741; Cardiff Life Department to Head Office Actuarial Department, 12 June 1950.   [32] *Bankers' Magazine*, 129 (1930), pp. 157, 325.

and 1940. The speciality in death duty cover shows up clearly: this was the most prolifically advertised of the tax-related instruments, with eleven separate publications devoted to this part of the market between 1916 and 1938.

But these devices were directed at the lesser currents of demand not the mainswell. At least a part of that force was pushing upon group life and pension business. Here the Phoenix seems not to have been an activist. The office did offer some early group life schemes to some very specialised groups – naval and military officers from 1912, bankers from 1915, and farmers with income-tax problems from 1918; but activity hardly broadened outside these categories in the 1920s and 1930s. The one exception was a discount rate for Europeans in India, which produced six promotional publications between 1918 and 1928, about as many as all other group life schemes put together.[33] Certainly, the Phoenix does not seem to have linked endowment assurances with group life business to any interesting degree before 1930. Much the same was true of group pension schemes, where the company appears to have limited itself to providing cover for big fire and accident customers who asked for this additional service. This market was developed rather by Legal and General and Standard Life, and a few colleagues.

Another part of the mainswell in the life market pressed towards the use of endowment assurances for house purchase. Here the Phoenix response was much more emphatic. By 1910 endowment assurances had already marked their presence in the Phoenix's books. They had reached this position after growing from about 5.3 per cent of all Phoenix life premiums in 1885 to 17.9 per cent in 1895. By 1920 they represented 30.2 per cent of premiums in the with-profits sector of business, and by 1930, 43.8 per cent.

It was in linking endowments to house purchase that the Phoenix probably did most to exploit the assurance opportunities of the interwar economy. From 1924 onwards the office was extremely active in issuing promotional literature on this theme: no less than twenty-three different prospectuses and proposals were generated in relation to housing and property purchases in the period 1924 to 1938. Phoenix created its own endowment-backed house-purchase scheme in 1924; then added an arrangement for borrowers from building societies in 1926; and finally produced an improved version of this, the New House Purchase Scheme, in 1934.

Priority was always given to pushing Phoenix's own schemes, but the

---

[33] And all of these examples were quite distinct from group insurance proper, where a single agency, such as an employer, sets out to buy protection for a particular community.

office responded positively to proposals from the building societies which often arose as a result of contacts between Phoenix local branch managers or agents and their opposite numbers in the neighbourhood societies. An example of this was an arrangement of October 1933 with the Bromley and South Eastern Building Society, which was secured through the intermediation of the manager of the Phoenix's South London Branch.[34] The most important link of the 1930s was the agreement of March 1934 with the Woolwich Equitable Building Society whereby the Phoenix agreed to issue twenty-year endowment assurances against the building society's loans and pay a commission of 2.5 per cent of the premiums to the society.[35] Besides the Bromley and the Woolwich, the Phoenix formed connections before the Second World War with the Cheltenham and Gloucester, the Newbury, the Newcastle and Gateshead, and the Portman societies, names which indicated both spread and seriousness of intent.[36]

The share of endowments in the Phoenix's sums assured peak exactly where they should, if they were tracking the housing boom, between 1925 and 1935. Other clues also suggest a connection between endowment business and mortgage business. If the endowment vehicle were being used for housing purchase, it would not be of variable length, but, most usually, for a fixed term. Contrariwise, if endowments were being used for retirement nest eggs, they would be aimed at normal retirement age and therefore vary in term according to the date of purchase. One Phoenix life specialist recalled that, in the interwar years, 'house purchase loans repayable by endowment assurance . . . produced a healthy flow of business'.[37] Another remembered that 'by far the commonest type of policy being issued in the late 1920s was the 20-year Endowment Assurance, with profits'.[38] This is exactly the type of fixed-term, investment-oriented policy which would have been involved in house-purchase schemes, and the type quoted to the Woolwich Equitable in the agreement of 1934.

First-hand evidence from contemporary experts is also confirmed by the formal record of the period. Ryan, in his last annual report, noticed that in regard to whole-life and endowment assurance, 'the proportions of these two classes of policy have greatly changed in the last few years'. And one of

---

[34] South London Branch to Head Office, 30 October 1933. Phoenix Bristol Life File 918, 918A.   [35] Ibid., 918A.

[36] However, Phoenix's most active period of association with the building societies seems to have been 1945–55, during which the office maintained arrangements with some twenty-seven different societies.

[37] A. G. Butler to R. G. Street, 18 January 1994. Mr Butler had recently celebrated his ninetieth birthday.   [38] A. W. Smith to R. G. Street, 25 January 1994.

his successors in 1939 stated unequivocally that, in the 1920s and early 1930s, 'the most popular policy of those days was a 20-year endowment policy'.[39]

By the late 1930s, however, a small fly had appeared in the actuarial ointment: some twenty-year endowments had begun to mature and it was now necessary for the Phoenix to start paying out on them. The Chairman of 1939 expected 'increased outgo under this heading in future years for we have now arrived at the period when we are making payment in respect of the increased business of 1919 onwards'.[40] In fact, 1940 was a record year for outpayments on endowments (which amounted to nearly £600,000). The Phoenix grinned and bore it, and, in congratulating the fortunate policy-holders, provided its own testimony to rising life expectations: 'it is of course a ground for satisfaction . . . that the robust vitality of so many of the assured enabled them to survive to the endowment age'.[41]

IV

The insurance business exhibited some complex responses to Britain's economic performance between 1919 and 1939, and indeed in the longer period 1870 and 1939. It is not really sufficient to say that the services sector of the UK economy did well in the later Victorian and Edwardian periods, nor to point a simple contrast with the manufacturing sector. Parts of the insurance industry, mainly the parts centred on Liverpool and specialising in transatlantic underwriting, were undeniably dynamic, and did much to promote the UK's remarkable expansion of invisible exports. But older London offices, the Phoenix among them, often remained quite as attached to conservative ways as their manufacturing counterparts until late in the century.[42] The services sector was not a monolith, it contained pioneers and new entrants, giants and minnows, the capital intensive and the lightweight, the old and the new, the staid and the sharp.

However, the rise of the composite offices, dealing in all types of insurance, in the 1900s created a new range of opportunities, even for the longest-lived insurers, like the Sun, the Royal Exchange, and the Phoenix. This increase in scale and scope had little to do with strategic initiatives executed by the kind of dashing business leadership which is the decisive force

---

[39] Chairman's Annual Reports, 10 June 1931; 24 May 1939.
[40] Ibid.   [41] Ibid.
[42] Phoenix did not resume direct trade in the USA until 1878, and then not through choice; until then the company relied on taking reinsurances from other offices. See Trebilcock, 'The City, entrepreneurship and insurance'.

in Alfred Chandler's explanation of growth in big corporate structures.[43] Indeed, the applicability of the Chandler formula to largescale business organisations in the services sector may be questioned, and the application is not attempted successfully in Chandler's own work. Yet the British insurance business certainly developed the classic multi-divisional corporate structure, with the multi-national spread, a branch system of organisation and a central executive group – the distinguishing features of Chandlerian scale – even before 1914. In this, the offices outpaced British manufacturers who, encumbered by an inheritance of small, family-based enterprises, were notoriously slow to effect the transition to the ideal business type.

In fact, the insurers had little choice. Scale and scope were imperatives for them from the start. If the miscellany of risks in a given field of insurance were to be covered effectively, a certain mass of resources was essential. This could be provided by a group of rich capitalists, by a larger group of partners from a shared profession (sugar-baking in the case of the Phoenix), or by an even larger group of the less rich (such as house-owners) clubbing together to find mutual relief from threat. In any event, scale was built in.

Admittedly, scope widened in the composite movement of the 1900s. But this is not easily traced to the entrepreneurial derring-do of Ryan and his peers. Rather, they were drawn along by the peculiarities of markets, costs, and very different 'technologies'. It was the insurance customer rather than the insurance entrepreneur who created the scope of the composite office. The customer desired to buy his accident insurance from the same vendor as his fire insurance, his life assurance from the same vendor as his cargo insurance. Convenience and reduced transaction costs were the main drivers of the movement. And high levels of competition and rising administration costs made it economical for the insurer to group the different insurance lines within the same business machinery.

But the insurance products and 'technologies' for generating them were very dissimilar; little in the way of organisational binding force came from this quarter. The tasks of insuring a ship's cargo, a domestic house, or a human life involve very different issues of title, risk appraisal, and probability management. As Barry Supple has written, in his own reflections on insurance, these various types of policy have 'little more in common than, say, the respective purchases of clothing, furniture, garden implements and food'.[44]

---

[43] See Alfred Chandler, *Strategy and structure* (Cambridge, Mass., 1962) and *Scale and scope: dynamics of industrial capitalism* (Cambridge, Mass., (1990).

[44] B. E. Supple, 'Insurance in British History' in O. E. Westell (ed.), *The historian and the business of insurance* (Manchester, 1984), p. 1.

The institutional systems and skills needed to market such very different commodities had not developed convergently. So, once the various insurance 'technologies' were brought under the same roof, there was little choice but to organise them within a divisional structure. The divisions of fire, life, marine, and accident did not have to be designed by the leadership cadre; they were ready-made. On the one hand, they gave the early composites a shape which could easily be mistaken for Chandlerian. On the other, they conferred upon the composites a certain resistance to economic recession which was not widely noticed inside the industry or outside it.

The insurance products on the composite counter spanned such a range of markets, such a width of contemporary social experience, that it became unlikely that all of the composite divisions would be afflicted simultaneously. Some were undoubtedly connected to parts of the outer economy which were experiencing bad times. Fire insurance tended to be overly bound up with cover upon derelict mills in Manchester or decrepit warehouses in Manila. Marine insurers were entirely stranded by the receding tide of world trade. Accident saw its premiums boom with the inexorable pressure of motorisation but could not get its profits to motor so well. Nevertheless, accident takings provided a buoyant cash flow and supply of investable funds. It was life assurance which found opportunities for both premiums and profits in an expanding sector of the interwar economy, as its salesmen tapped the growing consumerist tendencies of Inner Britain.

In the early 1920s, Ryan's reflections on insurance matters had stressed 'the close connection between Commercial Strength and Insurance Profits',[45] and insisted that 'insurance is a powerful, if not infallible, index to trade conditions generally'.[46] He had noticed the 'contrary motion'[47] under which different sections of the Phoenix experienced divergent fortunes in the same year, but he had not registered its significance. Realisation was slow in dawning. The Phoenix increased its dividend from 13 shillings to a historic high of 14 shillings per £1 share in 1928 and held this level in 1929 and 1930. Yet, amid the crashing stock markets and soaring unemployment of 1929, Ryan still thought that insurance was 'a barometer . . . reflecting unswervingly general trade conditions'. He then went to present the weather report on 1929: 'the disturbances in China . . . the financial troubles in America . . . the trade depression in our Dominions . . . at home the deep unrest caused by the deplorable amount of unemployment'. Yet the Phoenix's own barometer in King William Street did not

---

[45] Chairman's Annual Speech, 30 April 1924.   [46] Ibid., 29 April 1925.
[47] Ibid., 30 April 1924.

really reflect these horrors. At length Ryan grasped this; and had the grace to admit it. He reported on 1929, the year of the Great Crash, that 'our net result is not one we have any right to regard as unsatisfactory'.[48]

Even when the underwriting side of their activities were affected by the Crash, the insurers found recompense in the investment side of their accounts. Of course, the early 1930s were not a famously good time for investors, but not all of them had miserable results. As Ryan conceded: 'that is not our experience, nor the experience of the bulk of Insurance Companies'.[49] Long-maintained portfolios, cautious investment policies, large retentions of government paper, and a renewed interest in property, all held the offices firm while the gales of investment panic shredded the stock markets.

By such tactics, the best offices in 1930 were able to maintain dividends, salt generous amounts in reserves, and improve their financial position. Still confused by his faith in barometers, Ryan could only muse that, 'Surely it is a great tribute to the soundness of policy and efficiency of management that a storm like that which we passed through last year should have expended itself with so little effect on our Insurance Companies.'[50]

By the spring of 1931, Ryan had begun to realise a significant truth of the interwar years: that the insurance offices were less reflecting the behaviour of UK trade and industry than comfortably out-performing most participants in most sectors. Phoenix actually added to its balance carried forward in 1930 due to the movement in security prices and ended the year with its finances as 'solid as a rock'. Ryan concluded, 'We can scrutinise our Balance Sheet without any of the qualms which recent experience has shown to be necessary in the case of many large financial institutions.' Despite the collapse of the world economy, Ryan could celebrate his retirement in 1931, after fifty full years as Fellow of the Institute of Actuaries, by announcing the retention of the 14-shilling dividend; as he said, 'it was a very different story from that which is commonly related'.[51] Ryan had thus come into line with the best financial opinion: the *Bankers' Magazine* was also clear that 'the insurance industry is not depressed like other industries'.[52]

Of course, those parts of the insurance industry closest to depressed 'other industries', such as shipping, did not escape so lightly. But due to the corporate restructuring of the big offices and the advance of the composite form, nearly all major insurers now had several strings to their bows. The most powerful string was life underwriting.

[48] Ibid., 10 May 1930.   [49] Ibid., 10 June 1931.   [50] Ibid.
[51] Ibid.   [52] *Bankers' Magazine*, 128 (1929), p. 188.

The interwar years were a special era for the life assurance business. The institution of retirement first appeared in its modern form as a mass social phenomenon, and the actuaries adjusted to this well. The rise of the salariat and the spread of suburbia created consumer markets for new life products. And the industry responded with a showcase of devices from tax schemes to bachelor's policies, school-fee providers to pensions, low-cost options to endowment mortgages. The Phoenix showed well in this innovating sector, particularly in the area of house purchase. But, in many ways, the social conditions of the interwar years allowed the whole life sector of the insurance business to behave more as a 'new industry' than as a services 'old staple'.

When he first noticed the 'contrary motion' of the various insurance departments of the Phoenix in 1923, Ryan had wondered what would happen if they all pulled in the same direction at the same time. It is just as well that they did not. The contrary motion of the consumer-oriented life sector, together with its resilient investment power,[53] was the saving grace of the insurance industry in bad times. Another Phoenix Chairman spoke for many colleagues when, in 1940, he summarised the preceding two decades with the wholly accurate but scarcely predictable verdict: 'our Life organisation has never been in better shape than at present'.[54]

[53] This theme is explored more fully in C. Trebilcock, *Phoenix Assurance and the British insurance business, vol. II, 1870–1984* (Cambridge, forthcoming), ch. 8.

[54] Ralph Sketch, Chairman's Annual Speech, 29 May 1940.

7

Keynes, New Jerusalem, and British decline

PETER CLARKE

British economic management in the thirty years after the Second World War was distinguished by two features, not perhaps wholly peculiar to the United Kingdom but certainly salient in perceptions of British economic performance. One feature was the 'postwar consensus', premised on acceptance of a Keynesian approach to problems of economic policy, thus legitimising the development of a welfare state and the maintenance of full employment. The other was the mounting evidence that economic growth in Britain, though sustained at an historically high level, was fairly consistently lower than in many comparable industrial countries. The fact that Germany and France provided the nearest examples of apparently more successful strategies for national regeneration after the setbacks of the Second World War may, as Barry Supple suggests, have made such an impression on their insular European neighbours for psychological as much as for purely economic reasons (see above, ch. 1). Still, it is hardly surprising that, by the 1970s, these two factors had frequently become linked in a critique of the nature of British decline. This came to be represented as a long-term process, but one accelerated since 1945 by British weakness for the soft option of Keynesianism, allowing successive governments, from Attlee to Callaghan, to paper over the cracks in an old building which in fact needed structural restoration and reconstruction.

In the remaking of the political economy of the 1980s, such a scenario served as one of the ideological preconditions of Thatcherism. In the rewriting of the history of the postwar period, Correlli Barnett's *The audit of war* (1986) was an influential book. Its successor, *The lost victory* (1995), likewise focuses attention on global overstretch, which sapped Britain's strength externally, and the simultaneous pursuit of a New Jerusalem at home that 'loaded a second crushing burden on the economy'.

Since the abolition of mass unemployment 'had been from the start a fundamental tenet of wartime New Jerusalemism', it followed that, hardly less than the Beveridge Report itself, the White Paper on Employment Policy of 1944, which 'pledged that full employment would be maintained after the war by Keynesian manipulation of aggregate demand', was a fateful step, taken by the Coalition Government as a portentous signal of the road it intended its successors to follow. 'Thus did future postwar governments finally embrace "full employment" as the factor which must govern their entire economic strategy – not so much a *Schwerpunkt* as a shackle.' Thus was 'the debilitating artificial habitat of "full employment" and the "planned economy"' foisted on the unwitting victors – unlike luckier defeated Germans – as part of a fate 'brought down upon the British people by themselves and by the elite they had allowed to manage national policy in their name'. Accordingly, 'the pervasive harm of full employment' diverted attention from the real (supply-side) problems, which 'could not be cured, only temporarily masked, by turning up the Keynesian burner under the economy as a whole'. Little wonder that the Attlee Government failed to benefit from American assistance if it was 'stoking general inflation through commitment to the costs of both the world role and New Jerusalem ("full employment", the welfare state and costly housing programmes)'.[1]

Allegations that Keynes was 'in great danger . . . of going down to history as the man who persuaded the British people to ruin themselves by gambling on a greater illusion than any of those which he had shattered' are nothing new, as is shown by this taunt in a private letter from Hubert Henderson in June 1930.[2] The barb was all the more piquant since it came little more than a year after the two Liberal economists had collaborated in producing the pamphlet *Can Lloyd George do it?*, an early statement of the Keynesian agenda for public investment as a means of alleviating mass unemployment. With his recent appointment to a civil service post as secretary of the Economic Advisory Council, Henderson had meanwhile become impressed with the weight of Treasury anxieties about the Budget and sterling, imbuing his own policy advice with a new sense of scepticism about the narrow room for manoeuvre available.

[1] Correlli Barnett, *The lost victory: British dreams, British realities, 1945–50* (1995), quotations at pp. xiii, 345, 349–50, 4, 357, 347, 379 – mainly from ch. 18, 'The pervasive harm of "full employment"'. In concentrating my criticism below on the book's treatment of the salient Keynesian theme, I am not unmindful of its salutary attention to other points on which there would be more agreement between its author, Keynes, and indeed myself. My own thanks are due to Stefan Collini, Ewen Green, John Thompson, and Maria Tippett for reading an earlier draft.

[2] Donald Moggridge and Austin Robinson (eds.), *The collected writings of John Maynard Keynes*, 30 vols. (Royal Economic Society, 1971–89) (hereafter *JMK* with vol. and page numbers), XX, 364 (Henderson to Keynes, 5 June 1930).

Henderson's incipient doubts about the feasibility of what he and Keynes had urged in *Can Lloyd George do it?*, with its case for a purely temporary stimulus from public works to jolt the economy on to the track of spontaneous recovery, thus marked a growing breach with Keynes, both over immediate, pragmatic arguments over policy, and ultimately over more intractable issues of theory. Accordingly, when the committee of economists of the Economic Advisory Council sought to reach agreement on their recommendations to the Labour Government in October 1930, Henderson stood his ground. Believing that there was 'no alternative now but to face up to the disagreeable reactionary necessity of cutting costs (including wages) in industry and cutting expenditure in public affairs', he commented on Keynes's own draft: 'It seems to me to run away, under cover of complex sophistication, from the plain moral of the situation which it diagnoses.'[3] Observing ruefully, as an appalled bystander, the progress of Keynes's thinking towards the ideas of the *General theory of employment, interest and money* (1936), Henderson accused Keynes of generalising from an anomalous period of slump and advocating policies which would merely fuel inflation under other conditions. Unsurprisingly, therefore, he was to emerge, in wartime Whitehall, as the most scathing opponent of the proposals for a full-employment policy. Whereas Keynes commended the penultimate draft of the 1944 White Paper as 'an outstanding State Paper which, if one casts one's mind back ten years or so, represents a revolution in official opinion',[4] Henderson sarcastically pointed to its composite character:

Mix one teaspoonful of financial profligacy with three tablespoons of economic *laissez-faire*. Dilute liberally with verbal water, and add wishful thinking according to individual taste.[5]

Henderson was thus one of the first and one of the most persistent critics of Keynesianism, both in theory and in practice. Some of the questions he prompted are plainly still worth asking in the light of subsequent historical knowledge and controversy. Did Keynes take account of the structural problems of the British economy and its need for competitiveness in world markets? How far was his analysis premised upon decline? Did Keynesian economic policies take shape as an ingenious set of stop-gap expedients, serving to evade more deep-seated problems? Finally, did

[3] *JMK*, XX, 452–6 (Henderson, 'The drift of the draft report', 13 Oct. 1930).
[4] *JMK*, XXVII, 364 ('Postwar employment', 14 Feb. 1944).
[5] Henderson to Sir Wilfrid Eady, 13 Dec. 1943, in Alec Cairncross and Nina Watts, *The economic section, 1939–61* (1989), p. 85.

Keynes propagate a doctrine of fiscal irresponsibility which made him heedless of the burden that New Jerusalem would impose on the postwar British economy?

I

A couple of passages from the *Treatise on money* (1930) provide a suggestive starting point, the more so since they date from just the moment when the trajectory of Keynes's thought moved into a different orbit from that of Henderson's. The *Treatise* is a formidable academic work in two volumes, ostensibly concerned with economic theory at a high level of generality. But in fact Keynes's analysis was related in a number of crucial respects to the immediate problems of the British economy at the time of writing. One sign of this preoccupation is the fact that, unlike the *General theory*, the system is not closed but is that of an open economy, subject to exogenous influence from international forces.

Thus theoretical axioms that held true in general terms might not apply under real-world conditions in a particular special case. Even in volume I, *The pure theory of money*, Keynes departed from the abstractions of hypothesis in a pregnant way, with a scarcely veiled speculation that in 'an old country, especially one in which the population has ceased to expand rapidly', investment prospects would be less attractive than in 'new countries'. Funds would tend to flow abroad, thus putting more strain on competitiveness – especially if 'trade unions in the old country present great obstacles to a reduction of money wages'.[6] What Keynes was doing here, in an obvious reference to Britain, was taking the existence of wage stickiness as a fact of life; and in volume II, *The applied theory of money*, he was explicitly free to depart further from the plane of pure theory.

Here Keynes cursorily ruled out the practicability of enforcing reductions in money wages as a remedy for Britain's problem of competitiveness under the Gold Standard from 1925. Again he reflected that 'Great Britain is an old country', which, having lost 'the special advantages in manufacture which used to be ours' – and given, moreover, 'the high real wages (including in this the value of social services) to which our workers are accustomed as compared with our European competitors' – faced unprecedented difficulties in reviving its export trade.[7]

This haunting image of an 'old country' undoubtedly offers an insight

---

[6] *JMK*, V, 312.   [7] *JMK*, VI, 165 ff., at 168–9.

into the range of options which Keynes saw as available and therefore worthy of practical consideration. It would, however, be a distortion to suppose that he saw his mission in life as that of a doctor prescribing palliative care for a valetudinarian patient. He subsequently made it clear enough that he despised such a role. In his last speech to the House of Lords in December 1945, he had to take account of a strong feeling that his country had been shabbily recompensed for its heroic war record by its grasping American creditors. Warning the House that 'contemporary acts are generally directed towards influencing the future and not towards pensioning the past', Lord Keynes mordantly added:

> Nor, I venture to say, should it be becoming in us to respond by showing our medals, all of them, and pleading that the old veteran deserves better than that, especially if we speak in the same breath of his forthcoming retirement from open commerce and the draughts of free competition, which most probably in his present condition would give him sore throat and drive him still further indoors.[8]

There may have been some public posturing here, but the tone chimes with Keynes's privately expressed comment a month later that 'England is sticky with self-pity and not prepared to accept peacefully and wisely the fact that her position and her resources are not what they once were.'[9] Recognition that the old country faced historically generated problems represented not fatalism but, given Keynes's temperamental optimism, the spur to finding appropriate solutions in a new predicament. Only in this way, he pleaded, could Britain make the best of its opportunities, which were conditioned not only by its past experience but also by its present will, guided by a realistic appraisal of its future prospects.

This outlook is well illustrated in a paper which Keynes wrote for the cabinet in May 1945, in which he pointed to the gap in earnings between Britain and the USA as one historic difference which might be exploited. 'Even the celebrated inefficiency of British manufacturers', he observed drily, 'can scarcely (one hopes) be capable of offsetting over wide ranges of industry the whole of this initial cost-difference in their favour, though, admittedly, they have managed it in some important cases.' His point was not that the trick could be turned by juggling relative exchange rates or other macroeconomic variables but rather that a (microeconomic) struggle for competitiveness was indispensable. With little hope of reviving Britain's traditional staples, he put his faith in the new technologies fostered by war, adding the twist:

[8] *JMK*, XXIV, 610.　　[9] *JMK*, XXVII, 464 (Keynes to R. H. Brand, 29 Jan. 1946).

If by some sad geographical slip the American Air Force (it is too late now to hope for much from the enemy) were to destroy every factory on the North-East coast and in Lancashire (at an hour when the directors were sitting there and no one else), we should have nothing to fear. How else we are to regain the exuberant inexperience which is necessary, it seems, for success, I cannot surmise.

In this context, a fair financial settlement with the Americans was needed by Britain, not as a veteran's pension, but in order to 'face the economic future without any serious anxiety – except the perennial one of knocking some energy and enterprise into our third-generation export industries and of organising the new industries which our first generation is well qualified to conduct if the capital and the organisation can be arranged'.[10]

It should already be apparent that, in Keynes's advice on economic policy, he did not suppose that Britain could ignore the outside world or that it remained other than the open economy of which his *Treatise on money* had spoken. The reason that the *General theory* took a closed system as its model is not that Keynes had meanwhile become a super-protectionist, preaching 'full employment in one country' on the basis of autarky: it was obviously because a *general* theory had to apply to the system as a whole, with no leakages to breach the seal of its own universal assumptions. The gain here was, as in all exercises in pure theory, that of rigour in the analysis; the loss was that of realism in applying the theory to the case of any particular national economy, especially one like that of Britain, historically enmeshed in a web of worldwide commercial ties. It would, however, be wrong to suppose that the closed assumptions of the *General theory*'s model transformed the nature of its author's *policy* advice. In particular, he did not become more ambitious about the target figure to which he thought it feasible to reduce unemployment, nor more dirigiste about the means by which this might be achieved – if anything, the reverse. In short, as the transparency of its title ought sufficiently to indicate, Keynes's *magnum opus* was a work of theory, not a handbook for policy-makers; and the best guide to his thinking about postwar economic policy in Britain is the record of his own activities as a policy-maker, particularly in the last four years of his life when he addressed these issues directly.

II

The Keynes who emerges from these (published) documents bears an intermittent resemblance to the Keynes whom Barnett claims to have encoun-

---

[10] *JMK*, XXIV, 262, 290 ('Overseas financial policy in Stage II', May 1945).

tered in the files of the Public Record Office. Part of the reason for any discrepancy here is no doubt subjective. It is surely notorious that documents rarely speak for themselves but at best respond to purposeful interrogation from different historians, each with the research strategy driven by his or her own preconceptions about the right questions to ask. So it is only natural that different judgements may ensue, the more so since cogent exposition demands selectivity in the quotations chosen to illustrate those points – rarely susceptible of determinate proof – to which each historian attaches significance. These are among the ineluctable conditions under which historians work, and by which their writings must be judged, with no peremptory appeal to the authority of the archive being capable of settling many questions of interpretation and argument.[11]

The root of the trouble is not that Barnett is guilty of perpetrating a string of howlers in his citations – though one lapse is indicative of his own preconceptions. For when he lays out the severe nature of the constraints on British policy at the time of the American loan negotiations in 1945, he tightly anchors his judgement here to the contents of a file from 'J. E. Maude of the Economic Section of the Cabinet Secretariat', with only the caveat that 'even such objective minds as Keynes's and Maude's failed to draw the logical conclusion from their own analyses'. The prescient, objective, analytical mind of Maude – hitherto unrecognised in historical accounts – makes an obvious contrast with that of his dilettante colleague in the Economic Section, James Meade, the future Nobel laureate, whose role as 'a passionate New Jerusalemer' went along, all too predictably, with the fact that he had started life as a classicist, and become an Oxford don, before turning up as one of 'the Whitehall men of paper'.[12] Alas, Maude and Meade were, of course, one and the same person.

Keynes, too, leads a Jekyll-and-Hyde life through Barnett's pages. The

---

[11] These remarks are prompted by the letter, partly quoted below, which Barnett wrote in response to criticism of *The lost victory* from David Edgerton, *London review of books*, 21 Mar. 1996; see also issues of 7 March for the review, and 4 April, 9 May, and 23 May 1996 for further correspondence.
'David Edgerton writes that I don't "like" full employment "because of its inflationary effect, and the strength it gives to the trade unions." Yet my chapter on full employment cites as a key text an analysis by Hugh Gaitskell as Chancellor of the Exchequer in December 1950 in which he specifically makes these two points. It is therefore absurd and irrelevant for Edgerton to accuse me of not "liking" full employment.
This is only one example of David Edgerton's wholesale misrepresentation – misunderstanding perhaps – of my book. He acknowledges that it is based "almost entirely on research in the files of the Labour Cabinet and cabinet committees" and yet fails to acknowledge that my judgements are tightly anchored to the content of these files.'
[12] *Lost victory*, pp. 42–3, 185, 214.

Prologue is built around a memorandum for the new Labour Cabinet, written by Keynes in August 1945, that 'coldly pointed out the economic and strategic realities so blithely ignored in the successful marketing of New Jerusalem' – quite a tribute from Barnett. The passages quoted by him give a graphic impression of Britain's plight upon the imminent ending of the Lend-Lease arrangements, asking ministers whether they realised 'that the gay and successful fashion in which we undertake liabilities all over the world and slop out money to the importunate represents an over-playing of our hand'.[13] The first chapter of *Lost victory* concludes with several lengthy quotations from the same document, as Keynes developed his argument that 'very early and very drastic economies in this huge cash expenditure overseas seem an absolute condition of maintaining our solvency'.[14] Chapter 2 borrows Keynes's phrase, 'a financial Dunkirk', as its title and again quotes him at length on the ways in which he advised Britain to turn its reverses into a threefold strategy for survival, and on the consequences of failure.[15]

Enter Mr Hyde. For Keynes not only insisted on 'an intense concentration on the expansion of exports', as well as 'drastic and immediate economies in our overseas expenditure', but also on the need for assistance from the USA. Keynes's statement that this was needed '*to enable us to live and spend on the scale we contemplate*' (Barnett's italics) is glossed by the author as follows:

Keynes therefore reckoned that Britain would have to cadge a loan of about $5 billion from the United States. But spending 'on the scale we contemplate' included the extra future load of costs on the British economy represented by New Jerusalem, that 'happier future' for the British people promised by the Labour Party's election manifesto. Keynes did not go into this in detail, merely remarking that, if the Americans refused to be touched for $5 billion, it would render 'the economic basis of the hopes of the public non existent'.[16]

This may be an arguable contention, couched as it is in Barnett's own colourful language, but the judgements with which it is infused are anchored some distance away from Keynes's own moorings. The kind of spending which Keynes had in view throughout his memorandum, consistent with its title, 'The Present Overseas Financial Position of the UK', was

---

[13] *JMK*, XXIV, 400 ('The present overseas financial position of the UK', Aug. 1945); cf. 398, 407, also quoted in *Lost victory*, pp. 2–4 (with Public Record Office – hereafter PRO – references).

[14] *JMK*, XXIV, 408; cf. 401–2, also quoted in *Lost victory*, pp. 28–9.

[15] *JMK*, XXIV, 403, 405, 410, quoted in *Lost victory*, pp. 41–3; cf. *JMK*, XXIV, 372 for a slightly earlier use of the phrase 'a financial Dunkirk'.   [16] *Lost victory*, pp. 41–2.

overseas expenditure, affecting the balance of payments; and the *scale* on which he contemplated it to be made was, of course, that governed by the export drive for which he called, since higher exports would offset these costs; and all of this was projected to occur *after* the drastic cuts in overseas commitments which he envisaged. And to say that he 'did not go into detail' in any allusion to New Jerusalem is an example of litotes that suggests a sad decline in yet another formerly admired cottage industry – the British talent for measured understatement. In fact the nearest that the forty-four pages of the printed text came to hinting at the welfare state was in Keynes's paragraph on the worst-case alternative – when all three elements in his proposed strategy had failed – in which hypothetical event 'there would have to be an indefinite postponement of the best hopes of the new Government'.[17]

Nowhere does this lengthy document address the wholly separate issues of the British budget and the domestic costs of the welfare state – not because Keynes thought them unimportant in themselves but because he understood their lack of relevance to the problem of the external balance, which alone drove the analysis he offered and sufficiently made out the case for seeking aid from the USA. Even his final flourish about 'the hopes of the public' – which Barnett presses into service twice over, each time in juxtaposition to the costs of New Jerusalem – surely refers, in context, to the economic resources available to the country as a whole, especially the level of net imports it could finance, rather than to any schemes for internal redistribution or transfer via welfare legislation. The fact that Keynes (not to mention 'Maude') failed to draw the same conclusions from this analysis as Barnett, fifty years later, may indicate some difference in the relative levels of economic sophistication with which they approached the data.

III

Lost victory, as has been seen, attributes a pivotal role to the influence of Keynes's own economic analysis, relying here chiefly on a recapitulation of one (Hyde-ridden) section from *Audit of war*, which, while it stands virtually unchanged, ought not to stand unchallenged. Barnett represents the wartime discussions about employment policy as turning 'on one central

---

[17] *JMK*, XXIV, 410: 'that is, New Jerusalem', as Barnett glosses this phrase in *Lost victory*, p. 132, where the contingency is simply described as that which would exist 'without American handouts'.

issue: whether Keynes was right or not – whether full employment could be maintained by means of the government feeding money into the economy in order to keep general consumer demand at a level that would require virtually the entire labour-force to satisfy it'. By contrast, the Treasury is applauded for warning against 'a policy of deficit financing as a means of curing structural unemployment'.[18]

This depiction of the alternatives, however, makes for a simplistic polarisation of the argument. It is true that the Treasury at one point in 1943 seemed to be arguing that, except in a couple of prewar years, the problem of unemployment had been entirely structural, and thus confined to particular declining industries. 'I should have said that in almost every year of the prewar decade there was a deficiency of effective demand', Keynes commented, 'the actual level of unemployment being the result of a combination of this and of structural unemployment.'[19] It is also true that the (generally Keynesian) Economic Section had begun by arguing explicitly for regulation of demand through consumption, as well as through investment, thus using deficit financing to counter mass unemployment. But the shift of emphasis away from such an approach during 1943 was partly due to the fact that Keynes himself, let alone the rest of the Treasury, would not lend support to it. Instead Keynes was won over to supporting Meade's scheme for variable levels of insurance contributions, while the Economic Section retreated from the idea of regulating consumer demand through fiscal changes. Hence the tone of Keynes's advice to his Treasury colleagues in June 1943:

The proposals for deficit budgeting were, in my opinion, rather overstressed in the first version of the Economic Section's document, but they are not overstressed in the final version. Personally I like Meade's social security proposal. It is not open to many of the objections to other forms of deficit finance . . .

About other forms of deficit financing, I am inclined to lie low because I am sure that, if serious unemployment does develop, deficit financing is absolutely certain to happen, and I should like to keep free to object hereafter to the more objectionable forms of it.[20]

Keynes's own proposal was to separate the presentation of the public finances into a current budget, providing for ordinary revenue and expenditure, and a capital budget which would deal with public investment. This

---

[18] *Lost victory*, pp. 345–6; cf. *The audit of war: the illusion and reality of Britain as a great nation* (1986), p. 258.

[19] *JMK*, XXVII, 354 (Keynes to Eady, 10 June 1943); cf. Cairncross and Watts, *Economic Section*, pp. 81–2.   [20] *JMK*, XXVII, 352–3 (Keynes to Eady, 10 June 1943).

was wholly in line with his longstanding preference for tackling the British problem of domestic under-investment, rather than boosting consumption to stimulate the economy. Keynes thus cautioned Meade against putting 'too much stress on devices for causing the volume of consumption to fluctuate in preference to devices for varying the volume of investment'.[21] Keynes's position was that 'the ordinary Budget should be balanced at all times. It is the capital Budget which should fluctuate with the demand for employment.'[22] Not only is it a mistake to identify Keynes with the doctrine of 'feeding money into the economy' to boost consumer demand as the means to full employment: the actual course of British postwar fiscal policy did not in fact deliver a string of budget deficits. Though there was to be no immediate reform in the public accounts, the traditional category of expenditure 'above the line' broadly corresponded to what Keynes meant by the ordinary budget; and the fact is that, following the transition to peacetime finance by 1947–8, consecutive British budgets were to be in surplus above the line for the best part of a quarter of a century.[23]

Barnett alleges that 'certain crucial fallacies underlay the arguments of the Keynesians, especially popularising Keynesians like Beveridge in his report on full employment in 1944'. First, it is asserted that the Treasury was right to deny that, except between 1930 and 1933, there had been a general problem of unemployment; it had been, and was to remain, a structural problem in certain regions. Keynes's own response to this highly disputable contention has already been quoted above. Barnett seeks to support it with the argument that in south-east England, by 1938, demand had been sufficient 'to limit unemployment to 8 per cent of the labour-force – Keynes's and Beveridge's own definitions of full employment'.[24] This is a curious point to make since, if true, it is difficult to see what all the fuss was about – why on earth the Treasury should have had any qualms about a supposed postwar target for full employment that had already been achieved before the war ever came along to put their new colleague Lord Keynes into an office down the corridor! This really would have been what Keynes called one Treasury draft on employment policy: 'not much more than Neville Chamberlain disguised in a little modern fancy dress'.[25]

There is indeed a fallacy here: not, however, in the Keynesian argument

---

[21] *JMK*, XXVII, 319–20 (Keynes to Meade, 25 Apr. 1943).
[22] *JMK*, XXVII, 224–5 (Keynes to Sir Richard Hopkins, 20 July 1942).
[23] See my essay, 'Keynes, Buchanan and the balanced budget doctrine' in John Maloney (ed.), *Debt and deficits in historical perspective* (Cheltenham, 1997).
[24] *Lost victory*, pp. 346–7; cf. *Audit of war*, p. 259.
[25] *JMK*, XXVII, 358 (Keynes to Eady, 30 June 1943).

but one arising from Barnett's misunderstanding of the documents which he has seen. For there was a debate which rumbled on in Whitehall, right up to the publication of the 1944 White Paper, about the maximum average of unemployment at which the social insurance scheme could maintain its actuarial soundness. It was here that Beveridge cautiously set the figure at around 8 per cent. Likewise, in Keynes's discussions with Meade about the level at which counter-cyclical variations in social security contributions might be triggered, Keynes argued that 'if 5 per cent is the minimum practicable rate of unemployment, this ought not, I should have thought, to be the dividing line', but rather 'something more like 8 per cent'.[26] Obviously the more optimistic the view of postwar employment, the more relaxed the estimate could be about the burden of unemployment insurance; but Keynes and Beveridge ought surely not be criticised, by Barnett of all people, for making a conservative estimate of the costs of the scheme and ensuring its financial soundness.

When it came to giving his own definition of the average level to which employment might be reduced, Keynes stuck to the sort of target consistently suggested by him over the years since *Can Lloyd George do it?* in 1929. This was a figure around 5 per cent, which by 1942 he was coming to regard as 'a pessimistic assumption'.[27] Ironically, it was his erstwhile co-author, Henderson, who now challenged such a figure. Keynes accordingly defended the assumption on which he and Richard Stone had postulated their estimates of postwar national income:

it is a misunderstanding to suppose that the 5 per cent is a prophecy of what will happen if nothing is done and prewar methods, generally speaking, are continued. Mr Stone and I chose as our basic assumption 800,000 equivalent men out of work, chiefly on the ground that it seemed to us that this was about the highest that the public would stand in postwar conditions without demanding something very drastic to be done about it, coupled with the fact that it did not seem to us impracticable to take drastic steps which would bring down the figure to this total. If one was to put in, as Sir H. Henderson suggests, a figure approaching 2 million men normally out of work after the war, I should have expected the rejoinder that we were wasting our time in assuming a situation which could not possibly be allowed to happen.

Keynes thought that Henderson's scenario of enhanced austerity plus heavy unemployment betrayed a lack of realism in the paradoxical vision it

---

[26] *JMK*, XXVII, 208 (Keynes to Meade, 16 June 1942); and see the clear treatment in Cairncross and Watts, *Economic Section*, pp. 74, 82; cf. 92.

[27] *JMK*, XXVII, 287 ('National income and expenditure after the war', 28 May 1942); cf. 272, 280–1; and see Peter Clarke, *The Keynesian revolution in the making, 1924–36* (Oxford, 1988), pp. 316–17.

implied: 'It would cross someone's mind that it was not very sensible to suffer these severe privations with all that labour available to make something useful.'[28] Keynes remained consistent, therefore, in officially defending an unemployment target range of around 5 per cent, while privately considering this somewhat pessimistic; and when Beveridge became converted to a definition of full employment as 3 per cent, Keynes simply told him: 'No harm in aiming at 3 per cent unemployment, but I shall be surprised if we succeed.'[29]

A further fallacy which Barnett identifies is that of taking the war economy as an object lesson for postwar possibilities. He argues that 'wartime "full employment" was in truth entirely bogus', not only because it was supported by overseas credits from Britain's allies – which is obviously true – but also, more provokingly, because 'wartime "full employment" had in no sense been secured by an across-the-board boosting of demand and investment of a Keynesian kind'.[30] Plainly, the British economy was distorted into a particular shape by the demands of war, at the expense of the export trade, on which future viability would depend. But this point is nowhere put more forcefully than in Keynes's own memorandum to the Labour Cabinet in 1945. The combination of Lend-Lease from the USA, Canadian mutual aid, and the build-up of adverse balances with the sterling area had, he reminded ministers,

made it possible for us to mobilise our domestic man-power for war with an intensity not approached elsewhere, and to spend cash abroad, mainly in India and the Middle East, on a scale not even equalled by the Americans, *without having to export* [Keynes's italics] in order to pay for the food and raw materials which we were using at home to provide the cash which we were spending abroad.

And the result, Keynes said, 'leaves us far worse off, when the sources of assistance dry up, than if the roles had been reversed'.[31]

Keynes clearly did not suppose that demand management could fill this gap after the war; but he would have been very surprised to hear that the 'boosting of demand and investment' licensed during the war – by whatever means, and at whatever price, and at a huge cost in borrowing, regardless of fiscal rectitude – played no part in the *economic* explanation of wartime full employment of all resources, labour and capital alike. As early as 1940

---

[28] *JMK*, XXVII, 299, 302 (Keynes to Henderson, 3 June 1942). Henderson's figure implied a rate of about 12.5 per cent.   [29] *JMK*, XXVII, 381 (Keynes to Beveridge, 16 Dec. 1944).
[30] *Lost victory*, p. 347; cf. *Audit of war*, p. 260.
[31] *JMK*, XXIV, 398–9 ('The present overseas financial position of the UK', Aug. 1945); cf. 461–2 (Keynes press conference in Washington, 12 Sept. 1945).

Keynes had wryly wondered whether it was politically possible 'for a capitalistic democracy to organise expenditure on the scale necessary to make the grand experiments which would prove my case – except in war conditions'.[32] Though manpower may have been directed out of its peace-time pattern, it was still government action that was responsible for the rise in aggregate demand for labour. Indeed it was exactly this military spending which created 'an atmosphere of potential boom, with overwhelming demands which we are not in a position to meet', as Keynes put it in 1942, explicitly drawing the parallel between the economic impact of over-full demand in war or peace.[33] The fact that the biggest increase in wartime civilian employment was in the new technologies rather than the old, far from showing the irrelevance of a Keynesian analysis, provides some encouraging evidence for his persistent belief that the problem of labour mobility and transference, which had long bedevilled Britain's rigid industrial structure, could best be solved in a climate of expansion and full demand for labour.

Hence Barnett's final thrust against Keynesianism seems bafflingly mis-conceived. With incontestable accuracy, but a surely misplaced air of dialectical triumph, he discloses that: 'The magic wartime cure was actually provided by the demands of the armed forces of the Crown, civil defence and the swollen bureaucracy.'[34] Of course it was. Once more, Barnett's hindsight in spotting this line of argument turns out to have been antici-pated by a contemporary Treasury mandarin, whose 'query how 1 million in the army could be an offset to 1 million unemployed' received this answer from Keynes: '1 million in the army is in effect an additional demand for labour on that scale and, therefore, in so far as unemployment is due to an inadequate demand for labour, it ought to cure the problem nearly as well as any other additional form of activity.'[35]

A Martian with a degree in economics would have observed that in the early 1940s a large number of earthlings were paid (rather low) wages by rival groups of employers ('nation states') to dress up in uniforms and perform tasks of no greater social utility than that of digging holes in the ground and filling them up again. Transfer payments between different groups within the same country partly financed these make-work schemes, and to that extent made no impact on the balance of payments. Nor was this

[32] *JMK*, XXII, 149 (*New Republic*, 29 July 1940).
[33] *JMK*, XXVII, 302 (Keynes to Sir Alan Barlow, 4 June 1942).
[34] *Lost victory*, p. 348; cf. *Audit of war*, pp. 260–1.
[35] *JMK*, XXVII, 304 (Keynes to Hopkins, 4 June 1942).

affected by the fact that some of these employed workers delivered manufactured exports to foreign countries, often dropping them from aero-
planes, since there was no visible return (except perhaps through a crude
reciprocal exercise in barter the next night).

But there was an external dimension to the widespread deployment of
troops who contributed to the invisible earnings of their host countries as
involuntary tourists. In his memorandum of August 1945 Keynes noted
that 'there are certain items of *income* which arise out of the war and will
fade away with it', notably arising from 'the personal expenditure of the
American forces in this country (£115 million in 1944 and probably as
much as £60 million in 1945'.[36] A few months later, during the negotiations
over the postwar loan, the Americans looked for a solution to the British
balance of payments along similar lines. 'They calculate', Keynes reported,
'that with 100,000 Americans on the average of the year (presumably in
Oxford) each spending at the rate of £500 a year, the whole problem of what
we are now discussing is solved with something to spare.'[37] No uniforms for
these tourists, of course, but *plus ça change, plus c'est la même chose*. To mis-
construe the macroeconomic impact of putting men into the armed forces
is a disabling flaw, the more so since the whole argument about the costs to
Britain of its global overstretch depends on a clear understanding of what
the real costs were.

IV

Here was a problem with which Keynes was acutely concerned: what the
country could afford externally if it were to pay its way in the postwar world.
Moreover he was simultaneously concerned with a parallel problem: how
much strain the budget could bear internally if it had to finance the
Beveridge proposals. The distinction between the two problems was clearly
set out in the letter which Keynes wrote to the Secretary of the War
Cabinet in 1945:

I should make an even more emphatic distinction between the burden of overseas
expenditure and the burden of domestic expenditure. We can always manage more
of the latter, if necessary. Indeed, defence expenditure might prove one of the
methods of reaching full employment and hereby, partly at least, pay for itself as

[36] *JMK*, XXIV, 402; cf. 430, 469. On the eve of D-Day 1944 there were 1.67 million GIs sta-
tioned in Britain; see David Reynolds, *Rich relations: the American occupation of Britain,
1942–5* (1995), esp. p. 103.
[37] *JMK*, XXIV, 561 (Keynes to Hugh Dalton, 20 Oct. 1945).

compared with other alternatives in the short run. Moreover, I at any rate would not be shocked by some borrowing, if the case for higher expenditure on defence in the immediately-ensuing years is overwhelmingly made out, hoping to cover this up later on by the buoyancy of the national income. Within reason anything is possible financially in the way of domestic expenditure, if the case for incurring it is made out with sufficient strength. Nothing of the kind, however, is true of overseas expenditure.[38]

There is accordingly no inconsistency in what Keynes was saying about the two problems. 'Anything we can actually *do* we can afford', he assured a radio audience in 1942.[39] Accordingly, he lent his authority to the proposition that the country could afford a social security system, telling Beveridge at the first opportunity of his 'state of wild enthusiasm for your general scheme' and commending his eponymous Report as 'a grand document'.[40]

This was the same Keynes who, in 1944, told the War Cabinet that 'the assumption that we shall be able to import all the raw materials and foodstuffs necessary to provide full employment and maintain (or improve) the standard of life' was 'at present, an act of blind faith'. His message was that the time had come for Britain to stop playing 'Lady Bountiful' in the world.[41] It was in this context that he went on to add, 'in parenthesis, that the time and energy and thought which we are all giving to the Brave New World is wildly disproportionate to what is being given to the Cruel Real World, towards which our present policy is neither brave nor new'.[42]

Already 'uncomfortable about the possible cumulative effect of certain current decisions of higher policy (or, in the case of exports, lack of decisions) on our prospective financial position', Keynes sharpened his point in September 1944. 'We cannot police half the world at our own expense when we have already gone into pawn to the other half', he wrote. 'We cannot run for long a great programme of social amelioration on money lent from overseas.'[43] This was the clearest link he made between 'New Jerusalem' and the 'financial Dunkirk', and he made it as a general moni-

---

[38] *JMK*, XXIV, 295 (Keynes to Sir Edward Bridges, 23 Mar. 1945).
[39] *JMK*, XXVII, 270 (*The Listener*, 2 Apr. 1942).
[40] *JMK*, XXVII, 204, 255 (Keynes to Beveridge, 17 Mar., 14 Oct. 1942).
[41] *JMK*, XXIV, 34; cf. 37 ('The problem of our external finance in the transition', 12 June 1944).
[42] Ibid., 53. 'In sum, the New Jerusalemers chose to proceed on the best romantic principle that sense must bend to feeling, and facts to faith', is Barnett's gloss on this quotation (*Lost victory*, p. 128) which he uses as the heading for chapter 7.
[43] *JMK*, XXIV, 114, 125 ('Decisions of policy affecting the financial position in Stages II and III, Sep. 1944').

tory proposition, advanced eight months before VE Day, ten months before the Labour Government took office, nearly a year before VJ Day, one year before the American loan negotiations began, and a clear couple of years before the date at which the war was currently expected to end.

What Keynes sought to achieve was a variable strategy for coping with Britain's external financial problem – the nature of which he thought insufficiently appreciated – on the basis of what he called 'enterprise' (exports), 'ruthlessness' (overseas cuts) and 'tact' (American assistance).[44] It is obvious enough to us now that the scale of British commitments in the world betokened pretensions which were not only obsolescent in themselves but a serious impediment to the achievement of postwar economic success. Few saw this as clearly at the time as Keynes, or argued more consistently for a drastic reduction in British overseas commitments. He identified 'our position as a Great Power, equal in authority and responsibility and therefore equal in the assumption of burdens', as 'the ingredient of power and prestige – easily understandable, but nevertheless short-sighted if pride and prestige are, in fact, to be preserved'. He pointed not only to the economic impact but to the psychological origins – 'our reflex actions are those of a rich man' – of such an attitude, which now threatened to ensnare his country in its own historical legacy.[45]

In tackling this problem, Keynes foresaw the need for postwar assistance from the USA, as he recorded in an official paper circulated a full eighteen months before a Labour Government was elected in Britain. Indeed, right up until the actual declaration of the poll in July 1945, he was one of many in expecting another Conservative Government under Churchill. Even so, in 1944 Keynes anticipated the danger that American aid might make things 'too free-and-easy for the initial period', meaning that, after three years of transition to peace, 'we should have formed postwar habits and have relaxed controls'.[46] His fear that this might lead to disinvestment overseas, allowing the British people to live off repatriated capital, was wide of the mark as a prophecy, since part of the actual dollar shortage after 1945 was linked to the unanticipated growth of British investments in the sterling area.[47] Nor is the Attlee Government normally criticised for its haste in relaxing controls.

---

[44] *JMK*, XXIV, 410 ('The present overseas financial position of the UK', Aug. 1945).

[45] *JMK*, XXIV, 55–6, 64 ('The problem of our external finance in the transition', 12 June 1944); cf. 93.

[46] *JMK*, XXIV, 17 ('Notes on external finance in the post-Japanese-Armistice transitional period', 11 Jan. 1944); and see 376 on the 1945 election.

[47] See Alec Cairncross, *Years of recovery: British economic policy, 1945–51* (1985), pp. 153ff.

The fact is that the rationale for seeking American assistance, ultimately as a loan, was not to appease feckless Labour ministers in building a socialist Britain, but virtually the opposite. Many arguments were advanced, of course, but Keynes put to the War Cabinet, as 'a further, and in my judgment an overriding, consideration', the point that the alternative was a commitment to an isolationist command economy for half a generation, since 'nothing much less than Russian methods would have served our turn meanwhile'.[48]

The real ideological tincture to the Anglo-American negotiations became apparent when Keynes was actually negotiating on behalf of the Attlee Government in Washington, late in 1945. Convinced now that only the form of an interest-bearing loan would satisfy American opinion, Keynes was constantly warned by his Treasury colleagues at home of strong Labour antipathy to the whole idea – almost regardless of the price of breakdown. 'As regards the austerity consequences of anything less than complete success, I should judge the present Government to be much less frightened of the politics of that than their predecessors', Sir Wilfrid Eady wrote. 'Indeed, there is a risk that austerity for its own sake may become a little too fashionable, partly as a more noble way of life, partly as a sublimation of disappointment.' Paradoxical shades of New Jerusalem! Keynes was warned that ministers remained 'reluctant to admit that we are in any sense dependent upon the US' and needed constant persuasion from cautiously conservative Treasury officials that the external payments gap could be filled in no other way. 'One thing is pretty certain', Eady reiterated, 'They do not want to be under an obligation to the United States for one dollar more than they need for one minute more than is necessary.' Though a diffuse spirit of anti-socialism manifestly coloured the view of many American critics of the loan to Britain, within the formal negotiations themselves Keynes neither sought to invoke, nor had to defend, the costs of the domestic legislative programme of the Labour Government, since the need for the loan was perceived by the experts on both sides to rest on quite other grounds.[49]

Admittedly, Keynes was soon to be disillusioned about the use made of these hard-won dollars. He privately expressed exasperation that 'the mixed

[48] JMK, XXIV, 271–2, 275–6 ('Overseas financial policy in Stage III', May 1945).
[49] JMK, XXIV, 521, 544, 536 (Eady to Keynes, 28 Sep., 12 and 6 Oct. 1945); and see the American statements, 'Purpose of the credit', in JMK, XXIV, 629, 636. On the ideological background see the classic study by Richard N. Gardner, Sterling–dollar diplomacy in current perspective (1956; new edn, 1980), esp. pp. 236 ff; and the authoritative account in D. E. Moggridge, Maynard Keynes; an economist's biography (1992), pp. 799–818.

chauvinism and universal benevolence of the FO and other departments and the weakness of the Chancellor in these matters are slopping away on everything and everybody in the world except the poor Englishman the fruits of our American loan'.[50] In one of Keynes's last Treasury memoranda before his sudden death early in 1946, he commiserated with 'the hard-pressed British public' over the fact that 'not a single bean of sustenance for themselves or of capital equipment for British manufacturers is likely to be left from the American credit', since it was currently being used 'to cut a dash in the world considerably above our means'.[51]

According to Barnett, Keynes thought that Britain could – 'and more-over *should*' – use one part of the loan 'to bolster British pretensions to world-power status rather than to invest in modernising the real source of the United Kingdom's strength and wealth, the British industrial machine'; and use another part to build New Jerusalem 'on foreign tick'.[52] Keynes's own words show this to be wrong in almost every particular.

V

How, then, did Keynes actually suppose the Beveridge Plan feasible? One reason arises from the fact that he had himself represented the Treasury in the hard financial negotiations with Beveridge. The first forecasts of postwar national income were made by Keynes (and Stone) precisely in order to ascertain what was affordable, with Beveridge being asked to cut and trim provisions that were thought ideally desirable if the cost seemed prohibitive. Keynes favoured the preservation of an insurance 'fund', despite its rather fictional nature, as 'the only way by which to preserve sound accounting, to measure efficiency, to maintain economy and to keep the public properly aware of what things cost'.[53] Since Beveridge showed himself to be 'strongly of the opinion that the benefits must be paid for', this produced common ground in seeking financial viability through a rel-atively high level of initial contributions.[54] As Keynes reassured his col-leagues: 'It is the very large sums obtained in this way which make so far-reaching a proposal practicable at such modest cost to the Treasury.'[55] Had he gone ahead with his proposed maiden speech to the House of Lords

---

[50] *JMK*, XXVII, 463 (Keynes to Brand, 29 Jan. 1946).
[51] *JMK*, XXVII, 466 ('Political and military expenditure overseas', 11 Feb. 1946).
[52] *Lost victory*, p. 43 (Barnett's italics).
[53] *JMK*, XXVII, 225 (Keynes to Hopkins, 20 July 1942).
[54] *JMK*, XXVII, 237 (Keynes to Sir Horace Wilson, 11 Aug. 1942).
[55] *JMK*, XXVII, 251 (Keynes to Hopkins, 13 Oct. 1942); cf. 243.

in February 1943, he would have said that it was 'precisely because I am deeply concerned about the Budget position in the early years after the war that I welcome the Beveridge proposals'.[56] Indeed the real criticism, as Jose Harris makes clear below (pp. 182–3), turns on the extent to which current parsimony stored up longer-term problems of under-funding.

If the relatively modest scale of the final proposals assuaged Keynes's fears on budgetary grounds, he saw no other reason to oppose the welfare state in principle, however frail he knew the balance of payments to be. He understood that the real resources consumed by welfare, especially scarce imports or import substitutes, were a minor part of the costs, compared with the transfer of incomes between British citizens. And the problem of finding domestic resources was, in this sense, the obverse of the problem of sustaining full employment. 'We shall, in very fact, have built our New Jerusalem out of the labour which in our former vain folly we were keeping unused and unhappy in enforced idleness', was how Keynes put it in 1942.[57] Moreover, subsequent historical research, notably a cogent analysis by Jim Tomlinson, has confirmed that, since the welfare services were not only labour-intensive, but also drew heavily on an expanding number of occupied women, the diversion of suitable labour was not generally at the expense of (male-dominated) export industries. Indeed it is arguable how far the welfare state should be seen as a burden on, rather than a contribution to, the economy.[58]

Jose Harris has persuasively argued that it is anachronistic to project the more lavish welfare strategies of the 1960s back on to the austere 1940s, and curiously insular to ignore the fact that British spending on social security as a proportion of GDP was, for example, already outstripped by West Germany in 1950 and overtaken by France two years later.[59] In Britain the supposed uniqueness of the welfare state legislation of the Attlee Government has been exaggerated for various reasons – by those commending its redistributive effects as much as by those indicting a tax-and-spend New Jerusalem. Yet what Britain was doing, in ways that accorded with its own traditions of social legislation, was little different in scope or

---

[56] *JMK*, XXVII, 258.   [57] *JMK*, XXVII, 270 (*The Listener*, 2 Apr. 1942).

[58] Jim Tomlinson, 'Welfare and the economy: the economic impact of the welfare state, 1945–51,' *20th Century British History*, 6 (1995), pp. 194–219, esp. 196, 206–7.

[59] Jose Harris, 'Enterprise and welfare states; a comparative perspective', *Transactions of the Royal Historical Society*, 5th ser., 40 (1990), pp. 175–95, esp. 180, 189, 193. This fundamental critique of the social theme in *The audit of war* was one inspiration for my own essay, taking up the macroeconomic implications. The microeconomic case is trenchantly examined in David Edgerton, 'The prophet militant and industrial: the peculiarities of Correlli Barnett', *20th Century British History*, 2 (1991), pp. 360–79, esp. 372–6.

scale from what was soon implemented throughout western Europe. Indeed Alan Milward suggests that the reconstruction of the postwar state on the basis of the security and prosperity of its citizens, ushering in a unique era of both personal and public consumption, was a process that was relatively weak in insular Britain, compared with the increasingly integrated continent.[60] The story that emerges in a European context is of thirty years in which full employment and social security marched forward together. As Donald Sassoon puts it, this 'triumph of capitalism, *les trentes glorieuses*, was, in reality, the triumph of *regulated* capitalism: the countries under such a regime enjoyed democracy, peace and unparalleled prosperity'.[61]

To regard this whole era simply as one of decline, even for the relatively lagging British economy, is itself curious, as Barry Supple has long argued. To identify emerging problems of overload as peculiarly British, and to ascribe them to the influence of Keynes, is even less tenable. Recognising Britain as 'an old country', he wanted it to shed the real burden of an historically bloated world role. But he did not believe that the rather austere proposals for social reform which were generated in the 1940s were beyond the country's capacity; nor did he think that the finance of the Beveridge Plan implied deficits on the current budget. Nor, for that matter, did it; and the origins of the actual budgetary overload that became apparent thirty years later need a different explanation. 'We can do almost anything we like, *given time*', Keynes had cautioned in 1942. 'We must not force the pace – that is necessary warning.'[62] Though hardly, as Henderson had once suggested, 'the man who persuaded the British people to ruin themselves by gambling on a greater illusion than any of those which he had shattered', Keynes might well go down to history as a man whose emblematic posthumous fame long obscured the fact that his warnings had been insufficiently heeded.

[60] Alan S. Milward, *The European rescue of the nation-state* (1992), esp. pp. 3, 21–2, 27–8, 31–2, 43, 433.
[61] Donald Sassoon, *One hundred years of Socialism* (1996), p. 446.
[62] *JMK*, XXVII, 269 (*The Listener*, 2 Apr. 1942, Keynes's italics).

8

Social policy, saving, and sound money: budgeting for the New Jerusalem in the Second World War

JOSE HARRIS

I

Oh, won't it be wonderful after the war!
There won't be no rich and there won't be no poor,
We'll all get a pension about twenty-four,
And we won't have to work if we find it a bore.

Oh, won't it be wonderful after the war!
The beer will be better and quicker and more,
And there's only one thing I would like to explore;
Why didn't we have this old war before?

Set to the tune of 'The Mountains of Mourne', these words were sung by
A. P. Herbert, the well-known humourist and Independent MP, to entertain the guests at the wedding reception of Sir William Beveridge – held at
the Dorchester Hotel a few days after the publication of Beveridge's famous
social insurance Plan in December 1942.[1] Whether his host was amused is
not recorded, but Herbert's ditty sounded a note of scepticism and cynicism
about schemes for social welfare that was to haunt the reconstruction
movement throughout the 1940s and has been powerfully revived in recent
years by those who have viewed the welfare state as the albatross of Britain's
postwar economic decline. Over the past two decades public spending on
welfare since the Second World War has been variously blamed for high
inflation, low investment, erosion of work incentives, corruption of civic
values, and collapse of family life; while Beveridge, Keynes, and the whole
generation of wartime social reformers have been widely portrayed as sen-
timental utopians who debauched both the currency and the morals of the
nation in a vain search for the chimera of postwar 'social justice'.[2]

---

[1] William Clark, *From three worlds. Memoirs* (1986), pp. 20–1.
[2] T. B. Howarth, *Prospect and reality, Great Britain 1945–55* (1985); Corelli Barnett, *The audit of war. The illusion and reality of Britain as a great nation* (1986); P. Minford, 'Reconstruction and the UK. False start and new beginning', in R. Dornbusch, W. Nolling, and R. Layard

How far 'welfare' and 'decline' are causally related is clearly a matter of great economic and cultural complexity, but only recently have historians and social scientists showed signs of treating the question not merely as one of axiomatic theory but of concrete historical evidence about specific policies, individuals, institutions, and events. Micro studies of small samples of welfare claimants, drawing largely upon North American data, have indicated that potential beneficiaries of welfare do indeed adjust their patterns of behaviour in response to patterns of welfare spending (though not always precisely in ways that economic theory would predict).[3] Conversely, larger-scale institutional studies drawing mainly on British and European experience have suggested that the negative impact of welfare spending on the performance of different national economies has been much more limited than its critics would allow – and that, unexpectedly, postwar welfare spending by fast-growing 'Christian democrat' regimes in western Europe was consistently higher than by either Labour or Conservative governments in postwar Britain.[4] On both sides of the debate there has been some reluctance to differentiate between different *types* of welfare spending, or to concede the possibility that *some* social policies may have been economically and morally damaging whilst others may have not. This chapter will concentrate on one small aspect of this controversy – namely, the debate on the financing of social welfare that was carried on amongst economists and public administrators during and immediately after the Second World War. It will suggest that the priorities of this debate were very different from what has often been imagined, and that in the shaping of government policy abstract notions of 'social justice' consistently played second fiddle to the imperatives of postwar economic reconstruction and to fiscal and monetary restraint.

(eds.), *Postwar economic reconstruction and lessons for the East today* (Cambridge, Mass., 1993), pp. 115–38.

[3] Robert Moffitt, 'Incentive effects of the US welfare system: a review', *Journal of Economic Literature*, 30 (March 1992), pp. 1–61; John Ermisch, 'Impacts of policy actions on the family and household', *Journal of Public Policy*, 6, 3, (1987), pp. 297–318; S. Jenkins, J. Ermisch, and R. Wright, 'Adverse selection features of poverty among lone mothers', *Fiscal Studies*, 11 (1990), pp. 76–90.

[4] Harold Wilensky, 'Democratic corporatism, consensus, and social policy', in *The welfare state in crisis. An account of the Conference on Social Policies in the 1980s* (Paris, 1981): Jose Harris, 'Enterprise and welfare states: a comparative perspective', *Transactions of the Royal Historical Society*, 5th ser. 40 (1990), pp. 175–95; Jim Tomlinson, 'Welfare and the economy: the economic impact of the welfare state, 1945–51', *20th Century British History*, 6, 2 (1995), pp. 194–219.

II

Whitehall discussion of postwar social reform began at a surprisingly early date. Home Office, Ministry of Health, and Ministry of Labour officials were already toying with schemes for the postwar world in the autumn of 1939 – a fact which some historians have interpreted to mean that the war was less of a social catalyst than is often supposed and that 'reconstruction' evolved out of proposals for extending and rationalising the social services that had already been put forward in the mid-1930s. Up to a point this view is correct, and certainly much of the thrust towards 'universalism' that was to become associated with the name of Beveridge had already been articulated by bodies like Political and Economic Planning and certain sections of the Labour party several years before.[5] Nevertheless from the start of the war there were some important new factors in the social policy equation – of which the most crucial were the desire to use social policy to palliate the impact of wartime controls, the desire to ward off inflation, and the desire to avoid a repetition of the build-up of frustrated consumer demand that had exploded on the economy with such disastrous long-term consequences at the end of the First World War.[6]

Certainly it was these latter factors that dominated discussion of social policy questions among the influential group of economists involved in the government's Commitee on Economic Information, headed by Josiah Stamp, during the winter months of 1939–40.[7] As the war became more desperate this committee of economic notables was to be eclipsed by other more dynamic and less orthodox advisory bodies; but during those early months it was remarkably influential in inculcating the view that the war should be fought as far as possible on terms of strictest financial probity, and that Britain's major card in the forthcoming struggle with Germany was 'our financial strength'.[8] Sterling was to be protected at all costs; British non-military exports were to be positively expanded in order to build up

---

[5] *Report on the British Social Services . . . with proposals for future developments* (1937).

[6] Clay papers, Nuffield College, C8, file 18, Lord Stamp to Sir John Simon, 22 Nov. 1939.

[7] On the work of this committee see Alan Booth, 'Economic Advice at the Centre of British Government, 1939–41', *Historical Journal*, 29, 3 (1986), pp. 655–75. I have used the set of minutes and memoranda in the Clay papers, rather than the set in the Public Record Office (hereafter PRO), CAB 89/1.

[8] PRO, CAB 89/26, memorandum to Lord Stamp from B. S. Rowntree, 5 Dec. 1939; Clay papers, 9/19, 'Exchange Discrimination or Manipulation', by Lord Stamp, 1 Jan. 1940. (This approach directly reflected the view of the Prime Minister, Neville Chamberlain, that 'war is not won by arms and men alone, but rather by material reserves and credits' (Clay papers, C11/23)).

balances in strong foreign currencies; military expenditure was to be financed as far as possible from taxation rather than borrowing; an 'ethic of saving' was to be promoted at all levels of income; and wage-inflation resulting from longer working hours and absorption of unemployed workers was to be kept rigorously at bay.[9] In the booming climate of the early months of war (itself partly generated by a fall in sterling) this latter concern threatened a general 'show-down with labour' – a threat that sucked Lord Stamp and his advisers albeit reluctantly into questions of social welfare, in the hope that measures to protect the living-standards of the 'economically weakest members of the community' would appease the wage-demands of the more robust sectors of the industrial working-class.[10]

The earliest welfare concerns of the Stamp committee were very limited in scope, relating mainly to the relaxation of public assistance means-tests, and to the extension of food and rent subsidies (though such subsidies were seen as in themselves threatening a dangerous expansion of surplus income in the hands of the higher-paid sectors of the working-class).[11] More ambitious proposals came during the winter of 1939–40 from the Quaker chocolate manufacturers, L. S. Cadbury and Benjamin Seebohm Rowntree, who suggested that large firms should pay wartime family allowances and cost-of-living bonuses as a trade-off for wage-restraint;[12] and from J. M. Keynes, who published a series of articles linking social welfare with war finance, culminating in a short book on *How to pay for the war*. Keynes's book was highly critical of the 'business-as-usual' assumptions about the wartime economy emanating from the Chamberlain government and from the Stamp survey; but no less than Lord Stamp and his advisers, Keynes was adamant that government policy should avoid a repeat performance of the inflationary build-up of the First World War – an inflation which, he argued, had poured public money into the pockets of large-scale entrepreneurs whilst robbing small savers and giving nothing but paper gains to the industrial working-class. Instead the current war was to be financed by

---

[9] Clay papers, C8/17, Stamp Enquiry: Survey of War Plans, 33rd, 38th, and 41st meetings, Sept.–Oct. 1939.

[10] Clay papers, C8/17, 'Controlled materials price policy', by H. D. Henderson, 2 Oct. 1939; 38th and 50th meetings of the Survey of War Plans in the Economic and Financial Spheres. 11 Oct. and 8 Nov. 1939; C9/19, 'Sterling, exports and the vicious spiral', by H. D. Henderson, 17 Jan. 1940.

[11] Clay papers, C8/18, 'Control of prices and wages. Memorandum prepared in the Ministry of Labour, enclosed in a letter to Lord Stamp', 15 Nov. 1939; 57th meeting of the Survey of War Plans in the Economic and Financial Spheres, 27 Nov. 1939.

[12] PRO, CAB 87/26, B. S. Seebohm Rowntree to Lord Stamp. 5 Dec. 1939; *The Times*, L. J. Cadbury to the Editor, 17 Jan. 1941; Clay papers, C8/18, Survey of War Plans in the Economic and Financial Spheres, 55th meeting, 22 Nov. 1939.

steeply progressive taxation, compulsory saving, and the lowering of income-tax thresholds to incorporate for the first time the bulk of manual workers. The quid pro quo for this unprecedented tax regime was to be strict controls over the supply and prices of basic commodities, family allowances for dependent children, and the accumulation of 'deferred pay' or 'post-war credits' through weekly deductions from wages modelled on national insurance contributions. The latter would be encashable either when a worker became sick or unemployed, or when the economy had returned to normal after the end of the war.[13] The combined 'social justice and social efficiency' of his proposals, Keynes argued, would encourage wage-restraint without resort to punitive legal sanctions, ward off both present inflation and future unemployment, and at the same time spread 'the inevitable increase in the National Debt widely among every class in the community'. These arguments won the cautious support of trade unionists and of many members of the economics profession, among them Keynes's erstwhile and future adversary, F. A. Hayek.[14] But they were resisted by the Treasury, who at this stage of the war were considerably less 'austere' than Keynes about the probable future pattern of wartime finance.[15]

The notion of using social welfare spending to restrain rather than stimulate consumer demand had been a significant if little noticed aspect of Keynes's applied economic thought since well before the formulation of the rather different approach set out in the *General theory*.[16] Concern with balancing budgets, avoiding inflation, and palliating the impact of high taxation on low incomes was to characterise all his wartime writings that touched upon social policy, even after the collapse of 1940 had made inevitable a very high degree of dependence on American loans and on domestic monetary expansion. After the massive extension of direct taxation and compulsory saving imposed by the so-called 'first Keynesian budget' of 1941, Keynes proposed that the budget of the following year should be 'described as a *social policy Budget*, and should primarily aim at adjusting various social anomalies which have developed out of the war

---

[13] Donald Moggridge and Austin Robinson (eds.), *The collected writings of John Maynard Keynes*, 30 vols. (1971–89) (hereafter *JMK* with vol. and page numbers), IX, pp. 367–439 and XXII, pp. 41–51; Clay papers, 9/20, 'The Keynes Plan. Administration in the Lower Incomes. Note by Lord Stamp', 11 Mar. 1940.

[14] *JMK*, XXII, ch. 2 esp. pp. 49–51, 78, 95, 98–102, 116.

[15] Alan Booth, *British economic policy, 1931–49. Was there a Keynesian revolution?* (1989), p. 64.

[16] J. M. Keynes, 'The question of high wages', *Political Quarterly*, 1, 1 (Jan. 1930), pp. 110–24.

situation and also out of the previous Budget itself.[17] This proposal neatly dovetailed with the beginning of the Beveridge inquiry into social insurance; and a few months later Keynes pounced with alacrity upon Beveridge's draft insurance scheme as an ideal strategy with which to reinforce the habit of saving, to put a ring-fence around more extravagant forms of welfare spending, to legitimise the impact of a low threshold of taxation, and (incidentally) to strengthen the economic structure of family life. Keynes's contribution to the Beveridge report had nothing directly to do, as is sometimes supposed, with promoting Beveridge's famous assumption C (that social security would only be affordable in the long-term within a context of 'full employment'); on the contrary, it was entirely concerned with assisting Beveridge to limit the demands made by social welfare on postwar public expenditure. It was Keynes who persuaded Beveridge to prune down the early drafts of his social security plan, which threatened to add £500 million a year to postwar direct taxation, and helped him to substitute instead a much more modest scheme, whose total cost in its early years would add up to little more than that imposed by the normal growth of social services already in existence in 1939 – and whose contributory insurance aspects would help to stabilise the postwar economy with large 'extra-budgetary surpluses'.[18]

Support for social policies that would help to avoid a repetition of the inflation of 1919 to 1921 was widespread throughout reconstruction circles, even among economists who were normally much more favourable than Keynes to 'market' solutions for social problems. Lionel Robbins, for example, argued that only the introduction of a 'national minimum' could legitimise tight monetary controls at the end of the war.[19] Evan Durbin, personal economic adviser to Clement Attlee, envisaged that in the postwar world a growing proportion of national income would inevitably be absorbed by social services, but that such expenditure would play an important part in both political and financial 'stabilisation'.[20] Within the Economic Section of the War Cabinet there was great interest in the possibility of using social insurance as an antidote to postwar economic crisis – both by adjusting contributions to counteract the trade cycle, and by using benefits 'to maintain the demand for consumption goods and

[17] *JMK*, XXII, p. 355.
[18] Jose Harris, *William Beveridge. A biography* (Oxford, 1977), pp. 407–12; *JMK*, XXVII, ch. 4.
[19] PRO, CAB 117/2, 'War aims and reconstruction', by L. Robbins, 4 Feb. 1941.
[20] Evan Durbin, *The politics of democratic socialism. An essay on social policy* (1940), pp. 94–5, 114–5.

services in times of depression'.[21] The government's Committee on Reconstruction Problems (later the Reconstruction Secretariat) identified 'the process of eliminating the grosser forms of poverty' and the 'extension and consolidation of our great system of social services' as crucial to its task of drawing up 'skeleton plans . . . for the stern necessities of practical administration at the end of the war'.[22] A similar case was argued by R. H. Tawney in his classic mid-war article on 'The abolition of economic controls', which blamed the *laissez-faire* finance, unregulated inflation, and contraction of spending on public services between 1919 and 1921 for the interwar depression and world slump. Tawney's 'long and valuable memorandum' had been commissioned as an advisory paper by the government's Committee on Reconstruction Problems in February 1941, but was initially suppressed by the Treasury which took exception to its excessively 'critical' tone. Publication was only authorised more than two years later in an academic journal, after assurance had been given that its 'only readership' would be 'a handful of professors of history' (though it was subsequently widely circulated as a WEA discussion paper, and read as an indication of changed government priorities in the current war).[23] Yet 'The abolition of controls' was scarcely as subversive as the official mind appeared to believe, since its author fully shared the Treasury's belief that the main problem of the postwar economy would 'not be that of stimulating the effective demand for goods and services, but rather of controlling and directing it'.[24]

What of Beveridge himself, the 'great arch-planner' of the reconstruction movement, whose name is so often twinned with that of J. M. Keynes as co-author both of the rise of welfare and of long-term economic decline? Although Beveridge was to make use of Keynesian ideas in many of his wartime writings, he approached social welfare problems from a different angle from that of Keynes and was never more than a semi-detached and somewhat transient Keynesian. During the late 1920s and for much of the 1930s Beveridge had been strongly influenced both by a 'monetarist' interpretation of unemployment and by the belief that above-wage-level welfare benefits, particularly for women and for men with dependent children,

---

[21] PRO T.230/100: J. E. Meade to D. N. Chester, 15 June 1941; J. E. Meade to J. Jewkes, 15 June 1941; 'Some notes on the finance of social insurance', n.d.; 'Unemployment benefit and the mobility of labour', 20 Aug. 1941.

[22] PRO, CAB 117/3, 'War Cabinet outline of statement on reconstruction problems. Memorandum by the Paymaster-General', 4 Nov. 1942.

[23] R. H. Tawney, 'The abolition of economic controls, 1918–21', *Economic History Review*, 12 (1943), pp. 1–30. The story of the official commissioning, subsequent de-commissioning, and eventual private publication of Tawney's paper can be found in PRO, CAB 117/2 and CAB 117/40.   [24] PRO, CAB 117/7, R. Hopkins to G. Baster, 22 May 1942.

were undermining incentives to work. In the late 1930s he had modified these views in favour of social and economic planning, but as I have shown elsewhere his conception of planning centred on controls over supply, rather than on the Keynesian model of demand management.[25] Though both men continued to be 'liberals', there was a major difference in their approach to the priorities of the postwar world – Keynes being concerned to retrieve as much as possible of market capitalism, while Beveridge was much more sceptical about how far 'economic liberalism' could survive the mass destruction and material and cultural revolution entailed in global war. Beveridge's 'liberalism' in the early-1940s was mainly concerned not with salvaging capitalism but with making state regulation and collectivism compatible with the survival of largely non-economic 'personal freedoms'. Beveridge's thinking on this issue was complex and far from consistent: freedom in spending one's personal income was 'an essential citizen liberty', but freedom to own investment capital was not; freedom to strike and freedom to choose an occupation lay somewhere between the two.[26]

No less than that of Keynes, however, Beveridge's approach to social welfare was one of rigorous austerity and economy – an approach in which he was strongly supported by his civil service advisers, and in particular by the secretary of his Social Insurance Committee, D. N. Chester.[27] No less than Tawney and the economists of the Stamp survey Beveridge had at the forefront of his mind the disastrous inflationary boom that had engulfed the economy in 1919 – a boom that he blamed at least partly upon the short-sighted failure of Lloyd George and other first world war ministers to adopt the pre-emptive schemes for social security that had been devised by Beveridge himself and other Whitehall officials in 1916–17. When he first sketched out his new insurance proposals in the winter of 1941–2 Beveridge's initial aim was to fix the amount of social insurance benefits at a level of subsistence that would have absolute objective, 'scientific' valid-ity totally independent of individual circumstance, change through time, and the vagaries of the political process; but when it became apparent that this was impossible, he proved willing to adapt the strict 'subsistence' prin-ciple to the more pragmatic constraints of public finance.[28] Far from offer-ing pensions to all and sundry, Beveridge's final 'social security budget',

[25] Harris, *Beveridge*. pp. 428–34.
[26] Cmd. 6404, *Social insurance and allied services*, p. 12; W. H. Beveridge, *Full employment in a free society* (1944, 2nd edn, 1960), pp. 21–3.
[27] Chester papers, Nuffield College, box 23/2, 'Fixing rates of benefit', by D. N. Chester, 5 Jan. 1942; and 'Means Tests. Note by Mr. D. N. Chester', 8 Jan. 1942.
[28] For a full discussion of this issue, see John Veit-Wilson, 'Muddle or mendacity? The Beveridge Committee and the poverty line', *Journal of Social Policy*, 21, 3 (1992), pp. 259–301.

which was hammered out in close conjunction with Keynes and other Treasury advisers, offered full subsistence-level old age pensions only to those with at least a twenty-year record of insurance contributions – and then only when they had withdrawn from full-time work.[29] He was brusque to the point of rudeness with representatives of the old-age pensions lobby, who were pressing for a universal subsistence-level old-age pension payable at age sixty out of redistributive taxation.[30] And even for those on the full subsistence minimum, it was stressed that 'by minimum he meant minimum – no allowance for beer or tobacco or cinemas or for long train journeys or for specially high rents. Nor for waste – the minimum depended on a person making best use of the money he got.'[31]

The same notes of prudence and parsimony could be heard in many other aspects of the Beveridge Plan. Far from eroding incentives to work, the whole edifice of universal social security as envisaged in 1942 was implicitly built around the old utilitarian principle of less-eligibility – by using family allowances to maintain an incentive gap in the case of large families, and by preserving a substantial margin between benefits and wages ('the gap between income during earning and during interruption of earning should be as large as possible for every man').[32] A major economy was the decision to confine family allowances to second and further children – on the ground that support for the first child of a parent in paid employment 'may be described as wasteful and certainly [not] . . . indispensable for the abolition of poverty'.[33] It was Beveridge himself who insisted on the 'flat-rate' principle in both benefits and contributions, not merely for reasons of economy but to preserve what he believed to be the moral and civic virtue of voluntary personal saving.[34] For the long-term unemployed and for those who wilfully refused suitable jobs, benefit was to be reinforced by an extensive system of compulsory retraining and industrial discipline. Residual public assistance was to be subject to 'conditions as to behaviour . . . likely to hasten restoration of earning capacity': men and women who failed to support themselves and their families or to comply with 'reasonable just conditions'

[29] Cmd. 6404, *Social insurance and allied services*, p. 131.
[30] PRO, CAB 87/77, Social Insurance committee minutes, 20 May 1942, QQ. 2,713–816; John Macnicol, 'Beveridge and old age'; J. Hills, J. Ditch and H. Glennerster, *Beveridge and social security* (Oxford, 1994), pp. 83–93.
[31] Chester papers, box 27/1, notes on 'Social administration', 13 Apr. 1947.
[32] *Social insurance and allied services*, p. 154; John Macnicol, *The campaign for family allowances 1918–45* (1980), pp. 186–7.
[33] *Social insurance and allied services*, pp. 155–6.
[34] PRO, CAB 87/76, 'Basic problems of Social Security with heads of a scheme', by W. H. Beveridge, 11 Dec. 1941.

for the receipt of benefit were 'in the last . . . [to] be subject to penal treatment'.[35] Despite Beveridge's 'assumption of full employment', his social security budget allowed for an unemployment level of 8½ per cent, equivalent to 10 per cent under the prewar method of reckoning. Even 'assumption B' (for a universal national health service) was designed to have powerful cost-cutting overtones, since its main functions within the social security scheme were seen as the policing of improper claims and the rapid restoration of claimants to productive employment.[36] The morale-building rhetoric of the Beveridge report certainly looked forward to the abolition of poverty; and in real terms the benefits proposed (24 shillings for a single person, 40 shillings for a married couple) were higher and more comprehensive than those available under existing insurance schemes.[37] But beyond that the report conjured up a somewhat puritanical vision of the postwar world as an era of abstinence, hard work, public spirit, 'painful effort', and self-sacrifice; there would be 'no easy carefree times' ahead in the long-drawn-out process of social and industrial reconstruction.[38]

Beveridge's Plan – for 'universal' social insurance, backed up by full employment, family allowances, and a national health service financed largely from direct taxation – was published in an atmosphere of great public excitement and acclaim in December 1942. Even before its publication the report set off a series of alarm bells in official circles; and within the Treasury there was immediate criticism of Beveridge's proposed level of family allowances, and of the political impracticality of training schemes for the long-term unemployed. The plan provoked a large-scale inquiry in the Economic Section of the War Cabinet into 'estimates of the postwar income, and related taxable income . . . and whether Beveridge's proposals could be accommodated, together with other unexpected public sector demands, without an intolerable burden either on real resources or on the budget'.[39] Churchill himself declared that no commitment to large-scale social reform could be undertaken until after the war had been won; while the Chancellor of the Exchequer, Kingsley Wood, privately denounced the Plan as a dangerous threat to postwar economic recovery. Kingsley Wood's

---

[35] *Social insurance and allied services*, paras. 369 and 373.
[36] Chester papers, box 23/2, 'Notes on S.I.C.(41)20. Basic problems', 19 Jan. 1942.
[37] For both the unemployed and pensioners, non-contributory benefits available from the Assistance Board were in certain circumstances significantly *higher* than those envisaged by Beveridge.
[38] *Social insurance and allied services*, para. 447.
[39] Alex Cairncross and Nita Watts, *The Economic Section 1939–1961. A study in economic advising* (1989), p. 91.

prevarication during the parliamentary debate on the Beveridge Plan provoked widespread public suspicion that the scheme was to be pigeon-holed, and led to the setting-up of a nation-wide Social Security League that lobbied for its rapid implementation. The lurking popular misgiving that Conservative ministers were hostile to the Beveridge Plan, while Labour was enthusiastic for it, was an important strand in the leftward tide of public opinion in the later war years that was to culminate in the Labour victory of 1945.

Yet – despite certain strongly expressed views to the contrary – government archives of the period suggest that most ministers and officials ultimately came to agree with the view that the Beveridge Plan was 'the cheapest we ever had a hope of getting' and that there was nothing in it 'which need frighten a mouse'.[40] Kingsley Wood himself strongly favoured the insurance approach to social welfare (he was an old insurance expert, recruited into government from the country's largest 'approved society'), and he was well aware of Keynes's view that social insurance could both ward off wage-demands and help to broaden the tax base.[41] Churchill's closest adviser, Lord Cherwell, was impressed by the cheapness of the Beveridge scheme and convinced that it posed no financial threat to postwar industrial reconstruction.[42] The Ministry of Information seized upon the Plan as a classic example of British 'social invention' and 'social dynamism', embodying 'joint participation by citizen and state and [avoiding] the conception of a mere "Santa Claus" state doling out benefits to a passive citizenry'.[43] Within the Conservative party a secret committee under Ralph Assheton denounced the Plan as dangerously expensive; but many other Conservatives welcomed universal insurance as an institutional embodiment of thrift and of one-nation Toryism.[44] The official committee of permanent civil servants under Sir Thomas Phillips which reviewed the Plan on behalf of the Whitehall social policy departments reported in

[40] *JMK*, XXVII, pp. 256–61 and 263.
[41] PRO, CAB 87/12, War Cabinet Committee on Reconstruction Priorities, minutes, 28 Jan. – 17 May 1943; *JMK*, XXVII, pp. 226–30.
[42] Cherwell papers, Off.42.1, 'Economic effects of the Beveridge Plan', 22 Jan. 1942; this was an almost verbatim reproduction of a paper of the same title by Cherwell's economic assistant, Tom Wilson (Chester papers, 24/5).
[43] Chester papers, 24/2, Overseas Planning Committee, 'Report of Beveridge Committee on Social Services. Treatment in overseas propaganda', 23 Nov. 1942.
[44] Conservative Party archive, CRD 2/28/6, 'Beveridge Report Committee: note by the Chairman', 17 Dec. 1942; Woolton papers, Bodleian Library, 16, ff.9–10, R. A. Butler to Lord Woolton, 13 Sept. 1944, and f.196, 'Memorandum on postwar policy of Conservative Party', n.d.; Hugh Molson, The Tory Reform committee', *New English Review* (1945), pp. 245–52.

rather disparaging and grudging terms; but beneath the committee's ungracious and curmudgeonly tone lay almost total acceptance of Beveridge's substantive proposals – the only major issue of dissent being a refusal to recommend public commitment to the principle of subsistence.[45] The Phillips committee was followed by a further multi-departmental committee under Thomas Sheepshanks that produced a series of white papers on social insurance, family allowances, and the setting-up of a national health service – all of which indicated serious government commitment to Beveridgean reforms well before the end of the war.

III

Whence then came the suspicion that the Beveridge Plan was viewed by the coalition government as a blueprint for gross financial extravagance, on a scale that threatened the prospects of economic recovery? And, conversely, whence came the widespread popular impression (feared by some, welcomed by many) that the Plan promised large-scale fiscal redistribution and social levelling? The answers to these two questions to a certain extent overlap with each other. Both archive sources and the private recollections of those who worked in Whitehall at the time suggest that the most crucial ministerial objections to the Beveridge Plan (shared by some Labour ministers as well as Conservatives) were political, constitutional, rhetorical, and personal rather than economic and financial. Beveridge was not an effective operator within the inner circles of government, but he was a brilliant publicist and performer in the mass media. He was convinced that social security could give a mass sense of purpose to the war against Hitler; and he was convinced also that, if the history of the 1920s was not to repeat itself, the new system had to be ready *before* the war came to an end. With these aims in view he had relentlessly promoted his proposals through press, radio, pamphleteering, and public meetings for well over a year before his report was finally published – as he continued to do, in the USA as well as in Britain, throughout the rest of the war.[46] This media campaign

---

[45] PRO, PIN 8/85, Report of the Official Committee on the Beveridge report, 1943. Supporters of Beveridge in Whitehall were clearly surprised, in view of the hostile atmosphere in which this review committee had been set up, that the end result was so favourable (Piercy papers, British Library of Political Science, 8/22/D119 Soc, 'Official Committee on Beveridge Report', by D. N. Chester, 20 Jan. 1943; 'Papers on the Beveridge Report', by E. F. M. Durbin for the deputy Prime Minister, 5 Feb. 1943; and paper on 'Report of the Official Committee on the Beveridge Report', n.d., probably by Durbin).

[46] See Harris, *Beveridge*, pp. 421ff.

was perceived in government as driven by Beveridge's overweening personal ambition, and there can be no doubt that he believed himself to be more competent than many in power. But his prime objective, apart from morale-boosting, was to compel government not to repeat the fiasco of 1919 to 1921, by leaving the planning of postwar social security until it was all too late.

It was this media campaign, rather than the actual text of the Beveridge Report itself, that generated great expectations amongst an anxious, tax-burdened, and war-weary public.[47] But among Whitehall officials and orthodox constitutionalists the social security campaign aroused exactly the same kind of distaste and suspicion as had been evoked by Gladstone's rhetoric from railway trains half a century earlier – a suspicion made worse by the fact that in Beveridge's case he had no formal place in government and was not even an MP.[48] To ministers and officials of all political complexions it seemed improper and intolerable that major public decisions, even of an eminently modest and well-costed kind, should be precipitately forced upon government via press and radio rather than through the normal channels of high policy.[49] Within the Treasury (already smarting under its wartime loss of control over spending departments) it was regarded as particularly offensive that Beveridge should have called his financial proposals 'the Social Security Budget';[50] while within the Economic section of the War Cabinet it seemed that Beveridge's full employment proposals were trying to precipitate premature public commitment on a subject where expert opinion was deeply divided, and about which Beveridge himself knew very little.[51] The two men most directly concerned with translating Beveridge's insurance proposals into administrative action – Thomas Phillips and Thomas Sheepshanks – both disliked Beveridge personally and strongly resented his attempts to tell them how to do their job through the medium of the British and American

[47] Mass Observation archive, Beveridge Social Services Survey, Box 1, File F. *passim*.
[48] The comparison with Gladstone was explicitly made by widespread reference to Beveridge in the press as 'the people's William'.
[49] On the practical difficulties stemming from what was felt to be an overhasty commitment to universalist social reform, see D. N. Chester's paper for the Lord President of the Council, Clement Attlee, 'Old age and widows' pensions', 4 March 1943 (Chester papers, 24/2); and ibid., 27/2, 'Social insurance and assistance', n.d. (mid-1944).
[50] *JMK*, XXVII, p. 228. Throughout the war there were comments in Whitehall about Treasury officials artificially 'trying to create an atmosphere of tremendous difficulty' and being more than usually 'niggling and pernickety' in an effort to bolster their weakened hold over other departments (PRO, T.230/100, D. N. Chester to Lionel Robbins, 17 Oct. 1941, and D. N. Chester to Norman Brook, 22 Oct. 1941).
[51] PRO, CAB 123/43, Lionel Robbins to Sir John Anderson, 14 Jan. 1943.

press.[52] Among Labour ministers there was much irritation that Beveridge seemed to be demanding that 'the war ought to stop while his plan was put into effect . . . he seemed to imagine that he was going to be a leader of the nation or of the House of Commons'.[53]

A less explicit but no less important factor in some quarters was the suspicion that, far from being a well-meaning reformist liberal, Beveridge was at heart a thoroughgoing administrative authoritarian whose ultimate political ideal was not the universal friendly society but state coercion and 'the *ne plus ultra* of bureaucratic State planning'.[54] From such a perspective his crime was not that he connived at extravagance and inflation, but that he sought to abolish inflation by bureaucratic fiat ('As long as inflationary tendencies exist in the aftermath of war, war-time controls must be maintained').[55] There was almost no public sympathy for the view expressed by a handful of right-wing libertarians that the Social Insurance Plan constituted a veiled threat to personal freedom; but nevertheless Beveridge did not advance his popularity in government circles by sharing platforms with those who claimed that 'in a sheerly realistic sense, the Russian peoples are a great deal more free than we are'.[56] Moreover, not all contributors to the reconstruction debate, including many supporters of the Social Security League, were as austere and reticent in their budgetary calculations as Beveridge and Keynes. From the start of the war there were fears among fiscal conservatives that 'the intelligentsia of Whitehall and the City can . . . be observed whispering in corners that there may be something to be said for a spot of inflation'.[57] Among the younger and more radical economists in Whitehall there were some like James Meade who argued that contributory insurance was an outdated fiction which should be replaced by 'a general charge on public revenue'.[58] There were some reconstruction

---

[52] On the hostility of Sheepshanks, see Chester papers, 24/2, D. N. Chester to T. H. Sheepshanks, 30 Mar. 1943, and 24/3, S. C. Leslie to T. H. Sheepshanks, 11 May 1944; on Beveridge's poor relations with Sir Thomas Phillips, see Harris, *Beveridge*, pp. 374–5.

[53] Francis Williams, *A Prime Minister remembers* (1961), p. 57; Dalton papers, diary, vol. 28, Feb. 1943.   [54] Attlee papers, dep. 13, ff. 152–3, copy of article by A. J. Nock.

[55] Beveridge, *Full employment in a free society*, p. 338.

[56] G. D. H. Cole, 'Plan for living' in Fabian Society, *Plan for Britain* (1943), pp. 11. Beveridge's own contribution to this series of lectures, 'Freedom from idleness', was the most outspoken expression of his mid-war view that, as an economic though not as a political system, western liberal capitalism had come to an end.

[57] Clay papers, C9/19, 'Sterling, exports and the vicious spiral', by H. D. Henderson, 17 Jan. 1940. This remark was directed against reckless young Keynesians, but Henderson's perception was exactly shared by Keynes himself (*JMK*, XXII, p. 120).

[58] PRO, T.230/100, J. E. Meade to D. N. Chester, 15 June 1941. This was a view with which in theory Keynes himself agreed, though he thought it, at least in the short term, politically and administratively impractical (*JMK*, XXVII, pp. 223–8).

theorists who thought that not just the war but the costs of future social reform should be financed by a 'Grand once-for-all capital levy' – or by a shift to large-scale state-ownership of property, income from which would ultimately make taxes on individuals redundant.[59] And there were certain Keynesian young Turks on the fringes of Whitehall who hinted that in the postwar period budgetary constraints would have ceased to be a serious problem, because public debt could always be cancelled out by devaluation or the printing of money.[60] This latter line of argument was very far from finding acceptance within the centre of government at any time between 1939 and 1945; but it contributed to an atmosphere of unease about fiscal extravagance that was to link the welfare state – quite contrary to the intentions of it major founders – to reckless inflation and visions of Utopia.

IV

As mentioned above, large parts of the Beveridge Plan were accepted by the wartime Coalition Government before 1945; and the White Paper on 'Full Employment' of 1944 signalled at least partial Treasury acceptance of Keynesian ideas about demand management. The Family Allowances Act, which authorised weekly payments of five shillings to the mothers of second and further children, was passed with all-party support early in 1945. As is well known, with certain modifications of detail the Beveridge Plan formed the basis of the postwar Labour government's national insurance, national health, industrial injuries, and public assistance legislation of 1946 to 1948. This legislation, which was carried through in the teeth of the financial tornado that hit the British economy after the ending of the American Lend-Lease programme, has been portrayed in recent years as a damaging burden on postwar economic recovery – a burden which creamed off resources that might have gone into industrial investment, and that fatally fuelled the public debt. Yet by postwar European standards it was a relatively modest programme; and though for the first two years it was accompanied by an ambitious regime of low interest rates and monetary expansion there is little evidence to suggest that this regime was impelled by provision of the new social services. Indeed quite the contrary appears to have been

---

[59] Douglas Jay, *Who is to pay for the war and the peace?* (1941), p. 51; *JMK*, XXVII, pp. 213–14 (J. E. Meade to J. M. Keynes, 25 June 1942).
[60] Views ascribed to Joan Robinson and E. F. Schumacher, though whether this was quite what they meant seems doubtful (*Full employment in a free society*, appendix B; Susan Howson, *British monetary policy 1945–51* (Oxford, 1993, pp. 89–90)).

true: as Jim Tomlinson has persuasively argued, Labour's welfare spending in this period was consistently subordinate to the defence of sterling and maintenance of domestic and overseas investment; and (as Keynes had long envisaged) social policy played an important role in defusing inflationary pressures at a time of unprecedented peacetime shortage of manpower.[61] Even in Treasury circles there was some feeling in the postwar years that social services were affordable, that social security was a useful tool with which to stabilise demand, and that 'the maintenance of the better health, fitness, and working capacity throughout the working population as a result of the new insurance schemes is bound greatly to enhance the productive power of the nation'.[62] The most unexpectedly expensive of the new services was the National Health Service, but even here research in the early 1950s found that health spending in Britain was conspicuously lower than in many other industrialised countries – and arguably no higher than the exponential cost of equivalent services in 1939.[63] Some at least of the conservative and libertarian critique of Labour's social policies in the postwar period complained that the level of spending – particularly on housing, hospitals, and education – was not too high but too low (certainly by comparison with what might have been attainable through the voluntary sector and the market).[64] Throughout the 1950s there were periodic attempts to cure balance of payments crises by cuts in social welfare; but mainstream economic theory of the period blamed wage-push rather than welfare-spending for continuous inflation (a not unreasonable view, seeing that the percentage of GDP going to social services remained more or less static throughout the decade). It was not until the 1960s – when social policy had become a much more important tool of socio-economic engineering – that welfare spending began to grow significantly faster than national income.[65]

Why then have recent attacks on the welfare state as the *locus classicus* of British economic decline focused on the era of Beveridge, Keynes, and postwar reconstruction, rather than upon the apparently more free-

---

[61] Jim Tomlinson, 'Welfare and the economy: the economic impact of the welfare state, 1945–1951', *20th Century British History*, 6, 2 (1995), pp. 194–219.

[62] Attlee papers, 31, ff. 9–10, D. P. T. J[ay] to Clement Attlee, 4 Feb. 1946; ff. 12–13, Sir Bernard Gilbert on the 'National Insurance Bill'; f. 14, note by the Economic Section on 'Economic effects of national insurance'.

[63] *Report of the Committee of Enquiry into the cost of the National Health Service* (Cmnd. 9663, 1956), pp. 286–9.

[64] Cecil Palmer, *The British Socialist ill-fare state* (1952); John Jewkes, *The genesis of the British Health Service* (1961).

[65] Brian Abel-Smith, 'Public expenditure on the social services', Social Trends, 1 (1970), p. 19; Rodney Lowe, *The welfare state in Britain since 1945* (1993), pp. 336–7.

spending and inflationary era of Crossman and Crosland, Peter Townsend and Richard Titmuss, Noel Barber and Edward Heath? Why have a series of measures designed to buttress sound money, personal saving, hard-work, family solidarity, and very limited personal consumption been portrayed by historians as doing exactly the opposite? The full impact of the social policies of the 1960s lies outside the scope of this paper, but the question of correctly identifying the dominant policies of the 1940s calls for further comment. One part of the answer has already been suggested above: that the reconstruction movement was carried along upon a great tide of populist debate and democratic persuasion which promised something very much more open-handed and grandiose than the austere proposals of the Beveridge Plan and of *How to pay for the war*. This led many at the time and has led many ever since to mistake the early welfare state's true character (hence the somewhat barbed buffoonery of A. P. Herbert at Beveridge's wedding feast!). Another significant factor was that both Beveridge and Keynes were surrounded by groups of disciples who developed their ideas in directions very different from those envisaged by their masters; and certainly the expansionist social reform movements of the 1960s were full of *éminences grises* who had contributed energetically to the lower ranks of the reconstruction movement in the 1940s.

A further point that may be conceded is that, despite their overriding concern with budgetary purity, there were certain financial fault-lines concealed within the social policies of Beveridge and Keynes themselves; fault-lines that stemmed partly from their own personal perspectives, partly from the very narrow room for manoeuvre in the circumstances of the wartime era. Keynes's determination to use insurance as a device to counteract inflation was concentrated overwhelmingly upon the wartime and postwar years; he was happy in 1942 to unload part of the additional cost of pensions onto a date twenty years' hence, on the ground that 'the future can well be left to look after itself' (a manifestation perhaps of that enigmatic 'childless vision' about which so much has been written).[66] Beveridge was much more apprehensive than Keynes about the long-term inflationary impact of a rapidly ageing population; but he was constrained from fully addressing this problem by his absolute commitment to flat-rate contributions – and by the belief that wartime controls over both money and labour would continue indefinitely into the era of peace. Nor was it addressed by the 1944 National Insurance white paper, which (under conflicting pres-

[66] Beveridge Papers, IXa, 37(1), Keynes to Beveridge, 17 Mar. 1942.

sure from Treasury parsimony and the demands of current pensioners) proposed a single standard pension payable from the start of the new insurance scheme regardless of contribution record – but at a rate substantially lower than prevailing definitions of subsistence.[67] The authors of the white paper tacitly acknowledged that this meant the indefinite survival of non-contributory welfare provision, not in the residual form envisaged by Beveridge, but 'as a kind of universal poultice to cover the spots, all over the social system, where social security benefits will be inadequate'.[68] The result was that, even in the 'classic' era of the welfare state, pensions were under-funded, public assistance expanded rather than contracted, and – by comparison with similar European schemes – British social security was over-reliant on subsidies from direct taxation.[69] This reliance was actively encouraged by certain voices within the Treasury, where it was felt that too much funding mortgaged the future and limited the autonomy of Treasury control.[70] Thus, paradoxically, there was a sense in which the rigid economy of the reforms of the 1940s sowed the seeds of future financial problems – either by refusing to plan for the long term, or by harbouring over-optimistic expectations about the willingness of later cohorts of taxpayers to pick up an inherited bill.[71]

Perhaps the most important elements, however, in transforming the relationship of welfare to the wider industrial economy were simply the fading of social memory and the long-term postwar transformation in political and popular culture. A slightly curious feature of the wartime reconstruction movement was that, although people involved in it constantly talked about their visions of the future, they also wrote and spoke as though the heroic moment of war emergency – with its low material expectations and heightened acceptance of an ethic of communal sharing – would somehow last forever. Although there was some anxiety that peace might bring a revival

[67] Immediate payment of full pensions seems to have been offered as a placebo for rejecting the principle of subsistence. But as D. N. Chester pointed out, the compromise was significantly more expensive than Beveridge's proposals, and made nonsense of Treasury complaints about Beveridge's 'extravagance' (Piercy papers, 8/22, 'Progress of discussion on Beveridge Report', by E. F. M. Durbin, 5 Aug. 1943; D. N. Chester papers, 24/2, 'Old age pensions', 13 May 1944: *JMK*, XXVII, pp. 261–3).

[68] Piercy papers, 8/22, paper on 'Social insurance and allied services', n.d. (Jan. 1944).

[69] Peter Flora (ed.), *State, economy and society in Western Europe, 1815–1975. Vol. I. The growth of mass democracies and welfare states* (Frankfurt, 1883) pp. 462–551.

[70] Henderson Papers, 'The principles of the Beveridge Plan', 4 Aug. 1942, and 'Draft memorandum on the Social Security Plan', 22 Dec. 1942; Chester papers, 24/3, D. N. Chester to Muriel Ritson, 3 Feb. 1944.

[71] This was presciently predicted by some commentators at the time (e.g. Chester papers, 24/2, 'Second thoughts on Beveridge', memorandum by P.E.P., 29 Mar. 1943; 24/5, 'Old age pensions', by D. N. Chester, n.d. [early 1944]).

of 'profiteering', there was little anticipation among reconstruction enthu-
siasts that the mass of working people might grow tired of austerity and
regulation after the end of the war – or that state intervention in employment and social security might in itself generate changes in popular
expectations and habits. Beveridge himself referred uneasily in his Plan to
the problem of dealing with 'new classes not hitherto accustomed to industrial discipline', but concluded that this problem would largely resolve itself
through the spread of a sense of 'social security' and through the new public
ethic of citizen solidarity.[72] As we have seen, the hope that higher welfare
benefits would restrain wage-demands was a major feature of wartime social
security reform; but the possibility that in certain circumstances higher
benefits might actually accelerate wage-demands (on the ground that
workers would be 'better off on the dole') never crossed anyone's mind.
Despite the numerous poverty surveys of the interwar and early war years
there was still a very strong assumption in the 1940s that the concept of
poverty was scientific and static, rather than cultural and dynamic, and that
it could therefore be 'cured' for all time by a precisely calculated dose of
'subsistence minimum'. This is not to deny that a more relativist notion of
poverty had been emerging over many years in the surveys of Seebohm
Rowntree, who was Beveridge's chief source of information on the content
and definition of subsistence. But the data collected by Rowntree and the
other nutritionists who advised the Beveridge committee was overwhelmingly physiological in character; and Rowntree's conception of the requirements of human life beyond mere physical survival was a great deal
narrower even than the austere vision of Beveridge. There was no real fore-
shadowing here of the much more ambitious definitions of poverty that
were to emerge in the 1960s.[73] Moreover, there was no anticipation of the
fact that 'prosperity' might in itself generate 'poverty', by setting new standards of consumer comparison. Likewise there was almost no conception
in any wartime writing that easier access to welfare goods might over the
course of time transform their nature – that, for instance, 'health' might
cease to be a mere functional prerequisite of paid employment, and become
a major consumer good in its own right.[74] All these assumptions were to be
confounded, overturned, or drastically modified over the course of the
postwar decades, as citizens learnt to take for granted – and adapt their

---

[72] *Social insurance and allied services* (1942), paras. 130–1, 458–60.
[73] See, e.g., the physiological and dietary statistics in Chester papers, 22/5.
[74] Though there was a passing hint of this in a memorandum from Keynes to Sir Richard
Hopkins (*JMK*, XXVII, p. 249).

behaviour to – the culture of social security. If, therefore, the 'welfare state' has indeed been a cause of economic and moral decline (rather than an index and victim of such decline), then the case for the prosecution should shift away from the austere and orthodox 1940s, towards the much more ambitious, complex, consumerist, and libertarian welfare regimes of a later generation.

9

1945–1951: years of recovery or a stage in economic decline?

BERNARD ALFORD

There is, perhaps, something peculiarly British about the fact that widespread concern that the country was suffering economic decline should have arisen during the period since the Second World War while its economic performance exceeded the previous record by a significant margin. But it was, also, a period during which expectation sat in the air and the atmosphere increasingly became charged with a new form of national rivalry, popularly known as growthmanship. For nations as for individuals, it seems, prosperity or poverty are felt more as relative than as absolute conditions. Thus, concern in Britain rose to new levels from the late 1960s onwards as country after country came to match then, worse, to pass British levels of income per head.

Explanations of Britain's postwar economic performance have proliferated and, not surprisingly, the immediate postwar period has attracted particular attention. Most commonly, this period has been portrayed either as one of success in which those directing the economy achieved as much as could be expected, so that the explanation of any subsequent shortcomings in economic performance has to be sought elsewhere, or as one in which those in power sacrificed fundamental and longer-term economic needs to the teachings of the prophets of the New Jerusalem of the welfare state.[1] Parallel to these conflicting interpretations is another currently fashionable one which seeks to explain Britain's economic performance more directly in comparative international terms. Britain, it is claimed, did not benefit from the circumstances of postwar economic recovery in the way that other western European countries and Japan were able to do. For the latter, the events of the war, ending in ignominious defeat, acted as a profound shock

---

[1] In the former respect see A. K. Cairncross, *Years of recovery. British economic policy 1945–51* (1985); K. O. Morgan, *Labour in power, 1945–1951* (Oxford, 1984); K. O. Morgan, *The people's peace. British history 1945–1989* (Oxford, 1990). On the latter see C. Barnett, *The audit of war: the illusion and reality of Britain as a great nation* (1986); C. Barnett, *The lost victory. British dreams, British realities 1945–1950* (1995).

that helped to precipitate radical political and economic change which was central to what is defined as the process of catch-up and convergence.[2] Inexorably, the wide economic gap that existed at the end of the war between these countries and the USA, and to a lesser degree Britain, was closed. For Britain this resulted ultimately in a reversal of positions such that, by the 1970s, it had become a follower economy. But far from everything being lost, Britain, it is claimed, was now placed in a position from which, potentially, it could benefit from the process of catching up. For present purposes, however, the important point is that whilst this analysis accords the circumstances of the period a central role in this process, it is the economic shock effect that is crucial, rather than the specific events; and, so it is argued, such an effect can occur in other ways as, for example, with the oil price rises of the 1970s. For Britain, therefore, the experience of the postwar period is seen as part of the rhythm of swings and roundabouts of economic growth among the advanced economies in the latter half of the twentieth century, and not as something which cast Britain down into a position of long-term disadvantage.

These three major interpretations of Britain's economic performance under the two postwar Labour Governments form the framework for the analysis which follows. We shall attempt to show that none of them is convincing. That, whilst measurable economic performance between 1945 and 1951 could not have been much improved upon because of the sheer physical limitations, this is a very narrow basis on which to base judgement.[3] That in critical areas of policy the postwar Labour Governments contributed in a major way to reinforcing existing barriers to economic performance; and with the advantage of hindsight it is clear that, over the longer term, this contributed in a major way to Britain's relative economic decline.

---

[2] For a broad coverage of the literature see M. Abramovitz, 'Catching up, forging ahead and falling behind', *Journal of Economic History*, 46 (1986), pp. 385–406; B. W. E. Alford, 'British economic performance in the European perspective – A case of catch-up and convergence?', in C. A. Wurm (ed.), *Wege Nach Europa. Wirtschaft und Aussenpolitik Grossbritanniens in 20. Jahrhundert* (Bochum, 1992), pp. 17–30; S. N. Broadberry, 'Manufacturing and the convergence hypothesis: what the long-run data show', *Journal of Economic History*, 53 (1993), pp. 772–95; C. Feinstein, 'Benefits of backwardness and costs of continuity' in A. Graham and A. Seldon, *Government and economics in the postwar world: economic policies and comparative performance 1945–85* (1990).

[3] For an account that places great emphasis on the physical constraints to recovery see A. Robinson, 'The economic problems of transition from war to peace: 1945–49', *Cambridge Journal of Economics*, 10 (1986), pp. 165–85.

I

Those historians who place emphasis on the success of economic recovery between 1945 and 1951 do so after making full allowance for a number of crises and problems, largely external in origin, which, it is claimed, would have engulfed any government of the period. The key issues are the 1947 convertibility crisis, the yawning trade deficit, devaluation, and the intense administrative pressure on ministers and senior civil servants. It is by no means clear, however, that these exigencies were entirely independent of government action.

So far as the 1947 crisis is concerned, there was no obvious alternative way of dealing with it than the one adopted. Britain simply did not possess the capacity to sustain the convertibility of sterling against the dollar. But there is a major sense in which the crisis was of its own making. The position which Britain had taken in the negotiations that produced the postwar financial settlement was based on two preconceptions: that it would continue to play a major international role and that Europe should be kept firmly at arm's length. Responsibility for a reserve currency was seen as a necessary element of the wider role of leader and primary defender of a far-flung Commonwealth and empire.[4] The 1944 Bretton Woods agreement and the associated policy on the sterling area, not only set Britain on the path to the convertibility crisis but, just as directly, on the path to successive exchange rate and balance of payments crises in the decades that were to follow. The extent of commitment to this policy was reflected in the scale of the armed forces. The total strength amounted to 940,000 as late as 1948 and was still 790,000 in 1949; and all the while there was a shortage of labour on the domestic front.[5] Yet the commitment to an international role went even deeper than the public, Parliament, and most of the cabinet were aware of. Attlee and Bevin decided, virtually in secret, to commit resources to the development of nuclear weapons. In particular, 'Bevin insisted that

---

[4] The issues and events are well covered by R. N. Gardner, *Sterling–dollar diplomacy* (New York, 1969 edn); W. R. Louis, *Imperialism at bay 1941–1945: the United States and the decolonisation of the British Empire* (Oxford, 1977); L. S. Pressnell, *External economic policy since the war*. Volume I. *The postwar financial settlement* (1986); S. Stange, *Sterling and British policy* (Oxford, 1971); A. Van Dormael, *Bretton Woods: birth of a monetary system* (1978).

[5] See A. Bullock, *Ernest Bevin, Foreign Secretary 1945–51* (Oxford, 1985), pp. 233–4, 239–41, 244, 322–3, 330, 354, 522–4, 581–2 for Bevin's firm views on defence. Bullock's justification of Bevin's policy is considered below. For Attlee's views see PRO, CAB 21/2216, CM (47)9, 17 Jan. 1947. Cairncross, *Years of recovery*, pp. 385–99. The numbers for the armed forces are slightly variable between different sources mainly because of personnel on release but not yet in employment.

it would be politically dangerous to leave the United States with a monopoly of atomic weapons, and Attlee shared this view to the full.'[6] The continuing commitment to defence on a world scale is borne out by the fact that one of the last acts of the second postwar Labour Government was to agree to increased defence expenditure, with the result that by 1951 defence accounted for 20 per cent of total public expenditure or 7.6 per cent of GDP, and was higher than the corresponding figure (5.1 per cent in 1950) for the USA. Britain had firmly set its frontiers 'on the Himalayas'.[7]

The existence of large sterling balances and the obligations they imposed on Britain, especially to poor countries such as Egypt and India, clearly presented a problem under any circumstances. But the situation became critical only when those balances were allowed to become, in effect, an integral part of the mechanism for maintaining a fixed exchange rate for sterling under conditions of convertibility. Against this the government and the Bank of England were fully committed to maintaining sterling as an international currency, albeit necessarily as a second reserve to the almighty dollar. Thus from their standpoint any solution to the problem of the sterling balances could not be allowed to threaten the primary international financial role. Yet any kind of refinancing of the balances would necessarily involve the USA and, indeed, such schemes were being actively canvassed by US officials at that time. But these schemes came with conditions that were unacceptable to Britain since, one way or another, they involved conceding to US pressure to become more closely tied to continental Europe. The government's general position on this aspect of foreign policy was encapsulated by Bevin when he declared that Britain was not 'just another European country'.[8]

Britain's external financial position in 1946 was unsustainable. The irony is that the terms of the 1945 American loan which Britain had negotiated to finance what Keynes had calculated as its interim dollar deficit,

[6] See Morgan, *Labour in power*, p. 284, where Lord Zuckerman's opinion is affirmed that 'Attlee's decision to develop British nuclear weapons was taken solely to boost the nation's political power'.

[7] Based on R. Middleton, *Government versus the market. The growth of the public sector, economic management and British economic performance c. 1890–1979* (Cheltenham, 1996), pp. 91, 615. The confident allusion was made by Harold Wilson in the late 1960s.

[8] Bevin made the comment to the US under-secretary of state in June 1947, cited by A. S. Milward, *The European rescue of the nation-state* (1992), p. 354, n. 14. For more detail of Bevin's views see Bullock, Ernest Bevin, *passim*. It is clear that Bevin's anti-Europeanism was coloured by the fact that pro-European views in his own party were associated with figures of the Left, such as Laski, whom Bevin regarded as anathema.

precipitated the collapse of sterling.[9] The period during which sterling/dollar convertibility had to be achieved was radically shortened from the initial provision of five years to just one year. Convertibility was duly introduced in July 1947. The outcome has been well chronicled. Within a month Britain's dollar reserves evaporated and convertibility had to be suspended. The events of the summer of 1947 created a situation in which the issue of sterling once again became a matter of choice for Britain. There could hardly have been clearer or more dramatic proof of Britain's financial weakness.[10] Subsequent events resulted in a double irony, however. Whereas the collapse of sterling might have been expected to force Britain to bow to growing US pressure to revise the international role of the currency in association with a changed relationship with Europe, the growing threat of Communism from the East intervened and caused a rapid volte face in US foreign policy. Extensive financial assistance was provided to western Europe through the European Economic Recovery Programme (Marshall Aid). Sterling was patched up and allowed to soldier on. The Labour Government did not alter course. The commitment to sterling was deep. The reaction was determined. The exhortation was the 'Export Drive'.

The sponsoring department of the campaign was the Board of Trade under the near messianic leadership of Stafford Cripps. In broad terms, trade performance between 1947 and 1951 was impressive. Imports rose from an index of 100 to 125 whereas exports increased from 100 to 164. Moreover, the position was even more satisfactory than contemporaries were aware of because recording errors had led to an overestimate of the current account deficit by approximately 44 per cent in 1947.[11] But when these results are examined more closely the outcome is revealed as far less impressive. The growth of exports was largely the result of a general expansion of world trade, in part facilitated by the improved liquidity provided by Marshall Aid. Furthermore, British manufacturers faced a sellers' market in conditions of postwar recovery and reconstruction because their productive capacity, especially for basic consumer and capital goods, had survived the war more intact than that of their European competitors. At best the export drive was little more than an exercise in political rhetoric;

---

[9] Keynes's calculations led him to what proved to be a very optimistic view of Britain's postwar dollar balance – J. M. Keynes, 'The balance of payments of the US', *Economic Journal*, 56 (1946), pp. 172–87.

[10] First-hand evidence of the shock is provided by Robinson, 'The economic problems of the transition', pp. 171–4.   [11] Cairncross, *Years of recovery*, p. 154.

at worst it amounted to misplaced effort.[12] Far more serious, however, was the manner in which these conditions reinforced the traditional composition and direction of British trade, with the emphasis on the old staple industries and dependence on soft currency markets, in particular the white dominions, which accounted for nearly a quarter of visible exports in 1948.[13]

After a difficult postwar start, the export performance of the western European countries began to improve rapidly, based mainly on intra-European trade. Germany, in particular, began to recover its capacity for meeting European demands for the most advanced and new types of capital goods, which were beyond Britain's ability to supply. The critical turning point came during 1949 when the faster rate of growth of intra-European trade in comparison with British/world trade not only began to reverse the tables but also revealed the comparative ease with which the western European economies could cope with the recession in trade emanating from the USA; for Britain this set-back precipitated yet another balance of payments and exchange rate crisis.[14] In mitigation of the weaknesses of the quality of Britain's trade performance, it might be argued that it faced a dilemma in export markets in that any attempt to switch from soft to hard currency areas would have led to the former seeking imports from the latter, thus causing a drain on the sterling area dollar pool. But this is only another way of demonstrating the vulnerability that Britain had imposed on itself by choosing to operate a reserve currency. By late 1949, therefore, the nature of British trade, despite its recovery, had already severely reduced Britain's capacity to influence the form and direction of western European economic development. One leading commentator has gone so far as to state that the loss of capacity was already complete.[15]

The relationship with Europe was seen by the Labour Government in totally different terms from the commercial reality. Throughout the period the government continued to resist pressure from the USA to play a leading role in European reconstruction despite the opportunity it offered between 1947 and 1949. It was, no doubt, a measure of Bevin's skill and forcefulness, as his biographer emphasises, that he was able to cement the Atlantic alliance between western Europe and the USA, whilst maintaining an

[12] See for example A. Maizels, *Industrial growth and world trade* (Cambridge, 1963), pp. 200–1. A. S. Milward, *The reconstruction of Western Europe 1945–51* (1984), pp. 335–61, provides an excellent comparative analysis of British and western European trade performance that has direct bearing on this point.
[13] R. E. Rowthorn and J. R. Wells, *De-industrialization and foreign trade* (Cambridge, 1987), p. 185.   [14] Milward, *The reconstruction of Western Europe*, p. 339.   [15] Ibid.

independent international position for Britain 'that frequently exasperated the Americans to the point of angry protest'.[16] Further, it is claimed that Bevin's policy kept open options for change for future governments, especially for Britain's relationship with western Europe.[17] As a defence of Bevin's position we do not find these arguments convincing. Whilst Bevin was central to relations between Europe and the USA and exercised strong influence on the form of the Atlantic alliance, the fact remains that the fundamental change in US policy towards Europe was made in its own interests and was marked by the introduction of the Marshall Aid programme. This was a defining point for Britain's standing in the world and it is hard to see how Bevin's foreign policy recognised this fact.

So far as policy options are concerned, the nature of the international political and financial commitments Britain entered into created enormous obstacles to any future attempts to extricate itself from them. 1949 was the pivotal year in this respect, as has been noted. Britain's continued detachment from Europe facilitated French aims to build European political and economic development on a Franco-German axis.[18] Furthermore, the claim that the emerging Schuman plan did not fit British and Commonwealth interests entirely begs the question of how those interests are defined.[19] The false assumption was that Britain's international posture could be supported by rising levels of prosperity. There was no real questioning in official circles of whether the two elements might be in direct conflict. The effective exclusion of Britain from the region of fastest trade growth was not even seen as a competitive threat let alone as a fundamental political issue. It can at least be said in their defence that in their attitude to Europe Bevin and other senior ministers were no less percipient than a long line of leading British politicians who came after them.[20]

The government's reaction to the 1947 convertibility crisis was later matched by its handling of the devaluation of sterling in 1949, from $4.02 to $2.80.[21] Intense pressure in the financial markets made the devaluation

---

[16] Bullock, *Ernest Bevin*, p. 841 and more generally pp. 839–48.
[17] Ibid., pp. 783–4.
[18] Milward, *The European rescue of the nation-state*, pp. 345–433.
[19] Morgan, *Labour in power*, p. 398, goes so far as to state that 'the anti-Europeanism . . . of the Cripps' era was a practical imperative'.
[20] See for example Roy Jenkins's characterisation of the imperial commitments of George Brown, Denis Healey, and the Chiefs of Staff in 1967 as worthy of Jo Chamberlain, Kitchener, and Curzon – 'although it would be difficult to allocate the analogues', cited by Middleton, *Government versus the market*, pp. 534–5 from R. Jenkins, *Life at the centre* (1991), pp. 224–5.
[21] For an account of the events see A. Cairncross and B. Eichengreen, *Sterling in decline. The devaluations of 1931, 1949 and 1967* (Oxford, 1983), pp. 111–55.

unavoidable, though it was more a matter of the undervaluation of the dollar than the weakness of sterling, as most other countries followed suit in discriminating against the dollar; and the 30 per cent devaluation was reduced to 9 per cent when calculated on a trade-weighted basis. It was, nevertheless, a severe blow to the international standing of sterling, which is why for a while it was strongly resisted by senior ministers and officials. Sir Stafford Cripps, as Chancellor of the Exchequer, was the principal minister involved, and he did not remove his resistance to the devaluation until the last minute and then only with great reluctance and some detachment from the three junior ministers who finally took the initiative. The main reason for Cripps's attitude would appear to have been his conviction that devaluation was 'an act of foreign policy quite as much as economic policy'. In his opposition he was fully supported by Attlee and Bevin. This combination of ministerial opposition and dithering significantly reduced the potential trade advantage from the devaluation, since traders and speculators sold increasing quantities of sterling forward as it became quite clear to them that sterling could not hold its parity against the dollar. It is difficult, moreover, to square these events with the judgement that Cripps created an 'economic transformation . . . at the Treasury and was the real architect of the rapidly improving economic picture and growing affluence from 1952 onwards'.[22] More immediately, senior ministers and officials came to regard the devaluation as a necessary technical adjustment that in no way amounted to a surrender of the principle of sterling's international financial role.

As we have indicated, for a number of commentators on this period the convertibility crisis, the export drive, and devaluation were the peak events in conditions under which ministers and civil servants were subjected to intense and exhausting pressures. Allied to this view is the judgement that there is no evidence that civil servants attempted to obstruct government intentions in any serious respect.[23] That the pressures were great cannot be

---

[22] Morgan, *Labour in power*, p. 408. Among other things, the highly favourable assessment of Cripps by Morgan takes no account of Cripps's role in restoring the Treasury to dominance in government, unless it is assumed that this was highly desirable. See note 64 below.

[23] Ibid., pp. 85–9. But there is much evidence to the contrary. Cf. B. W. E. Alford, R. Lowe, and N. Rollings, *Economic planning 1943–1951* (1992), pp. 1–29; R. S. Barker, 'Civil service attitudes and the economic planning of the Attlee Government', *Journal of Contemporary History*, 21 (1986), pp. 473–86. Numerous examples of obstruction by senior civil servants can be found in A. Chester, 'Planning, the Labour Governments and British economic policy 1945–51', unpublished PhD thesis, University of Bristol, 1983. And on the dominant roles and conservative attitudes of Brook (Cabinet Secretary) and Bridges (Permanent Secretary to the Treasury) see P. Hennessy, *Whitehall* (1990 edn), pp. 137–52.

disputed. The nationalisation programme in particular absorbed large amounts of ministerial and official time as well as parliamentary time, particularly as opposition MPs prolonged debates and put down innumerable amendments to bills. The burden was borne mainly by three departments – Fuel and Power, Transport, and the Treasury – the last being concerned mainly with compensation and the financial aspects of the legislation.[24] And whilst it must be accepted that for a number of reasons the nationalisation programme was a political imperative for a Labour Government, this does not alter the fact that the political attention it demanded was, to that extent, at the expense of other policies. The actual record of the government must not be lost sight of, whatever the mitigating circumstances surrounding it. Nationalisation, also, required administrative adaptability. But what was involved was far less radical than it might seem from the political debate surrounding the policy and from the language of the Labour party's election manifesto, *Let us face the future*. The major cases of coal, rail transport, electricity, and gas were already highly regulated, and nationalisation completed a process well under way before the war.[25] What is more, each of these cases provided ample opportunity for the civil service to define the task as one concerned with devising systems of administration for the new corporate creations rather than addressing commercial needs, which were never clearly defined anyway.[26] Less directly, the activity generated by nationalisation served to divert attention away from other aspects of government/industry relations, an issue to which we shall return.

There is, however, another dimension to this issue. By focusing on policy, it is easy to ignore the mechanisms by which policy was formulated or to assume that they adjusted to need as required. To the contrary, accumulating evidence both in respect of developments during the period and subsequently reveals the inadequacy and inappropriateness of the machinery of government to the needs of the modern economy. International

[24] N. Chester, *The nationalisation of British industry 1945–51* (1975), p. 40.
[25] A. A. Rogow, *The Labour government and British industry 1945–1951* (Oxford, 1955), p. 157. The main reports involved were Bank of England (Macmillan), Coal (Reid), Electricity (McGowan), and Gas (Heyworth) – 'Conservative dominated fact-finding and special investigating committees'.
[26] For detailed examples see W. Ashworth (with the assistance of M. Pegg), *The history of the British coal industry*. Volume V. *1946–1982. The nationalised industry* (Oxford, 1986), pp. 221, 579, 613, 657; T. R. Gourvish, *British Railways 1948–73. A business history* (Cambridge, 1986), p. 27. More generally see Chester, *The nationalisation of British industry*, pp. 40–66, 122, 189. See also M. Chick, 'Competition, competitiveness and nationalization, 1945–51', in G. Jones and M. W. Kirby (eds), *Competitiveness and the state* (Manchester, 1991), pp. 60–77.

comparisons have brought out these weaknesses in even sharper relief.[27] Within the space available it is impossible to examine the full extent of this problem but it can be easily exemplified because of the dominance of the Treasury within government. Having lost its long-time pre-eminent position during the war, the Treasury experienced some difficulty in recovering it in the immediate postwar years; and its failure to predict the 1947 crisis did not help its cause. But the translation of Cripps to the Treasury in late 1947 brought with it the control of economic policy and this served, also, to restore the Treasury's grip on the administrative machine. The Treasury mandarins, under the dominance of the permanent secretary, Brook, showed themselves to be fully committed to the orthodoxies of sound public finance, the international role of sterling, and a limited government involvement with industry. Some adjustment was needed to accommodate Keynesian prescriptions but these were flexible enough; and the rhetoric of Keynesianism was easily adapted to Treasury commitment to the practice of macroeconomic management.[28]

Attempts by some elements in the government to honour the pledge on planning made in the election manifesto were the more easily deflected and resisted by senior officials, particularly by those in the Treasury and the Cabinet Office. Years of practice had produced an administrative system that was perfectly suited to official machination and prevarication. Superficially, major reforms in Whitehall had been made in 1947, but the continuing operation of a large number of ministerial, and more especially official, co-ordinating committees is a clear indication that under the surface not much had changed. Administrative reform is difficult under any circumstances, partly because what is called for can involve unwelcome and in some cases potentially self-destructive participation on the part of the administrators themselves. In addition, there are day-to-day demands that have to be met; and these demands were exceptional during this period. But exceptional conditions can often provide the opportunity for exceptional remedies. The Labour Government was possessed of an enlarged government machine and enormous political legitimacy, but these were not

[27] A comprehensive survey is provided by Hennessy, *Whitehall*, especially pp. 120–68. See also Alford, Lowe, and Rollings, *Economic planning*, pp. 12–29 where it is pointed out that Morris and Gaitskell, two ministers who might have been expected to promote administrative reform, were dismissive of the need. See, for example, S. Estrom and P. Holmes, *French planning in theory and practice* (1983); A. J. Nicholls, *Freedom with responsibility. The social market economy in Germany 1918–1963* (Oxford, 1994), pp. 136 ff. There were official studies of emergent European economic planning but the overall assessment was unenthusiastic – PRO, T 230 24; T 299 207, T 299 65 cited by Chester, 'Planning'.

[28] For detailed examples see Chester, 'Planning', pp. 237–79.

matched by a sufficiency of political will. And it was a matter of will since the administrative system had not been discredited during the war. The question is how far was it understood that wartime needs had caused both reorganisation and a shift of power within the administrative machine that could be exploited on the return to peacetime conditions.

This practical issue of government was of infinitely greater importance in determining policy than Labour's 'belief in parliamentary sovereignty', which one commentator sees as being of crucial importance. Indeed, there was nothing inconsistent between such a belief and major administrative reform. Bigger government was perhaps more clearly understood as control over a larger amount of public expenditure than as involving the potential for reform.[29] Whilst there was a diversity of aim among government ministers, and whilst it may ever be thus, the fact remains that the dominant will was exercised by Attlee, Bevin, and latterly Cripps, who were set on maintaining Britain's world role, replete with the accoutrements of sterling and large defence forces. It was these aims and not the commitment to the New Jerusalem that reduced the longer-term needs of the domestic economy to secondary importance. Indeed, as will be argued, not only is this antithesis based on flawed logic but also more attention and commitment to the New Jerusalem could have contributed a great deal to those needs. As it was, administrative vested interests under the lead of the Treasury were able to ensure that the system of government was, in essentials, restored to the *status quo ante bellum*. What clearer testimony could there be to the highly constrained radicalism of the Labour government's economic policy?

II

Given these guiding principles and the circumstances surrounding them, the economic policies of the postwar Labour Governments should be seen more as acts of commission or omission than as the forced outcomes of successive economic crises. Within the space available three areas of policy which are considered central to an assessment of the record will be briefly examined: government relations with business and industry, incomes policy, and technical education and training.

---

[29] This claim is made in J. D. Tomlinson, 'The iron quadrilateral. Political obstacles to economic reform under the Attlee government', *Journal of British Studies*, 34 (1995), pp. 90–111. For a comprehensive analysis of the growth in government in this context see Middleton, *Government versus the market*, pp. 85–132, 471–641.

The war effort had drawn heavily on co-operation between government and both sides of industry, even though at times relations became very strained particularly with the trade unions. Employers' organisations such as the Cotton Board and the British Iron and Steel Federation proved particularly useful in this process, somewhat paradoxically so since they had arisen as defensive organisations out of the difficulties facing these old industries in the 1930s. But together with this co-operation went increased status and bargaining power. So it was, also, with the unions.[30] The government thus became particularly sensitive to maintaining good relations with these bodies as part of a continuing contribution it was felt they could make to postwar economic reconstruction and recovery; an attitude that was reinforced by a concern to reassure the US authorities that a Labour Government was not a form of *dirigiste* anti-capitalism.[31] Nationalisation was not a contested area in this respect since, as has been noted, the major part of the programme followed on from official reports commissioned by Conservative administrations before the war. Steel was, however, the limiting case. Private enterprise was convinced that it owned something worth defending and it experienced no difficulty in securing fierce political support from the Conservative party in its opposition to steel nationalisation.

Ministerial concern not to antagonise private enterprise was readily supported by official advice, especially from the Treasury, that nothing should be done to discourage or divert the efforts of private industry in export markets. Accordingly, welfare expenditure should not be allowed to create disincentives to industry through the imposition of what would be regarded as punitive rates of taxation.[32] By 1948, the grand aims of the 1945 Labour party manifesto – *Let us face the future* – with its pledge to plan from the ground up, had been exposed as little more than rhetoric, though it has been claimed recently that during the last stages of the second Labour Government Gaitskell was attempting to revive a policy of central planning, albeit of a more refined and limited kind than had been hoped for in

[30] An interesting insight into government/industry relations is provided by M. Dupree (ed.), *Lancashire and Whitehall. The Diary of Sir Raymond Streat*. Volume II, *1939–1957* (Manchester, 1987). More generally see S. Blank, *Industry and government in Britain. The Federation of British Industry in politics, 1945–65* (Farnborough, 1973); H. Mercer, N. Rollings, and J. D. Tomlinson (eds.), *Labour governments and private industry. The experience of 1945–51* (Edinburgh, 1992); Rogow, *The Labour government and British industry*.

[31] For the views of Sir Norman Brook, the Cabinet Secretary, see PRO, CAB 21/2244.

[32] G. Peden, 'Old dogs and new tricks: the British Treasury and Keynesian economics in the 1940s and 1950s', in M. O. Furner and B. Supple (eds.), *The state and economic knowledge. The American and British experiences* (Cambridge, 1990), p. 23.

earlier, headier days.[33] The effusion of rhetoric did, nevertheless, contain a core of industrial policy made up of three elements which were central to any attempt to improve Britain's longer-term economic performance: improved productivity, industrial reorganisation, and the promotion of competition.

The policy on productivity ranged from sponsoring industry working parties and Joint Production Committees involving employers and union representatives (known as Tripartism), to the setting up of the Anglo-American productivity council in 1948. Not a great deal was achieved.[34] There was confusion in official circles such that productivity was viewed more in terms of labour efficiency with existing techniques rather than in relation to the wider application of technical and organisational change. The gap between British and American methods was glaringly obvious.[35] But there is much evidence of the determination and the success of industrialists to resist government interference even at the level of advice; and they were quick to exploit reciprocal demands in the promotion of the export drive. For the unions' part, traditional work practices and manning levels were the mainstay of collective bargaining. Against these interests, the policy to improve productivity was ill-specified and lacked the means for effective implementation. As potential agencies for change the Joint Production Committees were reduced to talking-shops. It would be foolish to deny, nevertheless, that the pressing needs of production made change difficult; even so, the point is that the most was made of these conditions to block innovation and, more seriously, this set the pattern for the future.

Industrial restructuring was to be achieved under the auspices of the Industrial Organisation and Development Act (1947). The Board of Trade was empowered to establish Development Councils, made up of representatives from employers, unions, and independent interests, and to raise funds from industry to finance research, promotion of exports, and a range of activities aimed at raising efficiency. Despite its practical and politically neutral character, this legislation achieved virtually nothing. Only four development councils were formed: three were in minor industries and one effectively involved the transfer of these responsibilities to the existing

---

[33] N. Rollings, '"The Reichstag method of governing"? The Attlee Governments and permanent economic controls' in Mercer, Rollings, and Tomlinson, *Labour governments and private industry*, pp. 15–36.

[34] For a survey of the main developments and the literature see J. Tomlinson, 'Productivity policy' in Mercer, Rollings, and Tomlinson, *Labour governments and private industry*, pp. 37–54.   [35] L. Rostas, *Comparative productivity in British and American industry* (Cambridge, 1948), which was a Board of Trade sponsored analysis.

Cotton Board which simply served to maintain existing practices. Strong opposition to the scheme came from trade associations, fierce in their defence of their war-won status. This reveals, also, that the focus by some commentators on the weakness of Tripartism, which was based on umbrella organisations such as the Federation of British Industries and the Trades Union Congress, misses the point that at the level of individual firms the lobbying of government was extremely effective.[36] An important case was that of steel in which the most efficient firms were keen to promote a plan for restructuring the industry but it was vehemently opposed by many of the remaining firms, which raised the spectre of local unemployment if the plan went through. These tactics were not lost on firms in other industries that were threatened with reorganisation or closure in the interests of efficiency.[37]

Attention has been drawn by one commentator on the period to the importance of the Ministry of Supply in government/industry relations, based on its responsibility for defence contracts. But whilst the ministry ostensibly exercised a powerful influence on industry through the placing of contracts for research and production, and although this was in a sense discriminatory, this hardly amounts to a coherent policy of government/industry relations. Indeed, the same writer stresses the manner in which the ministry (and particularly its officials) promoted the extension of private enterprise in the defence industries. Without detailed evidence to the contrary, and from what has subsequently been revealed about the costing methods of defence contracts, there are no grounds for claiming that the state was 'picking winners' in the sense that this is generally under-

---

[36] The Tripartism approach is stressed by K. Middlemas, *Politics in industrial society: the experience of the British system since 1911* (1979) and Tomlinson, 'The iron quadrilateral'. Examples of the successful lobbying of industrialists will be found, for example, in H. Mercer, *Constructing a competitive order. The hidden history of British antitrust policies* (Cambridge, 1995), especially pp. 104–24, 170–95. Numerous cases in the official record at the PRO are listed under firms' names in Alford, Lowe and Rollings, *Economic planning*. The willing responsiveness of the Board of Trade to such pressures is the subject of current research by S. Rosevear at the University of Bristol who has kindly made information available to me. For a general critique of the Tripartist analysis of Middlemas see R. Lowe, 'The Ministry of Labour: fact and fiction', *Bulletin of the Society for the Study of Labour History*, 41 (1980), pp. 23–7.

[37] M. Chick, 'Private industrial investment', in Mercer, Rollings, and Tomlinson, *Labour governments and private industry*, pp. 74–90. See S. Wilks, 'Institutional insularity: government and the British motor industry since 1945', in M. Chick (ed.), *Governments, industries and markets. Aspects of government–industry relations in the UK, Japan, West Germany and the USA since 1945* (Aldershot, 1990), pp. 157–79, which provides evidence of the effective opposition of individual firms (and trade unions) in the context of a seriously deficient industry.

stood. More to the point, this area provides classic evidence of economic policy being the creature of foreign policy.[38]

Whilst the government was committed to the creation of state monopolies through its nationalisation programme, in its approach to private industry monopolistic practices were officially anathema. Hence in 1948 the Monopolies and Restrictive Practices Act was passed which established a Commission to investigate monopolies (as defined) in order to discover whether they operated against 'the public interest', and in the light of these investigations the government was empowered to ban such practices. The Act, nevertheless, represented a significant watering-down of the pledges made in the Labour party's 1945 manifesto and this reflected persistent pressure from business interests who regarded such regulation as socialism rampant. The government, for its part, as in its broader industrial policy, was acutely sensitive to the maintenance of good relations with business. The weaknesses of the legislation were thus fully exposed in its practice. The Commission had a small staff, operated extremely slowly and possessed no effective enforcement agency. And the definition of 'the public interest' was so vague as to be easily open to challenge from those under investigation.[39]

The compliant attitude of the Labour Government to relations with private enterprise has to be set against its possession of a wide range of controls over industry; and whilst the return to peace inevitably meant the surrender of some control, the massively enhanced position of the government in the economy must be counted as a powerful opportunity for it to redefine its peacetime relationship with industry. The fact is that the Labour Government did not have anything approaching a clear intellectual position on its relationship with private industry, despite the strength of its political rhetoric. In the nationalisation programme there was a similar lack of coherent thought that was rawly exposed when it came to devising plans for the industries concerned. And when it came to economic planning the intellectual vacuum was quickly filled with Keynesian recipes.

The official source of expert economic advice available to the government was the Economic Section of the Cabinet Office which had been established at the outset of the war.[40] This body had made a valuable

---

[38] D. Edgerton, 'Whatever happened to the British warfare state? The Ministry of Supply, 1945–1951', in Mercer, Rollings, and Tomlinson, *Labour Governments and private industry*, pp. 91–116.   [39] Mercer, *Constructing a competitive order*, pp. 54–124.

[40] A. Cairncross and N. Watts, *The Economic Section 1939–1961. A study in economic advising* (1989).

contribution to the management of the war economy, especially through the development of techniques for economic control and the distribution of physical resources. National income accounting and annual economic surveys, the first of which was prepared in 1946, were instruments that seemed to herald significant changes in government/industry relations. This apparatus was supplemented by the Central Economic Planning staff in 1947, which was given the brief of co-ordinating the physical aspects of economic planning as the means to developing 'the long-term plan for the use of the country's manpower and resources'.[41] It was, moreover, a system that appeared to have much in common with the approach of the French government to postwar reconstruction under the Monnet Plan (1946). But all similarity began and ended at this point. Keynesian ideas soon proved to be the dominant influence at work among economists in the Economic Section.[42] And the Central Economic Planning Staff busied itself with immediate practical problems. This form of economic liberalism encouraged the government to concentrate on macro, demand-side economic management and to surrender micro, supply-side policies which were essential for overcoming Britain's deep-seated industrial weakness; moreover, it was a theoretical approach that adapted well to the Treasury's understanding of the mechanism of economic policy. Nevertheless, the economist in the Economic Section should not be seen as exercising a bewitching influence on ministers but rather as providing reassurance when ministers chose the line of least resistance.

The minimal nature of reform of government/industry relations during this period set a pattern that, we contend, proved costly to Britain's economic performance in the longer run. Olson's analysis in terms of the obstructive nature of the large number of British interest groups that survived the war in contrast with the radical shake-up experienced by the continental European countries, provides a pointer here.[43] As has been suggested, however, it may not be so much a matter of the number or even the size of such groups as of the values that sustained and underlay them.[44] The emphasis was more on self-interest than on the common interest. Reform of

[41] PRO, T 229 56, 20 March 1947.

[42] This attitude comes through strongly in the account by Cairncross and Watts, *The Economic Section*, though the authors appear a little reticent to recognise it fully. See in particular pp. 130, 285–301.

[43] M. Olson, *The rise and decline of nations: economic growth, stagflation and social rigidities* (1982). But see also J. Zysman, *Governments, markets and growth: financial systems and the politics of industrial change* (Ithaca, NY, 1983).

[44] D. Marquand, 'Political institutions and economic performance', in Graham and Seldon, *Government and economics in the post-war world*, pp. 315–22.

institutions to match changed and changing economic circumstances were correspondingly more difficult to achieve. Government/industry relations were a major case in point but the two remaining areas to be examined – incomes policy and technical education and training – present a similar picture.

III

Wage levels and the need for wage restraint were of prime concern to the postwar Labour Government, and this reflected a continuation of the importance attached to the issue in reconstruction discussions between ministers and officials during the later stages of the war.[45] What they had particularly in mind was the post First World War experience in which rampant inflation and substantial increases in wage rates accompanied by a reduction in hours were followed by deflation and high unemployment. This concern had, nevertheless, to be balanced against commitments made during the war, and enshrined in the Labour party's 1945 manifesto, to create a society in which there would be fair shares for all. Income tax was maintained at a significantly higher level than prewar, with increases above the basic rate as income rose. But fears of punitive taxation and, even worse, expropriation, that existed among wide sections of the better off, proved to be exaggerated. Substantially higher death duties had some immediate effect because the techniques of tax avoidance took a little while to catch up with the change.[46] For the rest, however, capital and capital accumulation remained unscathed. Moreover, whilst progressive taxation obviously had a redistributive effect it was in the nature of things that it had little effect on changes in the level of wages or incomes, except that higher tax rates probably added pressure to wage and income demands. In other words, a more progressive taxation system did not amount to an incomes policy.

A primitive form of incomes policy emerged through a series of White Papers beginning with the well-known one on *Employment policy*. In somewhat vague terms it declared the need for moderation in wage demands. Official concern increased as union bargaining in conditions of manpower shortages forced up wages at a rate not matched by productivity gains. The need for restraint led to another declaratory White Paper in 1947 following discussion between the government and both sides of industry. The

[45] R. Jones, *Wages and employment policy 1936–1985* (1987), pp. 15–33.
[46] See C. D. Harbury and P. C. MacMahon, 'Inheritance and the characteristics of top wealth leavers in Britain', *Economic Journal*, 83 (1973), pp. 816–33.

economic crisis of that year intensified matters and in 1948 yet another White Paper was issued around which a voluntary policy of restraint on increases in wages, salaries, dividends, and prices was achieved.[47] This agreement more or less held until early 1950 when it broke down. During 1950/1, under the lead of Gaitskell, new proposals were under consideration that aimed to link wage increases to the cost of living and changes in productivity and to reinforce such a system with parallel methods for determining dividends. These proposals came to nothing.

There were a number of reasons for the failure to establish an incomes policy despite the government's clear understanding of the need. First, whilst employers collectively subscribed to the principle of limiting the growth of wages – and this principle was represented by the Federation of British Industries – when it came to practical implementation they were individually resistant to government controls over prices and dividends; and in conditions of labour shortages, they were determined to retain individual freedom to bid for workers. Secondly, there was powerful opposition from trade unions towards a centrally determined incomes policy, even in the form of devolved systems of negotiation. The overriding aim was to return as quickly and as fully as possible to free collective bargaining with the emphasis on 'free'. In this aim, unions were powerfully supported at cabinet level by Ernest Bevin, when occasion demanded. Union opposition to an incomes policy effectively increased with time and at the 1951 Trades Union Congress a resolution which included a proposal for formulating a planned wages policy was heavily defeated.[48] Thirdly, ministers and officials reassured themselves that union leadership would exercise restraint on their members. There was some justification for this belief since the memory of high unemployment in the 1930s was still strong in the collective mind of organised labour. And from 1947 onwards, that restraint was clearly in evidence.

Lastly, expert opinion was increasingly influenced by alternative ideas on how to regulate wage increases. The Economic Section, in particular, came to view the problem as one of macroeconomic management in line with basic Keynesian principles. In short, upward pressure on wages could and

---

[47] Jones, *Wages and employment policy*, pp. 34–47. For more detailed analysis of this period see R. B. Jones, 'The wages problem in employment policy 1936–48', unpublished MSc thesis, University of Bristol, 1983.

[48] Cited by Rogow, *The Labour governments and British industry*, p. 40 and note 1. Evidence on the pressure for free collective bargaining is extensive but in general see L. Panitch, *Social democracy and industrial militancy* (Cambridge, 1976); H. F. Gospel, *Markets, firms and the management of labour in modern Britain* (Cambridge, 1992), pp. 105–67.

should be countered by policies that reduced the level of aggregate demand. They thus committed the major Keynesian fallacy of assuming that provided demand was taken care of supply would look after itself. Wages and incomes policy thus became a subordinate element of fiscal management. In the light of the centrality of wage bargaining to economic performance in the longer run, it is hard to deny the seriousness of the failure to devise an incomes policy during this period, based on agreed institutional arrangements. The restraint that had been achieved relied on *ad hoc* undertakings that owed much to personal relationships between ministers, and leading trade unionists.[49] Equally it would be foolish to ignore that subsequent attempts to solve the problem have proved no more successful; and there is no obvious way in which the task was easier during the immediate postwar period than it was, for example, in the late 1970s. But however understandable, the inability of the Labour Governments to establish a new basis for the determination of wages incomes must modify claims as to the economic transformation they achieved during this period. It is significant that James Meade, the director of the Economic Section at the time, later counted this failure as one of the most important of the period.[50]

IV

The 1944 Education Act, though the product of the wartime coalition, is correctly regarded as a legislative landmark in the return to peacetime. Fundamental to its aims was the replacement of a ramshackle system of education with a more coherent structure, albeit one that still placed heavy reliance on local authorities. As well as greater efficiency and cost effectiveness, it was claimed that it promoted social justice by means of equality of opportunity. In this respect, social welfare and economic need could be effectively combined. Tawney had vividly expressed the challenge in the early 1920s – 'Ill-health and ignorance are a burden which no society can afford to carry, and education which diminishes them is not a burden but an investment.'[51]

Tawney's warnings were by no means isolated polemicism. A few years later the Balfour Committee had drawn attention in sober detail to serious weaknesses in education and training in relation to commercial and indus-

---

[49] Even during the period, wage restraint had not curtailed wage drift.
[50] F. Cairncross (ed.), *Changing perceptions of economic policy* (London, 1981), pp. 259–66 comments by James Meade; see, more generally, J. Meade, *Stagflation*. Volume I. *Wage fixing* (1982).   [51] R. H. Tawney, *Education. The socialist policy* (1924), p. 57.

trial needs.[52] In 1938 the government-sponsored Spens Report argued in the strongest terms for expansion of technical education; and the strength of the case was fully recognised by the White Paper which preceded the 1944 Act.[53] The legislative outcome did not, however, match these arguments. R. A. Butler, the Minister of Education, purposefully commissioned the Norwood Committee in the expectation that it would make recommendations that would counter the Spens Report and enable him to compromise with powerful vested interests opposed to any changes in the system that threatened the survival of the grammar (and public) schools largely in their existing forms. Butler later appointed the Flemming Committee to report on public schools in order to deflect any attacks on them, and, again, in anticipation that the Committee would serve their interests. The 1944 Act effectively endorsed the Norwood Committee's proposal for a tripartite system of secondary education based on intellectual aptitude defined as 'abstract', 'mechanical', and 'practical'. The corresponding schools would be grammar, technical, and secondary modern. What has been described as a 'bland compromise' matched the educational and the social divisions already in existence.[54] The sheer prejudice which surrounded this policy was exemplified by two contemporary commentators: 'The quality of English private (including public, "private", and grammar) schools is the result of concentrating boys and girls, mainly from the middle classes, in one set of schools . . . and for that very reason they have the power to convert limited numbers of children from other than middle-class homes into middle-class personalities.'[55]

The extent of compromise and concession to vested interests embodied in the 1944 Act has been defended in terms of what are perceived to be the 'political realities' of the period. But, after all, such 'realities' are in the nature of the test of political principle and will. Even so, this issue need not detain us since, for all its shortcomings, the 1944 Act had kept open the possibility for developing greater provision of technical education. The case was further strengthened by two successive reports, the Percy Committee on Higher Technological Education in 1945 and the Barlow

---

[52] Committee on Industry and Trade (Balfour), *Factors in industrial and commercial efficiency* (1927).
[53] A useful survey and guide to further reading is R. Lowe, *The welfare state in Britain since 1945* (1993), pp. 193–234.
[54] J. Harris, 'Enterprise and welfare states: a comparative perspective', *Transactions of the Royal Historical Society*, 40 (1990), p. 192. The defeat of radical reform was more complete than perhaps even this author allows.
[55] R. Lewis and A. Maude, *The English middle classes* (Harmondsworth, 1953 edn), p. 195.

Report on scientific manpower in 1946, which in different ways strongly advocated the expansion of technical and scientific education at college and university levels.

In 1946 out of 1·269 million children in state secondary schools in Great Britain, only 60,000 (4·7 per cent) were in technical schools as compared with 488,000 (38·5 per cent) in grammar schools and 719,000 (56·7 per cent) in secondary modern schools. By 1950 a total state secondary school population of 1·670 million was divided into secondary modern (1·095 million or 65·6 per cent), grammar (0·503 million or 30·1 per cent) and technical (0·072 million or 4·3 per cent).[56] Technical education had, therefore, made virtually no headway and the indications are that the greater part of the potential number who would have benefited from a technical school were funnelled into the secondary modern sector. A smaller element was directed into grammar schools on the assumption that this was an appropriate way of educating those destined for the higher reaches of technical training. Judged against previous evidence, advice, and proposals on the need for much greater provision of technical education, this was nothing short of a record of failure.[57]

It has been pointed out that the provisions made for education during this period involved the commitment of substantial resources in difficult economic circumstances.[58] One third of school buildings had suffered war damage and this entailed a major programme of repair and rebuilding. Further resources were required to match the raising of the school leaving age to fifteen in 1947 and to meet the needs of the postwar boom in the birth rate. The abolition of grammar school fees, the expansion of free school milk and meals, and grants to university students added to costs. Moreover, it was not simply a matter of direct costs since the raising of the school leaving age removed 400,000 school leavers from the labour market at a time of severe labour shortages. Thus 'by honouring the 1944 commitment [to provide equality of opportunity] the Labour government revealed its ultimate determination not to sacrifice long-term social need to short-term economic demands'.[59] These achievements and the conditions under which they were made still do not amount to a satisfactory defence against the charge of failure to meet the needs of technical education. The very fact that central government had to allocate scarce materials and equipment to the school-building programme gave it a powerful bargaining position *vis*

[56] B. R. Mitchell, *British historical statistics* (Cambridge, 1988), p. 806.
[57] See D. H. Aldcroft, *Education, training and economic performance, 1944–1990s* (Manchester, 1992).   [58] Lowe, *The welfare state*, pp. 204–6.   [59] Ibid., p. 204.

à vis local authorities which had immediate responsibility for educational provision. The provision of more technical education would have increased total costs only marginally, if at all, since the same number of children had to be provided for. It was a matter of diverting resources to this purpose, made easier by the amount of new building involved. In some ways this failure was all the more surprising, given the apparent contemporary concern to improve productivity and labour efficiency though, as has been noted, the poor record in this area casts doubt on the depth of understanding of the problem. Whatever the case, the determination of central government to honour its pledge to provide equality of opportunity in education did not extend to altering the balance between the range of opportunities on offer. The possibility for changes existed under the terms of the 1944 Act, but in practice the Labour Government conceded to the dominant attitudes and vested interests that had done so much to shape it. Equality of opportunity was truly reduced to the conversion of 'limited numbers of children from other than middle-class homes into middle-class personalities'.

V

Our focus on the period 1945–51 has raised questions of how to balance the impact of what are generally acknowledged as being critical events during these years against longer-term elements of economic performance. Correspondingly, statistical measures of economic performance during the period are only a part of the story; and it is unconvincing to claim that the rate of economic growth could have been significantly higher, even though there were possibilities of higher productivity through improved business organisation and production methods. In similar vein, the argument that economic recovery would have been stronger and matched more closely that of Britain's competitors if, like them, less had been spent on the New Jerusalem of social welfare and more on re-equipping British industry, is both historically shallow and inherently inconsistent.[60] Not only was the commitment to greater social welfare a political imperative of the return to peacetime, it is simply not the case that Britain's spending on social security was comparatively out of line.[61] For example, in 1950 it accounted for a lower proportion of GDP than was the case in either Germany, Austria, or Belgium. Furthermore, expenditure on education, housing, and health are

---

[60] Barnett, *The audit of war.*
[61] Harris, 'Enterprise and welfare states', especially pp. 179–84.

central elements in improving the quality of human capital. The effectiveness with which such expenditures were made is, of course, another issue.

The charge that the Labour Government put 'parlours before plant' places heavy emphasis on the alleged ineptness of government in central areas of economic activity and on the need to release the forces of a free enterprise economy. Not only does this ignore the central problem of how to cope with acute shortages in the economy, more fundamentally it betrays deep confusion in relation to systemic weaknesses in a wide range of economic agents and organisations. How else did the economy reach the state of inefficiency and incompetence with which it is charged? Were businessmen any less to blame than governments or unions? Why should inept government be construed as an argument for less government rather than for more effective government in areas where market failure was all too obvious? In short, there is much confusion of cause and effect in this attack on the postwar Labour administrations. It is an interpretation of the past that reflects all the simplism of the Thatcherite environment in which it was conceived.

It was the failure to grasp the opportunities for economic and institutional change and reform that constitutes the serious indictment against the postwar Labour Governments. This failure was to prove critical in comparative economic performance in the second half of the twentieth century. Moreover, these opportunities were historically specific and not in the nature of substitute conditions available in alternative forms along a time-scale defined in terms of catch-up and convergence.

The striking thing is the persistence of the belief among those directing policy that Britain was correctly cast in performing its traditional world role, albeit with some modification that acknowledged the dominant power of the USA. This belief was defined practically not only in terms of political and military obligations but also in relation to international economic responsibility. The Prime Minister, Attlee, seems to have completely reversed his position of the 1930s when he had declared: 'The foreign policy of a Government is the reflection of its internal policy.'[62] To the extent that some duties were seen as burdens imposed as a consequence of the war, the perception was that these were more than counter-balanced by the rewards of victory which conferred the power to determine the conditions of the peace. There were, however, stark, alternative lessons to be learnt from the war. In the crisis years of 1940 and 1941 Britain had been

---

[62] Cited by Bullock, *Ernest Bevin*, p. 62. See also PRO, CAB 129/37, CP (49) 203, 25 Oct. 1949; CAB 128/16, CM (49) 62nd, 27 Oct. 1949.

faced with the frightening reality that it simply did not possess the physical capacity to sustain war against Germany. Equally clearly it was forced to accept that its continued efforts depended critically on assistance from the USA. Even this was far from enough to secure victory. The defeat of the Axis powers could only be achieved by a combination of American and Russian military might. And by the war's end the material cost and physical exhaustion suffered by Britain left it as a major casualty. The economic experiences of the war did not, however, fully inform the official approach to the peace. Not only did crucial lessons go unlearned but important lessons of the prewar period were either forgotten or ignored.

It was acknowledged that the solution to a recurrence of prewar economic problems depended to some extent on the establishment of a new exchange-rate system. Co-operation with the USA was fundamental to the achievement of this aim. Bretton Woods, as the solution, was different in form from the old gold exchange standard, yet in important respects it was similar in its consequences. It did not cause a radical shift in Britain's international financial role, as measured by its impact on domestic and foreign policy. There was a sense of making good the failures of the pre First World War period; Bretton Woods was some thirty years out of date at its inception. It may be added (perhaps in mitigation) that US attitudes to the war were in many ways comparable to those ruling in Britain, to the extent that up to 1947 the USA saw its international role as a transitory one in sponsoring and to a degree financing the return to a liberal international economic order that had much in common with the pre-1914 world. Even Keynes misjudged Britain's postwar economic capacity to meet the challenge of the now mighty dollar.[63] For the most part, however, the official position was based on a mixture of insufficient understanding of the recent past and determination to restore Britain to its true place in the world now that Germany had finally been tamed.

Central to this approach was the government's highly conditional policy towards western Europe. The powerful influence of Bevin and Attlee in this regard has been emphasised. The other powerful member of the Cabinet, Stafford Cripps, tended to complement this approach in his policies both as President of the Board of Trade and later as Chancellor of the Exchequer. He held a world view of British trade that was much more concerned with sterling and dollar markets than with European ones, and this was reinforced by his attitude to sterling most significantly revealed in his

---

[63] Keynes, 'The balance of payments'. For a detailed discussion of this matter and a sympathetic view of Keynes's position see Pressnell, *External economic policy*, pp. 432–65.

opposition to the 1949 devaluation. The surprising thing, perhaps, is that Cripps's attraction to economic planning at home did not lead him to a more European-focused outlook, though the consistency of his views during the period is open to a serious question.[64]

The degree to which the Labour Governments understood the full consequences of their international ambitions requires further research. But there are strong grounds for claiming that, in any event, they were unwilling to pursue radical policies in areas central to longer-term economic performance. This view has been supported by a brief analysis of three branches of policy: government/industry relations, incomes policy, and education and training. And common to all of them was the need to reform the machinery of government. More precisely, the manner in which the Treasury recovered and then reasserted its dominance over the government machine is one of the most significant events of the period. To the extent that this success is explained by the translation of Cripps from the Board of Trade via the short-lived Ministry of Economic Affairs to the Chancellorship in 1947, it only serves to emphasise the willingness among senior ministers to conform to orthodoxy.

Part of the explanation for the Labour Government's compliance in the face of vested interests is the extent to which party politics had recovered its vigour by 1947. It was not that the wartime consensus was breaking down; it is now clear that it had never been very firm anyway. It was that from 1947 onwards opposition to the government was becoming more threatening as the electorate grew increasingly irritated by rationing, controls, and the dreary exigencies of postwar austerity. Cripps, himself, became identified with austerity. Whatever radical intentions the government might have had, it was now placed within a more hostile political environment in which its sensitivity to the challenge of whether it was fit to govern was heightened. In these circumstances, and in part for want of a clearly articulated alternative, the siren-call of Keynesian macroeconomic management exercised powerful seductive appeal.

This chapter began by setting out three alternative interpretations of the

---

[64] The enlightened technocrat characterisation of Cripps is to be found, for example, in Morgan, *Labour in power*, pp. 398, 408; Tomlinson, 'The iron quadrilateral', pp. 95–8; Robinson, 'The economic problems of the transition", pp. 176, 181. But it is difficult to square this assessment with Cripps's earlier, more *dirigiste*, approach to planning as shown by Chester, *Planning*, especially chapters 3 and 6, or with Cripps's performance in the devaluation of 1949, Cairncross and Eichengreen, *Sterling in decline*. See also Edgerton, 'Whatever happened to the warfare state?', pp. 93–4. Cripps's translation to the Treasury in late 1947 seems critical in this respect. In short, there was a considerable change in his views and, at times, his technocratic skills were not a prominent feature of his actions.

economic achievements of the two postwar Labour Governments. Our analysis has attempted to show that ministers were not forced along unwillingly by the pressure of events; that whilst we share the view that there was a failure to match economic need with appropriate policy measures, this was not a consequence of a commitment to the New Jerusalem; and that to see the economic development of this period as part of a process of catch-up and convergence is far too passive an interpretation that ignores both the specific nature of contemporary policy and the strength of its longer-term influence on economic performance. What remains is that the Labour Governments' record between 1945 and 1951 formed a stage in Britain's continuing economic decline among the leading economies; though as Barry Supple has well reminded us (in ch. 1), Decline has still not become Fall.

10

The end of empire and the golden age

CHARLES H. FEINSTEIN

There is no more dramatic and visible index of Britain's decline than the end of the British Empire. In the Victorian and Edwardian era Britain had been the dominant world power. By the end of the 1960s her status had crumbled, her empire had gone. The bonds of empire had already weakened in the interwar period. The special position of four countries – Australia, Canada, New Zealand, and South Africa – had been recognised during the First World War, and their 'dominion status' was given legal force in 1931. A large part of their population was of British origin, and ties with the mother country of all kinds – military, economic, judicial, and social – were still extremely close. Nevertheless, these were sovereign countries, making their own decisions, in their own interests, on both internal and external affairs. Eire enjoyed broadly similar status from 1923, but without the same warmth of feeling towards Britain.

The critical changes came after the Second World War and the unexpected transformation in Britain's position was then swift and comprehensive. In 1945 ultimate power over more than 500 million colonial peoples was still exercised from London.[1] Twenty years later nothing of any consequence remained. India and Pakistan became independent in 1947, Burma and Ceylon a year later. After a slight pause the process resumed with Sudan in 1956 and the Gold Coast in 1957, and it was effectively all over within a decade. In every corner of the globe the symbols of power were eagerly taken up by the new Prime Ministers and their officials. The cockatooed colonial governors and their district officers and soldiers departed: in West

---

[1] One important exception to this must be noted. In 1919 the British Government accepted a convention on fiscal autonomy, allowing India to raise tariffs and develop domestic industries (notably iron and steel, and cotton textiles) behind protective duties. See Ian M. Drummond, *British economic policy and the empire, 1919–1939* (1972), pp. 121–40; Brian R. Tomlinson, *The political economy of the Raj 1914–1947* (1979), pp. 60–2, 104–38. There were also small constitutional reforms in 1935, carrying the implication of future movement to self-government and dominion status.

Africa from Nigeria, Sierra Leone, and the Gambia; in East Africa from Kenya, Tanganyika, and Uganda; in central Africa from Southern Rhodesia, Northern Rhodesia, and Nyasaland; in south-east Asia from Singapore, Malaya, Sarawak, and North Borneo; in the West Indies from Jamaica, Trinidad, and British Guiana; in the Mediterranean from Palestine, Malta, and Cyprus; in the Indian Ocean from Aden and Mauritius; in the Pacific Ocean from Fiji. The roll-call reminds us how large and diverse the empire had been.[2]

Stretching beyond even this vast empire had been the 'informal empire'. In Latin America and parts of the Middle East countries like Argentina, Peru, Iraq, and Egypt enjoyed nominal political independence, but relied heavily on British capital, trade, shipping, and finance, and could not easily deviate too far from policies acceptable to Britain. After 1914, however, a number of forces operated to undermine Britain's authority in these areas, including the costs of the two world wars and the liquidation of British investments, the moves towards imperial preference and closer ties with the empire in the 1930s, and the increasing economic and political power of the USA.[3] By the 1950s Britain's influence had disintegrated in Latin America, and the Iranian oil and Suez Canal crises made it painfully obvious that Britain could no longer exercise authority in the Middle East. The days of imperial power were drawing to a close.

At precisely the same time that this remarkable withdrawal from empire was in progress, the United Kingdom was enjoying an equally remarkable phase of successful economic performance, the best ever achieved in more than two centuries of modern economic growth. From 1951 to 1973 both the total output of goods and services (real GDP), and the efficiency with which that output was produced (output per hour worked), increased more rapidly than in any previous period since the start of the industrial revolution in the late eighteenth century.[4] Certain other countries may have been doing even better, but by Britain's historic standards this was a time of record economic achievement.

For output the average annual rate of growth in this 'golden age' was 3

---

[2] See John Darwin, *Britain and decolonisation* (1988) for a comprehensive analysis of the retreat from empire.

[3] D. C. M. Platt, *Finance, trade and politics in British foreign policy* (Oxford, 1968); D. C. M. Platt (ed.), *Business imperialism, 1840–1930: an inquiry based on British experience in Latin America* (Oxford, 1977); Rory Miller, *Britain and Latin America in the nineteenth and twentieth centuries* (1993).

[4] For a detailed analysis of these and other features of the postwar boom in an historical perspective see R. C. O. Matthews, C. H. Feinstein, and J. C. Odling-Smee, *British economic growth, 1856–1973* (Oxford, 1982).

per cent, compared with a previous best of 2 per cent from 1820 to 1870. For labour productivity it was 3.2 per cent per annum, compared with a previous record only half as good from 1913 to 1950.[5] The increase in the volume of United Kingdom exports was also exceptionally rapid during the golden age. At close to 4 per cent per annum it was not quite up to the standard achieved from 1820 to 1870 when Britain was the world's leading supplier of manufacturers, but it was well above the 3 per cent in the years before the First World War and far better than the stagnation of the period from 1913 to 1950.[6]

An important factor underlying the record rate of growth was the high level of domestic investment. In the years 1950 to 1973, 20 per cent of GDP was devoted to home investment, roughly double the ratio in former periods. This historically high rate of capital formation made an important contribution to economic growth, both by providing a powerful boost to demand, and by the direct effect of the expansion of productive capacity, with cumulative benefits from quicker incorporation of the latest technical advances in the stock of capital.

In addition to rapid economic growth and high investment, Britain also scored extremely high marks on three of the other principal tests of economic performance. First, for the quarter century following the Second World War there was full employment: no healthy worker who wished to have a job was unable to find one. Secondly, there was no serious problem of inflation, apart from the short-lived effect of the Korean War boom. Thirdly, growth was not only more rapid, it was also more stable: the amplitude of cyclical fluctuations in output and exports was milder than in earlier periods, particularly if comparison is made with the exceptionally disturbed years between the wars. Only the balance of payments position was consistently unsatisfactory. There was generally a surplus on current account, but it was too small and too uncertain to prevent recurrent sterling crises and fears that the currency would be devalued, as it was in 1949 and again in 1967.

The broad temporal coincidence of these two unique episodes, the dissolution of the formal empire and record economic performance, provides the central theme for this chapter. The loss of empire was obviously of the highest importance in political and strategic terms. The United Kingdom

---

[5] Estimates for 1820 to 1992 from A. Maddison, *Monitoring the world economy 1820–1992* (Paris, 1995), p. 41. For 1700–1831 see N. F. R. Crafts, *British economic growth during the Industrial Revolution* (Oxford, 1985), p. 45.

[6] Maddison, *Monitoring the world economy*, p. 74.

ceased to be a superpower, although it was to some extent able to conceal this fact behind the facade of the new Commonwealth, and by relying on the status it had acquired through earlier achievements, including its triumphs in the Second World War. However, the loss of military and naval bases, and of command over sea and air routes, could not be disguised. Britain could no longer claim in international gatherings to speak for one quarter of the world's population, nor rely in future conflicts on the heroic contribution to her armed forces which the empire had made in the two world wars.

In a hostile world the significance of these geo-political and military losses was not easily disentangled from the safeguarding of Britain's economic security. The blow to the country's pride and sense of national greatness from the loss of status associated with possession of a glorious empire may also have had an impact on morale and attitudes at all levels of British society.[7] But our concern is with the more immediate economic consequences of the end of empire, both formal and informal. What impact did this have on the metropolitan economy and the standard of living of the British people? Is it of any significance that Britain's record economic performance occurred at exactly the historical moment in which imperial domination came to an end?

In recent years a substantial programme of research and debate has explored the overall costs and benefits of British imperialism, and the role of specifically economic factors in the drive for colonies.[8] The main conclusion to emerge from these studies is that the empire was more burden than benefit, though Offer has made a strong case for the contrary view, adducing a number of factors to show that the principal cost of empire – the high level of defence expenditure – was not irrational, especially if the empire's contribution between 1914 and 1919 is brought into the reckoning. For

---

[7] The interesting idea of the empire as a status good is developed in A. Offer, 'The British Empire, 1870–1914: a waste of money?', *Economic History Review*, 46 (1993), pp. 215–38.

[8] See D. K. Fieldhouse, *Economics and empire, 1830–1914* (1973); Michael Edelstein, *Overseas investment in the age of high imperialism: the United Kingdom, 1850–1914* (New York, 1982); L. E. Davis and R. A. Huttenback, *Mammon and the pursuit of empire: the political economy of British imperialism, 1860–1912* (Cambridge, 1986); P. J. Cain and A. G. Hopkins, 'Gentlemanly capitalism and British expansion overseas, I, New imperialism, 1850–1945', *Economic History Review*, 40 (1987), pp. 1–26; P. K. O'Brien, 'The costs and benefits of British imperialism 1846–1914', *Past and Present*, 120 (1988), pp. 163–200; A. Hopkins, 'Accounting for the British Empire', *Journal of Imperial and Commonwealth History*, 16 (1988), pp. 234–47, A. Porter, 'The balance sheet of Empire, 1850–1914', *Historical Journal*, 31 (1988), pp. 685–99; M. Daunton, '"Gentlemanly capitalism" and British Industry, 1820–1914', *Past and Present*, 122 (1989), pp. 119–58; Offer, 'The British Empire'; Michael Edelstein, 'Imperialism: cost and benefit' in R. C. Floud and D. N. McCloskey, *An economic history of Britain since 1700*, vol. II (Cambridge, 2nd edn, 1994), pp. 197–216.

obvious reasons, however, this body of work has focused almost entirely on the period before 1914, and has sought to establish its conclusions from the evidence of the empire at its zenith.[9] This chapter looks at the same issues in the context of decolonisation, and attempts to evaluate the imperial contribution to Britain's economy in the period when the benefits of empire ceased to be available. There is space to consider only the direct economic aspects; political and military issues are not brought into the reckoning.

The interest of the question is enhanced by the observation that the retreat from formal empire applied equally to other European colonial powers. Yet in these same decades France, Belgium, and the Netherlands also experienced a golden age of dynamic economic growth – indeed, one even more impressive than Britain's – and they too enjoyed full employment, price stability, and weak cycles. In these countries, as in the United Kingdom, this prosperity was not what many had anticipated:

All agreed that economic disaster would follow the complete loosening of the ties between Europe and the European dependencies. This was clearly expressed by Captain Gammans when he discussed Dutch Colonial policy in Indonesia in private session. 'The Dutch are in a dilemma. They realise that without the Netherlands East Indies the economy of the mother country would suffer, or worse, would collapse.'[10]

II

The belief that the empire was a significant source of actual and potential economic importance for Britain was proclaimed both by critical opponents and by enthusiastic supporters of imperial unity. Bevin's remarks in the House of Commons in 1946, at the end of a rather rambling debate on foreign affairs, expressed a widely held – if often tacit – opinion: 'When I

---

[9]   The most substantial modern study of the post-1914 period is P. J. Cain and A. G. Hopkins, *British imperialism, crisis and deconstruction, 1914–1990* (1993), though the assessment of costs and benefits is incidental to the authors' main concern, which is to make a case for the significance of their concept of 'gentlemanly capitalism' and to establish its role in the continued dynamic of British imperialism. Some of the key issues affecting Britain's position after 1945 are raised in J. Strachey, *The end of empire* (1959) and Michael Barratt Brown, *After imperialism* (1963), but both were written too early to provide a full appreciation of the performance of the post-imperial economy.

[10]   FO 371/73039, Report of the Foreign Office representative at an International Study Conference on Overseas Territories of Western Europe held in Amsterdam in 1948, in R. Hyam (ed.), *British documents on the end of empire*, Series A, Volume 2, *The Labour Government and the end of empire 1945–1951*, Part II, *Economics and international relations* (1992), p. 434. Capt. Gammans, a Conservative MP, was a member of the UK delegation who had been in the Malayan Civil Service for many years.

say I am not prepared to sacrifice the British Empire, what do I mean? I know that if the British Empire fell . . . it would mean that the standard of life of our constituents would fall considerably.'[11]

Such views did not normally rest on an explicit and up-to-date analysis of overall costs and benefits, still less of their distribution between social classes. For a generation of politicians, including Bevin and Morrison, Churchill and Macmillan, it was a mindset created in an earlier age. In the labour movement it was a conviction held most strongly by those whose understanding of the nature of economic imperialism had been shaped by Lenin's doctrine that the workers in the metropolitan country shared in 'the super-profits obtained from the exploitation of the vast mass of the workers on a world scale, and especially of the impoverished and heavily exploited colonial and semi-colonial peoples'.[12] In other cases it was a paradoxical response to the analyses of imperialism, and the indictments of the treatment of colonial people, by liberal and socialist writers such as Hobson, Olivier, Woolf, Morel, and Barnes.[13] Even as they denounced imperialism, and demonstrated that the policy was, at best, in the interests of 'certain sectional interests', they helped to persuade their readers that such exploitation must be the source of a vast flow of tribute to the metropolitan powers.

In the Conservative party the same aspects of the imperial relationship were seen from a somewhat different perspective, but those who upheld the policies advanced by Disraeli, Salisbury, and Chamberlain in the nineteenth century believed with equal fervour that the empire was still the cornerstone of Britain's economic power in the twentieth century. 'We have got to be quite clear about it', Julian Amery informed the 1948 Conservative conference, 'Empire Preference is a foundation for our whole economic life.'[14] For millions more, it was simply pride in the splendour and significance of the empire which nourished the belief that it must be a vital

---

[11] *HCDeb*, 1365, 21 Feb. 1946. Cf. Strachey, *End of empire*, p. 146, 'The possession of an empire has been widely regarded as a condition for the improvement, or even the maintenance, of the standard of life of the British people.'

[12] R. Palme Dutt, *The crisis of Britain and the British Empire* (1953), p. 326. For more sophisticated discussions see M. H. Dobb, *Political economy and capitalism* (1937), pp. 246–7; E. J. Hobsbawm, 'Trends in the British Labour movement' in *Labouring men* (1964), pp. 330–1; Tom Kemp, *Theories of imperialism* (1967), pp. 79–82.

[13] J. A. Hobson, *Imperialism, a study* (1902, 3rd edn, 1938), Sydney Olivier, *White capital and coloured labour* (1906), Leonard S. Woolf, *Empire and commerce in Africa* (1919), E. D. Morel, *The black man's burden* (1920), Leonard Barnes, *Empire or democracy?* (1939). For an excellent survey of the views of these and other writers see Bernard Porter, *Critics of empire* (1968).

[14] Quoted by David Goldsworthy, *Colonial issues in British politics 1945–1961* (Oxford, 1971), p. 170.

element in their standard of living. This sentiment had been fostered ever since the Victorian era by incessant pageantry and propaganda, invoking crown and state in classroom and pulpit, scout hall and barrack, press and cinema.

When attempts were made to articulate a more explicit economic analysis of the rewards of empire, a number of different aspects were identified, either by those who wished to promote the extension of empire or by those whose aim was to prevent it. Many laid special stress on the role of trade. From the empire flowed cocoa, sugar, and tea; palm oil, timber, and rubber; nickel, copper, and tin; and a myriad other commodities which Britain could not produce at home. For some, what was important was privileged access to these supplies, especially in times of war. For others, the critical issue was the ability of the metropolis to acquire her imports on favourable terms.

The empire was also seen as an essential market for British exports. Those who foresaw a grim prospect of increasing foreign competition and declining sales, looked for a solution in the expansion of Britain's exports to the empire. At first this came about as a natural preference for British manufactures, exercised by those who came from, or looked to, the mother country. Later, it was reinforced by imperial preference, a process started on a small scale before 1914, and given its main impetus by the Ottawa Agreements of 1932. National prosperity, it was believed, required the continuous expansion of foreign trade; the empire was the means to achieve this.

In other studies it was the imperialism of capital which was crucial. Overseas investment was essential as an outlet for surplus British capital: without it, the attempt to invest the funds at home would drive down the rate of return. The continuous flow of interest and dividends derived by British bond and shareholders from investments abroad thus sustained the profitability of capitalism. Furthermore, imperial power enabled British firms to draw abnormal profits from the employment of colonial labour at wages far lower than would have to be paid in Britain. A further strand of this analysis was the contention that there were also significant benefits for the City: from Britain's role as the financial centre of the empire, the use of sterling as the major trading currency, and the reliance on British banking, insurance, and shipping. The interwar period also saw the origin of the system of sterling balances which was held to be of particular importance after the Second World War.

Yet another view saw the rewards of empire in terms of employment.

Migration to the dominions, and to a few of the more attractive colonial regions such as the highlands of Kenya, represented a valuable outlet for those for whom satisfactory work was not available in Britain. In the 1920s, when unemployment soared to unprecedented levels, transfer of the 'surplus population' seemed to some the only feasible solution, and the 1929 Colonial Development Act was specifically designed to relieve unemployment in Britain.[15] Administration and policing of the colonies also provided congenial employment for many of the middle class.

Indirect confirmation of the view that the economic gains from the empire must be significant came from the attempts of Germany and other rival powers to acquire their own colonies in the years before 1914; and from the attitude of the USA after 1940. In Anglo-American discussions during and after the Second World War the special privileges which Britain enjoyed were a major source of contention, and it was made perfectly plain that there was a price to be paid for the economic aid and political support which Britain desperately needed. She would have to give up those aspects of empire which denied the USA equal opportunities to purchase its raw materials, promote its exports, invest its capital, and expand its financial networks. The fact that the self-interest of the USA could be so readily harmonised with her own tradition of revolutionary struggle for independence from Britain, and presented as an altruistic demand on behalf of the colonies, made the policy so much more compelling to Americans. Their demands provoked Winston Churchill's famous response in 1942: 'We mean to hold our own. I have not become the King's First Minister in order to preside over the liquidation of the British Empire.'[16]

Finally, we must also note another angle of vision, in which the colonies are significant not for what they were, but for what they might be. This was a view frequently expressed in the dark days when Britain was struggling to come to terms with the grave economic plight in which it emerged from the war. One of the principal policy objectives in this situation, as formulated by a member of the cabinet in 1949, was to achieve 'the most rapid development practicable of our overseas possessions, since without such

---

[15] In the event the Act was completely ineffective; see Michael Havinden and David Meredith, *Colonialism and development. Britain and its tropical colonies, 1850–1960* (1993), pp. 147–8 and 199–200.

[16] At a later stage the USA moderated the urgency of its anti-colonialism in the greater interest of the crusade against communism, but this merely slowed the pace of the changes it demanded; see Wm R. Louis, *Imperialism at bay 1941–1945, the United States and the decolonisation of the British Empire* (Oxford, 1977) and Wm R. Louis and Ronald Robinson, 'The imperialism of decolonization', *Journal of Imperial and Commonwealth History*, 22 (1994), pp. 462–511.

colonial development there can be no major improvement in the standard of living of our own people at home'.[17]

This approach flowed naturally from the shift in colonial policy initiated with the adoption of the Colonial Development and Welfare Act of 1940, as extended in 1945 and carried forward under the influence of Creech Jones, Andrew Cohen, and other ministers and officials in the postwar Labour Government.[18] To this end the organisation of the Colonial Office was restructured and an Economic Intelligence and Planning Section created in the economic division, a new Colonial Development Corporation was established, increased grants and loans were made available to the colonies, and private firms were encouraged to expand the output of primary products. In the colonies a major effort was made to improve the machinery for development, each colony was expected to draw up a comprehensive ten-year development plan, completely new tasks and objectives were set for the colonial service, and they were expected to pursue a dynamic programme of economic development which would have been inconceivable before the war.

There was, however a danger in this emphasis on development, as the Cabinet Secretary, Sir Norman Brook, noted in a revealing minute to the Prime Minister in January 1948:

At recent meetings there has been general support for the view that the development of Africa's economic resources should be pushed forward rapidly in order to support the political and economic position of the United Kingdom. I wonder whether Ministers have considered sufficiently the difficulties of defending this policy against the criticisms, and misrepresentation, which it may provoke? It could, I suppose, be said to fall within the ordinary definition of 'Imperialism'. And . . . it might be represented as *a policy of exploiting native peoples in order to support the standards of living of the workers in this country*.[19]

Was this simply misrepresentation, or was Britain's standard of living really in some degree dependent on the empire? If one or more of the themes outlined above were correct, the rapid liquidation of the formal empire and the disintegration of the informal empire should have had serious adverse consequences for Britain. In fact, it is remarkably difficult

---

[17] CAB 129/37/3, CP(49)245, Annex A, memo by A. V. Alexander, Minister of Defence, quoted by Hyam, *The Labour Government and the end of empire 1945–1951*, Part I, *High policy and administration*, p. xxiii.

[18] See J. M. Lee, *Colonial development and good government* (Oxford, 1967) for a comprehensive account of the evolution of the new policy.

[19] PREM 8/923 in Hyam, *The Labour Government and the end of empire 1945–1951*, Part II, *Economics and international relations*, p. 257; my italics.

to ascertain any significant impact.[20] The British economy faced many grave economic problems in the postwar years, but the loss of the empire was not one of them. Difficulties arising from the direct economic consequence of decolonisation are barely mentioned in the copious selection of official papers published by the *British Documents on the End of Empire* Project.[21] The problem does not surface as a significant issue in the standard accounts of British economic policy and performance in this period.[22] What needs to be explained, therefore, is why the dissolution of the imperial bonds failed to have the economic impact which believers in the empire would have anticipated.

III

In order to understand why the loss of empire turned out not to matter we must undertake a more detailed scrutiny of the alleged economic benefits of imperialism. Consider first the traditional argument relating to the importance of the empire as a source of imports. In reality, it was not supremacy over her imperial domains that had enabled Britain to import large quantities of food and raw materials. It was her huge purchasing power as an industrial nation, reinforced – apart from a few concessions to the dominions – by a sturdy commitment to free trade. This determination to purchase in the cheapest market differentiated Britain from France, Germany, and other European powers which had preferred to introduce tariffs to protect their farmers from competition in wheat, sugar, meat, and dairy products.

Moreover, privileged access to empire products was only crucial if these were in short supply, as some were during the war and immediate postwar years. The more normal position was one of excess supply. This was the consequence of a number of factors, including over-production by many

[20] It could be argued that this was because the effects of the withdrawal were delayed. Lipton shows that this did happen for about a decade after Indian independence, but then 'post-colonial inertia broke down' and the process of disengagement accelerated sharply; see Michael Lipton, 'Neither partnership nor dependence: pre-decolonisation, inertia, diversification and para-protectionism in Indo-British relations since 1947', in W. H. Morris-Jones and Georges Fischer (eds.), *Decolonisation and after, the British and French experience* (1980), pp. 158–92.

[21] Hyam, *The Labour Government and the end of empire 1945–1951*; David Goldsworthy (ed.), *The Conservative Government and the end of empire, 1951–1957*, series A, vol. III (1994). The major exception to this comment on government concerns is the assessment of the effects of independence for the remaining colonies which Macmillan asked for in 1957; the answer he was given by his officials is that the 'economic considerations were fairly evenly matched'; see D. J. Morgan, *The official history of colonial development* (1989), vol. V, p. 102.

small producers unable to restrict their output or store their crops; low income elasticity of demand for food; technological improvements leading to economies in the use of raw materials; and substitution of synthetic for natural materials, a process enormously enhanced by the postwar development of the modern petrochemical industry. The scale of substitution is indicated by a 1955 GATT estimate that: 'without these domestically produced substitutes the demand of the industrialised countries last year for raw materials would have been some 40 per cent higher'.[23]

Nevertheless, in the years of postwar reconstruction there were still many who were persuaded that expansion of production in the colonies would both relieve the shortages of food and raw materials from which Britain suffered, and reduce hard-currency imports. An extreme example of this belief is found in a lengthy memorandum written by the Chief of the Imperial General Staff, Field-Marshal Lord Montgomery, following a tour of Africa late in 1947.

3. It is impossible to tour Africa without being impressed with the following points: (a) the immense possibilities that exist in British Africa for development. (b) the use to which such development could be put *to enable Great Britain to maintain her standard of living, and to survive.* (c) the lack of any 'grand design' for the development of British Africa and consequently the lack of a master plan in any colony.[24]

He continued: 'These lands contain everything we need'; minerals, raw materials, and labour 'exist in almost unlimited quantities'; food 'can be grown to any extent desired'; power 'can be developed economically, since coal is unlimited and can be obtained very cheaply'.

His report was taken very seriously. The Prime Minister expressed himself 'much interested', the Foreign Minister called for the report to be given 'serious and urgent study', and in January 1948 Attlee chaired a special committee of senior cabinet ministers convened to consider it.[25] The Field-Marshal's approach to matters of economic development (and of colonial politics) was clearly too simplistic, and the response produced by the Secretary of State for the Colonies observed sharply that the statements in paragraph 4 of the memorandum (quoted above) were 'greatly

[22] Andrew Shonfield, *British economic policy since the war* (1958); J. C. R. Dow, *The management of the British economy, 1945–60* (Cambridge, 1974); Frank Blackaby, *British economic policy 1960–74* (Cambridge, 1978); Alec Cairncross, *Years of recovery, British economic policy 1945–51* (1985); Alec Cairncross, *The British economy since 1945* (1992).

[23] Quoted in Barratt Brown, *After imperialism*, p. 232.

[24] DO 35/2380 no. 1 in Hyam, *The Labour Government and the end of empire 1945–1951*, Part II, *Economics and international relations*, pp. 188–9, my italics.

[25] Ibid., p. 188; see also pp. 193–206 for reactions from the Foreign and Colonial Offices, and the minute of the cabinet meeting.

exaggerated'. However, Montgomery was by no means alone, either in his belief that the development of the colonies should be vigorously pursued, or in his underestimation of the difficulties that this would involve.

These difficulties were made agonisingly apparent to all concerned when the government launched its great attempt to expand production of groundnuts in East Africa. In 1947, the cabinet (ignoring strong reservations expressed by the agricultural advisers) approved a proposal by the Minister of Food, John Strachey, supported by the Colonial Office. The scheme involved the use of large-scale mechanised agriculture to clear and cultivate an area of over 3,000,000 acres for an estimated capital outlay of some £25 million. This was expected to produce 800,000 tons of groundnuts a year to meet 'our desperate need for fats'.

The chasm separating Whitehall dreams and African realities could not have been deeper. By March 1949 only 46,000 acres had been cleared and this miserable effort had cost over £21 million. At the end of 1950 the cabinet was informed by Strachey: 'that the large-scale production of groundnuts could not be carried on in East Africa on a commercial basis, and that there was no hope of obtaining any significant supply of oil-seeds from this scheme. There was no escape from the conclusion that the project ... had proved a costly failure.'[26] That was effectively the end of large-scale plans to supply Britain with food and raw materials from the African colonies, although the government continued to press ahead with smaller plans whenever it saw an opportunity.

With respect to the price of imports, the United Kingdom had not normally claimed special advantages. Other developed countries (for example, non-imperialist Sweden or Switzerland) which wished to purchase food and raw materials from empire countries were equally able to do so, and on terms no less favourable than those available to Britain. This had been the position before the war and was seen as the appropriate policy for the postwar period. The official marketing policy for colonial products was:[27]

(a) that the colonies were entitled to a fair commercial deal on the basis of either current world market values or of a long term undertaking to provide an assured market at a reasonable price; (b) that the Colonies should not discriminate between buyers, i.e. that colonies should accept the best commercial offer, from whatever

[26] CAB 128/18, CM 83(50)4 in Hyam, *The Labour Government and the end of empire 1945–1951*, Part II. *Economics and international relations*, pp. 293–4. For further details see also Alan Wood, *The groundnut affair* (1950).

[27] CO 852/989/3, Minute of 14/1/47 by E. Melville in Hyam, *The Labour Government and the end of empire 1945–1951*, Part II, *Economics and international relations*, p. 26.

source it was forthcoming, taking account of course of the factor of assured market given by a long term contract.

It is certainly true that Britain enjoyed substantial benefits during the Second World War through bulk purchase arrangements and controlled prices, and the terms of trade moved sharply against those colonies which were forced to sell their produce on these terms. To give just one instance, the Ministry of Food was paying approximately £30 to £35 per ton for cocoa purchased in the Gold Coast and Nigeria when the New York spot price was £50. The total sum saved on imports of this one product in the war years amounted to some £24 million.[28] It was absolutely clear in London that the exigencies of the fight against fascism were sufficient to justify this contribution by the colonies to the Allied war effort; we cannot know – but may reasonably doubt – whether it was equally clear to the residents of the colonies that they should make this sacrifice.

These arrangements were not immediately abandoned once the war was over, and became something of an embarrassment to the Colonial Office. United Kingdom prices were appreciably increased, but so too were world market prices, and a large gap remained for all the major colonial agricultural products except cocoa and rubber, and for some non-agricultural products. In the minute quoted above the writer notes sharply that the assumptions specified 'have . . . been overlooked, if not actually set aside in the case of certain recent deals with the Ministry of Food and the Board of Trade'.[29] However, pressure internally from the Colonial Office, and externally from the United Nations and other critics of colonialism, forced the British government to accept that this was not a tenable position in the postwar world. By 1951 the United Kingdom was generally paying open market prices for its purchases of colonial produce.[30]

If, therefore, there is a persistent inequity in the exchange between manufacturing and primary producing countries, as some have argued, it was *not* because formal empire enabled the metropolis to impose unfair terms on colonial primary producers.[31] The explanation must be sought else-

[28] Calculated from data in P. T. Bauer, *West African trade* (1963), pp. 396–7. See also Havinden and Meredith, *Colonialism and development*, pp. 207–12.

[29] In a draft cabinet memorandum of March 1947, the Secretary of State, Creech Jones, gave some examples of the large discrepancy between the current UK bulk purchase price and the estimated current world values. For African palm oil the UK price was £45 per ton compared to a world price in the range of £70–100; for palm kernels the corresponding prices were £35 against £50–75; CO 852/989/3, no 17, Annex, ibid., p. 37.

[30] Bauer, West African trade, p. 287; P. H. Ady, 'The terms of trade' in G. D. N. Worswick and P. H. Ady (eds.), *The British economy in the nineteen-fifties* (Oxford, 1962), pp. 152–9.

[31] Cf. A. Emmanuel, *Unequal exchange* (1972). See John Spraos, *Inequalising trade?* (Oxford, 1983) for an acute and balanced assessment of these issues.

where; for example, in low income elasticities of demand and the other factors tending to excess supply of primary products mentioned above; or in the fact that the structure of production and marketing is generally much more competitive in primary producing than in industrial countries. In practice, it was the operation of these trends which ensured that Britain was not penalised by the restoration of open market purchases for its imports. After an initial rise, powerfully stimulated by the Korean War boom in 1951, commodity prices declined relative to those for manufactured goods, and over the following two decades Britain enjoyed a significant improvement in the terms on which she traded exports of manufactures for imports of primary products.[32] Any adverse consequences arising from the end of controls on colonial trade were thus more than compensated for by these favourable trends in world market prices.

One other factor which moderated any impact of Britain's changed position was the successful expansion of home agriculture. This policy had been started between the wars, and was subsequently pursued more vigorously, first to supplement the severely limited food supplies available during the war, and later to relieve the continuous balance of payments problems in the postwar decades. From the end of the 1950s the volume of food imports remained broadly constant and Britain moved close to self-sufficiency in a wide range of products.

On the other side of the trade account, the benefits supposedly available in higher exports to captive markets turn out to be equally elusive. In fact, Britain's basic problem in the initial postwar period was not lack of markets, but of resources. Successive governments were desperately anxious to expand exports, but this had to be done in competition with similarly pressing claims for scarce labour and materials for home investment, for consumption, and for rearmament and other government purchases. In a period of full employment and booming world trade as much was being sold abroad as could be produced.

At the start, demand for British products was also high because of the depressed level of output in Germany, Japan, Italy, and other belligerents. Once they had recovered from the devastation of the war they became formidable competitors, and from the early 1950s Britain was losing her former share of the market in many countries. However, this applied in

---

[32] Because of the variability of the import and export price series, the choice of years for comparison is critical; Britain's net barter terms of trade improved between 1951 and 1972, but were marginally worse in 1972 than in the 1930s; B. R. Mitchell, *British Historical Statistics* (Cambridge, 1988), pp. 527–8. For a detailed picture of the deterioration in the position of individual colonies see Havinden and Meredith, *Colonialism and development*, pp. 239–46.

empire and non-empire countries alike. The principal explanation was not the dissolution of imperial power, formal or informal; it was Britain's competitive weakness, evident in a variety of ways, including higher prices, less innovative design, inferior quality and reliability, and longer delivery dates.

In earlier periods the United Kingdom had been able to shelter from her competitors in empire markets. When the dominions imposed tariffs on manufactures to protect their infant industries they were willing to discriminate in Britain's favour at the expense of foreign countries. In the colonies Britain could demand more than this; they could be prevented from giving any protection to their nascent manufacturing industries if this threatened British exports. British businessmen were almost always hostile to the establishment of manufacturing industry within the empire.[33] If a tariff on imports became imperative as a source of revenue, the British government was persuaded to use its political domination to insist that a countervailing excise duty be imposed on locally produced goods at the same rate as the tariff.

The most important example of this policy was its application to the Indian textile industry in the interest of the Lancashire cotton manufacturers in the late nineteenth century and again in 1916. It was also applied in Uganda in the 1920s when a Japanese firm started to make matches from local timber. The attempts of local Asian capitalists to manufacture textiles in Kenya in the interwar period were thwarted by the colonial administration, and the threat of sanctions against Tanganyika's sisal exports was invoked when a sisal twine plant was established there in the early 1930s to manufacture products for the exports market.[34]

One of the more innovative attempts to estimate the benefits which accrued to Britain in 1913 from its influence over the level of empire tariffs is Edelstein's counterfactual exercise.[35] For this purpose he assumes that in the absence of British rule both dominions and colonies would have imposed a tariff of 40 per cent, approximately the average rate in the fully independent USA. As with all large-scale counterfactuals a number of debatable assumptions are then required to specify the alternative conditions, and the results are at best interesting orders of magnitude. His first

[33] Lee, *Colonial development*, p. 122.
[34] For India see Peter Harnetty, *Imperialism and free trade: Lancashire and India in the mid-nineteenth century* (Vancouver, 1972), pp. 7–35 and Tomlinson, *Political economy of the Raj*, pp. 15–16 and 110–13. Details of the East African cases are given in E. A. Brett, *Colonialism and underdevelopment in East Africa, the politics of economic change, 1919–1939* (1973), pp. 266–81.
[35] Edelstein 'Imperialism: cost and benefit', pp. 200–15. The full exercise also considers the offsetting gains to Britain from lower aid and defence costs, and the elimination of the lower return on investment in the empire.

assumption, in the scenario most relevant for our purpose, is that the absence of the imperial connections would not have adversely affected the standard of development – and thus of external trade – of the empire. The second, is that there would have been no additional costs to the United Kingdom from any reduction in demand for exports as a consequence of the higher tariffs, that is, the labour and other resources employed in those industries would have found equally profitable employment elsewhere. A third set relates to the responsiveness of demand to the change in prices following the imposition of the tariff. On the basis of these assumptions he calculates that the gain to Britain from the actual lower levels of tariffs was equivalent to 3.8 per cent of GNP in 1913.

A corresponding estimate for a later date would certainly be lower than this relatively modest figure. As noted earlier, India acquired fiscal autonomy in 1919 and swiftly took advantage of this to increase tariff rates, and the dominions had also raised their tariffs in the interwar years. Enforced 'free trade' was thus of much less significance to the United Kingdom after the Second World War. Moreover, imperial attempts to discriminate in Britain's favour along the lines adopted in 1932 at Ottawa – by raising even higher tariffs against foreign countries than against Britain – were now being vigorously opposed, especially by the USA. The whole thrust of postwar policy was for free multilateral trade.[36] Every time a hard-pressed British government turned to its American ally for loans or grants it was compelled to concede further ground to US pressure for the elimination of imperial trade discrimination.

The dwindling band of Tory supporters of the imperialist tradition fought back as best they could. L. S. Amery, the leading figure in the movement in the 1920s, once again argued the case for imperial preference at the 1952 party conference: 'at any moment, on sixty days notice, we can walk out of the GATT prison camp. Well, why not walk out and walk our own way in the world?'[37] He and his supporters campaigned energetically in the House of Commons and in the constituencies to promote a revitalised imperial preference in place of GATT, but made little progress.

The crucial defect in their proposals was that their aspirations for imperial unity were no longer shared by any of the major Commonwealth countries. Those with whom the preferentialists wanted a special relationship could now see no reason why they should not trade on the most favourable

---

[36] The wartime discussions on this issue are described in Richard N. Gardner, *Sterling–dollar diplomacy in current perspective* (New York, new edn, 1980).
[37] Quoted in Goldsworthy, *Colonial issues*, p. 291.

terms they could get, wherever they could get them. The long crusade for imperial preference was fatally crushed at the 1954 party conference. An amendment to an official motion demanding 'such revision of the General Agreement on Tariffs and Trade as will restore freedom of action in respect of imperial preference' was defeated by a substantial majority.[38] Britain was firmly committed to the fundamental principles of a worldwide multilateral trading system promoted by GATT.

The battle for and against imperial preference aroused strong emotions, but the pattern of British trade was moving in a totally different direction. The striking changes are summarised in table 10.1. Before the war, almost half of United Kingdom exports went to the empire (29 per cent to the five dominions, and 19 per cent to India and the colonies); and a further 15 per cent to Latin America and all other countries which might, on a generous definition, be treated as the 'informal empire' (see columns 3, 5 and 6 of table 10.1). After the war, once Europe had recovered from the devastation and dislocation of the conflict, there was a massive shift in the destination of Britain's exports towards the most developed nations. The share of western Europe and the USA increased steadily from 32 per cent between 1950 and 1954 to 55 per cent between 1970 and 1973. Both the former dominions and the former colonies became progressively much less important: the former's share fell over the same period from 30 to 17 per cent; the latter's from 23 to 10 per cent. The proportion going to the 'informal empire' remained broadly constant, but this conceals a sharp fall in the importance of Latin America (down from 8 per cent to 4 per cent), compensated for by the growing markets in the newly rich oil-producing countries of the Middle East.

Ultimately, what really mattered for United Kingdom exports was the sustained and vigorous expansion of world trade which was such a crucial ingredient of the postwar golden age. This world boom owed nothing to any residues of imperialism. On the contrary, it was nourished by the stability and flexibility of the international monetary system formulated at Bretton Woods, the reduction in tariffs on manufactures initiated by GATT, and the vital role of international trade in the diffusion of technological advances. A further critical factor in the difficult early years of recovery from the wartime destruction was the understanding by the USA of the importance of generosity and patience, exemplified by Marshall Aid and the acceptance of the need for members of the European Payments

---

[38] Ibid., pp. 292–3.

Table 10.1. *Direction of United Kingdom exports, 1935–1973 (per cent)*

	Western Europe (1)	USA (2)	Old dominions (3)	Eastern Europe, USSR, and Japan (4)	Former colonies (5)	Latin America Middle East, and rest of world (6)
1935–8	27	5	29	5	19	15
1950–4	26	6	30	1	23	14
1955–9	27	8	26	2	23	14
1960–4	35	9	22	4	17	13
1965–9	39	12	20	5	12	12
1970–3	43	12	17	5	10	15

Notes:
For 1935–8 to 1955–9 exports of UK products; for later years re-exports are also included. (1) excludes Irish Republic; (3) Australia, Canada, Irish Republic, New Zealand, and South Africa; (5) all former British territories not covered in (3); (6) includes all non-British territories in Asia and Africa.
Source: Annual abstract of statistics, various years.

Union to be allowed to discriminate against dollar suppliers for over a decade after the conclusion of the war. With world trade growing at an unparalleled 7 per cent annum, Britain could achieve an exceptionally rapid increase in its exports to the industrialised countries, even while it was losing market shares to more efficient competitors.

There was, however, one aspect of the imperial financial relationship which became markedly more important after 1945 and attracted a great deal of attention: the growth of the sterling balances and the contribution which the colonies made to the overall deficit of the Sterling Area with the USA and other countries in the dollar area. The colonies earned substantial sums from their exports of rubber, cocoa, tin, copper, and other raw materials to the dollar area, particularly after the rise in commodity prices in the early 1950s. At the same time they were 'persuaded' by Britain to be exceptionally frugal in their spending on imports from the USA. They were thus able to accumulate a large surplus which remained in the dollar pool for the benefit of the other members of the Sterling Area.

The contribution of the colonies to Britain's dollar problem was most important in the immediate postwar years, broadly from 1946 to 1952. In this period the United Kingdom had an overall deficit in gold and dollars on current and capital account of $9,850 million, and the additional deficit of the independent Sterling Area countries raised the total to be financed to $11,200 million. The colonies contributed their dollar surplus of almost $2,000 million, but this still left a terrifyingly large shortfall of $9,200 million. By far the largest source of the finance needed to cover this huge deficit, some $7,600 million, came in credits from the USA and Canada, and Marshall Aid; the balance was covered by smaller loans from the IMF and other sources, and by reductions in Britain's meagre gold and dollar reserves.[39]

The dollar surplus of the colonies thus helped Britain to get through this extremely difficult early period. However, if the government had not attempted to preserve the Sterling Area arrangements, the *net* loss of gold and dollars from the Commonwealth as a whole would not have been disastrous, and even the gross contribution from the colonies was not of fundamental long-term significance. By 1953 a combination of higher exports and lower imports had brought the United Kingdom dollar problem under control, and in the later years of the decade it was Australia, South Africa, and the other independent members which were the principal beneficiaries of the dollar pool operated by the Sterling Area. The role of sterling as an international currency was increasingly seen as a burden to the United Kingdom; at best it was a rapidly depreciating asset.[40]

The final aspect of the alleged gains from empire which needs to be considered is Britain's huge investment of capital overseas, and the return flow of interest and dividends earned from this. The essential point here is that only one-fifth of the capital invested overseas in 1938 was in the colonies liberated after 1945. As with trade, they were for the most part too poor to offer a good investment. It was the USA, the dominions and some of the South American countries, especially Argentina, that had provided the best opportunities for British investors.

During and immediately after the war Britain was forced to make large sales of securities, notably in India and the Argentine. In the subsequent period there were massive shifts in both the direction and the type of United Kingdom overseas investment. When new investments were made, the acquisition of government and railway stocks by individual rentiers – the characteristic form of foreign investment before 1913 and still important in the interwar period – was of relatively little significance. The dominant form of the new capital was direct investment abroad by companies.

[39] Cairncross, *Years of recovery*, pp. 115–20.
[40] For example, Shonfield, *British economic policy*; Benjamin J. Cohen, *The future of sterling as an international currency* (1971); Susan Strange, *Sterling and British policy* (1971).

Investment by the oil companies was one important component of this movement, but the most rapid expansion – and the biggest break with the past – consisted of investment in manufacturing. There were a variety of motives for this, including the desire to establish foreign manufacturing plants where exports would be kept out by tariffs or other protective devices, the ability to reduce transport and other costs by producing abroad, and the opportunity to diversify by investment in foreign companies. As a consequence of this change, by 1968 almost three-quarters of overseas direct investment was in the former dominions, the USA, and Europe. The share of the former colonies was still about one-fifth, but the importance of Latin America had fallen to less than 5 per cent.[41]

Despite this renewal of the United Kingdom stock of overseas assets, the net flow of interest and dividends from abroad has become progressively less important as a source of income. It was as much as 8 per cent of GNP in the Edwardian period, it was only half this in the interwar years, and by the 1960s it had shrunk to little more than 1 per cent of Britain's national income. In part this reduction in the net receipts reflected the rise in profits taken out of the country with the increase in the capital invested here by the United States and other countries. But even if we take the gross receipts from overseas holdings, the contribution to GNP (after payment of foreign taxes) was only 3 per cent between 1960 and 1969; of which the income derived from investments in the former colonies and the countries of the 'informal empire' could not have been more than a third, that is, about 1 per cent of GNP.[42] It is thus difficult to find any secure foundation for the notion that tribute from abroad was of critical importance in Britain's postwar growth and prosperity.

IV

Some benefits of colonialism may have been lost and not detected in the vast economic upheaval simultaneously caused by the war, some may have continued in the new relationship, working to the advantage of Britain in the same way as under the old regimes. The nature of 'imperialism without

---

[41] Figures for the book value of overseas direct investment in 1968 (excluding oil, insurance, and banking) from *Board of Trade Journal*, 23 September 1970. Estimates of the missing categories of direct investment, and of portfolio investment and other long-term private and public external assets are also available, but without a geographical classification; for the end-1968 position see *Bank of England Quarterly Bulletin*, 9 (1969), pp. 438–47.

[42] The postwar estimates are calculated from *National income and expenditure 1963–1973* (1947), tables 1 and 7.

empires' has been the subject of a large literature in recent years.[43] Several techniques have been suggested by which developed countries might continue to exploit their superior economic strength to the detriment of independent but impoverished countries in the Third World. In particular, much attention has been given to the role of multinational corporations and discriminatory transfer pricing.

Whatever the merits of these theories as an explanation for the continuing economic problems of Africa and some other former colonial areas, they cannot be invoked to revive the proposition that Britain's prosperity suffered to any significant degree from the loss of her empire. How would they make their impact on Britain if not along the channels of trade and investment we have already explored? The main conclusion must be, therefore, that the alleged direct economic gains from the formal and informal colonial empire were largely illusory by 1945, if not earlier. Liquidation of the empire did not significantly raise the cost of imports, did not diminish the market for exports, and did not reduce the income which could be obtained from overseas assets. Essentially, what determined the standard of living of workers in the United Kingdom, as of those in other advanced industrial economies, was that output increased more rapidly than population. The 'secret' consisted of savings and capital, technological progress and skilled labour, buoyant exports and a stable international economy, not exploited colonial possessions.

Each of the major potential rewards of empire has now been considered; each has been found to be of small or negligible importance to the postwar British economy. The belief that the empire was vital to Britain's standard of living has, nevertheless, proved remarkably persistent, especially in foreign countries. The most important reason for this tenacity is probably a failure to perceive that there was actually a profound asymmetry between the cost to the colonies and the benefit to Britain. Those aware of the immense harm done to the colonies – by appropriation of their land, exploitation of their labour, extraction of their natural resources – assumed too quickly that this must be offset by a commensurate gain to Britain. In fact, it was not a zero-sum game. Countries which were poor to begin with could suffer extensive and long-lasting damage to their economic interests

---

[43] Colin Leys, *Underdevelopment in Kenya* (1975), pp. 1–27, is a very good review of modern theories of underdevelopment and neo-colonialism. For an excellent analysis of the relevance of the factors highlighted by these theories to the poor performance of Africa after decolonisation see D. K. Fieldhouse, *Black Africa 1945–80* (1986), pp. 102–22 and 231–45.

and the well-being of their people, without any *corresponding* advantage accruing to the population of Britain or other imperial powers.

This is not to deny that there were substantial benefits for a few. Colonial governments were persuaded by mining and plantation companies to impose taxes payable in cash, and to restrict land rights, thus driving the local population into wage labour. This greatly damaged the indigenous agriculture and way of life, and permitted a small number of shareholders to gain great profit from the operation of mines and plantations on the basis of poverty wages. Only rarely was anything paid to the colonies in mineral royalties, and very little was collected in taxes. A small number of white settlers were similarly enabled to farm large estates at considerable personal advantage. But all this had little significance for the prosperity of the great majority of the people of Britain, and was even less important after 1945 than in earlier years.

A second reason for the persistence of the belief in the importance of empire may have been a failure to distinguish sufficiently between the dominions, especially Australia and Canada, and the colonies. It was a large empire, and both the visionaries who proclaimed its merits and the critics who attacked its evils generally thought it politic to stress its significance and power as a unity. In economic terms, however, the connections which really counted were those with the dominions, with their relatively high per capita incomes. But from the First World War onwards these were essentially sovereign states. Any advantages which Britain obtained in dealings with them – whether in military security or preferential trade – were granted in exchange for what the dominions regarded as compensating benefits for themselves. They were bargains struck between two broadly equal parties.

In the colonies, by contrast, Britain could usually impose its wishes in matters of trade and investment; the interests of the weak could be sacrificed to those of the strong. However, the large populations – but very low per capita incomes – of the colonies were generally of little consequence in the overall economic picture. India was in some respects an exception to this, but she had already gained a substantial degree of autonomy in relation to trade and finance before the Second World War. Thus the relationships which mattered economically did not change politically after 1945; the relationships which changed did not matter.

11

Macmillan's audit of empire, 1957

TONY HOPKINS

I should also like to see something like a profit and loss account for each of our colonial possessions, so that we may be better able to gauge whether, from the financial and economic point of view, we are likely to gain or lose by its departure. This would need, of course, to be weighed against the political and strategic considerations involved in each case.[1]

I

Macmillan's request was the last of its kind on the scale needed to provide answers covering what was still a very sizeable empire. From the 1960s, with the wind of change carrying the empire ever more rapidly towards decolonisation, there was progressively less to inquire into and a diminishing incentive to make the effort. Questions of costs and benefits became increasingly irrelevant because the answers were already known or could readily be predicted. At the setting of the sun, the decision to go to war with Argentina over the Falklands Islands had nothing to do with any plan for the remnants of empire, while the exit from Hong Kong was as irreversible as it was long expected. In the 1950s, however, it was impossible for policy-makers either to think about Britain without also thinking about the empire, or to formulate an imperial strategy without automatically placing Britain at its centre. The assessment provided by Whitehall in response to the Prime Minister's instruction is therefore of considerable historical interest. It offers a final, official view of the empire at a moment when, as we now know, it was poised between late expansion and manifest decline,

I should like to express my gratitude to Gerold Krozewski of the Graduate Institute of International Studies, University of Geneva, for generously placing his very considerable knowledge of the period and the issues at my disposal.

[1] Prime Minister (Macmillan) to Lord President of the Council (Lord Salisbury), 28 Jan. 1957, CAB 134/1555. The documents referred to in this essay are in the Public Record Office unless otherwise indicated.

between the transfusions that reinvigorated it after the Second World War and the transactions that converted colonies into Commonwealth with such unexpected haste in the 1960s.

Given the historical interest of the assessment commissioned by Macmillan, it is surprising at first sight to find that it has attracted so little scholarly attention. Much of the apparent neglect is readily explained by the thirty-year rule: the documents concerned were all marked 'confidential' or 'secret' and were not available for public inspection until 1988. With one exception, not even the most thorough of the studies of decolonisation published before that date made reference to the audit of empire.[2] The exception is D. J. Morgan, who published his *Official history of colonial development* in 1980. Morgan had privileged access to official documents and was able to provide a summary of what he called the 'balance sheet of empire'.[3] Nevertheless, the contrast with the Defence Review, which was also a product of Macmillan's determination to re-examine important areas of policy after he became Prime Minister at the start of 1957, is complete.[4] The White Paper, being in the public domain, was much discussed at the time and has featured in the literature on the period ever since, whereas the assessment of empire remains unknown outside a small group of specialist historians.[5]

The voluminous nature of the documentation on the end of empire now available for public inspection also helps to explain why the exercise commissioned by Macmillan has still not been fully investigated. Of the handful of scholars who have referred to the audit, most take their cue from Morgan; the judgements made so far are therefore derivative and, inevitably, brief. In 1988, Hargreaves interpreted Morgan's précis of the key documents as showing that 'the assessed advantages of the African colonies were hardly overwhelming'.[6] Darwin, writing in the same year, suggested a different emphasis: 'the notorious colonial cost-benefit analysis carried out in 1957 at Macmillan's instigation is sometimes cited in

---

[2] Tribute should be paid here to the enduring value of some of the pioneering studies of the final phase of empire, notably David Goldsworthy, *Colonial issues in British politics, 1945–1961* (Oxford, 1971), and J. B. D. Miller, *Survey of Commonwealth affairs: problems of expansion and attrition, 1953–1969* (Oxford, 1974). The opportunity should also be taken to draw attention to a work that deserves to be better known in this context: Yusuf Bangura, *Britain and Commonwealth Africa: the politics of economic relations, 1951–75* (Manchester, 1983).

[3] Vol. V: *Guidance towards self-government in British colonies, 1941–1971* (1980), pp. 96–102.

[4] Cmnd 124. Defence: outline of future policy, 1957.

[5] Whether or not the audit of empire merits the same attention as has been paid to the Defence Review is of course an entirely separate question.

[6] John D. Hargreaves, *Decolonisation in Africa* (2nd edn 1996), pp. 171–3.

evidence of the new mood. But its conclusions were scarcely drastic.'[7] Drawing on Morgan's study, Darwin concluded: 'on these criteria, there was little scope for rapid colonial disengagement'.[8] In 1991, Reynolds, referring to Fieldhouse (who in turn referred to Morgan), offered the opinion that decolonisation was not 'in any direct sense the outcome of economic considerations'.[9] Two years later, Tarling used Morgan to emphasise the opposition of the Colonial Office to 'premature withdrawal' from south-east Asia.[10]

A few of the most recent studies refer to the original documentation, but they too give the matter summary treatment because their main interests lie elsewhere.[11] In 1994, Louis and Robinson, writing about decolonisation primarily from the perspective of Anglo-American relations, concluded that the report 'found, ambiguously, that British trade might be better served if independence came sooner rather than later'.[12] Ovendale, writing in 1995, had his eye on a review of policy towards Africa that was conducted in 1959, and tended to skim over the accounting aspects of the exercise.[13] On the other hand, Murphy's detailed investigation of Conservative party politics, also published in 1995, quoted the conclusion of the audit that Britain's economic interests 'were unlikely in themselves to be decisive' in determining the pace of constitutional change.[14] McIntyre's survey in 1996 of the evolution and composition of the Commonwealth after the Second World War also cited this conclusion, but drew attention, in addition, to the political and strategic arguments advanced in the report against 'premature with-

---

[7] John Darwin, *Britain and decolonisation: the retreat from empire in the postwar world* (1988), p. 230.   [8] Ibid., p. 230.

[9] David Reynolds, *Britannia overruled* (1991), pp. 221–4, citing David Fieldhouse, *Black Africa, 1945–1980* (1986), p. 8.

[10] Nicholas Tarling, *The fall of imperial Britain in south-east Asia* (Oxford, 1993), p. 204.

[11] It has to be said that the audit has also been bypassed more frequently than it deserves. For example, it is scarcely mentioned in Richard Aldous and Sabine Lee (eds.), *Harold Macmillan and Britain's world role* (1995).

[12] Wm Roger Louis and Ronald Robinson, 'The imperialism of decolonisation', *Journal of Imperial and Commonwealth History*, 22 (1994), p. 487. The authors then link this conclusion to their (more important) argument that 'economic informalization' went hand in hand with 'political informalization' as Britain tried to perpetuate her influence by means that were in tune with moves towards independence.

[13] Ritchie Ovendale, 'Macmillan and the wind of change in Africa, 1957–1960', *Historical Journal*, 38 (1995), pp. 455–77. In particular, Ovendale misses the significance of the economic dimension of Macmillan's audit. On the other hand, he is right to note (p. 458) that Hilton Poynton at the Colonial Office had questioned the value of some of Britain's colonies in 1956. However, this scarcely counts as a major reassessment: while Lennox-Boyd remained Colonial Secretary, the Colonial Office adhered to established policies.

[14] Philip Murphy, *Party politics and decolonization* (Oxford, 1995), p. 22.

drawal'.[15] The latest assessment, by Krozewski, judges that a 'cost-benefit analysis of empire was almost inevitable, given the far-reaching economic and political changes in imperial relations',[16] and goes on to suggest that the report was permissive in that it provided grounds for supposing that the transfer of power could proceed if Britain's cardinal economic priorities were safeguarded.[17]

These diverse interpretations clearly require further investigation. Morgan's account, despite its brevity, has been used to support conflicting views of the final stage of decolonisation. But, even if his summary had produced unanimity among subsequent commentators, it cannot serve as a firm basis for generalising about the conclusions of a major report on the state of the empire, let alone about the procedures and bargains that led to the final verdict. Recent authors have also reached different conclusions, even though they have cited the original documentation. Was the audit 'ambiguous', 'inconclusive', or 'evenly balanced' in weighing the economic costs and benefits of empire? If so, did this conclusion allow 'political' or 'strategic' considerations to be more influential in determining British policy towards self-government and independence in the colonies? Or, was there a sense, whether direct or indirect, in which the economics of empire were essential to the view taken of the constitutional evolution of the colonies? Both sets of arguments have been put. To be able to choose between them, or perhaps to reconcile them, we need to know who set the agenda and why, whether the conclusions were consistent with the evidence, whether the evidence reflected observable realities, and what impact, if any, the report had on the rapid changes in policy (and practice) that were to speed the process of decolonisation from the close of the 1950s.

Asking pertinent questions, as all historians know, is easy; pertinent answers are another matter. The enquiry mounted here cannot be comprehensive: the issues raised by Macmillan's audit are as wide-ranging as the territories they referred to were far-flung. There is no guarantee, either, that the answers given here will be persuasive. More research is needed (as always) on related documents in at least half a dozen Whitehall departments.[18] Yet some firm conclusions can be drawn from a textual analysis of the reports that made up the audit – an exercise that has not yet been undertaken. As we shall

---

[15] W. David McIntyre, 'The admission of small states to the Commonwealth', *Journal of Imperial and Commonwealth History*, 24 (1996), pp. 259–60.

[16] Gerold Krozewski, 'Finance and empire: the dilemma facing Great Britain in the 1950s', *International History Review*, 18 (1996), p. 66.

[17] Gerold Krozewski, 'The politics of sterling and Britain's postwar imperial connection, 1947–1958' (unpublished PhD thesis, University of Geneva, 1996), pp. 277–81.

[18] As well as on the private papers of Lennox-Boyd, Macmillan, and others.

now suggest, the audit records the official mind at a point of transition from the thinking that characterised policy in the 1950s to that associated with the 'wind of change' in the 1960s. It is important for what it reveals about perceptions of empire at a moment when, in formal terms, decline was about to be encouraged, and for the evidence it offers on the causes and timing of what was the final, fundamental change in colonial policy.

II

On becoming Prime Minister in January 1957, Macmillan listed six big issues that compelled his attention. One of them was the Commonwealth, which, he recalled gratefully, had been supportive during the Suez crisis. 'But what of the future? I reflected that in the coming year both Ghana and Malaya were due to become independent. This process was bound to continue. Could it be resisted? Or should it be guided as far as possible into fruitful channels? Was I destined to be the remodeller or the liquidator of empire?'[19] It was not long before the answer to this question became apparent: with the appointment of Macleod as Colonial Secretary in 1959 the process of decolonisation accelerated rapidly, and Macmillan found himself steering towards the fate that Churchill had been so determined to avoid. It is possible to suggest that he had set course at an even earlier date, despite his support for military action during the Suez crisis. In 1956, as officials in Whitehall agonised about the discrepancy between the needs of the empire and the means available to fund them, Macmillan (then Chancellor of the Exchequer) declared that he was willing to consider 'a deliberate policy of shedding some of our colonial burdens'.[20]

Yet, if this was the outcome, it was not quite the intention. As Prime Minister, Macmillan was also determined that Britain should remain a great power, and a world role was inconceivable without a vibrant Commonwealth. The Churchillian injunction, with its implied rebuke for those who broke faith with the empire, remained with him. A year after becoming Prime Minister, and with the results of the audit known to him, Macmillan stated that he had 'no intention of presiding over the liquidation of the British empire'.[21] Of course, he may not have meant what he said, but what

[19] Harold Macmillan, *Riding the storm, 1956–1959* (1971), p. 200. This is the only clue Macmillan gave in his memoirs to his motives in calling for an assessment of the empire. He made no direct reference to the report itself, probably out of respect for its 'confidential' and 'secret' status.   [20] Morgan, *Guidance towards self-government*, p. 90.
[21] A speech in Singapore on 19 January 1958. Quoted in McIntyre, 'Admission of small states', p. 260.

he said was at least consistent with his belief that he could manage an imperial transformation: the empire was not so much 'breaking up' as 'growing
up'.[22] As one means of control disappeared, another was to be invoked. The
empire was to be remodelled to enable Britain to exercise a degree of informal sway over her former colonies once they became independent members
of the Commonwealth. Although shorn of material strength, the British
could still 'exert our influence in other ways', notably by 'living by our wits,
as we had in earlier periods'.[23]

It is therefore too simple to suppose that Macmillan set about dis-
mantling the empire in the aftermath of Suez. At the same time, it is clear
that, on this subject, he had an open mind and was beginning to fill it with
thoughts that, for many of his Conservative colleagues, were unthinkable.
He recognised that change was needed and he sought to profit from it. Had
he been content with the status quo, it is unlikely that he would have initiated, so promptly, such a wide-ranging review of the costs and benefits of
empire. From this perspective, liquidation was not a terminal event but part
of an evolutionary process. In expert and fast-moving hands, emancipation
and subordination could be made to resemble one another. The result of
these calculations was a new version of the theory of how to square the
circle: by exchanging an empire of dominance for a Commonwealth of free
states Britain could remain a world power, gain goodwill, and economise
on scarce resources.

Given these preconditions, it is not hard to see why alarm bells rang
when the Prime Minister's request reached the Colonial Office (by way of
the Colonial Policy Committee) in January 1957.[24] Lennox-Boyd, the

---

[22] The phrase is Macmillan's: ibid. It is worth noting that Macmillan greatly enjoyed his tour
of the Commonwealth in January–February 1958 and returned with a heightened impression of its potential and of the need for policy changes to deal with emerging issues. See
Macmillan, *Riding the storm*, pp. 410–13, and 379–80, 395, 413.

[23] Ibid.

[24] The Colonial Policy Committee (CPC) was formed in 1955 to improve communication
between the Colonial Office and the Cabinet and to ensure, in particular, that general
policy issues were kept in view by a small group of ministers and senior officials from different departments of state. The intention was that the committee would decide the main lines
of policy and the Colonial Office would implement them. The committee was first chaired
by the Lord President of Council, then by the Lord Chancellor (from April 1957), and
finally by the Prime Minister (from November 1958). The committee was dissolved in June
1962, and replaced by the Overseas Policy Committee. The Ministerial CPC was served
by an Official CPC, which was set up in January 1956 to consider problems referred to it
by its senior counterpart. The official CPC consisted of the Secretary to the Cabinet (Sir
Norman Brook), who also acted as chairman, and high-ranking representatives from the
Colonial Office, the Commonwealth Relations Office, and the Foreign Office. It was
wound up in December 1961. For further details see Morgan, *Official history of development*,
vol. V, pp. 58–67.

Colonial Secretary, responded in February expressing, as he was bound to, his full co-operation and enclosing a 'skeleton plan' of the 'comprehensive review' he proposed to commission.[25] But he also took the precaution of adding 'one or two glosses' to the Prime Minister's request.

The first of these sought to correct an important point of terminology. Macmillan had distinguished between colonies that would qualify for full membership of the Commonwealth and those that might attain 'independence' but could not aspire to full membership. 'I have assumed', Lennox-Boyd observed, 'that, in using the word "independence" in this context, the Prime Minister had in mind the status which we usually ascribe as internal self-government.'[26] We do not know precisely what Macmillan did have in mind, but the fact that he had blurred such a standard distinction at least suggests that it was not, in his view, of paramount importance. Nor was it an innocent slip: it was repeated in another part of his letter.[27] However, the distinction was central not only to Lennox-Boyd's thinking but also to Colonial Office policy in the 1950s. On returning to power in 1951, the Conservative Government continued a broadly bi-partisan policy on colonial affairs:[28] the aim was to promote the degree of economic and political development needed to support, in the fullness of time, internal self-government in the colonies. 'Viability' and 'readiness' were the phrases of the day; internal self-government was a long-term possibility for those who met the test.[29] Independence was an entirely different matter. Indeed, Churchill and Eden wanted to ban the use of the word in any discussion of the future of the colonial empire. As far as possible, Lennox-Boyd kept the faith. The phrasing of Macmillan's request suggested that withdrawal might be on the agenda. It therefore questioned both Colonial Office policy and a central tenet of Conservative imperialists.

Lennox-Boyd's second gloss on Macmillan's request expressed his concern that the audit should 'also take account of the obligations towards the peoples of any given territory', the reason being that 'nothing is more

---

[25] Lennox-Boyd to the Lord President of the Council (Lord Salisbury), 15 February 1957, CAB 134/1555; CPC (57), 6.   [26] Ibid.

[27] 'It would be good if Ministers could know more clearly which territories are likely to become ripe for independence over the next few years – or even, if they are not ready for it, will demand it so insistently that their claims cannot be denied.' Macmillan, Personal Minute No. M 19/57, 28 January 1957 CPC (57) 6.

[28] Murphy, *Party politics and decolonization*, provides the most detailed assessment.

[29] David Goldsworthy, 'Keeping change within bounds: aspects of colonial policy during the Churchill and Eden Governments, 1951–57', *Journal of Imperial and Commonwealth History*, 18 (1990), pp. 81–108 is a valuable guide to Conservative policy during this period.

dangerous than to gain a reputation for forsaking one's friends'.[30] If Britain were to withdraw from individual colonies 'without being able to hand over to a successor government which could be expected to govern reasonably well in the interest of all its inhabitants, the repercussions would be serious and widespread'.[31] Evidently, Lennox-Boyd was trying to forestall any 'premature withdrawal' from empire. The reference to Britain's obligations towards colonial subjects was an attempt to remind the Prime Minister that forces on the periphery mattered; they needed to be entered in the balance sheet and weighed against domestic and other international considerations. Colonies that lacked 'viability' and 'readiness' would also be politically unstable. The 'repercussions', as Lennox-Boyd needed only to hint, would affect Britain's trade, prestige, and effectiveness as an ally in the Cold War.

The exchange between Macmillan and Lennox-Boyd indicates that the two parties most closely involved in the review had different conceptions of the purpose of the exercise. As we shall now see, the basic dilemma between the wisdom of continuity and the merits of change in colonial policy was elaborated and further developed by representations from other powerful interests in Whitehall that had a presence on the Official Colonial Policy Committee (CPC), the body charged with undertaking the audit. The Treasury made a major contribution to the crucial economic aspects of the audit; the Ministry of Defence kept a close eye on the strategic role of the colonies; related interests were represented by senior officials from the Commonwealth Relations Office, the Foreign Office, and the Board of Trade.[32] Beyond Whitehall were other influences, which made themselves felt (to the extent that they were felt at all) indirectly: competing groups within the Conservative party; the views of colonial governors; the growth of nationalism; and the interests of the USA. Aspects of the wider context will be considered at a later stage; the immediate task, having assembled the auditors, is to consider their audit.

---

[30] Lennox-Boyd to the Lord President of the Council (Lord Salisbury), 15 February 1957, CAB 134/1555; CPC (57), 6.

[31] Ibid.

[32] The committee was chaired by Sir Norman Brook (Secretary of the Cabinet) and had seven other members. The composition altered to reflect the subjects under discussion at particular times, though two, and sometimes three, representatives from the Colonial Office were always present. I am grateful to the surviving members of the CPC, Sir Richard Powell (MoD) and Sir Denis Wright (FO), and to P. R. Odgers (of the CPC's two-man secretariat) for assisting me with their recollections of the committee, and above all to Sir John Moreton (Parliamentary Secretary to Lennox-Boyd) for some spirited and highly informative letters on this subject.

III

The Official CPC laboured on its audit from February to September 1957, producing, in the course of eight months, three secret Confidential Prints and a number of subsidiary papers. The first Confidential Print, which at seventy-six pages was also the largest, appeared in May 1957 under the title 'Future constitutional development in the colonies'.[33] Two more papers were ready in June. One, dealing specifically with economic and financial considerations, appeared in July as a secret Confidential Print of ten printed pages; the other, which covered the same issues in a more analytical way, remained for the time being in draft form.[34] The Official CPC reviewed the results of its inquiries in June and July and decided to circulate the two Confidential Prints to ministers as 'background documents', and to produce a 'general paper' divided into 'constitutional, economic, strategic and political sections' that would summarise and interpret the information presented in the Confidential Prints.[35] The general paper, consisting of eight printed pages, appeared as a Confidential Print in September 1957, thus completing Macmillan's audit of empire.[36]

Morgan, the only author so far to examine the principal documents, treats them as separate contributions.[37] In a literal sense, this is correct, but his approach gives insufficient emphasis to the connections between the reports and the ways in which they evolved in the course of the investigation. While it would be possible to base an assessment of the audit solely on the final report, examining all four reports in sequence is a more illuminating procedure because it shows how accretions and modifications were made as the process of consultation and reflection advanced. By tracing this evolution, it becomes possible to see how the main conclusions were reached and to suggest how they might be interpreted.

The first report, presented in May, adopted the rather uninspiring format of an encyclopaedia entry, in which each colony was treated under identical headings: political and constitutional, strategic, economic, 'obligations and repercussions', and a conclusion. Impartially, if also

---

[33] 'Future constitutional development in the colonies (economic and financial considerations)', CP(O) (57) 5, 30 May 1957: Colonial Office Print, GEN 174/012. All three confidential prints carried the same title; the second one was sub-titled.

[34] CPC (57) 28, 26 July 1957: Colonial Office Print, GEN 174/012. See also the earlier version in CP(O) (57) 4, 30 May 1957, and the revise enclosed in CP(O) (57) 6, 4 July 1957.

[35] CP(O) (57) 7, 12 July 1957.

[36] 'Future constitutional development in the colonies', CPC (57) 30 (revise), 6 September 1957. C.O. Confidential Print, GEN 174/012: see n. 34.

[37] Morgan, *Guidance towards self-government*, pp. 96–102.

unhelpfully, the report offered no general evaluation; the assessments with the widest implications were those attached to the largest colonies.

The flavour of the report can be judged from its survey of Nigeria, the largest and most important of the remaining dependent territories.[38] The political section emphasised the risk of instability should constitutional advance be accelerated. External threats existed, but were of little account. 'A small minority of the Muslims – but it includes some of the most influential and able – must be recognised as potentially hostile to us and what we stand for, and inclined to fanaticism and xenophobia.'[39] There was also a 'small Communist-inspired party . . . but it has little influence. All the Governments in Nigeria have publicly condemned international Communism as a threat to their own freedom, and so far Moscow has had little success.' The main danger came from ethnic and other rivalries within the country. This issue had already caused 'an acute crisis' that had 'nearly split the country' in 1953. 'If independence for Nigeria comes too soon, the North, or parts of it, may talk of secession.' Consequently, 'it will be our aim to proceed with constitutional advances at the Federal level as slowly as possible'. Specifically, 'we shall seek to ensure that no date is set for self-government for the country as a whole. But success will not be easy.'

The brief section on strategy underlined the importance of the airport at Kano, which was on the route to East Africa, the Arabian peninsula, and the Far East, and commented that 'so long as the Federal Government remains dependent, our strategic requirements are constitutionally secure. After independence, we shall have to rely on goodwill.' The analysis of economic connections estimated that allocations under the Colonial Development and Welfare Act between 1955 and 1960 involved a direct cost to the Exchequer of about £13 million. On the other hand, Nigeria's net dollar earnings amounted to about £5 million a year, so the Sterling Area would suffer a 'moderate loss' should she decide to leave it after becoming independent. Still, there was 'no evidence' that there was 'any strong incentive' for her to do so. 'If, however, she disintegrates an entirely new situation would arise.' As far as trade ties were concerned, the Nigerian market was 'a valuable one'. Exports would be affected 'if independence were accompanied by hostility to United Kingdom traders, but it is to be hoped that there will be no such hostility'.

[38] The Gold Coast and Malaya were excluded from the report because both were about to become independent (the former in March 1957, as Ghana, and the latter in August of the same year).

[39] The quotations in this paragraph, and the next six paragraphs, are all from GEN 174/012 cited in n. 33.

The general assessment was that 'if the British withdraw in the next half decade, it is quite on the cards that the North, or large parts of it, will secede, and if this happened a general disintegration might well follow'. It was probable, in any event, that there would be 'less freedom for minorities everywhere' and in some areas 'a reversion to much of the barbarism of pre-Colonial days'. This prospect meant that 'our restraining hand is thus really needed for a generation. But it is unrealistic to expect that we shall have so long.'[40] Despite 'its great promise, and several encouraging features, one cannot avoid forebodings as to the outlook for Nigeria, for the simple reason that we are unlikely to have long enough to complete our civilising and unifying mission'.

A similar message was delivered by the comments on Kenya, even though political and economic choices there, in marked contrast to Nigeria, were profoundly influenced by the presence of white settlers. 'Internally, the political pressures are those of an unstable multi-racial society', but the basic problem, achieving stability, was the same as in Nigeria. There were encouraging signs: 'the habit of compromise is growing and if the races can be yoked in a pattern subject to control from Westminster for long enough the habit of co-operation and acceptance one of the other may become the natural order of things'. However, there was bad news too: 'this prospect is menaced by the theories of democracy which the African has avidly accepted'. If only there were more leaders like the Sultan of Zanzibar, Seyyid Sir Khalifa bin Harub: he had come to the throne in 1911, and 'the years have brought him honours and wisdom, and an enduring loyalty to the British connection'. As it was, alien notions of democracy 'lure the African to stand out against co-operation until he can dominate by numbers'. Liberal England's reservations about the consequences of universal suffrage were here clearly in evidence, as was its instinctive elitism; both counselled against 'premature withdrawal'. This judgement was reinforced by an uncompromising statement of East Africa's 'great potential strategic importance'. It was just as well, the strategist concluded, that 'the early relinquishment by Her Majesty of jurisdiction in the region is, for present purposes, remote'.

On the economic front, the cost to the Exchequer, via the Colonial Development and Welfare Acts, was very limited. The main drain on Britain had been caused by the Mau Mau emergency, but the greater part of this had now been met. East Africa as a whole was a very minor dollar

---

[40] Nigeria achieved independence in 1960.

earner; it was in the interests of territories in the region to remain in the Sterling Area 'in view of their high requirements of external capital'; and 'it may reasonably be assumed that they would do so'. As far as commerce was concerned, Britain had a surplus on her visible trade with East Africa, which absorbed about 1.8 per cent of the value of her total exports. This stake was not thought to be seriously at risk: independence was not on the agenda, and the region was likely to remain in the Sterling Area. Admittedly, the British connection provided an incentive for official purchases of capital goods from the United Kingdom, and this might be reduced if territories in East Africa gained independence. But this prospect was offset by the optimistic thought that 'the existence of well-established British merchanting houses in East Africa provides a local loyalty which not infrequently overcomes marginal price advantages offered by non-British suppliers of consumer goods'.

The conclusion for East Africa was similar to that for West Africa, despite their different circumstances. The region was a 'testing ground' for 'multi-racial development'; the 'balance between racial groups' was maintained 'only by the jurisdiction of the United Kingdom'; without it, there would be political conflict, social disintegration, and economic bankruptcy. Premature withdrawal would lead to a 'disastrous decline in the prestige and influence of the United Kingdom', and would 'bring to a shabby conclusion an important and hopeful experiment in race relations'. The consequences would be widely felt: markets would be lost and the 'flank of Africa would be thrown open to subversive penetration from the Soviet Union'. However, doom could be averted, even if gloom continued to linger: 'a strengthening of United Kingdom interest would . . . pay dividends'. The Colonial Office followed this thought by putting in a bid for substantial loans (totalling £150 million) for East Africa during the period 1957–60, this being the 'essential provision to sustain wise policy'.

The tenor of the assessments of West and East Africa was repeated elsewhere. Few, if any, countries were ready for independence; some would never attain it. Premature withdrawal – a phrase that appears throughout the report – would be damaging both to Britain's prestige and to the welfare of colonial peoples, while also opening the way for subversive elements. Strategic considerations dictated a continuing British presence virtually everywhere. With few exceptions, it was expected that independence would have a very limited effect on Britain's economic interests. Independence was considered to be, for the majority of colonies, a remote prospect whose effects could not be judged with much accuracy; the judgements that were made took a generally sanguine view of Britain's ability to uphold the Sterling Area (especially given the broadly co-operative attitude of Ghana and Malaya) and, with it, her informal commercial influence.

While conducting its tour of the world, the CPC also focused on a number of specific issues, and particularly on the economic and financial aspects of Britain's relationship with the empire. In June, the committee considered two papers on these subjects. The first was a formal presentation of the balance of payments and sterling assets of the colonies and the volume of British investment in them;[41] the second was a broader and more analytical assessment of these and allied issues.[42] Putting the two together, the CPC reached the provisional conclusion that 'the economic considerations tend to be evenly matched and were unlikely in themselves to be decisive in determining whether or not a territory should become independent'.[43] The committee also noted that investment needs were 'well beyond the present capacity of the United Kingdom's resources', with the result (acknowledged for the first time) that 'there might be no alternative but to allow economic standards in the colonial territories to fall'.[44]

The first paper was circulated in a virtually unchanged form as a Confidential Print. It was drawn on later when the auditors prepared their final report, and will be referred to in that context.[45] The important economic analysis of the second paper, however, was revised with assistance from the Treasury and the Board of Trade so that a more precise assessment could be made of some key issues: Britain's trade prospects and independence; the effect of independence on the Sterling Area; the supply of capital for development in the colonies and newly independent states in the Commonwealth; the need to reconsider strategic priorities in the light of the defence review that was currently under way. When the new version of the Colonial Office's original document came before the CPC in July, it was decided to carry the conclusions forward for use in the final summary report that appeared in September.[46] This was a highly significant decision. As we shall see, the analysis contained in the revised paper altered the balance and direction of the final recommendations.

The final report was presented to the cabinet in September.[47] As far as

---

[41] CP(O) (57), 4, 30 May 1957.　　[42] CP(O) (57), 3, 30 May 1957.

[43] CP(O) (57), 2, 6 June 1957.　　[44] Ibid.

[45] C.O. GEN, 174/012, July 1957.

[46] CP(O) (57) 6, 4 July 1957. Further amendments were made (with assistance from the Treasury) on the subject of colonial sterling balances. See also CPC (57) 28, 26 July 1957.

[47] CPC (57) 30 (Revise), 6 Sept. 1957. The quotations in this paragraph, and in the next seven paragraphs, are all from this source.

constitutional advance was concerned, the committee's conservative predictions reflected the commonly held view of the day: independence for a
very small number of territories 'within the next ten years', and 'significant
developments in internal self-government' during the same period for a
larger number of less-advanced colonies. There was no suggestion that the
pace of change might be faster than this, despite the fact that the Gold
Coast and Malaya were attaining independence as the audit was being com-
piled; nor was there any sign that the Colonial Office's long-established
faith in the cure-all properties of federations might be misplaced, though it
was conceded that any move towards federation in Central Africa could
occur only when 'a numerical majority of all the inhabitants of whatever
race so desire'. Considered in retrospect, this is an uncontroversial statement; set against the assertive and disparaging remarks made in the committee's first report about the 'theories of democracy which the African has
avidly accepted',[48] it is clear that an important shift of principle had taken
place, even if its application was still regarded as being a long-term
consideration.

The economic dimension of Britain's relations with the colonies, the
most complex and time-consuming of the issues addressed by the committee, took up more than half the final report. The evidence and analysis confirmed the conclusions put forward in July, after the Treasury had left its
fingerprints on the draft prepared by the Colonial Office. In September, the
committee felt confident enough to state a new central principle: 'the economic and financial implications of the grant of independence to Colonial
territories do not flow from the grant of independence itself but from the
policies which may be followed by the particular countries after independence'. Constitutions were less important than policies, and policies were
to be influenced – to the extent that they could be influenced at all – increasingly by informal rather than by formal means. The new principle was then
applied to Britain's main areas of economic interest.

It was now thought that the sterling balances held by the colonies, long
a source of concern in official circles, could probably be managed without
precipitating a crisis for the pound and the Sterling Area. The importance
of this issue, and the reason why policy was moving from conserving the
balances to running them down, will be dealt with later. For the moment,
and in the immediate context of the CPC's final report, it can be said that
the Treasury was reassured by the realisation that the balances were less

[48] Quoted on p. 244 above.

liquid than had been thought, that they could be used to finance colonial development, and that two of the three major creditors, Malaya and Ghana, had agreed to adopt a 'responsible' attitude in drawing on their balances (and there were good prospects that the third, Nigeria, would also fall into line). Admittedly, withdrawals might put pressure on the United Kingdom's reserves, but there was a strong argument for dealing with the problem sooner rather than later – after the dollar gap had been closed and before sterling moved to full convertibility in 1958. Of course, the Treasury continued to climb a wall of worry: independence could open the way to 'rash policies of over-development', 'an inflationary situation', 'a call on resources', and 'a considerable strain upon the United Kingdom'. Nevertheless, the 'mere fact of the grant of independence should not in itself make any appreciable difference to the trend', even though 'standards of prudence would probably fall'.

The report also acknowledged the contribution made by the colonies to 'the strength of the Sterling Area in recent years', and expressed anxiety about the far-reaching consequences for the United Kingdom should the large dollar-earning colonies leave it. But here, too, the conclusion was reassuring: 'there is no reason to believe that any of the present candidates for independence would find it in their interests to leave the Sterling Area after independence'. Admittedly, premature withdrawal, if it led to 'a serious deterioration in political and economic conditions', might easily damage the Sterling Area. On the other hand, 'postponement and any pique resulting from it' would be 'more likely' to produce the same result.

A similar line of argument was applied to trade relations, which were also regarded as being of 'considerable importance'.[49] Any 'premature transfer of power which resulted in serious political troubles and a lasting deterioration in a territory's economic circumstances' would 'of course seriously affect' British economic interests. On the other hand, 'assuming an orderly transfer of power and no appreciable falling-off in a territory's economic activity, the grant of independence need not adversely affect the United Kingdom's trading position'. The colonies 'already pursue a very liberal trade policy'; imperial preferences existed but were of varying importance and would not necessarily be affected by independence; 'intangible trade advantages' arising from the imperial connection 'might well be diminished' but the 'dangers of this should not . . . be exaggerated'. 'Once more,

---

[49] In 1956 the colonies accounted for 13 per cent of UK exports and 10 per cent of UK imports; one quarter of all colonial trade (imports and exports) was conducted with the United Kingdom.

it is not so much a question of the grant of independence itself, but the policy pursued after independence.'

The budgetary implications of independence were one area where constitutional change did have an effect, formally speaking, on the United Kingdom's responsibilities. This was because ex-colonies ceased to be eligible for aid through the Colonial Development and Welfare Act and associated schemes, which were estimated to cost the British government about £51 million a year. In practice, however, 'the net saving in the foreseeable future would almost certainly be considerably less than is generally imagined'. The territories closest to independence were in general those least in need of assistance from the Exchequer; where help was imperative, as in the case of Malaya,[50] resources would have to be found. All the same, the Treasury was satisfied that the burden on the UK was not very great and that it was not writing a blank cheque for future development needs. Grants under the Colonial Development and Welfare Acts in the period 1955–60 accounted for only one-sixth of colonial expenditure on development; the remainder came from the colonies' own resources and from external loans. Since demand from colonial governments for loan finance on the London market was expected to be about £25–30 million a year during the next few years, it was comforting to know that newly independent states had an incentive to 'so order their affairs that their credit stands high enough to make this a practical proposition'. Nevertheless, recent evidence suggested that the City was reluctant to meet all the demands placed on it, mainly because investors lacked confidence in newly independent states. The problem, however, inspired a solution: the concept of 'sharing the burden'. Since the demand for investment was 'well beyond the present capacity of the United Kingdom's resources', 'any arrangement which served to transfer to some other Commonwealth or foreign country some part of the Exchequer burden, or the demand for investment, would be welcome'. Treasury cynics must have been as surprised as they were delighted to learn, shortly afterwards, that their call had received an answer.[51]

The conclusion to the economic section of the final report is worth citing in full because the first sentence, which has been quoted by several previous authors, needs to be seen in its context if it is to be interpreted correctly:

[50] '. . . in connection with the Emergency and the building up of her armed forces'.
[51] Canada, explicitly mentioned in the report in this connection, responded subsequently by expanding her aid programme; the USA, already investing in British (and French) colonies, followed suit.

To sum up, the economic considerations tend to be evenly matched and the economic interests of the United Kingdom are unlikely in themselves to be decisive in determining whether or not a territory should become independent. Although damage could certainly be done by the premature grant of independence, the economic dangers to the United Kingdom of deferring the grant of independence for her own selfish interests after the country is politically and economically ripe for independence would be far greater than any dangers resulting from an act of independence negotiated in an atmosphere of goodwill such as has been the case with Ghana and Malaya. Meanwhile, during the period when we can still exercise control in any territory, it is most important to take every step open to us to ensure, as far as we can, that British standards and methods of business administration permeate the whole life of the territory.

As already suggested, the argument of the report is not that economic considerations were unimportant, quite the contrary, but that preserving them depended on political relationships rather than on constitutional change. The disavowal of selfish motives for deferring independence, though honourable, was also easily made: the Treasury had already reached the conclusion that an orderly retreat could be signalled without loss, and in important respects was to Britain's advantage.[52] What mattered was that we did not outstay our welcome, but took steps to make friends and influence the people who would shape policies in the new states, when they came into being. The problem was one of transition, a matter, as Macmillan himself was soon to put it, of 'growing up' rather than 'breaking up'.[53]

The summary of Britain's strategic interests appears to have been little influenced by the Defence Review, though the presentation was less strident than it had been in the first report, probably because it had been shaped by the calming hand of the Cabinet Secretary, Norman Brook. Key bases in the Mediterranean, West and East Africa, and Singapore were still needed and had to be maintained, though a British presence was thought to be consistent with moves towards internal self-government. The section on political priorities was equally brief. It reaffirmed a 'Colonial policy of assisting dependent peoples towards the greatest practicable measure of self-government' without 'imposing any delays which could be interpreted as artificial'. At the same time, 'we must retain some measure of jurisdiction or protection where this is patently required'. This recommendation was followed by some trenchant statements that bore the imprint of Lennox-Boyd rather than Norman Brook. 'The United Kingdom stands to gain no

---

[52] It may be, of course, that the 'selfish interests' referred to were not those linked to business but to the right wing of the Conservative party.   [53] See n. 21 above.

credit for launching a number of immature, unstable and impoverished units whose performances as "independent" countries would be an embarrassment and whose chaotic existence would be a temptation to our enemies.' We should maintain our authority 'until a transfer of power can be shown to be generally desired by its people and they have shown they can live at peace with one another and are capable of sustaining independent status with a reasonable standard of government'. The report ended with a rallying cry that can also be seen as a final plea: 'the United Kingdom has been too long connected with its Colonial possessions to sever ties abruptly without creating a bewilderment which would be discreditable and dangerous'.

If the interpretation suggested here is correct, the reports prepared between January and September 1957 signalled a major change in Conservative policy, a shift from the evolutionary approach of Lennox-Boyd to the radical prescription that was shortly to be issued by Macleod. The first and longest report, produced in May, emphasised constitutional and political issues. Economic aspects were dealt with, but in a factual way that was virtually shorn of analysis. The perception that Britain's financial and commercial interests were not inevitably doomed by the advent of independence was already present, but it was not allowed to modify the central theme that political advance needed time and had to be based on a successful development programme. The papers produced and discussed in June and July, however, brought the economic dimension to the fore, and the imprint of the Treasury ensured that the analysis and the weight attached to it were kept prominently in view thereafter. The final report, made available in September, reflected this emphasis. The position originally taken by the Colonial Office was reduced in size and significance. There was no mention of 'viability' or 'readiness': the terms survived only in translation and, even so, were confined to the political context. Nor was there talk of a 'civilising mission', as there had been in May. Lennox-Boyd's 'glosses' on Macmillan's request had lost their shine: the distinction between self-government and independence was preserved only as a formality, while Britain's 'obligations' to colonial subjects were scarcely mentioned outside the political context. The bid for sizeable additional aid made by the Colonial Office in May was ignored.

Lennox-Boyd's position survived but in an attenuated form that was detached from the economic underpinning it needed. The rhetoric about the 'discreditable and dangerous' act of abruptly severing ties was left in the final document, allowing Lennox-Boyd to claim that policy remained unchanged.[54] In a letter written to R. A. Butler (the Lord Privy Seal) in 1958, Lennox-Boyd said of the report: 'I keep the product always by me and constantly refer to it', and his summary of the recommendations clearly shows that he interpreted them as supporting his own view of colonial policy.[55] But the new and expanded emphasis on economic considerations pointed in a different direction. Britain's important financial and commercial stake in empire could survive constitutional independence; her wider international ambitions might even gain from it. The report thus gave Macmillan what he wanted: an assurance that he could remodel the empire without damaging Britain's economic interests; indeed, remodelling was needed to preserve them. By playing the right cards, the British could still, in Macmillan's phrase, 'exert our influence in other ways'.[56]

IV

Macmillan's audit presents two contrasting perceptions of empire, each recorded at the last possible moment – just before rapid decolonisation made further calculations redundant. We can now see why the exercise has been cited in support of opposed interpretations, one emphasising the paramountcy of political forces, and the other stressing the weight of economic considerations. In taking such divergent positions, previous commentators have been faithful to parts of the evidence without being fully aware of the additions and subtractions that shaped the final document. The summary statement presented in September was the product of an established view and an emerging one, and it was impossible even for the emollient Norman Brook to reconcile them. According to the established view, Britain could still bring her civilising mission to a triumphant close, given reasonable time and resources, without any fundamental change to existing policy. From the new perspective, the empire had served its purposes and could now be transformed into a co-operative association of free states within the Commonwealth, complementing British interests, acting as a shield against the expansion of communism, and sustaining Britain's prestige as a world power. There was no talk of decline, even in documents classified as confidential or secret. Problems abounded, but problems were the stuff of political life. They were to be overcome, and it was Whitehall's task to produce solutions.

It is easy now to identify the weaknesses in both views. At the time,

---

[54] Murphy, *Party politics and decolonization*, p. 163; Goldsworthy, *Colonial issues in British politics*, pp. 34–5.

[55] Dated 14 Feb. 1958. I am most grateful to Sir John Moreton for allowing me to cite and quote this letter.   [56] See n. 22 above.

however, some of the flaws were not apparent to the participants, while others, though visible, were underplayed or even bypassed. Unexceptionally, advocates on both sides sought to verify their arguments: their views of the world took in what was supportive of their particular standpoint. However, being selective, their perceptions produced conclusions that were, to a greater or lesser degree unrealistic. Not for the first time, too, policy-makers were inclined to suppose that their interpretation of the world, being right, would be shared by others and ought therefore to prevail; they then confused what they wanted with the power to obtain it. The auditors, being honourable, did not cook the books, but they did deploy a form of instinctive creative accounting, first in trying to run together two irreconcilable versions of colonial policy, and then in adopting an over-sanguine view of the chances of realising either.

Lennox-Boyd's policy was, in essence, to hold what we already had. This meant, above all, preserving the empire while also steering it on its evolutionary course. This position is not to be attributed simply to nostalgia, an illustration of the principle that ideas continue to influence events long after their time has passed. The empire had proved its worth during the Second World War. There followed, not a retreat, but a 'second colonial occupation' that reinvigorated imperial ties and greatly helped Britain's postwar reconstruction.[57] The colonies became significant dollar earners; by continuing to operate within the Sterling Area they added considerably to the sterling balances they had accumulated during the war. These balances, being held in London, strengthened Britain's reserves and hence the pound, and made Britain less dependent on the USA than she would otherwise have been.[58] Without this support, Britain's gold and exchange position would have been, as the Governor of the Bank of England put it, 'in queer street'.[59] Even the Treasury knights, reflecting on the success of the postwar arrangements, allowed themselves a rare smile: 'we could scarcely have done better', commented Sir Robert Hall, 'if we had intended to exploit the Colonies'.[60]

---

[57] The phrase is from D. A. Low and J. M. Lonsdale, 'Towards a new order, 1945–63' in D. A. Low and Alison Smith (eds.), *The Oxford history of East Africa*, vol. III (Oxford, 1976), pp. 12–16. For an interpretation of this period and further references see P. J. Cain and A. G. Hopkins, *British imperialism: crisis and deconstruction, 1914–1990* (1993), ch. 11.

[58] These very large issues can be approached through two important recent studies: Catherine Schenk, *Britain and the Sterling Area* (1994), and Krozewski, 'The politics of sterling', which is now fundamental to all future studies of decolonisation. For an accessible outline see Gerold Krozewski, 'Sterling, the "minor" territories, and the end of formal empire', *Economic History Review*, 46 (1993), pp. 239–65.

[59] Cobbold, Minute 5 March 1956, BoE, ADM 14/44.

[60] Minute, 12 November 1954, quoted in Morgan, *A reassessment of British aid*, p. 57. The Treasury remained convinced that 'the Area and the system have in general brought us great advantages'. Sir Leslie Rowan, Minute 31 December 1957, BoE, OV 44/65.

If the empire was to function as the political expression of the Sterling Area, it needed the backing of the USA and the acquiescence of the colonies. The USA, enmeshed in its own tangle of anti-Communist imperialism, found itself supporting the reconstruction of the British (and French) empires and agreeing to the perpetuation of the Sterling Area and imperial preferences – while still proclaiming the principles of anti-colonialism and free trade.[61] The colonies acquiesced because they had no choice: that was why they were colonies. Admittedly, subordination required coercion in some parts of the empire, such as Malaya and Kenya, but the results, though scarcely triumphant, were at least satisfactory in defending Britain's key interests and fending off Communism and its presumed accomplice, anarchy. In many parts of the empire, however, nationalism, though clearly visible and vociferous, was not the irresistible force it presented itself to be or was eventually to become. In the mid-1950s, nationalist leaders in a number of colonies made secret deals with the Colonial Secretary, Lennox-Boyd: they were well aware that they were ill-prepared to move at the speed they themselves were demanding; accordingly, and at their request, Lennox-Boyd undertook not to agree to their public demands for an increase in the pace of change.[62] Thus, in the decade after the war there were still grounds for thinking that nationalist forces could be tamed or managed, as circumstances dictated. Taken as a whole, it seemed possible that Britain could orchestrate economic development and political advance in the empire in such a way as to bring colonies to self-government, in some cases perhaps even independence, at the point when they had passed the tests of viability and reliability.

The problem with this perception of the world was not that it was out of line with reality (or at least with prospects for managing it) when it was formulated, but that it failed to take account of realities that were beginning to emerge in the mid-1950s. A key development, reflected in the prominence given to economic considerations in the auditor's final report, was the decision to move towards convertibility and in the direction of liberalisation generally, for this put the role of the sterling club, as it had functioned since 1945, in doubt. In the early 1950s, Conservative imperialists on the right of the party had made a determined effort to strengthen imperial ties by increasing trade preferences. The attempt failed: the view taken, in line with City interests and international obligations, was that Britain should

---

[61] Louis and Robinson, 'The imperialism of decolonization', is the most recent and most convenient route into this subject.

[62] See Morgan, *Guidance towards self-government*, p. 22.

move towards convertibility and a more open economy.[63] The City progressively reopened its doors to international business during the 1950s; the
pound attained *de jure* convertibility in 1958. Convertibility pumped up
pressure on Britain's resources; liberalisation was expected to increase the
demand from ex-colonies to withdraw or convert their sterling balances.

These considerations explain the preoccupations expressed in the auditors' final report with the fate of the sterling balances, with maintaining
future loyalty to sterling, and with strengthening Britain's reserves by
reducing the burden of overseas aid.[64] These imperatives were closely
related to the main aim of Britain's external economic policy in general, as
reflected in the Treasury's frequently affirmed commitment to maintain the
'cohesion of the sterling system' and, with it, the value of the pound.[65] The
phrasing of the report also expressed the Treasury's view that these problems could be contained, at least within the colonial context, and that, if
sterling were to be launched successfully on its new enterprise as the major
international currency alongside the dollar under the regime of free
exchange, the rising priority was not to preserve what we had, but to cultivate what we needed, in particular to release unwilling subjects in the hope
of turning them into co-operative allies. From this perspective, decolonisation was an act of constitutional reform designed to realign political

[63] The sources cited in n. 58 provide the best entry to the sizeable literature on this subject,
but direct reference should also be made to the valuable commentary by J. B. D. Miller,
Survey of Commonwealth affairs: problems of expansion and attrition, 1953–1969 (1974), and to
Susan Strange's masterly study, *Sterling and British policy: a political study of an international
currency in decline* (Oxford, 1971). In 1957, the Bank of England and the Treasury decided
to take a 'new look' at the Sterling Area to see 'whether the postwar transitional period does
not now need some radical change'. Cobbold to Bridges, 18 November 1955, BoE ADM
14/44.

[64] It is sometimes said that overseas aid (in the form of grants and loans to the colonies) constituted an exception to the policy of 'cut and run' that was increasingly adopted after 1959.
It is perfectly true that the Commonwealth Trade Conference in Montreal in 1958 (which
is often cited in this connection) promised a sizeable increase in development capital for
the colonies, and that an increase took place between 1958 and 1960. However, a good deal
of the new lending was tied, formally and informally, to the purchase of British goods, a
constraint that limited the amount of money taken up. The sum available was still trivial in
relation to total public expenditure and represented a diminishing percentage of GNP.
Although the Treasury was willing to develop the poorer colonies so that they could
contribute to the balance of payments of the Sterling Area, it kept a firm grip on the amount
available, and was determined not to write a blank cheque to meet limitless development
needs. Aid policy was not, therefore, an exception to the general policy of disengagement
initiated in 1959.

[65] Sir Leslie Rowan, Minute 31 December 1957, BoE, OV 44/65. The four stated aims were:
to maintain the international value of sterling, to ensure the cohesion of the sterling system,
to secure the 'steady expansion and freeing' of world trade, and to have a share in world
trade 'equitable to our needs'.

relationships so that they continued to serve the main aim of policy: upholding sterling as a world currency. Of course, the fate of sterling depended on international considerations that were far more important than any role the colonial empire could play. All the same, it was better to have friends than enemies in distant places, and if friendship could be sustained without burdening the Exchequer, a shift to informal influence had much to commend it.

Other perspectives on British policy tended to point in the same direction. There were signs, particularly through the growth of inter-industry trade and the redirection of overseas investment, that the expansion of the international economy would take place increasingly between advanced economies. These trends found formal expression in 1956 in Plan G, which foreshadowed the formation of the European Free Trade Area (EFTA) in 1959, and in the Treaty of Rome, which was signed in 1957.[66] They were complemented by a decline in primary produce prices, which had boomed between 1945 and the end of the Korean War in 1953. Colonial trade, like colonial investment, was becoming less attractive. The pattern of specialisation that had promoted economic integration in the world economy since the nineteenth century was beginning to weaken, and the empires that were its political expression were losing their rationale.[67]

These economic considerations appear to have been the main influence on the auditors' final report. However, they almost certainly kept one eye, too, on signals coming from Washington. There were indications, particularly after the Suez crisis, that the USA was becoming restless with the pace of change in the British empire. Greater progress was needed on all fronts if Soviet influence was to be kept at bay. In March 1957, when the audit was still at a preliminary stage, British and American officials (engaged in an entirely separate exercise) agreed that the African colonies were to move 'towards stable self-government or independence' as rapidly as possible, 'in such a way that these governments are willing and able to preserve their economic and political ties with the West'.[68] Fortunately for British policy,

[66] The negotiations over Europe deserve more space than can be made available on this occasion. For an exploratory essay that is consistent with the general argument put here, see Catherine R. Schenk, 'Decolonization and European economic integration: the Free Trade Area negotiations, 1956–58', *Journal of Imperial and Commonwealth History*, 24 (1996), pp. 444–63.

[67] For the argument and further references, see Cain and Hopkins, *British imperialism*, pp. 285–91, and on the fit with the case of France, Jacques Marseille, *Empire colonial et capitalisme français: histoire d'un divorce* (Paris, 1984).

[68] Agreed US–UK paper, 'Means of combatting Communist influence in tropical Africa', 13 March 1957, FRUS, 1955–57, XXVII. Quoted in Louis and Robinson, 'Imperialism of decolonisation', p. 487.

the view from Washington fitted with the new direction marked out by the Treasury's own assessment of Britain's future interests. Sorcerer and apprentice were already preparing to fashion a new order in Africa.

As for the periphery itself, no new significance seems to have been attached, in 1957, to nationalist forces. The emergency in central Africa in 1959 undoubtedly helped to move policy on, but it did so principally by discrediting Lennox-Boyd's constitutional approach to imperial problems, by emphasising that the costs of control far outweighed the meagre returns, and by advertising the fact that unrest was bad for the image of the free world. When the wind of change began to blow early in the 1960s, nationalist leaders were among those unexpectedly caught by it.[69]

For all these reasons, the Treasury view fitted emerging realities in 1957 much better than did established Colonial Office policy. Indeed, had the audit been produced by the Treasury rather than by the Colonial Office, it would almost certainly have pointed unambiguously towards rapid decolonisation. The reorientation of trade and finance towards the developed world, the negotiations over the European Economic Community, the independent stance adopted by the old Commonwealth, and the declining value of the new, all indicated that the imperial connection, in whatever form, was an option from the past – not one for the future. Above all, the commitment to full convertibility and liberalisation made direct political control for economic purposes irrelevant. As it was, these arguments left their imprint on the audit in a form that made decolonisation permissive rather than mandatory. In this matter, however, time was on the side of the Treasury: from 1958 the economic arguments for decolonisation became increasingly compelling, while Colonial Office policy began to depart more visibly from emerging realities.

Yet the revisions put forward in the September report themselves rested on ambitious assumptions that were acted on before they had been thought through. The Treasury, so perceptive in scrutinising the plans of others, took a much more indulgent attitude towards its own ideas. The chief and also the most comprehensive error arose from an excessively optimistic view of the prospects for sterling and the Sterling Area under conditions of free exchange and free trade. Early in 1957, Britain's liabilities were officially estimated to be over £4,000 million and her reserves at about £700 million.[70] Given the overhang of debt, the risks attached to convertibility, and the need to fund overseas investment, the Treasury reached the conclusion that

[69] Krozewski, 'Politics of sterling', p. 376.
[70] Economic Policy Committee (EPC), CAB 134/1676, EA (57) 52, 21 May 1957.

Britain needed a regular surplus on current account of about £400 million every year.[71] Without this, there was little prospect of retaining confidence in the pound; if confidence went, so would the Sterling Area. The Suez crisis had sent up the appropriate signal: the pound fell even though Britain's trading position was, momentarily, sound.[72] Yet the grounds for supposing that Britain might be able to sport a surplus of the order required were at best very slender. In 1958, the year of *de jure* convertibility, sterling received crucial backing from the balances held in London.[73] To re-launch a world currency on the basis of support from the ruler of Kuwait and other allies in the Middle East was indeed to build a future on sand. As is well known, Britain was unable to produce a surplus of the designated size during the 1960s. The pound struggled on, renewed hope yielding to successive crises, until devaluation in 1967, which presaged the end of the Sterling Area in 1972.[74] Put to the test of the open market, which the Treasury had advocated with such enthusiasm, sterling was unable to sustain the world role assigned to it. The end of an era for sterling was also the end of an empire for Britain.

Optimism about sterling was compounded by false hopes about prospects for success in closely allied areas. Too much was presumed of the future loyalty of existing members of the sterling club. Neither gratitude nor inertia sufficed to hold the membership once the attractions of the dollar were made available.[75] As for gaining new members, the Treasury already knew that few applicants were knocking on the door.[76] Similarly, the recommendation that Britain should lend less and borrow more in order to maintain confidence in sterling was itself an admission of weakness that, in any case, proved incapable of being implemented.[77] The assumption that trade ties between Britain and the colonies would remain essentially unchanged underestimated the diversification that took place after independence following the trend (that ought to have been visible in Whitehall) set by India after 1947. As Macmillan should have known, and perhaps did, 'growing up' was also associated with leaving home.

[71] Sir Leslie Rowan, Minute, 31 December 1957, BoE, OV 44/65.
[72] EPC, CAB 134/1675. EA (57) 12, 4 February 1957. Suez frightened the Treasury and the Bank of England by suddenly revealing the vulnerability of sterling. Discussion thereafter became preoccupied with the need to strengthen Britain's balance of payments.
[73] EPC, CAB 134/1675, EA (57) 20, 3 March 1957; Miller, *Survey of Commonwealth affairs*, p. 284.
[74] Alec Cairncross and Barry Eichengreen, *Sterling in decline: the devaluations of 1931, 1947 and 1967* (London, 1983), ch. 5; Bangura, *Britain and Commonwealth Africa*, pp. 97–119.
[75] Bangura, *Britain and Commonwealth Africa*, pp. 97–9, 112, 118–19.
[76] EPC, CAB 134/1875, EA (57) 20, 3 March 1957. There was even some (desultory) discussion at this time about drawing Germany into the new sterling club.
[77] EPC, 134/1676, EA (57), 21 May 1957; EPC, 134/1674, EA (57) 14, 29 May 1957.

V

Macmillan's audit had no immediate consequences, which is perhaps one further reason why it has been neglected. However, the explanation is not that the final report was discarded, or, as the Colonial Office used to say, 'put by', but that action was frozen, for political reasons, until Macmillan secured his position following the general election in October 1959. Until then, Lennox-Boyd continued with his measured and increasingly unrealistic plans for constitutional advance. After the election, the right wing of the party was no longer so influential, at least in imperial affairs; as is well known, Macmillan brought in Macleod to review policy and to make more rapid progress towards decolonisation.[78] As is less well known, the policy review already lay to hand; in it, too, lay the maxim that Macleod was to make his own by referring repeatedly to the judgement that the risks of moving too fast were outweighed by the dangers of moving too slowly.[79] Macmillan's audit had given the green light; Macleod drove through with his foot on the accelerator.

The British empire did not decline because imperial policy was intransigent or backward-looking. On the contrary, Macmillan's audit makes it clear that policy was moving with emerging realities and in some respects was moving ahead of them. Far from merely reacting to events, policy in the colonial field helped to create them. If decline meant abandoning Britain's world role, then it was not on the agenda; change, however, was, and change was defined as evolutionary advance. As Britain could manage the transition from a closed to an open economy, so the empire could be transformed into an association of free Commonwealth states that would be a useful adjunct to her wider international ambitions. For the custodians of a great empire, there was always another horizon. The problem lay elsewhere – with the underpinnings of this expansive policy both within and beyond the empire. After the war, Britain was crippled by debt, and in the 1950s she also began to suffer competition from revived and reconstructed rivals. When measured against her aspirations, she could not now pass the tests of 'viability' and 'readiness' that Lennox-Boyd had set for the colonies.

[78] There has been no space here to do justice to the variety of opinion underlying the stereotypes of right and left wings of the Conservative party. This subject has now been thoroughly explored by Murphy, *Party politics and decolonisation.*

[79] 'Of course there were risks in moving quickly. But the risks of moving slowly were far greater.' Iain Macleod, *Weekend Telegraph*, 12 March 1965. Quoted in Miller, Survey of Commonwealth affairs, pp. 114–15; Goldsworthy, *Colonial issues in British politics*, pp. 34–5, 362.

This was the visible reality that could either not be seen or, if seen, could not be acted on. Amidst their disagreements, Whitehall and Parliament were united in the belief that Britain still had a major role to play on the world stage. The idea that she might become a second or third-rate power was so unpalatable as to be inconceivable. When this prospect, the largest of realities, finally began to imprint itself, Britain was left to contemplate the thought that the fate of The Netherlands and Denmark, two former imperial powers whose history had habitually been cited in high places as an example to avoid, might after all be desirable – if it were still attainable.

12

Apocalypse when? British politicians and British 'decline' in the twentieth century

DAVID CANNADINE

There can be no doubt that since the last quarter of the nineteenth century, Britain has in many ways been a nation 'in decline'.[1] The empire on which the sun never set has become one with Nineveh and Tyre. The waves which Britannia once ruled so mightily have long since been subdued and sailed by other navies. The first industrial nation, the veritable workshop of the world, is now among the less successful economies of the west. Not surprisingly, God is no longer an Englishman but a multicultural deity of indeterminate gender. But this is only part of the story. Much of Britain's international decline has been relative rather than absolute. It took – and is still taking – a long time, and it has been sometimes halted, though rarely reversed. Meanwhile, on the home front, changes have been in precisely the opposite direction: emphatically for the better rather than visibly for the worse. During the last hundred years, levels of output, income, and national wealth have increased unprecedentedly. Today, for most people, life in Britain is more rich, prosperous, varied, abundant, and secure than it was for their late Victorian forebears one hundred years ago – a paradox suggestively explored by Barry Supple (ch. 1).

It is, then, impossible to describe the whole of Britain's recent historical experience in such morbidly evocative phrases as 'the eclipse of a great power', the 'contraction of England', or 'Britannia overruled'.[2] The British Empire may (or may not) have been won 'in a fit of absence of mind', but as far as the majority of the population seems to have been concerned, it

---

Earlier versions of this chapter have been given as lectures or seminar papers at Cambridge, Columbia, London, Princeton, and Yale Universities, and I have greatly benefited from the comments and criticisms made on these occasions. Thanks also to Andrew Adonis, Lord Gilmour of Graigmillar, and Lord Jenkins of Hillhead.

[1] The concept of national decline as explored here owes much to J. H. Elliott, 'The decline of Spain', *Past and Present*, 20 (1961), pp. 52–75; J. H. Elliott, 'Self-perception and decline in early seventeenth-century Spain', *Past and Present*, 74 (1977), pp. 41–61.

[2] K. Robbins, *The eclipse of a great power: modern Britain, 1875–1975* (1983); D. A. Low, *The contraction of England* (Cambridge, 1983); D. Reynolds, *Britannia overruled? British policy and world power in the twentieth century* (1991).

was given away in a fit of collective indifference. Nor were Britain's governing classes and policy makers as obsessed with 'the orderly management of decline' as the ample evidence for that decline suggests they should have been.[3] Gladstone regarded the rise of the USA with relative equanimity. Salisbury feared 'disintegration', but never enough to disturb his calm and imperturbable conduct of affairs. Asquith and Attlee were first and foremost domestic reformers, Baldwin was a domestic conciliator, Macmillan lacked the necessary crusading zeal, while Wilson vainly sought solace in the white-hot technological revolution. To be sure, all of them lived and ruled in an era of vanishing supremacies. But none had careers, or cultivated images, which could most appropriately be summed up by the phrase 'the statesman in an age of decline'.[4]

Yet from the 1880s to the 1980s, there were three unusual, indeed extraordinary, figures in British politics who might best be described by this rather double-edged term, and who were in part so unusual and so extraordinary precisely because that label fits them so well. All three were heroic egotists, possessed of a powerful, obsessive, unreflective sense of messianic self-identity. Each developed a coherent, doom-laden, and apocalyptic vision, part historical, part geopolitical, and part prescriptive. They were compulsively preoccupied by enemies without and by enemies within: internationally, they feared that Britain was being pushed to the margins of events by more vigorous overseas competitors; domestically they regretted what they saw as the moral decline in national character and national calibre. All of them looked back appreciatively (and selectively) to an earlier golden age of vigorous virtues, robust will, splendid endeavour, and unchallenged supremacy. They advocated reform, renewal, and regeneration as essential and imperative. And each one of them believed that they, and they alone, could lead the nation out of the abyss of despair and despond into which they claimed it had sunk, towards the broad, sunlit uplands of rebirth and revival.[5]

---

[3] Sir John Seeley, *The expansion of England* (1883), p. 8; J. G. Darwin, 'The fear of falling: British politicians and imperial decline since 1900', *Transactions of the Royal Historical Society*, 5th ser. 36 (1986), pp. 29, 39–43.

[4] A. Ramm (ed.), *The political correspondence of Mr. Gladstone and Lord Granville, 1876–86* (2 vols., 1962), vol. I, p. 85; H. C. G. Matthew, *Gladstone, 1875–1898* (Oxford, 1995), p. 24; P. Marsh, *The discipline of popular government: Lord Salisbury's domestic statecraft, 1881–1902* (Hassocks, 1978), pp. 10–11, 276–77; J. H. Elliott, *The Count-Duke of Olivares: the statesman in an age of decline* (1986), esp. pp. 89–94, 116–19, 230–1, 394–5.

[5] In addition to the works of Sir John Elliott cited above, I have been much helped by the following: R. Starn, 'Meaning-levels in the theory of historical decline', *History and Theory*, 14 (1975), pp. 1–29; P. Burke, 'Tradition and experience: the idea of decline from Bruni to

The individuals in question were Joseph Chamberlain, Winston Churchill, and Margaret Thatcher. All of them were members of Conservative administrations, yet their relations with the party were often difficult and acrimonious. They were regarded as outsiders, as social misfits, with excessively authoritarian attitudes and overbearing personalities. They were much disliked by traditional Tories from the shires, and that dislike was fully reciprocated. They were criticised for hijacking the party, for wrenching it out of its traditional trajectory, and for turning it in new and unwanted directions. But while they were much hated, they were also much admired: indeed, they were each made the centre of a personality cult in ways that have been true of no other twentieth-century British politicians. They all became obsessed with the problem of decline relatively late in their political careers, and there was nothing in their early years in public life to suggest that this would happen. And all three left office with a sense that their mission was incomplete, and with the fear, born out by subsequent events, that their chosen successors would let them down. How, indeed, could it have been otherwise, given that their efforts to reverse Britain's twentieth-century decline were in no case lastingly successful?

I

Joseph Chamberlain has rightly been described as the first leading British politician 'to propose a drastic method of averting the sort of national decline which he saw as otherwise inevitable'.[6] Yet there was nothing about his boyhood, his business, or his early career in local and national politics to suggest that 'messianic catastrophism' would become his creed and his crusade. For Chamberlain, born in 1836, had grown to maturity in the mid-Victorian era of liberalism and internationalism, when British industry and British power were both at their most pre-eminent. He was a Londoner by birth, but made his fortune in Birmingham as a manufacturer of screws. He

Gibbon', *Daedalus*, 105 (1975), pp. 137–52; C. M. Cipolla (ed.), *The economic decline of empires* (1970); M. Olson, *The rise and decline of nations: economic growth, stagflation and social rigidities* (1982); S. Friedlander et al., *Visions of apocalypse: end or rebirth?* (1985); P. M. Kennedy, *The rise and fall of the great powers: economic change and military conflict from 1500 to 2000* (1988).

[6] P. F. Clarke, *A question of leadership: Gladstone to Thatcher* (1991), pp. 75–6. The essential books for Chamberlain's life are: J. Boyd (ed.), *Mr. Chamberlain's speeches* (2 vols., 1914); J. L. Garvin and J. Amery, *The life of Joseph Chamberlain* (6 vols., 1932–69); P. Fraser, *Joseph Chamberlain: radicalism and empire, 1868–1914* (1966); R. Jay, *Joseph Chamberlain: a political study* (Oxford, 1981); M. Balfour, *Britain and Joseph Chamberlain* (1985); P. Marsh, *Joseph Chamberlain: entrepreneur in politics* (1994).

retired from business in 1874, having already entered local politics as an advanced Liberal. He was a legendary reforming Mayor of Birmingham, was elected one of the town's MPs in 1876, and within four years was a member of Gladstone's second administration, as President of the Board of Trade. As the first self-made industrialist to reach the highest echelons of British public life, Chamberlain's career until the mid-1880s reads like something out of Samuel Smiles.

Thus described, he was the coming man in the new age of quasi-democratic politics: radical, nonconformist, undeferential. He had no time for the aristocracy, and precious little for Queen Victoria. He viewed Birmingham as a latter-day Venetian city state, proud, free, and independent.[7] And he viewed the world beyond Britain as a market for exports rather than as regions ripe and ready for conquest. Not for nothing was he the political protégé and colleague of John Bright.[8] Yet this was the man who, in the ten years from 1886, was transformed from 'Radical Joe' into the 'First Minister of the British Empire'. He abandoned the Liberals and from 1895 to 1903 served under Lord Salisbury and A. J. Balfour as Colonial Secretary, thereupon resigning to launch a national campaign for Tariff Reform. In and out of office, his all-consuming obsession remained the same: to alert the British people to their country's economic and international decline, and to urge them to accept his audacious programme for revival and renewal. Here is Chamberlain, in 1903, in full apocalyptic spate:

All history is the history of states once powerful and then decaying. Is Britain to be numbered among the decaying states: is all the glory of the past to be forgotten? . . . Or are we to take up a new youth as members of a great Empire, which will continue for generation after generation the strength, the power and the glory of the British race?[9]

To Chamberlain, the evidence of British decline was as ample as it was alarming. The very year that he had retired from business had witnessed the end of the mid-Victorian boom, which was soon followed by the late-Victorian 'great depression'. It was primarily a depression of prices, profits, and interest rates, and the metal trades of Birmingham and the Black Country were especially hard hit.[10] But this first 'great depression' also

---

[7] The Venetian iconography of Chamberlain's Birmingham still awaits its historian. For some suggestive hints, see: Marsh, *Chamberlain*, pp. 87, 97, 100, 102, 139–40; N. Pevsner, *Warwickshire* (1966), p. 170; A. P. D. Thomson, 'The Chamberlain Memorial Tower, University of Birmingham', *University of Birmingham Historical Journal*, 4 (1954), pp. 174–9.

[8] R. Quinault, 'John Bright and Joseph Chamberlain', *Historical Journal*, 28 (1985), pp. 623–46.   [9] Boyd, *Chamberlain's speeches*, vol. II, p. 181.

[10] Marsh, *Chamberlain*, pp. 10, 74–6, 104, 181–2; B. Semmel, *Imperialism and social reform: English social-imperial thought, 1895–1914* (1960), pp. 84–90.

coincided with the rise to industrial might of Germany and the USA – larger nations, with richer natural resources, bigger populations, and greater markets. Gradually but inexorably, Britain's manufacturing supremacy was challenged then overwhelmed: in output, in productivity, in investment, in innovation, and in exports. To protect their own industries, other nations adopted tariffs, which made it even harder for Britain, stubbornly adhering to Free Trade, to compete, let alone retaliate. And the battle for overseas markets ushered in a new era of imperial rivalries. To be sure, Britain obtained the lion's share of the spoils in the 'Scramble for Africa'; but the increase in the amount of territory in the formal empire was matched by a decline of informal control of a much larger area. In China, Latin America, and the Middle East, the easy supremacy of an earlier era was gone. Everywhere, it seemed, the economic and imperial climate had turned harsh, cold, and bleak.[11]

Thus were Britain's enemies massing without, and as befitted someone of his background, Chamberlain was the most significant politician to catch and share the resulting mood of domestic anxiety and unease. 'Our competitors', he warned 'are gaining upon us in that which makes [for] national greatness.'[12] And there were also enemies within, who sought to weaken Britain at the very time when the country needed all its united strength to face and fight the world outside. These quislings came in two forms: Irish nationalists, who from 1880 made violence and subversion their stock in trade; and British Liberals, who showed every indication that they would give in to such threats. Here, indeed, was the great divide which opened up between Chamberlain and Gladstone. Gladstone regarded Home Rule as a legitimate concession, which would help to keep the Irish in the empire. Chamberlain saw it as an unpatriotic policy of appeasement, which would lead to the break-up of the United Kingdom, and portend the dismemberment and dissolution of the empire. Even worse, he feared that it would send an unmistakable signal to the world that Britain's will to rule had been mortally weakened, and that 'the sceptre of dominion' had 'passed from our grasp'.[13]

These anxieties, both economic and political, domestic and international, were rendered more credible and more urgent for Chamberlain by

[11] R. Hyam, *Britain's imperial century, 1815–1914: a study of empire and expansion* (1976), pp. 92–102; B. Porter, *The lion's share: a short history of British imperialism, 1850–1983* (1975), pp. 75–151.   [12] Marsh, *Chamberlain*, p. 164.
[13] J. Chamberlain, 'A bill for the weakening of Great Britain', *Nineteenth Century*, 35 (1893), pp. 545–58; J. Loughlin, 'Joseph Chamberlain, English nationalism and the Ulster question', *History*, 77 (1992), pp. 202–19; N. M. Marris, *The Rt. Hon. Joseph Chamberlain: the man and the statesman* (1900), p. 263; Boyd, *Chamberlain's speeches*, vol. II, pp. 272, 335.

the writings of Sir John Seeley, whose book, *The Expansion of England*, he much admired. It is often read as a paean of praise to the British Empire. But in the context of its times, it was more pessimistic than celebratory. The great empires of the past, Seeley argued, had been seaborne: the Portuguese, the Spanish, the Dutch, and the French. But they had all declined and, thanks to the steam engine and electricity, the great empires of the future were much more likely to be land based: in particular the Russian and the American, with their huge populations and resources. As a result, Britain would soon be faced with an unprecedentedly severe challenge. Its greatness depended on the successful maintenance of the last surviving seaborne empire. Without it, Seeley contended, Britain would decline into the ranks of a second-rate power – or worse. Accordingly, the most urgent and immediate task was to find a way of preserving and consolidating the British Empire so that it could hold its own in this challenging era of new, land-based super-states.[14]

From the mid-1880s until the end of his life, Chamberlain was haunted by these fears of national decline, and by the dread that 'the empire is being attacked on all sides'. He felt 'great alarm at the prospect of the future', and saw Britain as 'the weary Titan, staggering beneath the too vast orb of his own fate'.[15] In industry after industry, Britain's manufacturing supremacy was being lost, and with it the strength he regarded as essential for continued great-power status. A nation with an economy increasingly dominated by bankers and brokers, rather than by entrepreneurs and innovators, was not going to last long in an ever more alien and hostile world. Such structural change – away from industrial production and towards financial services – itself spelt economic decadence, and Chamberlain was appalled by the thought that Britain might become another Holland, 'an inconsiderable force in the world', a 'third-rate power', a 'fifth-rate nation'. As

[14] Garvin and Amery, *Chamberlain*, vol. I, p. 498; Marsh, *Chamberlain*, pp. 176–78; Seeley, *Expansion of England*, pp. 15–16, 39–44, 51–5, 72–6, 133–4, 157–9, 293–308. See also: D. Wormell, *Sir John Seeley and the uses of history* (Cambridge, 1980), pp. 95–6, 154–6, 162–3; P. Burroughs, 'John Robert Seeley and British imperial history', *Journal of Imperial and Commonwealth History*, 1 (1973), pp. 191–212; P. M. Kennedy, *Strategy and diplomacy, 1870–1945* (1989), pp. 41–86.

[15] Marris, *Chamberlain*, pp. 249, 318; Marsh, *Chamberlain*, p. 521; P. M. Kennedy, *The rise and fall of British naval mastery* (1976), p. 220. See also A. L. Friedberg, *The weary Titan: Britain and the experience of relative decline, 1895–1905* (Princeton, 1988), pp. 21–88; G. R. Searle, *The quest for national efficiency: a study in British politics and political thought, 1899–1914* (Oxford, 1971), pp. 5–13; P. J. Cain and A. G. Hopkins, *British imperialism, vol. I, Innovation and expansion, 1688–1914* (1993), pp. 202–25; E. H. H. Green, *The crisis of Conservatism: the politics, economics and ideology of the British Conservative party, 1880–1914* (1995), pp. 11–18, 27–56, 59–77, 194–206, 223–41.

'Brummagem Joe', he had been impressed by Venice in its prime; as Colonial Secretary, he was no less impressed by Venice in decline. 'The days', he believed, echoing Seeley, 'are for great empires and not for little states.'[16]

Having absorbed Seeley's analysis, Chamberlain sought to rise to Seeley's challenge: for his self-appointed task was to prevent Britain declining from a great empire into a little state by rousing the nation to the threats which it faced, and by implementing a practical and comprehensive policy of resistance and regeneration. Industry must be protected, the union preserved, and the empire consolidated. Yet despite the great campaigns he waged, the powerful organisation he created, the formidable array of academic advisors he assembled, and the confidence he felt in the appeal of his message, he actually accomplished very little. To be sure, he played a major part in defeating Gladstone's Home Rule Bills of 1886 and 1893, and in wrecking the Liberal party for a generation.[17] And with the House of Lords both able and willing to exercise its powers of veto, it looked as though the union with Ireland was safe for the foreseeable future. But in 1911, the Liberal Government passed the Parliament Act, and Chamberlain lived just long enough to experience the bitter defeat of knowing that a Home Rule Bill would finally make its way to the statute book in 1914.

As Colonial Secretary, his record was no less disappointing. He certainly raised Britain's imperial consciousness, with the Diamond Jubilee, the conferences of colonial premiers, the Boer War, and the Australian federation.[18] But he signally failed to convert sentiment into structure: the formal unification of the empire into one consolidated superpower eluded him. His preferred solution was some kind of imperial federation, involving Britain, Canada, South Africa, Australia, and New Zealand. But the colonists' growing sense of their own autonomy meant that this was never practical politics, even in the immediate aftermath of the Boer War.[19] Chamberlain's alternative approach, which kept the same ultimate end in view, was some form of transoceanic Zollverein – a massive imperial free-trade area, protected from the rest of the world by high tariff walls, within

---

[16] Boyd, *Chamberlain's speeches*, vol. II, pp. 5, 108, 144–8, 177, 217, 267–8, 368; Garvin and Amery, *Chamberlain*, vol. IV, p. 177; Green, *Crisis of conservatism*, pp. 35, 53–4.

[17] Boyd, *Chamberlain's speeches*, vol. I, pp. 238–9, 244–6, 255.

[18] For the broader background, see: J. E. Tyler, *The struggle for imperial unity, 1868–95* (1938); B. H. Brown, *The Tariff Reform Movement in Great Britain, 1881–95* (New York, 1943).

[19] Marris, *Chamberlain*, pp. v, 4, 320, 374, 378–80, 383–6; Boyd, *Chamberlain's speeches*, vol. I, pp. 322–3; vol. II, pp. 67–72, 110, 366–9; R. Quinault, 'Joseph Chamberlain: a reassessment', in T. R. Gourvish and A. O'Day (eds.), *Later Victorian Britain, 1867–1900* (1988), pp. 84–5.

which the colonies would provide both the raw materials and the markets for the goods produced by revived British industry.[20] But the colonies were as jealous of their own infant industries as they were of their recently acquired sense of political autonomy, and Chamberlain's proposals were decisively rejected at the imperial conference of 1897.

Having failed to consolidate the empire from within the government, Chamberlain took his greatest gamble, by resigning from the cabinet in 1903 and carrying his campaign for Tariff Reform directly to the British people.[21] This time, his immediate aim was to overturn Free Trade in favour of imperial preference – an elaborate system of tariffs and duties which, while not creating a Zollverein, would promote greater trade within the empire, would make possible the revival of British industry, and might be the prelude to imperial federation. But again, it did not work. The Conservative party was deeply and bitterly divided, went down to a massive electoral defeat in 1906, and did not recapture power in 1910, even though by then Tariff Reform had become its official policy. Four years previously, Chamberlain had himself been incapacitated by a stroke, and his eldest son and heir-apparent, Austen, failed to obtain the leadership of the Tory party on Balfour's resignation in 1911. Instead, the task fell to Andrew Bonar Law, who was himself sympathetic to Tariff Reform, but who felt obliged to repudiate most of the programme in 1913. 'We are beaten', Austen wrote to his wife, 'and the cause for which Father gave more than life itself is abandoned.'[22]

Chamberlain's last years were thus barren and unfulfilled. The self-appointed task to which he had devoted the second half of his career – the maintenance of 'Britain's position in the world' – had proved impossible, both for him and for his chosen successors.[23] Neither the electorate at home nor the colonies abroad could be persuaded to embrace his schemes for imperial unity. There were many parts of Britain beyond Birmingham which his vision did not encompass (especially the country and the City of London) and many parts of the empire beyond the four great dominions of which the same may be said (especially India).

[20] Boyd, *Chamberlain's speeches*, vol. I, pp. 365–72.
[21] There is a large literature on this subject. In addition to the biographies of Chamberlain, see: J. H. Zebel, 'Joseph Chamberlain and the genesis of the Tariff Reform controversy', *Journal of British Studies*, 7 (1967), pp. 131–57; R. A. Rempel, *Unionists divided: Arthur Balfour, Joseph Chamberlain and the Unionist Free Traders* (Newton Abbott, 1972); A. Sykes, *Tariff Reform in British politics, 1903–13* (Oxford, 1979).
[22] Marsh, *Chamberlain*, p. 661; Darwin, 'Fear of falling', p. 32; A. Chamberlain, *Politics from the inside* (1936), p. 508.
[23] L. S. Amery, *My political life* (3 vols., 1953–5), vol. III, p. 225.

Moreover, there is no evidence that protective tariffs would have led to a revival of Britain's manufacturing base, while Chamberlain seems to have had little interest in such new industries as chemicals or cars.[24] Above all, in the prosperous Edwardian years of *la belle époque*, there were many who simply refused to accept his doom-laden analysis. He may have been correct in despising Balfour's languid and lethargic indifference to Britain's decline, and in so doing he certainly prefigured Margaret Thatcher's later hostility to the Tory 'wets'. But his great schemes of national revival and imperial consolidation were simply beyond the bounds of practical politics.[25]

II

One relatively junior but excessively ambitious politician who shared neither Chamberlain's diagnosis of Britain's decline, nor his prescription for it, was Winston Churchill. Indeed, it was in part because young Winston believed in Free Trade and opposed Tariff Reform that he left the Conservatives and joined the Liberals in 1904. For him, as for many, Free Trade and British greatness were indissolubly linked: Tariff Reform would thus not be a cure for British decline, it would be the cause of it. For the world in which Churchill grew up – he was born in 1874 – was not for him the gloomy, battle-scarred landscape that it had seemed to Chamberlain. To be sure, it was an age of competition, of Darwinian struggle.[26] But it also seemed to be an age in which Britain's greatness was regularly and repeatedly reaffirmed. At the frontiers of empire – in India, the Sudan, and South Africa – Churchill saw and celebrated the extension of British rule. As a Liberal reformer, he sought to make life more stable and secure for ordinary men and women. And as First Lord of the Admiralty, he relished the challenge of creating the mightiest navy the world had ever seen. For him, as he later recalled, 'the nineteenth century ended amid the glories of the

---

[24] Marsh, *Chamberlain*, pp. 668–72; Hyam, *Britain's imperial century*, pp. 114–18; Green, *Crisis of conservatism*, pp. 230–8; P. J. Cain, 'Political economy in Edwardian England: the tariff reform controversy', in A. O'Day (ed.), *The Edwardian age: conflict and stability, 1900–1914* (1979), pp. 48–59.

[25] For comparisons between Chamberlain and Thatcher, see: P. Jenkins, *Mrs. Thatcher's revolution: the ending of the socialist era* (Cambridge, Mass., 1988), p. 53; H. Young, *Iron Lady: a biography of Margaret Thatcher* (New York, 1990), p. 100.

[26] P. F. Clarke, 'Churchill's economic ideas, 1900–30', in R. Blake and W. R. Louis (eds.), *Churchill* (New York, 1993), pp. 84–8; P. Addison, 'The political beliefs of Winston Churchill', *Transactions of the Royal Historical Society*, 5th series, 30 (1980), pp. 28–30; J. R. Colville, *The fringes of power: 10 Downing Street diaries, 1939–1955* (New York, 1985), p. 345.

Victorian era, and we entered upon the dawn of the twentieth century in high hopes for our country, our Empire and the world'.[27]

The first forty years of Churchill's life were, as they had earlier been for Chamberlain, a time of hope, progress, and improvement. But thereafter, like Chamberlain again, the skies suddenly and unexpectedly began to darken. In personal terms, Churchill's meteoric career crashed into ruins in 1915 in the aftermath of the Dardanelles fiasco, and political rehabilitation was to prove a long, slow, and painful process. And even someone as much in love with war as he had been was appalled by the cost – in men, in money, and in materials – of fighting the Germans. Like so many members of his generation, the domestic and international landscape which Churchill surveyed in the aftermath of victory in 1918 was one he scarcely recognised. He was disturbed and disoriented by the collapse of settled values and ancient institutions, and saw contemporary Europe 'relapsing in hideous succession into bankruptcy, barbarism or anarchy'. And as he was to discover in his years as Chancellor of the Exchequer, even Free Trade, the very underpinning of British greatness, was no longer a viable proposition. 'The compass has been damaged', he regretfully concluded. 'The charts are out of date.'[28]

Under these abruptly changed circumstances, Churchill's thoughts, writings, and rhetoric became increasingly apocalyptic, as he became obsessed with what he saw as Britain's domestic and international decline from the golden era before 1914. On the home front, the man who had attacked the peerage with such glee in 1910 now lamented the demise of the great governing families of England. The one-time Liberal reformer, anxious to improve the condition of the working classes, pronounced the new Labour party unfitted to rule. The restricted franchise that had existed before the Fourth Reform Act of 1918 had been superseded by the 'universal mush and sloppiness' of mass democracy, with its rootless and ignorant electorate, its caucuses, wire-pullers, and soap boxes, and with a Parliament incapable of discharging its responsibilities.[29] The great men of his youth – Curzon, Morley, Asquith, Balfour, Rosebery – had been replaced by interwar mediocrities such as Ramsay MacDonald ('the boneless wonder') and Stanley Baldwin ('the greatest of non-statesmen'). The result was deteriorated

---

[27] W. S. Churchill, *In the balance: speeches, 1949 and 1950* (Boston, 1952), p. 41.

[28] Clarke, 'Churchill's economic ideas', pp. 88–95; Addison, 'Political beliefs of Winston Churchill', p. 46; R. S. Churchill and M. Gilbert, *Winston S. Churchill* (8 vols., 1966–88), vol. IV, pp. 914–15.

[29] D. Cannadine, *Aspects of aristocracy: grandeur and decline in modern Britain* (1994), pp. 156–60; M. Cowling, *Religion and public doctrine in modern England* (Cambridge, 1980), pp. 284, 305; P. Addison, *Churchill on the home front, 1900–55* (New York, 1970), pp. 329–33.

democracy, and weak and infirm government, described and dismissed by Churchill in one of his most elaborate rhetorical flights: 'decided only to be undecided, resolved to be irresolute, adamant for drift, solid for fluidity, all-powerful for impotence'.[30]

Weakness at home was bad enough by itself. But for Churchill it was made worse by the fact that it inexorably led to weakness abroad. For Churchill as for Chamberlain, Britain's standing in the world was indissolubly linked to its will to rule and to retain its empire. But their conceptions of empire were very different. Chamberlain was most concerned with the great and growing British communities transplanted across the oceans. Churchill, by contrast, was most concerned with India. Without India, he believed, Britain's international prestige would be irretrievably damaged. And without the Indian Army, Britain would simply cease to be a great military power.[31] Hence his vehement opposition from 1930 to 1935 to the National Government's effort to grant a modest amount of constitutional reform in India. It was wrong because it indicated that the will to rule had been replaced by 'unimaginative incompetence and weak compromise and supine drift'. And it was wrong because this would mean the end of the Indian Empire, and thus the end of British greatness:

> The continuance of our present confusion and disintegration will reduce us, within a generation, and perhaps sooner, to the degree of states like Holland and Portugal, which nursed valiant races and held great possessions, but were stripped of them in the crush and competition of the world.[32]

For Churchill, as for Chamberlain before him, and like Thatcher after him, willpower, resolution, robustness, and determination were all-important attributes. They were the very fibre and sinews of Britain's greatness. By contrast, the policies of appeasement so zealously and misguidedly pursued by the governments of the 1930s proclaimed to the world that Britain was a nation and an empire in decline, suffering from a potentially fatal 'disease of the will'. This was not how a great power should behave – or could behave. Appeasement in India was wrong because it was the nega-

---

[30] Colville, *Fringes of power*, p. 278; D. Cannadine (ed.), *'Blood, toil, tears and sweat': the speeches of Winston Churchill* (Boston, 1989), p. 121.

[31] Hyam, *Britain's imperial century*, p. 118; S. Gopal, 'Churchill and India', in Blake and Louis, *Churchill*, p. 459; W. R. Louis, *'In The Name of God, Go!' Leo Amery and the British Empire in the age of Churchill* (New York, 1992), p. 20.

[32] Cannadine, *'Blood, toil, tears and sweat'*, p. 105; Addison, 'Political beliefs of Winston Churchill', pp. 37–41; Robert Rhodes James, *Churchill: a study in failure 1900–39* (Harmondsworth, 1973), pp. 217–23; R. Rhodes James (ed.), *Winston S. Churchill: the complete speeches* (8 vols., New York, 1974), vol. V, p. 4990.

tion of Britain's imperial mission. And the appeasement of Germany was also wrong because it represented the abdication of Britain's historic duty to ensure a continent free from tyrants and dictators. Giving way to Hitler was as bad as giving way to Gandhi: both were proof that 'the long, dismal, drawling tides of drift and surrender' had been elevated into government policy.[33] What was needed, Churchill insisted, in dealing with Nazi Germany, was a rediscovery of lost virtues, so as 'to raise again a great British nation, standing up before all the world'. There must be a 'supreme recovery of moral health and martial vigour', so the country could 'arise again, and take our stand for freedom as in olden times'.[34]

By the 1930s, Churchill has thus developed into a fully fledged alarmist, seeing enemies everywhere. Abroad, the foes were, successively, Lenin, then Gandhi, then Hitler. At home, they were the Labour party, the trades unions, and the National Government. No wonder that David Low drew a cartoon of a fabulous, snarling beast called 'The Winstonocerous', the caption beneath which read 'Destroys Imaginary Enemies With Great Fury.' But for Churchill, the enemies were very real, and during this period his rhetoric became increasingly apocalyptic, full of dark stairways, deep abysses, and mortal perils.[35] Only by a reassertion of the national will, and by a return to the heroic values of an earlier age, preferably under his own leadership, could Britain's decline be averted. But as contemporary critics and later historians have pointed out, this hardly amounted to a credible policy. On India, as Leopold Amery noted, Churchill was 'utterly and entirely negative, and devoid of constructive thought'. And on Germany, he was little better: 'fantastic', according to Lord Hankey, 'ignoring many realities'.[36] All he offered was rhetoric and resolution. This may have been admirable, but it was scarcely a solution to the underlying problem facing successive British governments during the 1930s: namely, of trying to reconcile too many commitments abroad with too few resources at home.

But in 1940, when Churchill finally became Prime Minister, rhetoric and resolution were precisely what were needed. Or perhaps it would be more accurate to say that they were virtually all that was available. They served Churchill, and Britain, brilliantly, and never to more telling effect than in the peroration of his great speech of 23 June, where he warned of 'the abyss

---

[33] Rhodes James, *Study in failure*, p. 224; W. S. Churchill, *The Second World War, vol. I. The gathering storm* (Boston, 1948), p. 257.

[34] Cannadine, *'Blood, toil, tears and sweat'*, p. 143; Rhodes James, *Study in failure*, p. 355.

[35] Rhodes James, *Study in failure*, pp. 237, 273, 354.

[36] Rhodes James, *Study in failure*, pp. 235, 265; Louis, *'In the name of God, go!'*, pp. 109–10; D. Cameron Watt, 'Churchill and appeasement', in Blake and Louis, *Churchill*, pp. 199–214.

of a new dark age', while also holding up the prospect of the nation's 'finest hour'. But the very notion of 'their finest hour' carried with it the unacknowledged implication that, thereafter, things would only decline still further. And so, very soon, they did.[37] Rhetoric and resolution had worked magnificently in Britain, but they conspicuously failed in Hong Kong, Malaya, Singapore, and substantial parts of north-east India, which were soon overrun by the Japanese. To make matters worse, Churchill now found himself with two allies, Russia and the USA, both of whom disliked the British Empire, while cherishing, as he feared, imperial designs of their own. Once again, he responded defiantly. He did everything he could to thwart demands in London, New Delhi, and Washington that he should undertake to give India self-government after the war. And in November 1942, he made this ringing declaration: 'We mean to hold our own. I have not become the King's first minister in order to preside over the liquidation of the British Empire.'[38]

But for all this defiant rhetoric, the reality of the matter was that the British Empire could only be recovered and retained on the sufferance of the Americans and the Russians. In 1945, it was the Iron Curtain and the Pax Americana which were expanding, while the British Empire in India was very soon to be in retreat. The bi-polar world, dominated by the two great land-based super-states, which Seeley had earlier foreseen, had now came into being, leaving an exhausted and depleted Britain with much less freedom of manoeuvre than hitherto: not for nothing did Churchill call the last volume of his war memoirs *Triumph and tragedy*.[39] But as Leader of the Opposition after 1945 he soon returned to the apocalyptic rhetoric of the 1930s, laying the blame for what he saw as Britain's continued but avoidable decline squarely at the feet of the Labour Government. The last six years, he thundered in 1951,

have marked the greatest fall in the rank and stature of Britain in the world, which has occurred since the loss of the American colonies two hundred years ago. Our Oriental Empire has been liquidated, our resources have been squandered, the pound sterling is only worth three quarters of what it was when Mr. Attlee took over from me, [and] our influence among the nations is now less than it has ever been in any period since I remember.[40]

[37] Clarke, *A question of leadership*, p. 143.
[38] Louis, '*In the name of God, go!*', pp. 123–78; Gopal, 'Churchill and India', pp. 461–6; R. J. Moore, *Churchill, Cripps, and India* (Oxford, 1979); W. R. Louis, *Imperialism at bay: the United States and the decolonization of the British Empire* (Oxford, 1970), esp. pp. 147–58, 198–210, 349–54, 433–60.
[39] Kennedy, *Rise and fall of the great powers*, pp. 347–437; Colville, *Fringes of power*, p. 564
[40] W. S. Churchill, *Stemming the tide: speeches, 1951 and 1952* (Boston, 1954), p. 142.

All this, to Churchill, was the inevitable result of ministerial 'apathy, indifference, and bewilderment', and of a lack of 'moral strength and willpower' on the part of the government. Once more, he insisted, what was needed was 'the regeneration of theme and spirit', and a 'new surge of impulse' to 'bring back all our true glories', so that Britain might 'rise again in its true strength'.[41]

As Churchill saw it, his task on returning to power in 1951 was thus to take on again 'the hard and grim duty of leading Britain and her empire through and out of her new and formidable crisis'.[42] But, once more, there were limits to what could be accomplished in practical terms. To be sure, he was himself the most admired statesman in the world. He sought to re-establish the 'special relationship' with America. And he ensured that Britain possessed the hydrogen bomb. But he could not conceal Britain's continued economic weakness, and its growing military dependency on the USA. And, as he had himself predicted twenty years before, without India, Britain was no longer the power in the world it had previously been. Indeed, without India, much of the remainder of the British Empire in Africa was no longer necessary or worthwhile. Hence, in 1954, the withdrawal of British troops from the Suez Canal zone, an act denounced by die-hard Tories for the very same reason that Churchill had denounced the National Governments of the 1930s: it showed to the world that Britain's will to rule had gone.[43] But even Churchill had by now come to recognise that resolution alone was not enough. The 'liquidation of the British Empire', begun by Attlee in 1947, continued.

After his retirement in 1955, it gathered momentum. In the final months of his premiership, Churchill had come to believe that his chosen successor, Anthony Eden, was not up to the job, and his mishandling of the Suez crisis amply vindicated that view. On Eden's abrupt resignation, Churchill recommended Harold Macmillan, who promptly wound up most of what was left of the empire. Like Chamberlain, Churchill's successors let him down and, like Chamberlain again, his last years were disappointed and unhappy. From 1930 onwards, he had devoted himself single-mindedly and whole-heartedly to what he described as 'the maintenance of the enduring greatness of Britain and her Empire'.[44] But by the time of his death in 1965,

---

[41] W. S. Churchill, *Europe unite!: speeches, 1947 and 1948* (Boston, 1950), pp. 24–5, 46–7, 187, 354, 357–60, 429–31; Churchill, *In the balance*, pp. 131, 160, 267–8.

[42] Churchill, *In the balance*, p. 214.

[43] Darwin, 'Fear of falling', pp. 37–8; W. R. Louis, 'Churchill and Egypt, 1946–1956', in Blake and Louis, *Churchill*, pp. 473–90.

[44] Colville, *Fringes of power*, pp. 259, 709; Addison, *Churchill on the home front*, p. 359.

these great causes had long since become lost causes, something that his own magnificent state funeral tacitly acknowledged. For as everyone recognised on that January day, but no one dared mention, the ceremonials were not only the last rites of the great man himself: they were also a requiem for Britain as a great power. In that sense, Churchill, like Chamberlain, had striven and fought in vain. Perhaps that was what he meant, when he observed, towards the close of his life, 'I have achieved a great deal – in the end to achieve NOTHING.'[45]

III

To move from Winston Churchill to Margaret Thatcher is thus to take a much bigger step down the slope of British 'decline', than it was to move from Joseph Chamberlain to Churchill, as the empire-state was superseded by the much-diminished island-state. Moreover, compared with Chamberlain's 'catastrophical theory of politics', and with Churchill's apocalyptic alarmism, Thatcher's rhetoric was less spacious and highly coloured. But it was much more explicit, straightforward and insistent, with the words 'decline' and 'renewal' constantly appearing in her speeches as Conservative leader and British Prime Minister. Yet once again, there is a familiar pattern: for there was nothing in her life or career between 1925 and 1975 to suggest that she would later become so preoccupied with the parlous state of Britain, and so determined to revive it by the single-minded exertion of her own Napoleonic will. From the Grantham corner shop, via Oxford University, marriage to a rich businessman, election to the Commons, and the Ministry of Education under Edward Heath, hers was a story of upward social mobility surpassing that of Joseph Chamberlain.[46] And for her generation, external circumstances were equally propitious: victory in war, the successful establishment of the welfare state, thirteen years of Conservative dominance, and 'you've never had it so good'.

But it is at that point that the pattern ceases to repeat itself. Or perhaps it would be more accurate to say that by that stage of Britain's 'decline' it

[45] J. Morris, *Farewell the trumpets: an imperial retreat* (1978), pp. 545–57; J. Dimbleby, *Richard Dimbleby* (1975), pp. 384–8; B. Levin, *The pendulum years: Britain and the sixties* (1970), pp. 403–11; A. Storr, 'The man', in A. J. P. Taylor, Robert Rhodes James, J. H. Plumb, *et al.*, *Churchill: four faces and the man* (Harmondsworth, 1973), p. 219; A. Montague Browne, *Long sunset: memoirs of Winston Churchill's last private secretary* (1995), pp. 161–4, 168–9, 183, 208–9, 249, 302–3, 307, 328.

[46] The most thoughtful account of Thatcher's early years remains Young, *Iron Lady*, pp. 3–80. But see also M. Thatcher, *The path to power* (1995), pp. 3–240.

was no longer possible for the pattern to repeat itself. For the Thatcher transformation during the late 1970s, from welfare-state handmaiden and Heathite acolyte to monetarist prophet and apocalyptic crusader, was not based on sudden disenchantment with the present, by comparison with which the immediately preceding decades seemed bathed in the mellow light of a nostalgic, golden age. On the contrary, Thatcher came to believe that the problems of the late 1970s, culminating in the miners' strike, stagflation, and the Winter of Discontent, were merely the end point of a century-long period of national decline, mismanagement, and retreat, of which the years since 1945 had been the worst of all. It is still unclear precisely when, how, and why she formulated these ideas. Certainly, there is no evidence that she was developing them during her time as Education Minister. But under the influence of Sir Keith Joseph, they soon took hold of her after she became Leader of the Opposition in 1975.[47]

Thatcher's account of Britain's decline thus encompassed her own era, as well as those of Chamberlain and Churchill. By this time she came to political prominence, it had therefore been going on much longer, and was correspondingly more advanced, than it had been in the 1900s or the 1930s. The rot had set in at precisely the time that Joseph Chamberlain had first noticed it: during the last quarter of the nineteenth century.[48] Sapped by the effete, insidious doctrines of the aristocracy, the civil service, the Church of England, the public schools, and Oxbridge, the entrepreneurial spirit that had previously made Britain great was gravely weakened. The rise of trade unionism and of the Labour party at the same time only made matters worse. After the Second World War came the welfare states, with too much socialism, too much planning, too much government spending and too much high taxation, which further eroded the spirit of enterprise.

[47] B. Harrison, 'Thatcher and the intellectuals', *20th Century British History*, 5 (1994), esp. pp. 209–17; Thatcher, *The path to power*, esp. pp. 135–6, 250–7. The book is dedicated to 'the memory of Keith Joseph'.

[48] M. Wiener, *English culture and the decline of the industrial spirit, 1850–1980* (Cambridge, 1981); C. Barnett, *The collapse of British power* (1972); C. Barnett, *The audit of war: the illusion and reality of Britain as a great nation* (1986). For a critique of these views, see: B. Collins and K. Robbins (eds.), *British culture and economic decline* (1991); J. Harris, 'Enterprise and welfare states: a comparative perspective', *Transactions of the Royal Historical Society*, 5th series, 40 (1990), pp. 175–95; D. Edgerton, 'The prophet militant and industrial: the peculiarities of Correlli Barnett', *20th Century British History*, 2 (1991), pp. 360–79. There is also a Marxist account of British decline which develops a very similar argument, albeit with a different vocabulary: A. Gamble, *The decline of Britain* (1981); S. Hall and M. Jacques (eds.), *The politics of Thatcherism* (1983); H. Overbeck, *Global capitalism and national decline: the Thatcher decade in perspective* (1990). For a helpful discussion, see P. Warwick, 'Did Britain change? An inquiry into the causes of national decline', *Journal of Contemporary History*, 20 (1985), pp. 99–133.

And in the 1960s came the permissive society, which added moral decay to economic degeneration. No wonder that, by then, Britain was widely regarded by the rest of the world, not as a great power, but as something between a national tragedy and a national joke.

According to Thatcher, this was the process whereby Britain had declined – morally, economically, and internationally. As an historical account, it owes much to Martin Wiener and Correlli Barnett, and it is set out in full as the prologue to Thatcher's prime-ministerial memoirs, where the phrase 'reverse national decline' is interminably repeated like some religious incantation.[49] Nor is this mere retrospective invention. For the speeches Thatcher delivered between 1975 and 1979 had been full of the same stark simple message: decline, decay, and degeneration on the one hand, and recovery, revival, and renewal on the other. She quoted Churchill's words, which had indicted the National Governments of the 1930s, and turned them into an indictment of the Labour Government of the 1970s: 'the long, dismal, drawling tides of drift and surrender'. And in the 1979 election campaign she was even more apocalyptic:

Unless we change our ways and our direction, our glories as a nation will soon be a footnote in the history books, a distant memory of an offshore island, lost in the mists of time, like Camelot, remembered kindly for its noble past.

Or, as she put it more pithily in her last televised election broadcast: 'Somewhere ahead lies greatness for our country again. This I know in my heart.'[50]

How, then, did Thatcher set about halting and reversing what she saw as Britain's century-long decline and fall? In part, she was herself her own answer. Like the Elder Pitt in 1757, she genuinely seems to have thought that she could save the country single-handedly, and that she alone could. More even than Joseph Chamberlain or Winston Churchill, she believed that Britain's decline could be arrested and averted by the sustained exertion of political will. In her eyes, the major failure of the Heath Government – indeed, the major failure of *all*

[49] M. Thatcher, *The Downing Street years* (1993), pp. 4–15, 30, 38, 42. See also D. Young, *Enterprise regained* (1985), pp. 5–8; D. Young, *The enterprise years* (1990), pp. 25–9; Harrison, 'Thatcher and the intellectuals', p. 237; B. Porter, '"Though not myself an historian . . . ": Margaret Thatcher and the historians', *20th Century British History*, 5 (1994), pp. 252–5. For a discussion of Thatcher's preoccupation with national decline, see: Jenkins, *Thatcher's revolution*, pp. xiii–xviii, 30–49; P. Riddell, *The Thatcher era and its legacy* (Oxford, 1991), pp. 6–7, 70–1.

[50] Young, *Iron Lady*, p. 130; Riddell, *Thatcher era*, p. 7; M. Thatcher, *Let our children grow tall* (1977), pp. 43–4, 77, 88, 93; M. Thatcher, *The revival of Britain* (1989), pp. 22, 57–8, 84–95.

British governments since 1945 – had been a lack of firmness and resolution, and it was a mistake she was determined not to repeat.[51] By her own example, she intended to 'renew the spirit and solidarity of the nation'. She worked prodigiously hard, relished confrontation, delighted in making enemies, dominated her cabinet, the civil service, and parliament. As the Iron Lady, who was emphatically 'not for turning', she was determined to show that 'decline is not inevitable'. On the contrary, it was primarily an enfeebling and demoralising state of mind which could, should, and must be changed. Such was Thatcher's 'inner conviction', on assuming power in 1979.[52]

For Thatcher, national decline was a *moral* question, and Thatcherism was thus a crusade, a cultural counter-revolution, to restore lost virtue.[53] In her eyes, the key to the revival of Britain was moral recovery and regeneration: the hedonism of the 1960s and the dependency culture of the welfare state must both be renounced, and the more vigorous and admirable qualities which had once made the nation great, and which could make it great again, must be re-discovered, proclaimed, and espoused. Hence her celebrated remarks about those 'Victorian values' which she had learned at her father's knee: thrift, sobriety, patriotism, hard work, self-help, independence, personal responsibility.[54] As several historians have subsequently had the temerity to point out, this was a very selective picture of Victorian virtues, which also completely ignored Victorian vices. And it was far from clear how the values evolved in mid-nineteenth century Britain could be grafted on to the very different economic and social structure of the later twentieth century.[55] Nevertheless, 'Victorian values' became the *leitmotif* of the Thatcher years: the idealisation of the past so as to bring about a better future.

In what seemed an appropriately self-validating way, Thatcher's forceful leadership, and her campaign for moral regeneration, brought

[51] Thatcher, *Downing Street years*, pp. 10, 46; Jenkins, *Thatcher's revolution*, p. 173; D. Kavanagh, *Thatcherism and British politics: the end of consensus?* (2nd edn, Oxford, 1990), p. 194.

[52] Thatcher, *Revival of Britain*, p. 158; Riddell, *Thatcher era*, p. 7; I. Gilmour, 'The Thatcher memoirs', *20th Century British History*, 5 (1994), p. 274.

[53] Jenkins, *Thatcher's revolution*, pp. 66–77; Riddell, *Thatcher era*, p. 8; S. R. Letwin, *The anatomy of Thatcherism* (1992), pp. 22–3.

[54] Young, *Iron Lady*, p. 6; Riddell, *Thatcher era*, p. 3; Thatcher, *Downing Street years*, p. 627; N. Ridley, *'My style of government:' The Thatcher years* (1991), pp. 18–19.

[55] J. Walvin, *Victorian values* (1988); E. M. Sigsworth (ed.), *In search of Victorian values* (Manchester, 1988); G. Marsden (ed.), *Victorian values* (1990), T. C. Smout (ed.), *Victorian values*, Proceedings of the British Academy, 78 (1992).

with them two spectacular and perfectly placed victories: one over the enemy without (General Galtieri), and the other over the enemy within (Arthur Scargill). Both were presented as triumphs of willpower and determination, as no doubt to some extent they were. Both were important because they avenged earlier defeats which had themselves been key episodes in the humiliating story of national decline. The Falklands atoned for the fiasco of Suez, which had itself been a vain attempt to blot out the humiliation of Munich; and victory over the miners was revenge for the defeat suffered at their hands by Edward Heath's Conservative Government in 1974.[56] And both were presented as emphatic evidence that decline had been halted, and that regeneration was under way. 'We are no longer a nation in retreat', Thatcher proclaimed in the aftermath of the Falklands War. 'We rejoice that Britain has rekindled that spirit which has fired her for generations past, and which today has begun to burn as brightly as before.' Or, as the Conservative manifesto put it more succinctly for the 1987 general election: 'Great Britain is great again' – 'confident, strong, trusted'.[57]

That was, and still is, Thatcher's claim: that she 'restored Britain's reputation as a force to be reckoned with in the world'. But victories which matter because they atone for earlier defeats (the 'we have licked the Vietnam syndrome' syndrome) might also be seen as further evidence of the very decline which it is claimed they are denying. In any case, apart from these two symbolic successes, the rest of Thatcher's record is much more mixed. In foreign affairs, she was certainly a star on the international stage, who raised Britains standing in the world.[58] But there is much less evidence to suggest that she lastingly reasserted British power or fundamentally changed British foreign policy. Try as she might (and she tried very hard indeed), she could not halt Britain's growing integration into Europe, nor could she prevent German reunification. She may have restored the 'special relationship' with the USA: but that was based on her close friendship with Ronald Reagan, it did not survive their departures from office, and there was never any doubt as to who was the more powerful partner. And for all her defiance over

---

[56] Thatcher, *Downing Street years*, pp. 8, 173, 264, 340–1, 377, 645; Jenkins, *Thatcher's revolution*, pp. 161, 225; Gilmour, 'Thatcher memoirs', p. 274.

[57] Thatcher, *Renewal of Britain*, pp. 164, 225, 235; Thatcher, *Downing Street years*, pp. 235, 254–5, 320; Young, *Iron Lady*, pp. 280–1, 371.

[58] Sir Anthony Parsons, 'Britain and the world', in D. Kavanagh and A. Seldon (eds.), *The Thatcher effect* (Oxford, 1989), p. 158; Riddell, *Thatcher era*, pp. 184–5, 203; Jenkins, *Thatcher's revolution*, p. 165.

the Falklands, Thatcher was much more flexible and accommodating when dealing with such other remnants of empire as Rhodesia, Northern Ireland, and Hong Kong.[59]

Nor did she regenerate Britain domestically in the way that she hoped and claimed. True, there was talk during the early stages of the Lawson boom of a 'British economic miracle', on a par with those of Germany and Japan. But this soon ended when the boom collapsed and, taking the whole of her period of power, her record is no better than uneven. The chief gain seems to have been that productivity improved, although levels are still considerably below those of Britain's international competitors. But investment and rates of growth remained slow and sluggish, the manufacturing base was eroded far beyond anything Joseph Chamberlain had feared, and what has survived of British industry is still internationally uncompetitive.[60] Nor was intrusive and inhibiting government rolled back: the overall tax burden was not significantly reduced, centralised spending remained high, and the reach of the state was extended rather than withdrawn. As for popular attitudes, there is little evidence to suggest that Thatcher's cultural counter-revolution got very far. The welfare-state mentality has survived, the enterprise-spirit is distinctly lukewarm, the 'permissive' legislation of the 1960s was not repealed, and 'Victorian values' were preached but not practised.[61]

Had Thatcher gone 'on and on and on and on', as she herself once threatened, her regenerative revolution might have cut deeper. But in the end, her messianic, hectoring intolerance proved her undoing, and she was deposed in November 1990. As with Chamberlain and Churchill, her self-appointed successor let her down. She supported John Major to thwart Michael Heseltine. But she already had her doubts, and his subsequent tenure of her office merely confirmed that he was 'wobbly', 'drifts with the tide', and was thus undoing her life's work.[62] Yet Thatcher's 'life's work', as she came to see it, only lasted from 1979 to 1990. As anyone who lived through those years can attest, it was an extra-

---

[59] Reynolds, *Britannia overruled*, pp. 256–89; Thatcher, *Downing Street years*, pp. 789–96, 813–15.

[60] I. Gilmour, *Dancing with dogma: Britain under Thatcherism* (1992), pp. 9–29, 45–75; N. Lawson, *The view from Number 11: memoirs of a Tory radical* (1992), p. 339.

[61] Riddell, *Thatcher era*, pp. 69–86, 171, 214–15, 244–5; I. Crewe, 'Values: the crusade that failed', in Kavanagh and Seldon, *Thatcher effect*, pp. 239–5; D. Willetts, 'The family', in Kavanagh and Seldon, *Thatcher effect*, p. 267.

[62] Thatcher, *Downing Street years*, pp. 719, 721, 724, 757, 832, 861; Thatcher, 'Don't undo my work', *Newsweek*, 27 April 1992, pp. 36–7.

ordinary performance. But only her most besotted and uncritical admirer would claim that her deeds matched her words. Here, instead, are the verdicts of two by no means unsympathetic journalists. Peter Jenkins concluded that Britain's decline had 'been temporarily arrested, although I doubt permanently reversed'. And Peter Riddell was more terse: 'she did not halt decline, no one could do that'. Perhaps, in her rather sad and deteriorated retirement, she has belatedly reached a similar conclusion. As she ruefully notes in her memoirs, in the manner of someone who has made an original and important discovery: there are no 'final victories' in politics, because 'arguments are never finally won'.[63]

IV

In a sense, of course, every major figure in British political life during the last 100 years could be described as 'the statesman in an age of decline'. But very few of them were, or became, so obsessed with diagnosing that problem and proposing a solution as to merit that characterisation. And even the three to whom that label may most appropriately be attached were in some significant ways extremely unalike. Joseph Chamberlain was a self-made industrialist, who never rose higher than the Colonial Secretaryship. Winston Churchill was the grandson of a duke, whose national leadership was more vigorous in war than in peace. And Margaret Thatcher was a shopkeeper's daughter, who had eleven uninterrupted years in which to impose her will on the country. Nor are these their only dissimilarities. In Chamberlain's time, Britain was a much greater force in the world than it was in Churchill's time. And in Churchill's time, it was a much greater force in the world than it was in Thatcher's. All of which is merely to say that they were different people, dealing with different phases of national decline, with different resources at their disposal, and with different policies in each case.

But for all these real variations in time and temperament, in circumstances and character these three leaders conform to a recognisably atypical and charismatic type: messianic crusaders, convinced that they alone could reverse national decline, and bring about national regeneration. Like all such figures, from the Count-Duke of Olivares to General Charles de Gaulle,[64] they were exceptionally difficult individ-

---

[63] Thatcher, *Downing Street years*, pp. 676, 755; Jenkins, *Thatcher revolution*, p. xviii; Riddell, *Thatcher era*, pp. 206, 245.

[64] This was a comparison which Thatcher greatly liked: Thatcher, *Downing Street years*, p. 82.

uals – scornful of political conventions, adversarial in their style and rhetoric, frequently battling against their own erstwhile supporters, and more concerned to mould and mobilise public opinion than to follow it. At a particular stage in their lives – in each case, interestingly enough, soon after the onset of middle age – they repudiated their earlier political beliefs, moved markedly to the right, became obsessed with the question of Britain's decline, and determined to change the course of the nation's history by their own exertions. But all three ended their political careers disappointed that they had accomplished less than they had set out to do. The most that can be said is that without Chamberlain, Churchill, or Thatcher, Britain might have declined more rapidly than it has. They may have slowed decline, but they neither halted nor reversed it.

Indeed, how could it possibly have been otherwise? For the whole point about a nation in a state of deeply rooted historical decline is that, by definition, that decline can be neither halted nor reversed. The diagnosis may be accurate, and the prescription the right one. But the patient not only refuses to recover: he stubbornly persists in getting worse. Chamberlain may have been correct in fearing the industrial might of the USA and the disintegration of the empire. But there was nothing he could do about either. Churchill was prescient in fearing Indian independence and foreseeing German dominance. But notwithstanding his great efforts, India has been independent for nearly half a century, and Germany is once again the dominant power in Europe. And Thatcher may have been right about Britain's lack of an enterprise culture and its loss of sovereignty to the Brussels bureaucracy. But however hard she tried, there was little she could to to promote the one or to prevent the other. At the individual level, these were specific failures and particular disappointments. Yet collectively, they suggest that there was, and there still is, something inexorable and irreversible about Britain's twentieth-century decline. *Pace* Thatcher, it is not clear the 'decline is not inevitable'.

There is, however, a less gloomy and less self-lacerating way of putting this. For it cannot be too often stressed that the economic, naval, and imperial dominance which Britain enjoyed in the heyday of 'Pax Britannica' was in many ways a fluke – the accidental result of early industrialisation, an empire run on the cheap, and the lack of credible continental rivals.[65] Once other, bigger nations caught up, once empires

[65] Reynolds, *Britannia overruled*, pp. 5–35.

became harder to defend, and once military equipment became more expensive, it was inevitable that, sooner or later, Britain would revert – as it is, today, still in the process of reverting – to being what throughout most of its history it has always been: a small group of islands off the coast of Europe. Given the size and natural endowments of other countries and other empires, it was (and is) inconceivable that Britain could permanently or persistently play a very significant or autonomous part in international affairs. As Barry Supple argues (ch. 1 above), a country with such a small proportion of the world's resources and population cannot indefinitely deal on equal terms with developed nations bigger by anything between 50 and 400 per cent. Thus described, British 'decline' is not the moral or economic or military or imperial catastrophe of Chamberlain, Churchill, and Thatcher: it is no more than a necessary (and perhaps even belated?) return to the normal state of affairs.

In believing that decline, thus reformulated and better understood, could be halted and reversed, these three leaders were all equally incorrect. But that was not the only error of judgement which each of them made. For it is also the case that their alarmist predictions of impending apocalypse have been no less mistaken. Britain may indeed have fallen in the world rankings of prosperous and powerful nations. But it is still, despite everything that has happened during the last hundred years, one of the most prosperous and powerful nations in the world. And there seems no good reason to suppose that it will cease to be so in the foreseeable future. That, in turn, suggests an explanation for this second mistaken judgement: all three figures spoke the doom-laden language of *absolute* decline, when Britain was in fact – and is still, in fact – experiencing only *relative* decline. Moreover, compared with earlier nations and empires 'in decline', Britain's retreat from greatness has been remarkably stable and trouble-free – no enemy invasions, no civil wars or revolutions, no end to civilisation. Britain's decline has not only been relative, in a contemporary sense; it has also, in historical terms, been relatively gradual and relatively gentle.

Nor, despite many gloomy forebodings, has there been the sort of internal economic collapse which has usually accompanied nations and empires 'in decline'. Quite the contrary. For it bears repeating that most Britons today enjoy a standard of living of which their late-Victorian forebears could scarcely have dreamed. A great power has surely been eclipsed, England has undeniably contracted, and Britannia has without doubt been overruled. But for the majority of the population, life has been getting, and is still getting, better and better and better. Small wonder, then, that the apocalyptic warnings of Chamberlain, Churchill, and Thatcher fell on ears which were rarely less than half deaf, and were often considerably more so. And small wonder, too, that the majority of the nation's leaders this century have left the issue of national decline very much alone. By definition, being a self-appointed 'statesman in an age of decline' is always rather a thankless task. It is even more thankless when, as in the case of twentieth-century Britain, that age of decline is also an age of affluence.

13

Measuring economic decline

PETER TEMIN

Barry Supple has convinced us all that Whig history cannot be the sole guide to our research. In buoyant economic times, Whig history is deservedly popular. But an exclusive reliance on improvements may not be defensive even then. In the uncertain world of today, we do not want to rule out historical evidence from any range of economic activity.

Supple has analysed British economic decline in both the nineteenth and twentieth centuries. Most of the chapters in this volume follow his lead. I want to deviate slightly and broaden the concern to Britain's most prosperous former colony: the United States of America. I will compare the British economic decline of a century ago with the purported US economic decline of today. In doing so, I will introduce a measure of economic decline that I hope may be useful in other comparisons.

I

Economic decline is a complex and multi-faceted concept. Supple recently has distinguished three dimensions of economic decline. I will discuss their relevance to the USA and add a fourth on which I then will focus.

The first aspect of economic decline noted by Supple (in ch. 1 above) is a fall in relative standing. Britain went from being the first industrial nation to being just another industrial nation. It went from having living standards higher than its continental neighbours to lagging behind at least a few prominent competitors. The first part of this process was happening even before the First World War, but the second awaited the conclusion of what Churchill called the Second Thirty-Years War.

This process goes by the name of convergence in the USA. America defines the frontier in this story, and other countries approach it over time. That living standards may be higher in other countries does not enter into the story; it is attributed to special circumstances, like OPEC. That the USA, like Britain, may be falling behind other industrial countries in its per capita GDP or productivity per worker is deeply disturbing.

It is worth commenting in passing that the shift in official statistics from GNP to GDP itself reflects a conception of economic decline. The former concept measures production by resources owned by citizens of the USA; the latter, production within the boundaries of the USA. The difference of course is foreign investment.

The USA imported capital on a large scale in the nineteenth century, long before anyone thought of these arcane concepts. It then exported capital for much of the twentieth century while GNP was the preferred measure of economic achievement. But when the USA began to import capital again in the 1980s, the use of GNP threatened to accentuate the sense of economic decline, to hasten the relative fall in American incomes. Switching to GDP moved Honda and Toyota production in the USA from Japanese GNP to American GDP.

The McKinsey Global Institute has issued a series of reports in recent years arguing that productivity in specific sectors of the American economy has fallen behind the analogous sectors of the German or Japanese economies. There always are sectors in which the USA excels, but the tone of these comparisons is far different from the condescending comparisons of the productivity commissions after the Second World War.[1]

Convergence is considered a good thing among economists, if not among politicians. But loss of leadership, however that illusive concept is defined, is more troubling. If, following Supple, leadership is taken to represent the highest per capita income, then the USA may indeed have lost its pre-eminent position. If there is a set of countries that have converged more or less to the same level, then it will be hard to say that any one of them is the leader. This may not be comforting to a former solitary leader.

For Britain, loss of economic leadership was accompanied by loss of international power. For the USA, convergence in living standards has meant if anything a divergence of political power. With the collapse of the Soviet Union, the USA has emerged as the sole superpower. The

---

[1] McKinsey Global Institute, *Manufacturing productivity* (Washington, D.C., 1993); L. Rostas, 'Productivity of labour in the cotton industry', *Economic Journal*, 55 (June–September 1945), pp. 192–205.

'convergence club' consists solely of capitalist countries; but the world stage until very recently contained a military power that was the very antithesis of capitalist. It seemed for a while as if the Soviet Union too was part of the 'convergence club', but this belief was one casualty of the Cold War's end.

Even if the specific historical events of the past decade had not taken place, the economic decline of the United States and Britain would have different political consequences. As with people when incomes and nutrition improve, the child is so much bigger than the mother. The USA is one of four large countries that dwarf all others in land area and particularly population. The other three – China, India, and Russia – are much poorer than the USA. Even so, they cannot be ignored from a political and even military point of view. The USA would have to suffer a far more precipitous economic decline than anyone envisages to become only a minor player in the world politics.

As in Britain, the American economic decline was accompanied by changes in the economy, by de-industrialisation. This in turn has been accompanied by the same kinds of worries. *Manufacturing matters* is the title of a book written by the Berkeley Round Table a few years ago, to be soundly criticised by Bhagwati.[2] The new aeroplane to be built jointly by the USA and Japan, the FSX, exposes to some jeremiads the end of US independence. More concretely, de-industrialisation is associated with the decline in good jobs for high-school graduates.

Supple noted that the British discussion of a century ago was led by Joseph Chamberlain and directed towards policies designed to reduce the loss of export markets. So too in the USA today. De-industrialisation goes hand in hand with the perception that everything bought in America was made in Japan or some more distant Asian country. I will explore this theme more thoroughly in the next section.

The final dimension of economic decline chronicled by Supple is 'the frustration of felt needs and aspirations'. This appears to be a world phenomenon at this moment. Residents of the less-developed countries are frustrated as they try to attain the good life held out to them in the global media of movies and television. People living in formerly socialist economies are discouraged by the enormity of the task in front of them: simultaneously to attain the living standards of capitalist societies

---

[2] Stephen S. Cohen, *Manufacturing matters: the myth of the post-industrial economy* (New York, 1987); Jagdish Bhagwati, 'Review of *Manufacturing matters*', *Journal of Economic Literature*, 27 (March 1989), pp. 121–3.

and recreate the presumed prosperity of their recent socialist past. And citizens of the USA are fearful of their economic future.

The root cause of this uncertainty is the decline in the growth of productivity that has dogged the world economy for the past twenty years. This is a phenomenon for which we have no convincing explanation and – at least partly as a result – no encouraging antidote. This slow growth has been accompanied by growing inequality, and the poorest members of society have seen their incomes go down even as the average continues to rise slowly.

Aspirations appear to lag behind events – when they do not race ahead of them. Even if their incomes have been rising in the recent past, most Americans are apprehensive about the immediate future. One reason for this apparent disharmony comes from the increasing participation rate of women. Families have experienced rising incomes in the past twenty years even if the wages of the man of the house went down. Women have increased their hours of paid work substantially, generating a rise in family income even if wages for any given job stagnate.

This source of income growth produces adverse expectations for two reasons. First, the gain comes because of a transition, much as total income grew in the nineteenth century when workers left agriculture for other pursuits. Women now are working almost full time; there is no way that their increased participation can raise family incomes in the next twenty years. The past in this case cannot be extrapolated into the future. Second, the gain in income has not translated into an equivalent rise in welfare. The paid work of women has come partly at the expense of home-making work and partly – one suspects – at the expense of sleep. The 'comforts of home' have decreased and frustration has increased.[3]

Most of the various dimensions of economic decline that Supple sees in Britain therefore can be seen as well in the USA. I want to take this parallel seriously and ask if there is a metric that allows us to compare the two economies along any of the dimensions noted by Supple.

II

International trade is an obvious measure of economic well-being. Long before the concepts of GNP and GDP were formulated, observers

---

[3] Frank Levy, 'Where did all the money go? A layman's guide to recent trends in US living standards', MIT IPC Working Paper 96–008 (July 1996).

could follow the fortunes of individual exports and imports and even of the balance of trade. They were early indicators of Supple's first two aspects of decline: lower relative income and de-industrialisation. A persistent theme in the literature on British economic decline has been Britain's loss of export markets in the past century. I will discuss this literature in this section and derive a measure of economic decline from it in the next.

The literature on Britain's export performance before the First World War was already old when I took it up as a graduate student. It had been an issue among contemporaries at the turn of the century, and there were well-known debates on tariffs. I want here only to note Edwin Cannan's view that it was foolish to talk of English commercial superiority and to use military metaphors to describe international trade.[4] Cannan's view foreshadows that of Krugman in the debate about US trade today.[5]

The issue arose again after the Second World War. The failure of British entrepreneurship was an issue at Harvard when Barry Supple visited in the late 1950s. Cole and Sawyer at the Business School were championing the role of British businessmen, while Gerschenkron at the Department of Economics was reviling them for ignoring the role of coal. Habakkuk weighed in with a nuanced discussion of competing explanations. His fine shading however was overwhelmed by his use of colourful language. His assertion that, 'Great generals are not made in time of peace; great entrepreneurs are not made in non-expanding industries', has been quoted more often than other, more subtle, parts of his discussion.[6] Landes, who arrived at Harvard a few years later, gave the entrepreneurship theory another full airing. While insisting that the matter was very complex, Landes nonetheless came down at the end to the importance of entrepreneurship. He wrote with an implicit list of causes for the British economic decline. Having rejected almost all of them, entrepreneurship was the residual.[7]

I confronted the identification problem in this discussion in an analysis of British steel exports. Britain grew slowly and had, apparently, poor

---

[4] Edwin Cannan, 'The practical utility of economic science', *Economic Journal*, 12 (1902), p. 470, quoted in Donald N. McCloskey, *Economic maturity and entrepreneurial decline* (Cambridge, Mass., 1973), p. 11.
[5] Paul R. Krugman, *Pop internationalism* (Cambridge, Mass., 1996).
[6] H. J. Habakkuk, *American and British technology in the 19th century* (Cambridge, 1962).
[7] David S. Landes, *Prometheus unbound: technological change and industrial development in Western Europe from 1750 to the present* (Cambridge, 1969), pp. 352–8.

entrepreneurs. Which was cause and which effect? Looking at the slow growth of the British home market, I argued that the British steel industry would have grown slowly in the late nineteenth century even if it had retained its share of open export markets. (Germany's market of course was protected by high tariffs.) I inferred that the slower-growing British steel industry would have older capital than its rivals in Germany and the USA with higher costs as a result. The loss of export markets then was the result of slow growth at home, not its cause.[8]

McCloskey agreed with my position on the identification problem. But he did not use my reasoning to do so. He followed Landes's pattern of exhausting explanations for the British decline, leaving entrepreneurship as the residual. But where Landes had found a gap at the end that needed to be explained, McCloskey was able to account for British decline in steel without invoking entrepreneurship. Quite the contrary, he asserted that the competitive nature of the British steel industry would have doomed poor entrepreneurs to bankruptcy and penury. In his concluding words: 'Late nineteenth-century entrepreneurs in iron and steel did not fail. By any cogent measure of performance, in fact, they did very well indeed.'[9]

Elbaum returned to this debate some years later with a new slant. He did not see the need to choose sides in a debate between entrepreneurship on the one hand and the rate of aggregate growth on the other. Instead, he argued that the industrial history of Britain restricted the choices open to British entrepreneurs. It is not that British steel makers made poor choices from a wide menu; the menu itself was deficient.[10]

The recent literature on the cotton industry has echoed the latter part of this intellectual trajectory. Sandberg argued that the cotton textile industry was making a successful transition to the new technology before the First World War, moving from mules to rings where appropriate and maintaining mules for higher count yarns where they were more profitable. This is the analogue of the arguments that the slower growth of the steel industry was due to causes beyond the control of the British entrepreneur.[11]

---

[8] Peter Temin, 'The relative decline of the British steel industry, 1880–1913' in H. Rosovsky (ed.), *Industrialization in two systems: essays in honor of Alexander Gerschenkron* (New York, 1966), pp. 140–55.

[9] McCloskey, *Economic maturity and entrepreneurial decline*, p. 127.

[10] Bernard Elbaum, 'The steel industry before World War I', in Bernard Elbaum and William Lazonick (eds.), *The decline of the British economy* (Oxford, 1986), pp. 51–81.

[11] Lars Sandberg, 'American rings and British mules', *Quarterly Journal of Economics*, 83 (1969), pp. 25–43; Lars Sandberg, *Lancashire in decline* (Columbus, Ohio, 1974).

Lazonick, in a series of papers, took strong exception to Sandberg's view. He argued that the British cotton industry was not making an efficient adaptation to new technology. Its fragmented structure and antiquated work rules precluded the needed changes. The cotton industry's inability to break out of this prewar institutional straightjacket was the cause of its incapacity to adapt to new circumstances after the First World War.[12]

The influence of industrial structure was absolved of responsibility by Saxonhouse and Wright. They argued, as McCloskey had for the steel industry, that cotton entrepreneurs were maximising profits before the First World War on the basis of prices existing at the time. They admitted that these decisions did not lay a good foundation for the conditions of the 1920s, but they did not criticise the industry for its inability to predict the future.[13]

This gave rise to an acrimonious exchange which shows how difficult it is to maintain a hypothesis of institutional constraint. Lazonick said, 'My use of the phrase, "nineteenth-century constraint" was never meant to be taken literally.'[14] Saxonhouse and Wright responded, 'the entire claim that British persistence with mule spinning before World War I was in any way inappropriate reduces to the argument that this choice channelled sales into certain markets rather than others, markets which later proved vulnerable even though no one at the time foresaw this or could reasonably have been expected to foresee it'.[15] This debate casts doubt on both Lazonick's argument about the cotton industry and on Elbaum's similar argument on the steel industry.

At about the same time that these issues were being disputed hotly in reference to Edwardian Britain, they were raised about contemporary America. The hypothesis that institutional constraints were impeding growth was raised in two forms. In one, the influence of the capital market was said to enforce myopic views on industrial leaders in the USA. Investments could have no longer horizon than the next quarterly

---

[12] William Lazonick, 'Factor costs and the diffusion of ring spinning in Britain prior to World War I', *Quarterly Journal of Economics*, 96 (1981), pp. 89–90; William Lazonick, 'The cotton industry', in Elbaum and Lazonick, *The decline of the British economy*, pp. 18–50.

[13] Gary R. Saxonhouse and Gavin Wright, 'New evidence on the stubborn English mule and the cotton industry, 1878–1920', *Economic History Review*, 37 (November 1984), pp. 507–19.

[14] William Lazonick, 'Stubborn mules: some comments', *Economic History Review*, 40 (February 1987), pp. 80–6.

[15] Gary R. Saxonhouse and Gavin Wright, 'Stubborn mules and vertical integration: the disappearing constraint', *Economic History Review*, 40 (February 1987), pp. 87–94.

statement.[16] In the other, the mass production that would be supported by the putative investment was impugned as innocent of the new 'flexible specialisation' and 'lean production'. This argument was applied first to US industry as a whole and then specifically to the automobile industry.[17]

American entrepreneurs in the late twentieth century are accused of being in the same position as their British counterparts a century earlier. They are unable to keep up with a rapidly changing world. Even without the shock of the First World War, they find themselves unable to compete in the new markets. The technology is different: just-in-time delivery systems instead of hard-driving and mules. But the accusation is the same.

The discussion is muted at the moment, as the American economy booms and Japan stagnates, at least relative to its past performance. Discussion of current events is dominated by conditions of the moment. But the long-run trends are still there. The future of the American labour force is in question. The education system in the USA is under fire as was the British educational system of the late nineteenth century.[18]

The literature briefly surveyed emphasises the similarity between discussions of economic decline. The debate about Britain that Supple summarises appears to be a model for the debate about economic decline in any modern country experiencing active economic competition. But is the experience the same? Is the USA not declining faster or slower than Britain was before the First World War?

III

The task is to take these discussions of specific industries and industrial sectors and generalise to the economy as a whole. To do this I generalise from the balance of trade in each specific good to the balance of trade in all goods and services, the balance on current account less interest receipts.

[16] Robert Hayes and William J. Abernathy, 'Managing our way to economic decline', *Harvard Business Review*, 58 (July–August 1980), pp. 67–77; Richard D. Ellsworth, 'Capital markets and competitive decline', *Harvard Business Review*, 63 (September–October 1985), pp. 171–83.

[17] Michael Piore and Charles Sabel, *The second industrial divide* (New York, 1984); James P. Womack, Daniel T. Jones, and Daniel Roos, *The machine that changed the world* (New York, 1990).

[18] Robert B. Reich, *The work of nations: preparing ourselves for 21st-century capitalism* (New York, 1991).

Think of Britain in its late-Victorian decline. It was, according to the authors surveyed in the previous section, losing its comparative advantage in steel and cotton. By implication – and by explicit extension in monographic work – Britain was losing its comparative advantage across the board.

This statement of course does not make sense. The theory of comparative advantage is based on the assumption of balanced trade. As Ricardo taught us, countries can have absolute advantage in everything – or nothing – but comparative advantage in only some of their traded goods and services.

There are assumptions in this Ricardian theory that are so familiar that they often are not worth noting. They merit emphasis here because they play a critical role in the calculations to come.

Ricardo assumed flexible exchange rates and no capital movements. Flexible exchange rates allow the exchange rate to move in order to balance trade. Comparative advantage in everything then implies a strong exchange rate rather than unbalanced trade. Capital movements by contrast permit trade to be unbalanced. Ricardo clearly did not want to complicate his model to distract from the concept of comparative advantage.

I will discuss these assumptions in turn because I want to relax them in order to construct a measure of economic decline, more properly, an ordinal measure of one dimension of economic decline. The first assumption is of flexible exchange rates. Britain had flexible exchange rates for the period of the Napoleonic Wars when Ricardo was writing, but it returned to gold shortly thereafter. Britain was on the Gold Standard during the period of purported economic decline in the late nineteenth century, and the Ricardian mechanism of trade could not work according to his model.

The value of the British pound could not fall as Britain's export industries began to fail. If individual prices could not adjust due to costs in Britain, then quantity adjustments would replace price changes. Exports of, say, steel fell as they would have under flexible exchange rates when Britain was losing its comparative advantage. Without a compensating fall in the value of the pound, steel exports fell more than they would have under flexible exchange rates.

But exports of other goods and services in which Britain was not falling behind, or at least in which the economic problems discussed above were not so prominent, would not rise. Britain therefore would find its balance of trade declining over time. If the balance of trade was not declining, then either Britain's steel industry was not declining, some other exports were gaining comparative advantage conveniently as steel faded, or domestic British prices were falling to make the real exchange rate fall.

Ricardo's second assumption, of no international capital flows, also does not apply to the period of Britain's climacteric. Capital flowed across national boundaries with great ease in the years before the First World War. Britain of course was the major capital exporter. The existence of these large capital flows meant that Britain's balance of trade need not have been balanced. Even if other countries not so intimately involved with the international flow of capital were disciplined by capital flows, Britain was not. Britain's balance of trade could easily have deteriorated as it lost comparative advantage in specific industries; the accompanying capital exports need only have diminished a bit to pay for the trade deficit.

Turning now to the late-twentieth century and to the USA, we find a slightly different scenario. Exchange rates now are flexible, as they have been for quarter of a century. The Ricardian equilibration method could be working now to compensate for any loss of American comparative advantage. But it need not be, since international capital movements again are easily accomplished. The USA today therefore is closer to the simple Ricardian model than Britain a century ago although still not a text-book case.

Accordingly, I must use a two-step test to see if Britain or the USA in their various periods were or are falling behind their competitors and losing their comparative advantage in a range of goods. First, I will examine the Ricardian adjustment mechanism: the exchange rate. Was or is the real exchange rate falling? This is more likely for the USA today than for late nineteenth-century Britain.

Second, I check that the balance of trade was not turning adverse. If it was, this implies that the exchange rate would have been lower than it was in the absence of offsetting capital flows. Fortunately, I do not have to answer the question whether the balance of trade is exogenous and capital flows endogenous or vice versa. I define the Ricardian exchange rate as the exchange rate determined by comparative advantage in the absence of capital flows. Then if capital is flowing into a country, the actual exchange rate is above the Ricardian exchange rate. In normal parlance, the exchange rate is overvalued.

The issue of overvaluation is most pressing at this moment for Latin American countries. The Mexican peso crisis of December, 1995 is widely credited to the preceding overvaluation of the peso. Not everyone agrees that overvaluation was the main problem, but it is still the leading hypothesis. More recently, Dornbusch has created a media sensation by claiming that the Brazilian currency is overvalued.[19]

This two-part measure appears to be binary: either the exchange rate fell or it did not, subject to the balance of trade staying constant. There are two problems with this toggle. First, the concept of decline is a multi-dimensional one with many nuances, as Barry Supple has emphasised. To apply this measure, one would like to know whether the evidence in question is strong or weak, large or small, rather than just present. Second, the aim in this chapter is comparative: Britain a century ago versus the USA today. The test should order their decline – in the sense described here – rather than say which one is or is not in decline.

I therefore define an ordinal measure. The country (of the two in question here) which has the greatest fall in what I have called the Ricardian exchange rate is suffering the worst decline. The two steps just described will allow this determination to be made.

Britain of course was on the Gold Standard in the years before the First World War; it was the conductor of the international orchestra in Keynes's phrase. Britain's nominal exchange rate therefore was stable. There were no changes in the gold value of the pound or of the currencies of Britain's principal trading partners. Latin American countries, among others, failed to uphold the Gold Standard from time to time, but they were not major trading partners even if they were connected to the British capital market.

Britain's real exchange rate from 1870 to 1914 is shown in figure 13.1. It too was stable. This is hardly surprising. It is a well-known discipline of the Gold Standard to keep international prices in line. This was true even in such extreme conditions as the early 1930s when prices were falling rapidly all over the world.[20] It clearly was true also in the years before the First World War.

I turn now to the second part of the measure I am using: the balance

[19] Rudiger Dornbusch, 'The Latin triangle', MIT World Economy Laboratory Working Paper 96–09 (1996).
[20] Peter Temin, 'Transmission of the Great Depression', *The Journal of Economic Perspectives*, 7 (Spring 1993), pp. 87–102.

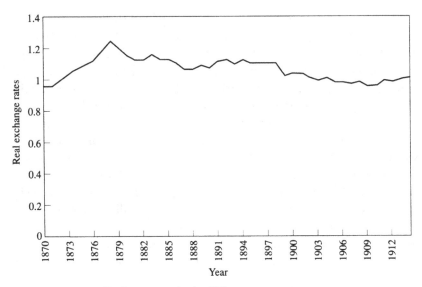

Fig. 13.1 Exchange rate in the UK

on current account. The Gold Standard enforced roughly uniform international prices. Britain's loss of comparative advantage should then have shown up in declining exports. As described in the previous section, Britain was losing exports in specific industries. This is a natural process of economic evolution. The fortunes of individual industries rise and fall in response to myriad influences. If the fall in British exports of steel were offset by rising exports of other goods, then a focus on the steel industry alone paints an excessively gloomy picture of the British economy.

The test here is not to survey all possible commodities and services looking for those that were expanding. It is instead to look at the total balance on current account. Most British commodity exports were manufactures at this time, as they had been throughout the nineteenth century. The cotton industry peaked as a share of exports in the 1830s.[21] But no one talks of British decline even before Crystal Palace. Instead, historians have noted that the exports of British cotton were being overtaken by exports of other British goods as the British economy expanded. The question is whether this same process was still happening sixty or seventy years later.

[21] Ralph Davis, *The Industrial Revolution and British overseas trade* (Leicester, 1979).

Table 13.1. *British trade figures, 1870–1913 (annual averages; millions of pounds)*

Quinquennia	Balance of trade	Balance of goods and services
1871–5	−62.50	24.58
1876–80	−124.56	−31.48
1881–5	−104.28	−3.20
1886–90	−91.10	3.42
1891–5	−130.30	−41.94
1896–1900	−190.60	−59.88
1901–5	−174.58	−63.90
1906–10	−142.10	−5.58
1911–13[a]	−134.30	18.17

Note:
[a] Three years
Source: Albert H. Imlah, *Economic elements in the Pax Britannica* (Cambridge, Mass., 1958)

Table 13.1 shows Britain's balance of trade and of goods and services from Imlah.[22] Both measures tell the same story. Britain was not suffering from a persistent trade deficit in the late nineteenth or early twentieth century. Despite the extensive capital exports of these years, Britain maintained an approximate balance in its trade of goods and services.

Arraying these well-known facts in this matter then, suggests the following conclusion. While Britain was losing its comparative advantage in some exports, it was gaining it in others.

The historical record discussed so far suggests that Britain may not have been as much in decline during its climacteric as conventionally thought. But this conclusion is not warranted at this stage of the argument. For this is only one example. Perhaps all countries in economic decline have balances of payments that look like this. As noted above, a comparison is needed. I use here the USA in its present state of possible economic decline.

Figure 13.2 shows the US real exchange rate for the past quarter of a century. We are no longer on the Gold Standard nor on any other stable exchange-rate regime. Nominal exchange rates vary, as do relative price levels in different countries. If these movements offset each other, the real exchange rate stays stable. If not, the real exchange rate moves.

[22] Albert H. Imlah, *Economic elements in the Pax Britannica* (Cambridge, Mass., 1958).

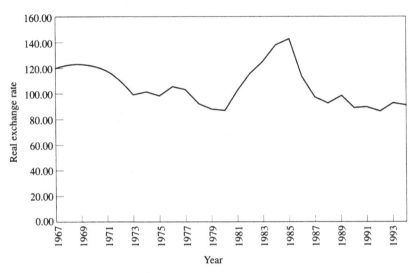

Fig. 13.2 US real exchange rate

This was the case for the USA. Its real exchange rate fell by one quarter during the 1970s, then rose above its level in 1970 by 1985 and fell again by the end of the decade to its previous low. The 1990s so far look like a continuation of the decline in the 1970s.

The overall decline suggests that the USA has been losing its comparative advantage in former export leaders and that other exports have not risen to take their place. The exchange rate then had to fall to bring the balance of trade back into balance. This observation however ignores the rise in the real exchange rate during the 1980s. How do the wild gyrations of the real exchange rate affect this measure?

The second part of the test is to look at the balance on current account (less interest receipts). Table 13.2 shows the US balance of trade and of goods and services for recent years. The USA had enjoyed a favourable balance on current account for the years preceding 1970. This positive balance eroded rapidly in the late 1960s and turned negative in the early 1970s. It reached a peak of over $100 billion in 1987 – just after the real exchange rate peaked – and then declined unevenly to its still negative level today.

Many pages have been filled attempting to understand the relationship between the real exchange rate and the trade balance in the 1980s. The problem with easy answers has been that the real exchange rate fell precipitously, while the trade deficit fell far more slowly. As a result,

Table 13.2. *US trade figures, 1966–1994 (annual averages; millions of dollars)*

Quinquennia	Balance of trade	Balance of goods and services
1966–70	2,292	1,628
1971–5	−873	−653
1976–80	−25,513	−21,413
1981–5	−73,255	−65,810
1986–90	−131,174	−115,791
1991–4[a]	−117,223	−62,848

Note:
[a] Four years
Source: US Council of Economic Advisors, *Economic Report of the President* (Washington, D.C.: Government Printing Office, 1996), p. 392.

simple relationships between the two magnitudes do not appear to fit the data after 1985 even if they fit wonderfully before then. Recent work has tended to resuscitate the theory that the trade balance is indeed responsive to real exchange rates.[23]

The test here does not require a detailed answer to this difficult question, only the assurance that trade flows are responsive to real exchange rates. What I have termed the Ricardian real exchange rate was below the actual real exchange rate after about 1970. I am not aware of any strict relationship between the size of the trade deficit and the gap between the actual and Ricardian real exchange rate, but I suspect it is monotonic. If so, then the Ricardian real exchange rate was far below the actual in the mid-1980s.

In other words, the temporary rise in the real exchange rate in the 1980s may not represent a rise in the Ricardian real exchange rate at all. I therefore ignore it. The trade balance today is worse than in 1970; the Ricardian exchange rate has fallen.

The trade balance is of roughly the same magnitude as it was around 1980. The real exchange rate is too. Consequently it is possible that the decline in the Ricardian real exchange rate happened quite precipitously

[23] Robert Z. Lawrence, 'US current account adjustment: an appraisal', *Brookings Papers on Economic Activity*, 2 (1990), pp. 343–89; Paul R. Krugman, 'Has the adjustment policy worked?' in C. Fred Bergston (ed.), *International adjustment and financing: the lessons of 1985–1991* (Washington, D.C. 1991), pp. 275–322.

in the 1970s and has not continued. Whenever it happened, the real exchange rate has fallen by at least one-quarter in the past thirty years.

The conclusion therefore is that the American economic decline of the past generation has – in this dimension and by this measure – been more severe than the British economic decline in the generation before the First World War. This is not to say that the British climacteric failed to occur. It is instead to provide a metric of economic decline. In comparison with at least one other economic decline, the British economic decline in the Edwardian period does not look so bad.

Alternatively, one could say that convergence is more apparent now than before the First World War. More countries have joined the 'convergence club'. Modern manufactures and other exportable goods and services are made in more parts of the world at competitive costs. Decline then, as noted above, can be taken as success as much as failure. The USA has been more successful, by this measure, than nineteenth-century Britain in teaching people around the world how to produce efficiently in order to live better. Even if leadership in this dimension is disappearing, perhaps leadership in another dimension is emerging. This of course brings us back to Supple's assertion that leadership has many dimensions.

IV

This chapter has tried to expand Supple's analysis of the literature on economic decline in two ways. First, I have exposed similarities between the discussion of British and American economic decline. Many of the points Supple implies are unique to Britain appear to be components of writing on economic decline wherever it occurs. Second, I have introduced a metric for one dimension of economic decline. On this metric the USA today is declining more rapidly than Edwardian Britain. If so, then the events being described by the literature on economic decline may need to be amended or even rethought. We even might come to think of the loss of leadership as a good thing!

Publications by Barry Supple

1 BOOKS (AUTHOR)

Commercial crisis and change in England, 1600–42: a study in the instability of a mercantile economy (Cambridge, 1959)

Boston capitalists and western railroads: a study in the nineteenth-century investment process (Harvard, 1967), co-author with Arthur M. Johnson

The Royal Exchange Assurance: a history of British insurance, 1720–1970 (Cambridge, 1970)

Vol. IV of *The history of the British coalmining industry, 1913–46: the political economy of decline* (1987)

2 BOOKS (EDITED)

The experience of economic growth: case studies in economic history (New York, 1963)

Essays in British business history (Cambridge, 1977)

The state and economic knowledge: the American and British experiences (Cambridge, 1990)

The rise of big business (Cheltenham, 1992)

3 CONTRIBUTIONS TO BOOKS

The experience of economic growth: case studies in economic history (New York, 1963), editor and contributor. Introduction and Part I, pp. 1–46, 'Economic history, economic theory, and economic growth'

'Can the new economic history become an import substitute?' in Donald N. McCloskey (ed.), *Essays on a mature economy: Britain after 1840* (1971), pp. 423–30

'The state and the industrial revolution', in C. M. Cipolla (ed.), *The Fontana economic history of Europe*, vol. III (1971, 1973), pp. 301–57

'Legislation and virtue: an essay in working-class self-help and the state in the early nineteenth century', in Neil McKendrick (ed.), *Historical perspectives: studies in English thought and society in honour of J. H. Plumb* (1974), pp. 211–54

'Private investment strategy in Britain', in Herman Daems and Herman Van Der Wee (eds.), *The rise of managerial capitalism* (Leuven and The Hague, 1974), pp. 73–95

'The nature of enterprise, 1450–1750', in E. E. Rich and C. H. Wilson (eds.), vol. V (*The economic organisation of early modern Europe*) of *The Cambridge economic history of Europe* (Cambridge, 1977), pp. 394–461

Essays in British business history (Cambridge, 1977), editor and contributor. Introduction, pp. 1–8; chapter 1, pp. 9–30, 'A framework for British business history'; chapter 4, pp. 69–87, 'Corporate growth and structural change in a service industry: insurance, 1870–1914'

'Material development: the condition of England, 1830–1860' and 'The governing framework: social class and institutional reform in Victorian Britain', both in Laurence Lerner (ed.), *The Victorians* (1978), pp. 49–69 and 90–119

'Income and demand, 1860–1914' in Roderick Floud and Donald McCloskey (eds.), *The economic history of Great Britain since 1750* (Cambridge, 1981), vol. II, pp. 121–43

'"No bloody revolutions but for obstinate reactions?" British coalowners in their context, 1919–20', in D. C. Coleman and Peter Mathias (eds), *Enterprise and history: essays in honour of Charles Wilson* (Cambridge, 1984), pp. 212–36

'Ideology and necessity: the nationalisation of coal mining, 1916–1946' in N. McKendrick and R. B. Outhwaite (eds.), *Business life and public policy: essays in honour of D. C. Coleman* (Cambridge, 1986), pp. 228–50

'Introduction to multinational enterprise', in Alice Teichova, Maurice Lévy-Leboyer and Helga Nussbaum (eds.), *Historical studies in international corporate business* (Cambridge, 1989), pp. 1–6

The state and economic knowledge: the American and British experiences (Cambridge, 1990), editor and contributor. Introduction (with Mary Furner), pp. 3–39, 'Ideas, institutions and state in America and Britain'; chapter 10, pp. 325–53, 'Official economic inquiry and Britain's industrial decline: the first fifty years'

'Beyond the welfare state', in Michael Lacey and Mary Furner (eds.), *The state and social investigation* (Cambridge, 1992)

The rise of big business (Cheltenham, 1992), Introduction, pp. xi–xxix

'British economic decline since 1945', in Roderick Floud and Donald McCloskey (eds.), *The economic history of Great Britain since 1750* (Cambridge, 2nd edition, 1994), vol. III, pp. 318–46

4 ARTICLES

'Thomas Mun and the commercial crisis, 1623', *Bulletin of the Institute of Historical Research*, 27 (1954), pp. 91–4

'Currency and commerce in the early seventeenth century', *Economic History Review*, 2nd series, 10 (1957), pp. 239–55

'A business elite: German-Jewish financiers in nineteenth-century New York', *Business History Review*, 31 (1957), pp. 143–78

'Economic history and economic growth', *Journal of Economic History*, 20 (1960), pp. 548–56

'Economic history and economic underdevelopment', *Canadian Journal of Economics and Political Science*, 37 (1961), pp. 460–78

'Has the early history of developed countries any current relevance?', *American Economic Review*, 55 (1965), pp. 99–103

'The entrepreneur in the preindustrial age', *Annales Cisalpines d'Histoire Sociale* (1970), pp. 21–36

'Economic history in the 1980s', *Journal of Interdisciplinary History*, 12 (Autumn 1981), pp. 199–205

'The political economy of demoralization: the state and the coalmining industry in America and Britain between the wars', *Economy History Review*, 41 (1988), pp. 566–91

'The ordeal of economic freedom: Marshall on economic history' (with R. C. O. Matthews), *Quaderni di storia dell'economia politica*, 9 (1991), pp. 189–213

'Fear of failing: economic history and the decline of Britain', *Economic History Review* 47, 3 (August 1994), pp. 441–58

5 REVIEW ARTICLES

'From business to government', *Business History Review*, 33 (1959), pp. 87–105

'American business history – a survey', *Business History*, 1 (1959), pp. 63–76

'The great capitalist man-hunt', *Business History*, 6 (1963), pp. 48–62

'Revisiting Rostow', *Economic History Review*, 37 (1984), pp. 107–114

'Scale and scope: Alfred Chandler and the dynamics of industrial capitalism', *Economic History Review*, 44 (1991), pp. 500–14

Index